DYNAMICS *of* MEANING

DYNAMICS
of MEANING

Anaphora,

Presupposition,

and the

Theory of

Grammar

Gennaro Chierchia

The UNIVERSITY *of* CHICAGO PRESS

Chicago *and* London

GENNARO CHIERCHIA is professor of linguistics at the
University of Milan.

The University of Chicago Press, Chicago 60637
The University of Chicago Press, Ltd., London
© 1995 by The University of Chicago

All rights reserved. Published 1995
Printed in the United States of America

04 03 02 01 00 99 98 97 96 95   1 2 3 4 5

ISBN: 0-226-10434-6 (cloth)
ISBN: 0-226-10435-4 (paper)

Library of Congress Cataloging-in-Publication Data

Chierchia, Gennaro.
    Dynamics of meaning : anaphora, presupposition, and the theory of
grammar / Gennaro Chierchia.
        p.   cm.
    Includes bibliographical references and index.
    1. Semantics.   2. Grammar, Comparative and general—Syntax.
3. Anaphora (Linguistics).   4. Presupposition (Logic).   5. Generative
grammar.   I. Title.
P325.C383   1995
401'.43—dc20   94-42522
                                                                CIP

⊗ The paper used in this publication meets the minimum requirements
of the American National Standard for Information Sciences—
Permanence of Paper for Printed Library Materials, ANSI Z39.48-1984.

To Lele and Antonia Chierchia

Contents

Preface

A well-established thesis on the relation between form and meaning in natural language is the following. Simple expressions are associated with objects. In virtue of this, complex expressions (i.e., well-formed arrangements of simple expressions) can be used to codify information about ways in which objects may be arranged. This gives to complex expressions (e.g., to sentences) their content (e.g., the propositions that sentences express or the truth conditions they have). To know a language is to know which configuration of expressions is associated with which arrangement of objects (e.g., which sentence is associated with which proposition). Grammars embody this knowledge.

The view just sketched comes in many forms. For example, there is disagreement as to the nature of the objects that expressions are associated with. They can be regarded as actual pieces of the external world, abstract platonic essences, internal constructions of the mind, and more. But whatever stand one wants to take on issues of this sort, there is a trait common to any variant of the way of relating form to meaning that I have just impressionistically outlined: the primary task of semantics is taken to be that of identifying the informational *content* of expressions. We might call this the "view of meaning as content."

It should immediately be added that researchers working in this tradition are acutely aware of the commonplace observation that language is not a static association of forms and contents. We surely do many different things with words. We use them to make assertions, entertain hypotheses, create metaphors, and so on. This is, however, generally viewed as a matter of language *use:* the content associated by grammar with expressions can be used to play a wide variety of language games in interaction with our extra-grammatical cognitive capacities (and as a result of this, the very association of expressions with their content may be modified as we go along). The identification of informational content must be supplemented by a consideration of how it is used in actual linguistic interaction. Semantics must be integrated with pragmatics, theories of processing, and so forth. At the same time, most questions of language use do not enter directly in the recursive, compositional characterization of the informational content of expressions of various types.

What I have just given is an extremely oversimplified picture of a wide-spread linguistic practice—a practice that has proven itself quite fruitful, I believe. I do think that semantics crucially involves the characterization of circumstances under which two expressions share the same informational content, and that this should be kept separate from issues of language use, even though content and use interact in pervasive and interesting ways. Now, a question has recently come to maturity that I think is important and affects this picture. The question concerns, in part, how much should be built into the recursive characterization of a system of semantic values and how much should be left out. In the following paragraphs, I will try to spell out this question in a preliminary and informal way, building on the views put forth in Stalnaker 1978.

Consider the act of asserting. What is it to assert something in a given context? When illocutionary agents engage in a conversational exchange, there is a set of assumptions they share—a body of knowledge and beliefs that must be taken as common background. For example, illocutionary agents must know which language is to be used, have access to the same information from the immediate environment, and be collectively aware of some basic facts concerning how the world may be. Such common ground can be viewed as the information state that constitutes the input to an act of asserting. Typically, an information state specifies a number of things and leaves others open. Asserting a sentence S modifies the common ground. Drawing from his or her own system of knowledge and beliefs, an agent normally utters a sentence S that updates the common ground by ruling out a number of alternatives previously left open. There are, of course, various complications that would require restructuring information states in ways more complex than the simple addition of a piece of information to the common ground (e.g., an agent might be wrong as to what is contained in the common ground). But, in first approximation, let us abstract away from these complicating factors. In general, what emerges is that an assertion can be thought of as a way of getting from one common ground to a new common ground, that is, as a function from one information state to another.

Now there are two ways of looking at what is going on. On the view of meaning as content, we might simply say that the utterance of a declarative sentence in a given context will naturally prompt us to enter its content into the common ground—and that is the end of the story. The second way to go is to view sentences as actually having as semantic values functions from information states into information states. On this second view, context updating would be an integral part of the compositional system of meanings. I will call this the "view of meaning as context change."

It is fair to say that the view of meaning as content is less dynamic than the view of meaning as context change, in the sense that on the latter view, certain aspects of language use enter directly into the compositional core of a semantic system. However, this contraposition should not be considered an absolute one. The view of meaning as content does provide us with a serious and powerful approach to the dynamics of language use. Conversely, the view of meaning as context change will still need pragmatics, theories of processing, and the like in dealing with many phenomena. The point is simply that the view of meaning as context change claims that certain aspects of interpretation viewed so far as essentially pragmatic are best regarded as part of the calculus that builds up recursively the semantic values of expressions. This claim has been explicitly articulated by some researchers a few years ago (see, e.g., Kamp 1981 or Heim 1992) on the basis of a number of empirical facts. The relevant facts have to do with the semantics of definite and indefinite NPs, their anaphoric behavior (e.g., what has come to be known as "donkey anaphora"), adverbs of quantification, and the way presuppositions are compositionally projected from simple expressions to complex ones. To this date, however, issues are far from being settled. The ongoing debate as to whether the analysis of the phenomena just mentioned really supports a more dynamic view of meaning is still wide open.

In the present book I go over the main stages of this debate as I understand it, and try to come up with new facts that might bear upon it. I first present and discuss the range of phenomena just mentioned (i.e., (in)definite NPs and their anaphoric and presuppositional properties) and argue that, properly understood, they indeed provide evidence in favor of the view of meaning as context change. I then individuate some empirical generalizations that I argue constitute new, independent evidence in favor of a dynamic approach to semantics. These empirical generalizations concern backwards anaphoric dependencies (like, e.g., *In his$_i$ youth everyone$_i$ makes mistakes*), the presuppositional properties of determiners, and the interpretation of pronouns in discourse. I will also address central aspects of what is known in linguistics as the theory of binding, Weak and Strong Crossover, and Reconstruction. While discussing these topics, we will run into some very basic questions concerning what should be dealt with by making specific assumptions about the nature of syntactic representations and what should be dealt with in terms of assumptions concerning the nature of the interpretive procedure, and we will have to take a stand on such issues. I think that even those who will not be convinced by my arguments in favor of dynamic semantics, or by my hypotheses on the nature of syntactic representations, will find in the present work a nontrivial set of partly novel facts and puzzles.

In making my case, I adopt a version of the Principles and Parameters framework, according to which grammar is viewed as a set of principles and generative devices that determine well-formed pairings of strings of sounds (i.e., Phonetic Representations) with Logical Forms. I proceed first by gradually setting up a dynamic interpretation of Logical Forms (in the guise of a mapping of Logical Forms into a dynamic logic) and then by exploring the empirical consequences of this step. Some of my points are internal to the view of syntax adopted here, others are largely independent of it. In the course of the book, I will try to indicate which of my arguments are less theory bound.

As far as prerequisites are concerned, I have tried to keep them to a minimum. A fairly basic knowledge of syntax and semantics (say, a graduate-level introduction to these disciplines) should be sufficient to follow the bulk of the argumentation presented here. I use the material in this book (integrated by some of the relevant papers) in courses of introduction to dynamic semantics. The first two chapters are supplemented by exercises for the reader.

In writing this book I have been helped by many colleagues and friends, more than I can acknowledge here. I have also been helped by many audiences to which portions of it have been presented over the past couple of years. My greatest debt, evident throughout, is owed to the work of and the (at times heated) discussions with Irene Heim, Jeroen Groenendijk, and Martin Stokhof. I must also individually acknowledge at least the following colleagues: David Beaver, Andrea Bonomi, John Bowers, Greg Carlson, Paolo Casalegno, Molly Diesing, Polly Jacobson, Hans Kamp, Angelika Kratzer, Fred Landman, David Pesetsky, Tanya Reinhart, Mats Rooth, Anna Szabolcsi, and the University of Chicago Press referees.

Since no person is an island, writing a book affects the life of many around you. Presumably for this reason, one often finds in prefaces like the present one noble words of thanks to those who have provided help not just in the form of professional advice. I will be no exception to this well-established tradition, also because in the art of sounding noble, I think I am second to few.

This book was started in the United States, which was home to me for almost 15 years, and completed in Italy, which looks like it might be home to me again, at least for a while. I cannot express here in a simple and clear way what living and working in the States has meant to me. The last and longest portion of my time in the United States was spent in Ithaca, working at Cornell University. It has been a good place to be, professionally and otherwise. Let me just say that among the many things I will miss are the joint seminars and intense discussions with John Bowers, Molly Diesing, Fred Landman, Sally McConnell-Ginet, Carol Rosen, Magui Suñer, and John Whitman. I will also miss the pizza and wine after grueling department meetings, and the lunches with Piero Pucci.

A characteristic of academic jobs is that they can absorb you more intensely than most other jobs. When you are thinking about an issue, it can stick with you rather obsessively. Writing a book that not many will read and even fewer will like is a rather weak reason for taking so much time away from being with your spouse and your kids. In this connection, I can only say that without the day-to-day presence, patience, impatience, and love of Isa, Gabriele, Tommaso, and Matteo my thoughts on semantics would have eaten up my mind like termites.

Who knows whether coming back to Italy was right. If you can't decide for yourself what to do, you better have somebody around you who can. This has two advantages. First, it saves you from paralysis. Second, in the case of success, you can partake of the credit, and in the case of failure, you are not to blame. And the art of eschewing responsibilities of this kind is another thing in which I am second to few. At any rate, many things have contributed to making this return to the Old World possible and worthwhile. Among them I must mention at least Anna and Andrea Bonomi's caring presence, Marco Santambrogio's unfailing advice, and Adriana and Luigi Rizzi's being in the same boat. Also absolutely crucial were the support of Lele and Antonia Chierchia, of Elda and Lodo Orvieto, of many old friends who are still there, of Gianni Marinangeli, and of my brother Luigi. He was probably always the brightest of us, and now he has also grown to be the wisest.

Milan
March 1994

1 The Two Souls of Discourse Representation Theory

1.1 INTRODUCTION

A great deal of work in linguistics (as well as in philosophy and A.I.) centers on anaphora. In particular, much attention has recently been devoted to the phenomena illustrated in (1).

(1)   a.   [No student]$_i$ believes that he$_i$ is treated fairly.
          b.   *Every professor that met [no student]$_i$ will soon meet him$_i$.
          c.   Every farmer that has [a donkey]$_i$ beats it$_i$.

In (1a), as the coindexing indicates, *he* can be naturally understood as being anaphoric to *no student*. This, however, is impossible in (1b). Restrictions of this kind have generally been attributed to the fact that quantified NPs like *no student* must bear a certain syntactic relationship to pronouns in order to bind them: the quantified NP must be "higher up" in the syntactic tree. Being "higher up" in the relevant sense is often formulated in terms of the notion of c-command:

(2)   A *c-commands* B iff A does not dominate B and the first branching node that dominates A also dominates B (cf. Reinhart 1983a,b).

No student c-commands *he* in (1a), and the anaphoric link is well-formed, while this does not happen in (1b) where the anaphoric link is ill-formed. The ungrammaticality of (1b) on the intended interpretation contrasts strikingly with the acceptability of (1c). In (1c), *a donkey* can antecede *it* without c-commanding it. Since the seminal work of Frege and Russell, indefinites are generally taken to be existentially quantified NPs. And yet they seem to behave differently from other quantified NPs in that they are able to antecede pronouns that they do not c-command. The phenomenon illustrated by (1c) has come to be known as "donkey anaphora," because of the type of examples used originally by Geach (1962) to illustrate it.

    Discourse Representation Theory (DRT)[1] constitutes the most articulated attempt to address the challenge posited by data such as (1). In the present work I would like to individuate some problems that DRT leaves open and propose a solution to them. I will also present and analyze new data that appear to be closely related to the phenomena in (1). In the course of our discussion, we will find out that DRT has two "souls." One soul deals with the relevant issues by essentially syntactic means. That is, it manipulates the structure of sentences like (1c) and sets up abstract "logical forms" easy to interpret by standard techniques.[2] The other soul deals with the problem by keeping the syntax simple and making meanings fancier, that is, more "dynamic."[3] Questions of this kind constantly arise in the investigation of problems that lie at the intersection of syntax and semantics. What aspects of a phenomenon are syntactic in nature and what aspects semantic? Given two alternative accounts of a given set of facts, one predominantly syntactic, the other predominantly semantic, how do we choose between them? We each may come to these questions with our own methodological biases. But whatever our biases may be, the way to optimally slice the pie between syntax and semantics will depend on the specifics of the phenomena at hand and is ultimately an empirical issue. I will argue that in dealing with (1c) and related phenomena, an approach based on a principled enrichment of the traditional notion of meaning (viz., the notion of meaning as truth-conditional content) is to be preferred on empirical grounds over more syntacticy approaches that stick to this traditional notion. This work, therefore, is directly inspired by the second of the two souls of DRT mentioned above and tries to offer new evidence in favor of it.

This chapter provides some essential background necessary to understand and put in the right perspective the issues sketched above. First we will outline more explicitly the problem of donkey sentences and the basic tack DRT takes on them. Then, after having spelled out some general assumptions concerning syntax and the overall organization of grammar, we will discuss in more detail what we have been referring to as "the two souls of DRT."

1.2 THE EMPIRICAL CHARACTERISTICS OF "DONKEY ANAPHORA"

Let us begin by considering in more detail the way in which indefinites differ from other quantified NPs.

1.2.1 Coordination

Consider the contrast in (3).

(3) a. *John introduced [every new student]$_i$ to the chairperson, and Bill introduced him$_i$ to the dean.
     b. *John introduced [every new student]$_i$ to the chairperson. Bill introduced him$_i$ to the dean.
     c. John introduced [a new student]$_i$ to the chairperson, and Bill introduced him$_i$ to the dean.

d.   John introduced [a new student]$_i$ to the chairperson. Bill introduced him$_i$ to the dean.

The anaphoric links in (3a–b) are ill-formed. This can be taken as an indication of the fact that an NP like *every new student* cannot be assigned scope over a conjunct or across a sequence of sentences, which in turn might be taken as an instance of the requirement that a pronoun must be c-commanded by its antecedent for it to receive a bound-variable interpretation. In other words, (3a–b) cannot be interpreted as in (4).

(4)   every$_x$ [x is a student][John introduced x to the chair and Bill introduced x to the dean][4]

However, as the well-formedness of (3c–d) shows, an indefinite can reach out across a conjunction or across sequences of sentences. One way to intuitively understand the contrasts in (3) is by assuming that indefinites "set up discourse referents" that may be picked up in subsequent discourse, while NPs like *every student* do not.[5]

Two observations should be added at this point. The first is that the well-formedness of (3c–d) is not just due to the fact that indefinites can be intepreted specifically, that is, in the case at hand, as referring to a specific, contextually salient student. This can be seen by embedding (3c–d) in a context where such a specific interpretation is not available.

For example:

(5)   In the old days, John would introduce [a new student]$_i$ to the chairperson, and Bill would introduce him$_i$ to the dean.

Clearly, no natural context for (5) allows for a specific interpretation of the indefinite. The second observation concerns the fact that ungrammatical anaphoric links such as those in (3a–b) become well-formed if we use plural pronouns:

(6)   a. John introduced [every new student]$_i$ to the chair and Bill introduced them$_i$ to the dean.
      b. [No new student]$_i$ came to the party. They$_i$ didn't know about it.

If (6a) and (6b) are to be analyzed using the same device, it appears prima facie implausible that such a device can be variable binding of the usual sort. For consider what we would get if we assumed that the scope of *no new student* in (6b) spans across both sentences:

(7)   no$_x$ [x is a new student] [x came to the party and x didn't know about it]

This says that no new student x is such that x came to the party and x did not know about the party, which clearly is not the right way to analyze (6b). What seems to be going on here is that every quantified noun phrase can make salient a set of entities (roughly, the set associated with its head noun). This set can then be referred to in subsequent discourse. Plural anaphora is a highly complex phenomenon, and we will not have much to say about it. But whatever line one chooses to take on it, it is a fact that while NPs like *every student* or *no student* can normally antecede singular pronouns, they cannot do so in an environment like (3a–b)—a fact that suggests that the phenomena in (3) are distinct from those in (6).

So the first difference between indefinites and other quantified NPs concerns the fact that the former, unlike the latter, can antecede pronouns across a conjunction or a sequence of sentences.

1.2.2 If/When-Clauses

The second class of cases involves conditionals and *when*-clauses and is exemplified by the following:[6]

(8)   a.   If John owns [a donkey]$_i$, he beats it$_i$.
       b.   When [an Italian is tall]$_i$, he$_i$ is also blond.
       c.   *If John owns [no donkey]$_i$, he wants it$_i$.
       d.   *When [every Italian]$_i$ is tall, he$_i$ is also blond.

Here too we find that indefinites behave differently from other quantified NPs. These examples are particularly challenging in view of the fact that there seems to be no way to interpret (8a–b) while sticking to the assumption that indefinites are existentially quantified. To see why, let us try to interpret (8a). There are two possibilities, namely:

(9)   a. [a$_x$ [x is a donkey and John has x] $\rightarrow$ John beat x]
       b. a$_x$ [x is a donkey and [John has x $\rightarrow$ John beat x]]

In both (9a) and (9b) we are interpreting the conditional in terms of the material implication '$\rightarrow$', but the point would also go through on other interpretations of the conditional. In (9a) the existential quantifier 'a$_x$' has narrow scope relative to the conditional. Hence the occurrence of 'x' in the consequent remains unbound. This means that its semantic value will be independent of the value of the first occurrence of 'x' in the antecedent. So the pronoun 'it' on this rendering would not be anaphoric to 'a donkey'. In (9b) the indefinite 'a donkey$_x$' is assigned wide scope relative to the conditional and consequently 'it' will be anaphoric to it. But the truth conditions we get are not right: the formula in (9b) will be made true by any value of x that makes the antecedent false, independently of what John does to his donkeys.

A better approximation to the meaning of (8a–b), suggested by Geach (1962), would be something like (10):

(10)   a. every$_x$ [x is a donkey and John owns x] [John beats x]
        b. every$_x$ [x is Italian and x is tall] [x is blond]

The question then becomes why it is that the indefinite has universal force in these examples. One may try to account for this shift by relating it to genericity. Indefinites are known to have generic uses, as in (11):

(11)   a. A dog barks.
        b. Gn$_x$ [x is a dog] [x barks]

Here 'Gn$_x$ [φ Ψ]' is meant to stand for something like 'It is generally true that if x satisfies φ, it also satisfies Ψ'. While spelling this out is very complicated, the quantificational force of the operator Gn is clearly (quasi-)universal. Perhaps we are dealing with generic uses of indefinites in (8a–b) and this is why indefinites in such sentences exhibit universal quantificational force.

While conditionals and generics may well be related, there are several reasons to doubt that a simpleminded account of donkey anaphora in terms of genericity, such as the one I have just sketched, will work. Let me illustrate why. First, notice that in isolation the antecedent of (8a) is clearly nongeneric:

(12)   a. John owns a donkey.
        b. a$_x$ [x is a donkey and John owns x]
        c. Gn$_x$ [x is a donkey] [John owns x]

The interpretation of (12a) is (12b), where the indefinite is interpreted existentially; not (12c), where it is interpreted generically. If the meaning of (8a) is a function of the meaning of (12a), as compositionality would demand, it remains a mystery how a shift in the quantificational force of the indefinite from existential to generic could occur.

Moreover, it seems that phenomena wholly parallel to (8a–b) occur in sentences that clearly are not generic. For example:

(13)   All the times yesterday when [a student]$_i$ walked in, John was rude to him$_i$.

Here again, the indefinite *a student* appears to have universal force, but the sentence is clearly episodic. So the shift in quantificational force of indefinites in *if/when*-clauses from existential to universal seems to be independent of genericity.

In fact, the quantificational force of indefinites in *if/when*-clauses appears to be more variable than it may prima facie appear. Consider the following paradigm:

(14)　　a. If an Italian is tall, he is always blond
　　　　　　 ≈ Every tall Italian is blond
　　　　b. Usually, if an Italian is tall, he is blond
　　　　　　 ≈ Most tall Italians are blond
　　　　c. Often, if an Italian is tall, he is blond
　　　　　　 ≈ Many tall Italians are blond
　　　　d. Sometimes, if an Italian is tall, he is blond
　　　　　　 ≈ Some tall Italians are blond

What emerges from this is fairly clear: adverbs of quantification determine the quantificational force of indefinites in *if/when*-clauses (and, more generally, in sentence-initial adverbial clauses). It is as if in the antecedent of an *if/when*-clause, indefinites lacked a quantificational force of their own. In light of these data, the universal quantificational force that indefinites take on when there is no overt adverb of quantification (as discussed above) appears to be a kind of "default" option. In other words, if no adverb of quantification is overtly realized, indefinites in conditionals are interpreted universally. Again, this behavior sharply separates indefinites from other quantified NPs.

1.2.3 Relative Clauses

Relative clauses give rise to problems that appear to be in some way parallel to those of conditionals. Consider the following:

(15)　　a.　Every man that has [a donkey]$_i$ beats it$_i$.
　　　　b.　No man that has [a donkey]$_i$ beats it$_i$.
　　　　c.　Most men that have [a donkey]$_i$ beat it$_i$.
　　　　d.　*Every man that has [no donkey]$_i$ wants it$_i$.
　　　　e.　*Every man that has [every donkey]$_i$ beats it$_i$.

Here, too, an indefinite appears capable of anteceding a pronoun across a relative clause boundary, while other NPs don't. Moreover, it is unclear how to obtain the meaning of sentences like (15a–c) compositionally. Let us illustrate by looking at (15a). There appear to be two options, as follows:

(16)   a. every$_x$ [x is a man and a$_y$ [y is a donkey and x has y]] [x beats y]
       b. a$_y$ [y is a donkey and every$_x$ [x is a man and x has y] [x beats y]]

In (16a) 'a donkey' has scope at the level of the relative clause. Consequently it does not bind the rightmost occurrence of 'y' and the pronoun is not interpreted as anaphoric to it. In (16b) the indefinite is assigned wide scope and the interpretation we get is 'There is a donkey such that for every man x, if x owns it, x beats it'. While this is arguably a possible reading for (16b), it surely isn't the most prominent one. A reasonable first approximation to the meanings of (15a–c) is given in (17a–c), respectively:

(17)   a. every$_{x,y}$ [x is a man, y is a donkey, and x owns y] [x beats y]
       b. no$_{x,y}$ [x is a man, y is a donkey, and x owns y] [x beats y]
       c. most$_{x,y}$ [x is a man, y is a donkey, and x owns y] [x beats y]

where a formula of the form '$Q_{x,y}$ [A] [B]' is taken to be true just in case Q-many pairs $\langle x,y \rangle$ that satisfy A satisfy B. In particular, (15a) is interpreted as a universal quantification over pairs.[7] So here, too, we see that indefinites can reach beyond their syntactic scope and appear to display a chameleonic behavior.

1.2.4 Accessibility

There is a further important property of the kind of anaphora under discussion. It concerns the issue of what domain conditions such anaphora must obey, if any. It would seem that indeed there are certain conditions that have to be met for an anaphoric link between an indefinite and a pronoun to be possible. Consider, for example, the following cases:

(18)   a. *Every man who has [a donkey]$_i$ beats it$_i$. It$_i$ isn't happy.
       b. *Always, if John has [a donkey]$_i$, he beats it$_i$. It$_i$ isn't happy.
       c. *John doesn't have a donkey$_i$. He wants it$_i$.

The anaphoric links in (18) between *a donkey* and the last occurrence of *it* are ill-formed, in spite of the fact that normally an indefinite can reach out of a sentence into the next one (cf. section 1.2.1). While the NP *a donkey* can antecede the first *it*, it cannot antecede the second. In (18c), we notice that the presence of negation blocks anaphora. How can we describe the relevant environments? How can we differentiate (18) from the well-formed sentences in (3) above? Observe that *every man* in (18a) and *always* in (18b) c-command the first occurrence of *it* (i.e., the one which is in fact anaphorically linked to the indefinite) but not the second occurrence of *it*. Notice, moreover, that negation in (18c) does not c-command the pronoun *it*. Perhaps it is to these facts that the impossibility of the anaphoric links in (18) is to be associated. Let us try to be a bit more explicit. What appears to affect the quantificational force of an indefinite is the closest c-commanding adverb of quantification or the closest c-commanding NP (which is not itself an indefinite) or the closest c-commanding negation. Let us call such an element the *binder* of the indefinite. As a first approximation, then, we can state the following domain condition:[8]

(19)   a. An indefinite α can antecede a pronoun β iff the lowest binder that c-commands α c-commands β.[9]
        b. Binder: adverb of quantification, quantificational (non-indefinite) NP, or negation.

If the condition in (19a) is met, we say that the antecedent is *accessible* to the pronoun. As it is, this condition is simply meant as a description of the facts.

Let us check the correctness of the hypothesis in (19) by considering a variety of other cases:

(20)   a. Usually, if a man has [a donkey]$_i$, it$_i$ gets beaten.
        b. *Usually, if **every man** has [a donkey]$_i$, it$_i$ gets beaten.

(21)   a. John met a farmer who had [a donkey]$_i$ and examined it$_i$.
        b. *John met **every farmer** who had [a donkey]$_i$ and examined it$_i$.

(22)   a. Always, if John sees a woman with [a hat]$_i$, he stares at it$_i$.
        b. *Always, if John sees **every woman** with [a hat]$_i$, he stares at it$_i$.

In all these examples, the relevant anaphoric link is possible in the (a)-cases and impossible in the (b)-cases. The (b)-cases arise by replacing an indefinite in the (a)-cases with a universally quantified NP (boldfaced in the examples). This introduces a binder for the lower indefinite. And we see that whenever such binder doesn't c-command the pronoun, the anaphoric link is impossible. The introduction of a binder creates a "screen" that the indefinite cannot pierce. So the domain condition in (19) seems to be empirically adequate.

There are cases where an indefinite NP can antecede a pronoun which is not accessible to it. The following sentences illustrate this.

(23)   a. Either Morrill Hall doesn't have [a bathroom]$_i$ or it$_i$ is in a funny place.   (B. Partee)

    b. I think that John has [an apartment]$_i$ in Paris, and I hope he hasn't sold it$_i$.   (P. Seuren)

    c. Every chess set comes with [a spare pawn]$_i$. It$_i$ is taped under the box.   (P. Sells)

    d. It is not the case that John doesn't have [a car]$_i$. It$_i$ is parked outside.

How the anaphoric links in (23) are to be treated is pretty much open. In chapter 2 we will discuss some possibilities. But however we want to treat them, it can be argued that they constitute a phenomenon which is distinct from plain donkey anaphora. The key observation in this connection is that anaphora across inaccessible domains is highly sensitive to various aspects of the context—what is known or presupposed by the speaker, the specific properties of the lexical items involved in interaction with what the extralinguistic facts are, and so on. This can be illustrated in a number of ways. Contrast, for example, (23b) with the following:

(24)   ??I hope that John has [an apartment]$_i$ in Paris. I believe he hasn't sold it$_i$.

(24) is structurally isomorphic to (23b). We have merely switched around the main verbs, but this suffices to make the anaphoric link much harder to interpret. Notice that if we insert the adverbial *still* in the first conjunct of (24), things improve again:

(25)   I hope that John still has [an apartment]$_i$ in Paris. I believe he hasn't sold it$_i$.

The presence of *still* triggers a presupposition that there was an apartment John used to have. Such a presupposition suffices to make the anaphoric link in (25) well-formed.

    Consider next the following discourse:

(26)   ??John doesn't have [a car]$_i$. Paul has it$_i$.

Out of the blue, the anaphoric link in (26) appears to be hard to interpret. Suppose now that we know that John used to have an old car which he was planning to sell to Paul. If we imagine uttering (26) against this background, it improves dramatically. And introducing an adverb like *anymore* makes the sentence perfect:

(27)   John doesn't have [a car]$_i$ anymore. Paul has it$_i$.

This shows that a shift in what facts are known or believed suffices to make the relevant link interpretable.

This contrasts sharply with what happens with anaphora in accessible domains, that is, "plain" donkey anaphora. Plain donkey anaphora appears to be no more affected by contextual and pragmatic factors than ordinary c-command anaphora. For example, swapping around the verbs in (28a) does not affect the well-formedness of the relevant anaphoric link in any way:

(28)   a. Every man who owns [a donkey]$_i$ beats it$_i$.
        b. Every man who beats [a donkey]$_i$ owns it$_i$.

These considerations suggest that plain donkey anaphora is governed essentially by structural factors, just like c-command anaphora, while the phenomena in (25) are clearly affected by various aspects of the context. Thus, prima facie it would appear to be plausible to separate them off from each other and study them independently (which does not mean that the two kinds of anaphora do not interact in interesting ways). For the time being we will concentrate on anaphora across accessible domains.

1.2.5 Summary

The anaphoric and quantificational nature of indefinites differs significantly and systematically from that of other NPs. These differences show up in coordinated structures, in preposed *if/when*-clauses, in relative clauses, and in the presence of quantificational adverbs. It is not prima facie obvious how to deal with them. For example, saying something along the following lines certainly will not do:

(29)   NPs like *every man* can antecede a pronoun only under c-command (at the relevant level, whatever that may turn out to be). Indefinites are not subject to such restriction.

As we have seen, if we go by this hypothesis, we are left in the dark as to how to derive the right truth conditions for the constructions in question. Moreover, it appears that donkey anaphora is subject to quite stringent structural conditions: it can only take place if the antecedent is accessible to the pronoun. Anaphora across inaccessible domains is also possible, but it appears to be governed by pragmatic factors in a way that plain donkey anaphora is not. So we seem to be confronted with a genuine knot of problems. If we want to figure out what constitutes a possible anaphoric link in the languages of the world, we have to untie it.

1.3 "CLASSICAL" DISCOURSE REPRESENTATION THEORY

Discourse Representation Theory (henceforth DRT) constitutes a highly productive and diversified line of research whose original nucleus can be found in Lewis 1975. In this section we will review, in an informal way, the main ideas of what constitutes "classical DRT," that is, the theories developed in Kamp 1981 and Heim 1982.

The assumptions that appear to be fundamental to all variants of classical DRT are the following:

(30)   i.   Indefinites have no quantificational force of their own. They are, in this respect, like free variables.

ii.   The quantificational force of indefinites is determined by the first available binder, that is, the lowest c-commanding quantifying determiner (*every, no, most,* etc.) or adverb of quantification (*always, usually,* etc.). These quantifying elements are *unselective.* They bind all free variables in their domain.

iii. A binder Q sets up a tripartite structure of the form Q[A][B], where A is the *restriction* of the binder and B its *(nuclear) scope.*

iv.   A rule of *existential closure* assigns existential force to indefinites that are not otherwise quantified.

Let us see how these ideas work in some of the key cases. Consider first the following kind of discourse anaphora:

(31)   A man walked in. He was wearing a hat.

Since indefinites are assimilated to free variables, the logical form of (31) can, in first approximation, be represented as in (32):

(32) $man(x) \wedge walked\text{-}in(x) \wedge hat(y) \wedge wear(x,y)$

This representation is obtained under the assumption that discourse sequencing is interpreted conjunctively and that the pronoun in (31) is associated with the same index (i.e., the same variable) as the indefinite *a man.* Since in (32) there are no quantifying elements, the indefinites get existential force by default (cf. (30iv)). This default quantification can be thought of as an existential quantifier that operates globally on the discourse as a whole and binds all free variables associated with indefinites, yielding the following:

(33) $\exists_{x,y}$ [man(x) $\wedge$ walked-in(x) $\wedge$ hat(y) $\wedge$ wear(x,y)]

In this way, we derive the fact that indefinites appear to be able to bind across stretches of discourse.

Consider next a relative clause like (34):

(34)   [Every man]$_i$ who owns [a donkey]$_j$ beats it$_j$ with [a stick]$_k$.

Here we have a quantifying element, namely *every*. Quantifying elements take two arguments: a restriction and a scope. In the case of (34), the restriction is given by the common noun phrase *man who has a donkey* and the scope by the verb phrase *beats it*. Thus the logical form of (34) can be taken to be, in first approximation, something like (35a):

(35)   a. every [man who owns a donkey] [beats it with a stick]
        b. every [man(x) $\wedge$ donkey(y) $\wedge$ own(x,y)] [stick(z) $\wedge$ beat-with (x,y,z)]

Since indefinites are free variables, (35a) becomes (35b). Moreover, quantifying elements are unselective; consequently they bind all variables which are free in their restrictive clause. We thus get:

(36) $\forall_{x,y}$ [man(x) $\wedge$ donkey(y) $\wedge$ own(x,y)] [stick(z) $\wedge$ beat-with(x,y,z)]

The variable z in the right argument of the quantifier in (36), being, as it were, "left over," receives existential force by default (i.e., by an automatically inserted existential quantifier, parallel to the one in (33)), which finally gets us to (37):

(37) $\forall_{x,y}$ [man(x) $\wedge$ donkey(y) $\wedge$ own(x,y)] $\exists_z$[stick(z) $\wedge$ beat-with(x,y,z)]

Formula (37) transparently yields the desired truth conditions for (34).

Consider finally a conditional like (38):

(38)   Usually, if [a man]$_i$ owns [a donkey]$_j$, he$_i$ beats it$_j$ with [a stick]$_k$.

Here the derivation of the desired reading proceeds pretty much as in the previous case. The quantifying element is the adverb of quantification *usually* (which in terms of its quantificational force corresponds to *most*). The restriction of *usually* is the *if*-clause, while its nuclear scope is the main clause. The result is (39):

(39)   most [a man owns a donkey] [he beats it with a stick]

Indefinites are interpreted as free variables, which gives us (40):

(40)   most [man(x) $\wedge$ donkey(y) $\wedge$ own(x,y)] [stick(z) $\wedge$ beat-with(x,y,z)]

The quantifier *most* in (40) binds the variables in its restriction, while the remaining free variable in the right argument gets existential force by default:

(41)   most$_{x,y}$ [man(x) $\wedge$ donkey(y) $\wedge$ own(x,y)] $\exists_z$[stick(z) $\wedge$ beat-with(x,y,z)]

Formula (41) assigns the desired truth conditions to (38), namely that for most pairs $\langle x,y \rangle$ such that x is a man, y a donkey, and x owns y, there exists a stick z such that x beats y with z. The semantics for (38) we are assuming here is somewhat simplified, for adverbs like *usually* arguably have a modal dimension, which we are ignoring for the time being. In spite of this simplification, an immediate consequence of the present view is that the quantificational force of an indefinite in an *if/when*-clause will be determined by the quantificational adverb. So for example, a sentence like (42a) will be interpreted as in (42b):

(42)   a. Sometimes, if [a man]$_i$ owns [a donkey]$_j$, he$_i$ beats it$_j$ with [a stick]$_k$.
        b. $\exists_{x,y}$ [man(x) $\wedge$ donkey(y) $\wedge$ own(x,y)] $\exists_z$[stick(z) $\wedge$ beat-with(x,y,z)]

Within classical DRT it is also assumed that if an *if/when*-clause lacks an overt adverb of quantification, a null adverb of quantification with a semantics similar to that of *always* or *usually* is present. This assumption reflects the idea, defended in Kratzer 1986, that the sole semantic contribution of an *if/when*-clause is that of restricting an adverb of quantification or a modal operator. Accordingly, the semantics of a sentence like (43a) can be represented as in (43b):

(43)   a. If [a man]$_i$ sees [a donkey]$_j$, he$_i$ beats it$_j$.
        b. Gn$_{x,y}$ [man(x) $\wedge$ donkey(y) $\wedge$ see(x,y)] [beat(x,y)]

In (43b) the implicit adverb of quantification whose presence is posited in (43a) is taken to be 'Gn', the (or a) generic operator. This reflects the view that sentences of this kind are interpreted generically (i.e., quasi-universally).[10]

Even on the basis of this very informal presentation, it should be clear that the hypotheses put forth in (30) show some promise in accounting for the complex behavior of indefinites and anaphoric pronouns in donkey anaphora contexts. In particular, the fact that the scope of an indefinite appears to extend across conjuncts and multisentential stretches of discourse follows from the fact that their quantificational force in these cases stems from a text-level process of existential quantification. The chameleonic properties of indefinites in relative clauses and conditionals derives from the fact that what binds the indefinite in these cases is the quantifier associated with the head of the relative or the adverb of quantification.

These assumptions also seem to explain *why* this type of anaphora displays the structural properties noticed above—that is, why an indefinite can only antecede a pronoun accessible to it. In (19a), repeated here as (44), accessibility was characterized as follows:

(44)   An indefinite α can antecede a pronoun β iff the lowest binder that c-commands α c-commands β.

It is not hard to see that (44) follows from the assumptions in (30). In general, for two variables to covary they must be in the scope of the same quantifying element. In the present system, where indefinites are assimilated to free variables, this will only be the case if a quantifying element c-commands both the variable associated with the indefinite and the pronoun coindexed with the indefinite. Consider one of the impossible anaphoric links discussed above:

(45)   *Usually, if [**every man**]$_i$ has [a donkey]$_j$, it$_j$ gets badly mistreated.

Let's focus on the reading of the *if*-clause according to which every man has a different donkey. On this reading, the two quantifying elements, *usually* and *every*, would have the following arguments respectively:

(46)   usually [every [man] [has a donkey]] [it gets badly mistreated]

By applying the procedure based on (30) we get:

(47)   most [$\forall_x$[man(x)] $\exists_y$[donkey(y) $\wedge$ has(x,y)]] [gets-mistreated(y)]

This formula makes it clear that the occurrence of 'y' in the right argument of 'most' is not in the scope of '$\exists y$'. Hence the value of this variable will be independent of the value of any previous occurrence of 'y'. The impossibility of the anaphoric link in (45) is a consequence of this fact. This constraint is of course fully general, and applies in the same way to all the ungrammatical cases in (20)–(21). So the descriptive generalization in (44) becomes a consequence of the assumptions in (30) and does not have the status of a constraint that must be independently assumed in the grammar.

The above considerations are largely informal. We have used the principles in (30) to provide a kind of derivation of quasi-formulae that are meant to express the desired truth conditions. To actually test the correctness of the claims made here, we will want to be more explicit about this procedure, by providing a formalism within which the assumptions in question can be fleshed out. But before we do that, we should address a further preliminary issue. DRT treats donkey pronouns as bound variables. However, it is conceivable that some pronouns are interpreted in a different way, namely as proxy for a description whose content can be systematically reconstructed from the context. A prime candidate for such an interpretation are the pronouns in following examples:

(48)   The man who gave [his paycheck]$_i$ to his wife is wiser than the man
        who gave it$_i$ to his mistress.   (Karttunen 1969)

Here the antecedent of the pronoun *it* is the NP *his paycheck*. Yet it seems impossible to analyze *it* as being bound by or coreferential with *his paycheck* (for that refers to the paycheck of the first man). More plausibly, *it* simply stands for another occurrence of *his paycheck* (one where the pronoun *his* is bound by a different NP). These pronouns are sometimes called "pronouns of laziness" (Geach 1962) or *E-type pronouns*.[11] One might regard them as descriptions in disguise. In (48) the content of the description (namely, 'the paycheck of x') is provided by the previous explicit occurrence of *his paycheck*. The availability of this pronominalization strategy raises the issue of its applicability to donkey anaphora. In other words, while the assumptions in (30) seem promising, a strategy based on the idea that pronouns are description-like (i.e., the E-type strategy) might yield an analysis that is equally successful, if not superior. So before pursuing DRT further, we now turn to a preliminary comparison of such a strategy of analysis with the E-type strategy.

1.4 UNIQUENESS

Let us illustrate how the E-type strategy—(i.e., the possibility of interpreting pronouns as descriptions in disguise—could be applied to various cases of donkey anaphora. Let us begin by considering stretches of discourse like (31) above, repeated here:

(31)   A man walked in. He was wearing a hat.

If we regard *he* as a description, a plausible candidate for the content of such description might be something like this:

(49)   A man walked in. The man that walked in was wearing a hat.

Uttering the first sentence in (31) provides us with an identifying property (being a man that walked in) which we can use to get at the intended referent of the pronoun *he*. This will only work, however, if we can maintain that whenever we refer to something introduced in previous discourse, a *uniqueness presupposition* is present (in the case of (31), the presupposition that only one man walked in).[12]

While the details of an approach along these lines remain to be worked out (and may turn out to be quite tricky), it is clear that such an approach has a fair amount of initial plausibility, at least to the extent that the presence of a uniqueness presupposition can be justified. Let us see what happens if we look at other typical donkey anaphora contexts in this light. Let us begin by considering conditionals:

(50)   a. If John has a donkey, he beats it.
        b. If John has a donkey, he beats the donkey he owns.

Extending in an obvious way the reasoning adopted in connection with (31), we can analyze (50a) as in (50b). Here it is the antecedent of the conditional that provides us with the property necessary to identify the referent of the pronoun. The analysis in (50b) claims that (50a) presupposes that John has just one donkey. Here intuitions are not so sharp. Contrast (50a) with (51):

(51)   If someone is in Rhodes, he is not in Athens.   (Heim 1982)

As Heim points out, we don't want to analyze *he* in (51) as 'the person who is in Rhodes', for that is certain to be an improper description (in the relevant contexts, there will be many people who are in Rhodes). One way out of this situation is to appeal to the idea that conditionals and *when*-clauses generally involve a quantification over eventualities or situations. One can argue, for example, following Davidson (1967), Parsons (1990), and many others, that verbs have internal arguments for eventualities (i.e., states, occasions, situations or the like), so that sentences like (52a–b) are interpreted as in (52c–d).[13]

(52)   a. John sings.
        b. Agesilaus is in Rhodes.
        c. ∃o [sing(o,j)]
        d. ∃o [in(o,Rhodes,a)]

In particular, (52a) is analyzed as saying that there exists an occasion at which John sings. By the same token, (52b) is analyzed as saying that there is a state or situation in which Agesilaus is in Rhodes. Now, the variable over eventualities/situations can be taken to be what adverbs of quantification quantify over in conditionals. So for example, we could analyze (51) as follows:

(53)   For any (minimal) situation s such that someone lives in Rhodes in s, the person who lives in Rhodes in s does not live in Athens in s.

In this way, uniqueness is appropriately relativized to situations. We consider states of living in Rhodes that contain just one person and quantify over those. We can then pick the unique person that such state contains and say something about him or her. The interpretation that we get as a result is adequate and can be compositionally worked out. And it relies on the idea that pronouns are (suitably relativized) descriptions of a kind.

   A major problem that this line runs into is constituted by sentences of the following kind:

(54)   a. If a man lives with another man, he shares the housework with
           him.   (J. van Eijck)
        b. If a cardinal meets another cardinal, he blesses him.
        (H. Kamp)

What description are the pronouns in the consequent associated with? The problem is that the predicates in the *if*-clauses are symmetric. In any minimal situation in which a man lives with another man, there are going to be two men, undistinguishable as to the role they play in that situation. So how do we pick one or the other by means of a suitable description in a non–ad hoc way? Relativization to states of affairs doesn't seem to help us in this connection.[14]

   Let us now turn to relative clauses. Sentence (55a) could be interpreted as (55b):

(55)   a. Every man that has a donkey beats it.
        b. Every man that has a donkey beats the donkey he owns.

According to the analysis in (55b), sentences like (55a) only say something about men that own exactly one donkey. Again, it seems difficult to decide whether this is correct just by looking at our intuitions. However, Heim (1982) points out the following kind of counterexample to the claim that the pronoun *it* in (55a) carries a uniqueness presupposition:

(56)   a. Every man who bought a sage plant here bought five others with it.

    b. Every house around here that has a barn has another one next to it.   (Kratzer 1988)

A sentence like (56a) would be appropriate in a situation where sage plants are only sold in cartons of six. Clearly, it makes no sense to analyze *it* in (56a) as 'the sage plant that x bought'; it is just not obvious what description to use. Kadmon (1990) has suggested that there is a way in which sentences like (56) are special. These types of sentences, she argues, are appropriate only in cases where it is assumed that one's choice of object for interpreting the pronoun makes no difference to the truth conditions of the sentence. Here is what she proposes regarding (56a):

> I believe that speakers accept this example because it can't make any difference which sage plant the pronoun *it* stands for, out of all the sage plants that a buyer x bought (for each buyer x). Given an individual who bought at least one sage plant, there are two possibilities: (i) She bought at least six plants. In that case no matter which plant you pick, it is true that she bought five others along with it. (ii) She bought 5 plants or less. In that case no matter which plant you pick, it is false that she bought 5 others with it. (Kadmon 1987, p. 317)

So, Kadmon concludes, even sage plant sentences display uniqueness, albeit of a special kind. However, I find this way of dealing with the issue problematic on several counts. What exactly does it mean that the choice of referent for a pronoun cannot make a difference to the truth conditions of a sentence? We may try to explicate this by saying that in order to interpret such sentences we need a context where it follows from the common ground that the choice of referent for the pronoun does not affect the truth conditions. A context where it is known that sage plants are sold by the half dozen only would satisfy this condition for (56a). But what would such a context be in the case of (56b)? We don't want to say that (56b) is felicitous only in a context where it is known that houses have two barns, for in such a context it would be pointless to utter (56b). Another class of cases that appears to be problematic in this connection, discussed in Rooth 1987 and Heim 1990, is the following:

(57)   No father with a teenage son lends him the car on weekdays.

There clearly isn't any uniqueness presupposition here; that is, in uttering (57) we do not confine our attention to fathers who have just one teenage son. So if Kadmon's suggestion is on the right track, it should make no difference to the truth conditions of (57) which son we choose. Yet in a situation where a father has more than one son and lends the car to some but not all of them, it does make a difference which son we pick as the referent of the pronoun. Thus, as Heim (1990, p. 160) puts it, Kadmon's account leads us to expect that our intuitions in the case of (57) should be shakier than they are.

We could weaken Kadmon's position and say that the uniqueness presupposition gets suspended when the choice of referent for the pronoun makes no difference to the truth *value* (as opposed to the truth *conditions*) of the relevant sentence. But this amounts to simply giving up uniqueness presuppositions altogether. It is no more than saying that a pronoun may or may not carry a uniqueness presupposition.

To sum up the discussion so far, the prima facie plausibility of the E-type strategy in analyzing donkey anaphora seems to run into a series of difficulties related to the fact that (in the form considered here) it requires a uniqueness condition. And, there appear to be no systematic uniqueness presuppositions in donkey sentences (contra Kadmon). Perhaps the only case in which such uniqueness presuppositions seem to be systematically present are coordinated narrative sequences such as (31) above. In those cases, appealing to scalar implicatures looks like a plausible first guess as to what is going on.

The outcome of this preliminary discussion provides supporting evidence for DRT in two ways. First, the Geachean truth conditions that DRT assigns to donkey sentences can be successfully defended against allegations of inadequacy on grounds that a systematic uniqueness presupposition is being missed. Second, the appeal to the E-type strategy, where pronouns are interpreted as singular descriptions, appears to be difficult to defend; the claim that such pronouns are bound variables, as DRT maintains, thereby gains support.

There is, however, a different line one can take, which may make the E-type strategy more viable. Instead of regarding donkey pronouns as singular definite descriptions, one might regard them as plural (or rather, number-neutral) ones. So, for example, one might analyze (58a) as (58b):

(58)   a. Every man that has a donkey beats it.
        b. Every man that has a donkey beats the donkey(s) he owns.

This analysis, which is defended, for example, by Lappin (1989) and Neale (1990), assigns to (58a) virtually the same truth conditions Geach had proposed. According to this analysis, while the pronoun *it* in (56a) is morphologically singular, it is semantically neutral as to whether it ranges over an individual or a group of individuals.

I believe that there is something right about this idea, but I don't think that taken by itself it constitutes an alternative to DRT. In chapter 2, I will present a version of the number-neutral approach to E-type pronouns and defend the view that such analysis is a complement, not an alternative, to DRT. For the time being, we seem to have enough motivation for exploring DRT further. But in order to do so, we must spell out some basic assumptions about syntax.

1.5 SYNTACTIC BACKGROUND

A lot of what I have to say is neutral with respect to syntactic frameworks, in the sense that it relies solely on widely shared assumptions on the nature of syntax and on the syntax-semantics map. But for explicitness' sake, I do need to rely on a specific syntactic framework; the one I will adopt here is a version of the Principles and Parameters approach (cf. e.g., Chomsky 1981, 1992). Besides more theory-neutral considerations, there are also aspects of my proposals that hinge directly on particular features of this syntactic approach and have general consequences for it. I will try to signal where this is the case.

To make things easier for the reader, I will first sketch my main assumptions in a relatively theory-neutral way. Then I will outline the aspects of the Principles and Parameters approach I will be adopting.

1.5.1 Weakly Theory-Bound Syntactic Assumptions

In order to interpret an expression, one needs, among other things, a way to determine the scope of quantifiers and other scope-bearing elements. I assume, therefore, that what is interpreted is a representation of (surface) constituent structure, augmented by a representation of scope and one of anaphoric relationships (indicating which pronouns are anaphoric to what). Semantics will then take the form of a compositional mapping from this level of syntactic representation into truth conditions. Such a mapping can be formulated either directly or by compositionally translating natural language into a logic like, for example, Montague's Intensional Logic (IL).

Concerning the representation of scope, there is evidence that in general, scoping in natural language must be a clause-bounded phenomenon. For example, in the following sentence, the universal quantifier in the embedded clause cannot have scope over the indefinite NP in the higher clause:

(59) a. Someone is claiming that everyone cheated.
         This sentence does *not* have the reading:
      b. For every x, there is a y such that y claims that x cheated.

By the same token, in the following sentence *everyone* cannot have scope over the negation that occurs in the higher clause:

(60) a. It is not the case that everyone will pass.
         This sentence does *not* have the reading:
      b. For every x, x will not pass.

These examples illustrate what appears to be a quite general constraint, namely that it is impossible to scope an embedded quantifier over another scope-bearing element in a higher clause—a fact that would follow from the clause-boundedness hypothesis. The only apparent counterexamples to this generalization seem to be constituted by de dicto/de re ambiguities. A sentence like (61) is ambiguous:

(61)   Ralph believes that someone is a spy.

On one reading, Ralph's belief is that there are spies. This belief is purely "general" or "conceptual," in the sense that whatever evidence might prompt Ralph to hold it is not evidence that directly links Ralph to any specific individual. This reading is called the *de dicto* reading. The second reading is one according to which Ralph's belief is about a specific individual (in the sense of being somehow caused by that individual), and this constitutes the *de re* reading. Since the pioneering work on quantified modal logic by Carnap, Quine, and others, it is customary to regard the ambiguity in question as a scopal one. The de dicto reading can be represented by assigning scope to the quantifier at the embedded clause level, while the de re reading is represented by scoping the quantifier at the matrix clause level.

The scopal theory of de dicto/de re ambiguities and the claim that quantifier scope is clause bound cannot both be right. If we adopt the former, we are left in the dark as to why facts like (59)–(60) obtain. If we adopt the latter, we are left in the dark as to how de dicto/de re ambiguities come about. Recently, Kratzer (1991) has developed an alternative to the traditional theory of de dicto/de re ambiguity which does not resort to scope and is therefore consistent with the claim that quantifiers cannot escape the minimal clause that contains them. I will assume here that a non-scopal approach to de dicto/de re ambiguities (such as Kratzer's) is on the right track; this will enable us to maintain that quantifier scope is a clause-bounded phenomenon.

A further important assumption we will make concerns dislocated constituents such as those in (62).

(62)   a. Here is the boy that Mary think John will not invite t.
        b. Who does Mary think that John will not invite t?
        c. This boy Mary thinks that John will not invite t.

In order to interpret dislocated constituents one needs to link their meaning to the position of the gaps (indicated by 't' in the above examples). I assume that gaps are encoded in the syntax by phonologically null elements and that each dislocated constituent is associated with one such element. The relation between dislocated constituents and the corresponding gaps is subject to locality conditions, which have been widely studied in the literature. Note, for instance, the ungrammaticality of the following:

(63)   *Who$_i$ does John like [the boy]$_j$ that e$_j$ invited e$_i$?

In (63) we are trying to question something out of a relative clause, which is impossible in English. I will adopt all of the canonical constraints on long-distance dependencies (like the Complex NP Constraint or the *Wh*-Island Constraint).

There are also a number of constraints on anaphora; these have been extensively studied in a wide variety of frameworks and will play a role in what follows. I will mention some of them here.

It is well known that reflexive pronouns must find their antecedent nearby. This generalization is stated in (64a) and illustrated in (64b–c).

(64)   a.   A reflexive must be bound *locally*.
        b.   John$_i$ likes himself$_i$.
        c.   *John$_i$ claims that Mary likes himself$_i$.

What exactly "locally" means in different languages is an object of controversy (even though much progress has been made in our understanding of the nature of locality). We will not try to settle this issue here, remaining rather vague on the locality condition involved.

A related generalization is that nonreflexive pronouns *cannot* have a local antecedent:

(65)   a.   A nonreflexive pronoun must be locally free.
       b.   *John$_i$ likes him$_i$.
       c.   *[Every man]$_i$ likes him$_i$.

It can be argued that, with some important qualifications, the environments where a reflexive must find its antecedent are those within which a nonreflexive cannot have one.

Yet another well-known constraint is that a pronoun cannot both precede and c-command its antecedent. The following is a typical paradigm that illustrates this restriction.

(66)   a.   *He$_i$ likes [every man]$_i$.
       b.   *He$_i$ thinks that John$_i$ is a genius.
       c.   *It$_i$ is happy when [a cat]$_i$ meows.
       d.   When it$_i$ meows, [a cat]$_i$ is happy.

The restriction just discussed is related to a further important observation, namely that, generally speaking, a quantified NP cannot bind a pronoun to its left, even if the pronoun does not c-command it:

(67)   a.   *His$_i$ mother likes [every boy]$_i$.
            This sentence *cannot* mean:
       b.   For every boy x, x's mother loves x.

Similarly, *wh*-elements cannot bind something to the left of their gap:

(68)   a.   *Who$_i$ does his$_i$ mother like t$_i$?
            This sentence *cannot* mean:
       b.   For which x, x's mother loves x.

This phenomenon is known in the literature as *Weak Crossover*.[15] Note that sentences like (66d) appear to be exceptions to Weak Crossover. We will come back to this issue in chapter 3.

Any theory of anaphora in natural language must account for the above generalizations, to the extent that they appear to be constitutive of the way languages work. This can be done in a number of ways. Moreover, it is possible to implement the generalizations in question in frameworks different from the one I am adopting (e.g., in a categorial setting or in a Generalized Phrase Structure one).[16] But as mentioned, I will pursue here a more or less traditional transformational approach, whose specifics I will now briefly outline. What follows is a rather cut-and-dry summary of the basics of the Principles and Parameters framework we will be assuming. It can be skipped with no harm by those familiar with that theory.

1.5.2 The "Official" Framework

According to the Principles and Parameters framework, grammars are generative devices organized as follows:

(69)

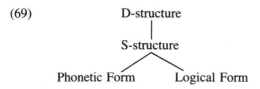

D-structure is a direct projection of the lexical properties of expressions into syntactic (phrase) structure. D-structure is mapped into S-structure via 'Move α', a transformation that freely moves constituents. Passive and raising (i.e., NP movement) as well as relativization and question formation (i.e., *wh*-movement) are the main instances of this transformation. S-structure is the input to phonetic interpretation and to the mapping into LF, which is also done via Move α. Scope is represented at LF, by adjoining NPs to S (Quantifier Raising). For example, the two possible readings of a sentence like (70a) are represented as in (70b) and (70c), respectively.

(70)   a. An engineer inspected every plane.
        b. [an engineer$_i$ every plane$_j$ [t$_i$ inspected t$_j$]]
        c. [every plane$_j$ an engineer$_i$ [t$_i$ inspected t$_j$]]

To be licensed as well-formed, a sentence must be well-formed at every level. The interaction of a set of (parametrized) principles prevents Move α from overgenerating. A standard system of relevant subtheories is the following:

(71)   a. X$'$-theory (which determines the admissible phrase-structural configurations)
        b. Theory of government (which characterizes the modes of interaction of constituents that are in construction with one another)
        c. Theory of bounding (which determines locality conditions on Move α)
        d. Theta theory (which determines how argument-taking items are linked to their arguments)

e. Case theory (which determines, via conditions on case, many of the distributional properties of NPs)

f. Binding theory (which determines what constitutes a well-formed anaphoric relation)

g. Control theory (which deals with the interpretation of PRO, the null subject of infinitives and gerunds)

Thus, for example, the generalizations about the distribution of reflexive and nonreflexive pronouns briefly recalled in the previous section are dealt with in the binding theory, one of whose formulations (cf., e.g., Chomsky 1981) is the following:

(72)   *Chomsky's (1981) Binding Theory*
Principle A: A reflexive must be bound within its minimal governing category.
Principle B: A nonreflexive pronoun must be free in its minimal governing category.
Principle C: An R-expression (i.e., a nonpronominal NP) must be free.

An expression α is bound iff it is coindexed with an expression β that c-commands it. The exact definition of 'minimal governing category' (or, in Chomsky's 1986 theory, 'minimal complete functional complex') is controversial. For our purposes, we can assume a relatively simple notion of minimal governing category, as, say, the minimal category that contains a governor for α and a subject.

To illustrate another module, we might briefly consider X'-theory. According to this theory, admissible phrase structure configurations are just those licensed by the following templates:

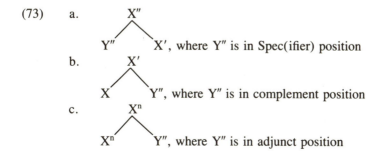

(73)   a.   X″
            Y″   X', where Y″ is in Spec(ifier) position
        b.   X'
            X   Y″, where Y″ is in complement position
        c. X^n
            X^n Y″, where Y″ is in adjunct position

For instance, the structure of a simple sentence is taken to be the following:

(74)

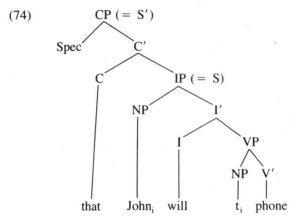

Clauses are taken to be the projection of Inflection, which contains tense and agreement, and the complements of Complementizers. Subjects originate in the Specifier of VP and, in languages like English, move into the Spec of IP (for evidence in favor of this view, see, e.g., Kuroda 1988 and Koopman and Sportiche 1988). Categories like C or I are functional categories, while N or V are lexical categories. It is also generally assumed that the I-node is split into further functional heads (where the information about tense, agreement, and so on is located), but I will omit making reference to these intermediate projections except when directly relevant. In fact, when simplicity calls for it, I will switch back from the notation in (74) to the more traditional one using S and S'.

The other modules of the Principles and Parameters approach are organized in a similar manner. Recently, Chomsky (1992) has proposed some interesting modifications of the model just sketched that eliminate the need to resort to intermediate levels of representation (i.e., D-structure and S-structure), thereby making the Principles and Parameters framework more "minimal." What I have to say is consistent with such a "minimalistic" revision of the model. However, I will keep referring to D-structure or S-structure on occasion, for purely expository purposes. Also, I will introduce further notions as needed. What I have presented above should suffice to give a rough indication of the main mechanisms that we will be relying on in subsequent discussion.

1.6 THE FIRST SOUL OF DISCOURSE REPRESENTATION THEORY

We can now take a closer look at how the basic assumptions of DRT can be implemented. This will enable us to test their consequences and flesh out the differences between what we have been referring to as "the two souls of DRT." We will begin by introducing and discussing the theory developed in Heim 1982 (chapter 2), which is based on a set of construal rules.

1.6.1 The Construal Component

Heim starts out from the standard assumptions that each NP carries a referential index and that all nonpronominal NPs are adjoined to S by Quantifier Raising (QR). Heim adds to these a number of further rules designed specifically to cope with donkey anaphora. First, we have a rule called *Quantifier Construal* (QC) that adjoins a quantifying element (quantificational determiner or adverb of quantification) to the left of the lowest S node containing it. Here are a couple of sample derivations:

(75)   Every man likes him.
        QR
        $\Rightarrow$ [every man$_i$ [t$_i$ likes him$_j$]]
        QC
        $\Rightarrow$

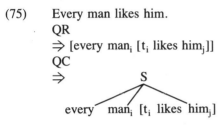

(76)   If a man sings he is usually happy.
        QR
        $\Rightarrow$ [S [a man$_i$ [t$_i$ sings]] [he$_i$ is usually happy]]
        QC
        $\Rightarrow$

$$\text{usually [a man}_i \text{ [t}_i \text{ sings]] [he}_i \text{ is happy]}$$

Notice that while QR is an instance of Chomsky Adjunction, QC is one of daughter adjunction and creates tripartite structures. The second constituent in these structures forms the restriction of the quantifier, while the third is its nuclear scope.

The next rule takes care of default existential quantification. It comes in two parts. The first part—Existential Closure, or ∃-Closure—says: "Insert ∃ in the nuclear scope of an operator" (where an operator is a quantifier or negation). Here are some examples:

(77)   [Every man]$_i$ likes [a cat]$_j$.
        QR
        $\Rightarrow$ [every man$_i$ [a cat$_j$ [t$_i$ likes t$_j$]]]

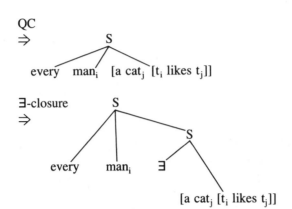

(78) a. It is not the case that John likes a woman.
    b. [not [a woman$_i$ [John likes t$_j$]]]

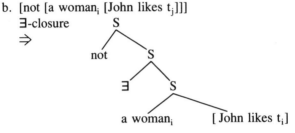

This first part of the rule of Existential Closure is designed to capture the fact that indefinites in the scope of a quantificational element (or in the scope of negation) are interpreted existentially. The second part of the rule—Text Formation—deals with multisentential discourses. Heim assumes that a discourse is constituted by adjoining a sequence of sentences under a text node. For example:

(79) [$_S$ A man walked in] [$_S$ He was wearing a hat]
    QR
    $\Rightarrow$ [$_S$ a man$_i$ [t$_i$ walked in]] [$_S$ [a hat$_j$ [he$_i$ was wearing t$_j$]]
    Text formation
    $\Rightarrow$ [$_T$[$_S$ a man$_i$ [t$_i$ walked in]] [$_S$ [a hat$_j$ [he$_i$ was wearing t$_j$]]]]

Then, Existential Closure is assumed to adjoin an existential quantifier to the T node, yielding in the case of (79):

(80) [$_T$ $\exists$ [$_T$ [$_S$ a man$_i$ [t$_i$ walked in]] [$_S$ [a hat$_j$ [he$_i$ was wearing t$_j$]]]]]

In all the structures considered so far, indefinites are interpreted as formulae containing a free variable. For example, a man$_i$ is interpreted as man(x_i). Their quantificational force is determined by the closest c-commanding quantifier. This is captured by a further rule that determines the indices each quantifier gets associated with:

(81)   *Quantifier Indexing:* Copy the index of each indefinite onto the lowest c-commanding quantifier (where the remnant of a quantified NP [e.g., *man$_i$* in (77)] counts as an indefinite).

For the examples considered above (repeated here with the same numbering), this yields:

(77')

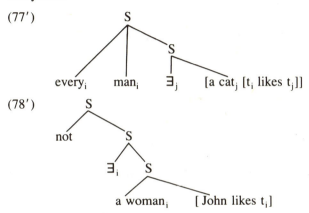

(78')

(80') $[_T \exists_{i,j} [_T [_S$ a man$_i$ [t$_i$ walked in]] $[_S$ [a hat$_j$ [he$_i$ was wearing t$_j$]]]]

The indices associated with a quantifier are called its *selection indices*. Keeping track of selection indices in this way is necessary because we must prevent a quantifier from binding a variable which is already bound higher up or whose value is indexically specified. Consider, for example, sentence (75), repeated here:

(75)   Every man$_i$ likes him$_j$.

Here we must prevent the unselective quantifier *every* from binding the pronoun *him$_j$* and yielding the following:

(82)   every$_{i,j}$ [man$_i$ [t$_i$ likes him$_j$]]

The LF in (82) would have the following truth conditions: For every x and every y, if x is a man, x likes y.

There is a further constraint that must be invoked for the system discussed so far to work. In the present framework, NPs are indexed freely. Then, general well-formedness constraints filter out undesirable coindexing. For example, in sentences like (75) something has to prevent *every man* and *him* from being coindexed, for otherwise (75) would erroneously be interpreted as equivalent to 'Every man loves himself'. In Chomsky's (1981) binding theory, this is accomplished by means of Principle B. Consider now sentence (83a). As far as standard coindexing constraints go, nothing would prevent the occurrences of *an Italian* and *an American* from having the same index.

(83) a. ??Always, if an Italian$_i$ is tall, an American$_i$ is blond.
      b. Always, if an Italian$_i$ is tall, he$_i$ is American and also blond.

By the rules adopted so far, (83a) should be perfect and have the same reading as (83b), which doesn't seem to be the case. In order to account for this, we must assume that indefinites are subject to a novelty condition: their index must always be new.

(84) *Novelty Condition (NC)* (first version): An indefinite cannot carry the index of an NP on its left (at LF).

The NC reflects the idea that indefinites *introduce* something. In its present form, it is simply a formal condition on LF, with a status analogous to, say, the principles of the binding theory.

   To sum up, in this first implementation of the basic ideas of DRT, Heim adopts the following rules and conditions on LF:

(85) a. Quantifier Construal
      b. Existential Closure
      c. Quantifier Indexing
      d. Novelty Condition

Exercise 1

(a) Give the LFs for the following sentences:
   (i) If a man sees a donkey he sometimes beats it with a stick.
   (ii) John gave every boy who likes an actor a book about him.
   (iii) A student guide showed every visitor around.
   (iv) Most men who have a donkey beat it.
(b) What rules of construal would be needed to set up suitable LFs for the following type of sentences?
   (v) Every man plays with his dog if he has time.
   (vi) Every man sings when he showers.

It is not hard to see that the LFs generated by these rules are designed to make the interpretation procedure as direct as possible. Even though it is pretty clear where this approach is headed, it might be worth going through some of the steps needed to spell out the interpretation.

1.6.2 The Interpretive Component

We will first consider how to give a direct semantics for the LFs we have set up, following Heim (1982). We will then provide a semantics via translation, following Kamp (1981).

The models with respect to which the semantics is specified are standard intensional structures. They are triplets of the form $\langle W,A,Int \rangle$, where W is a set of worlds, A a set of individuals, and Int assigns intensions to constants. That is to say that for every constant α, $Int(\alpha)$ is a function from worlds into extensions of the appropriate kind. In particular, if α is an n-place predicate, then for every $w \in W$, $Int(\alpha)(w) \subseteq A^n$ (where $A^n = A \times \ldots \times A$, n times). Assignments to variables are construed as infinite sequences of members of A of the form $a = \langle a_1, a_2, \ldots, a_n, \ldots \rangle$. If a is such a sequence, a_i is its ith member. Sequences of this form can be viewed as assignments of values to variables as follows: for any variable x_i, its value relative to a sequence a is a_i.

Since we are interpreting LF-structures using logical techniques, it is useful to map the standard syntactic terminology into the one used to describe logical languages (i.e., 'variable', 'predicate', 'operator', etc.). Accordingly, we shall adopt the following conventions:

(86)   *Variables:* pronouns, traces of NPs, indices on common nouns
        Predicates: common nouns, verbs
        Operators: negations and Q_s, where s is a sequence of indices and
        Q is *every, always,* $\exists, \ldots$

These are the logical categories in terms of which we will determine which LF-structures count as formulae. Note that certain elements, like the definite and indefinite articles, are assigned no category. Formulae are characterized as follows:

(87)   *Atomic formulae:* minimal constituents including a predicate and n
        variables
        Examples: $donkey_3$
                  $[_S t_1 \text{ beats } it_3]$
        Molecular formulae: constituents that have one or more formulae as
        their immediate constituents
        Examples: $[_N donkey_3]$
                  $[_{NP} a [_N donkey_3]]$
                  $[_S a donkey_3 [every_1 [man_1 [t_1 \text{ likes } t_3]]]]$
                  $[_T [_S a man walked in] [_S he_2 was bald]]$

Operator-headed formulae: formulae whose leftmost constituent is an operator

Examples: $[_T \exists_{1,3}$ [a man$_1$ [t$_1$ walked in]] [a hat$_3$ [he$_1$ was wearing t$_3$]]]

[every$_{2,3}$ [man$_2$ who has a donkey$_3$] [t$_2$ beats it$_3$]]

[always$_{5,1}$ [if a man$_5$ has a donkey$_1$] [he$_5$ beats it$_1$]]

[not [John sings]]

The semantics proper is defined in two stages by recursion on the logical categories defined in (87). First in (88) we define a *satisfaction relation* $Sat_{w,a}(\phi)$ (to be read, "a satisfies ϕ in world w"). Then in (100) we shall use this satisfaction relation to define *truth* relative to a world w and a context c (in symbols, $T_{c,w}(\phi)$).

(88)   *Satisfaction*

a. If ϕ is atomic and consists of a predicate β and variables $x_{i_1}, \ldots,$ x_{i_n} (where i_k, for $1 \leq k \leq n$, is the kth index), then $Sat_{w,a}(\phi)$ iff $\langle a_{i_1}, \ldots, a_{i_n} \rangle \in Int(\beta)(w)$.

Examples:

   i. $Sat_{w,a}(donkey_3)$ iff $a_3 \in Int(donkey)(w)$

   ii. $Sat_{w,a}$ ([$_S$ t$_1$ beats it$_3$]) iff $\langle a_1, a_3 \rangle \in Int(beat)(w)$

b. If ϕ is cumulative molecular, with $\phi_1, \ldots, \phi_n$ as immediate constituents, then $Sat_{w,a}(\phi)$ iff $Sat_{w,a}(\phi_1), \ldots,$ and $Sat_{w,a}(\phi_n)$.

Examples:

   i. $Sat_{w,a}([_{NP}$ a [$_N$ donkey$_3$]]) iff $Sat_{w,a}([_N$ donkey$_3$]) iff $a_3 \in Int(donkey)(w)$

   ii. $Sat_{w,a}([_T$ [$_S$ a man$_2$ [t$_2$ walked in]] [$_S$ he$_2$ was bald]]) iff $Sat_{w,a}([_S$ a man$_2$ [t$_2$ walked in]]) and $Sat_{w,a}([_S$ he$_2$ was bald]) iff $a_2 \in Int(man)(w)$ and $a_2 \in Int(walk\ in)(w)$ and $a_2 \in Int(bald)(w)$

c. If ϕ is an operator-headed formula, then:

if ϕ is of the form [NEG ϕ'], then $Sat_{w,a}([NEG\ \phi'])$ iff it is not the case that $Sat_{w,a}(\phi')$;

if ϕ is of the form $\exists_s \phi'$, where $s = \langle i_1, \ldots, i_n \rangle$, then $Sat_{w,a}$ ($\exists_s \phi'$) iff for some assignment b such that $b \approx_s a$ (where $b \approx_s$ a is to be read as "b agrees with a except possibly that on the members of s), $Sat_{w,b}(\phi')$;

if ϕ is of the form [every$_s$ ϕ_1 ϕ_2], then $Sat_{w,a}$ ([every$_s$ ϕ_1 ϕ_2]) iff for every assignment b such that $b \approx_s a$, if $Sat_{w,b}(\phi_1)$, then $Sat_{w,b}(\phi_2)$.

The definition of satisfaction given so far deals only with extensional operators and is very close to the definition of satisfaction for classical first-order logic. The main difference consists of the fact that quantifiers operate on a set of indices rather than on one index at a time. Let us see the definition in (88) at work by means of a simple computation. In going through the example, we will skip some irrelevant details.

(89)   Every man who has a donkey beats it.
        Satisfaction conditions: For any a and any w:
        Sat$_{w,a}$([every$_{5,1}$ [man$_5$ who has a donkey$_1$] [t$_5$ beats it$_1$]])
        iff for every b $\approx_{\{5,1\}}$ a, if Sat$_{w,b}$([man$_5$ who has a donkey$_1$], then Sat$_{w,b}$([t$_5$ beats it$_1$])
        iff for every assignment b identical to a except in the values assigned to 5 and 1, if b$_5$ ∈ Int(man)(w) and b$_1$ ∈ Int(donkey)(w) and ⟨b$_5$,b$_1$⟩ ∈ Int(has)(w), then ⟨b$_5$,b$_1$⟩ ∈ Int(beat)
        iff for every pair of individuals ⟨u,v⟩ such that u is a man, v a donkey, and u has b, u beats v.

Exercise 2

(a) Give a more complete logical form for the example in (89) and fill in the missing steps of the evaluation.
(b) Give the two LFs associated with *Every man loves a woman* and show that by the definition in (88) they are assigned the same satisfaction conditions as ∀x[man(x) → ∃y[woman(y) ∧ love(x,y)]] and ∃y[woman(y) ∧ ∀x[man(x) → love(x,y)]], respectively.

We will now give a semantics for modalized unselective binders (and for conditionals without an overt binder). As we will slightly depart from Heim's approach here, some discussion may be appropriate. Heim argues that modals such as *must* or *may* are unselective quantifiers, similar to *every*. The distinguishing feature of modals is that they bind worlds as well as the indefinites free in their scope. The idea that modals are unselective binders is based on examples like the following:

(90)   a. If a cat is exposed to 2,4-D, it must be taken to the vet immediately.
        b. If a woman's coat is missing from the coatrack, she may have gone out.

Heim suggests that *a cat* in (90a) has universal force and attributes this to the presence of *must* (standardly analyzed as a universal quantifier over accessible possible worlds), and that *a woman* in (90b) has existential force due to the presence of *may*. She then assumes that in donkey sentences that lack an overt quantificational element, there is an invisible necessity operator which is responsible for their universal quantificational force. She doesn't provide an explicit semantics for adverbs of quantification, though it seems fairly clear that she takes them, too, to be unselective binders of some kind.

As far as the intensional character of modals is concerned, Heim essentially follows the analysis developed by Kratzer (1981). According to that analysis modals are quantifiers over worlds, where the relevant set of worlds (the "modal base" in Kratzer's terminology) is contextually selected as part of the conversational background.[17] For example, *John can beat Bill* can be understood as a statement about John's strength (in which case the relevant set of worlds would be those in which John's and Bill's respective physical strength is as in the actual world) or it can be understood as saying that John is somehow entitled to beat Bill (in which case the relevant set of worlds would be those where whatever convention entitles John to do so holds), and so on. Heim's addition to Kratzer's approach is the idea that modals quantify not only over the worlds in the modal base but also over indefinites.

The reason why I will depart from Heim's approach on the semantics of modals (and conditionals) is basically that I disagree with Heim's judgment concerning (90b). I tend to read (90b) as a generic statement about women, roughly equivalent to "It is generally the case that if a woman's coat is missing from the rack, she may have gone out," where *a woman* is understood as having quasi-universal force, not quasi-existential one as suggested by Heim. This seems to suggest that modals do not directly affect the quantificational force of indefinites and, in fact, may not be unselective binders. Consequently, what determines the quantificational force of indefinites in the absence of an overt binder must be more akin to a null adverb of quantification than to a null modal.

Further evidence in favor of this hypothesis stems from the following considerations. Adverbs of quantification are known to be sensitive to the focal structure of a clause (a fact that we will discuss in more detail in chapter 2). Consider the following:

(91)   a. John usually beats BILL
           ≈ In most cases where John beat someone, it is Bill
        b. JOHN usually beats Bill
           ≈ In most cases where Bill gets beaten, it is John who beats him

Capitals in (91) indicate focal stress. The natural way to understand (91a–b) is as indicated by the paraphrases. Clearly, the unfocused part of the sentence is what provides the restriction for the adverb of quantification (i.e., what sets up the cases to be considered).[18] The different restrictive clauses in (91a) and (91b) are responsible for the difference in truth conditions between these two sentences. By contrast, modals do not appear to be so sensitive to focal structure. Contrast (91) with (92):

(92)   a. John can beat BILL.
        b. JOHN can beat Bill.

While these two sentences have different presuppositions, the modal base seems to be unaffected by their difference in focal structure, in the sense that focus doesn't seem to affect the quantificational domain of the modal in the way it affects the domain of a quantificational adverb. The final observation is that conditionals, *when*-clauses, and the like are highly sensitive to focal structure, as often pointed out in the literature. Thus Rooth (1985) presents the following example:

(93)   a. If A SOLDIER dates a ballerina, he doesn't takes her to dance.
        b. If a soldier dates A BALLERINA, he doesn't takes her to dance.

Sentence (93a) is about ballerinas. It says that all (or most) ballerinas dated by a soldier are not taken to dance. Sentence (93b) is about soldiers. It says that all (or most) soldiers who date a ballerina don't take her dancing (perhaps in order not to feel inferior). These sentences can be shown to have different truth conditions. The point we want to make here is that this sensitivity of the truth conditions of conditionals to focal structure is to be expected if their semantics involves an implicit adverb of quantification, for adverbs of quantification are known to be sensitive to focus. If instead the semantics of conditionals involves a null modal, as Heim proposes, their sensitivity to focal structure would be unexpected.

I thus conclude that what is responsible for the quantificational force of indefinites in preposed adverbial clauses with no overt quantifying element is an implicit, modalized, *always*-like quantificational adverb. This is what is responsible for the quantificational force of the indefinites in Heim's example (90), as well as for the quantificational force of indefinites in conditionals without modals, illustrated in (94) with examples also taken from Heim 1982.

(94)   a. If a cat is exposed to 2,4-D, it is taken to the doctor.
        b. If a woman's coat is missing from the coatrack, she is no longer around.

We are now ready to give the satisfaction condition for *always*.

(95)   If ϕ is of the form [always$_s$ ϕ_1 ϕ_2], then Sat$_{w,a}$([always$_s$ ϕ_1 ϕ_2]) iff Sat$_{w',b}(\phi_2)$ for **every** w′ and **every** b such that

i. $b \approx_s a$
ii. $w R w'$
iii. $\mathrm{Sat}_{w',b}(\phi_1)$

The semantics for *usually* would be the same, except that the quantifiers in boldface in (95) would be replaced by *most;* the semantics for *sometimes* would also be the same, except that the quantifiers in boldface would be replaced by *some;* and so on. The semantics for adverbs like *normally* or *generally* would have the same rough format, but the modal component of such semantics would have to be elaborated further. The relation R in (95ii) is the contextually specified accessibility relation (i.e., it characterizes the modal base). Condition (95) says that "always if ϕ_1 then ϕ_2" is satisfied by an assignment a in a world w iff for every world w' accessible to w and every assignment b identical to a except for the variables in s, if b satisfies ϕ_1 in w', then b satisfies ϕ_2 in w'. This is essentially the semantics Heim gives for *must,* applied here to *always* instead. As I don't see good evidence in favor of treating modals as unselective binders, I would analyze *must* more standardly as a (selective) quantifier over worlds.[19]

Let us now illustrate how (95) works for a concrete example. Take the following classical donkey sentence and its (simplified) LF:

(96)   a. Always, if a farmer owns a donkey, he beats it.
        b. [always$_{2,4}$ [if a farmer$_2$ owns a donkey$_4$] [he$_2$ beats it$_4$]]

Here the relevant modal base might, for example, pick the sets of worlds where farmers are disposed to act toward donkeys as they do in the actual world. The satisfaction condition in (95) yields the following results:

(97) $\mathrm{Sat}_{w,a}$([always$_{2,4}$ [if a farmer$_2$ owns a donkey$_4$] [he$_2$ beats it$_4$]]) iff
        $\mathrm{Sat}_{w',b}$([he$_2$ beats it$_4$]) for every w',b such that
        i. $b \approx_{\{2,4\}} a$
        ii. farmers in w' have the same dispositions as farmers in w
        iii. $\mathrm{Sat}_{w',b}$([a farmer$_2$ owns a donkey$_4$])
        iff $\langle b_2, b_4 \rangle \in$ Int(beat)(w') for every $_{w',b}$ such that
        i. $b \approx_{\{2,4\}} a$
        ii. farmers in w' have the same dispositions as farmers in w
        iii. $b_2 \in$ Int(farmer)(w') and $b_4 \in$ Int(donkey)(w') and $\langle b_2, b_4 \rangle \in$ Int(own)(w')
        iff u beats u' in w' for every u, u', and w' such that farmers in w' have the same dispositions as farmers in w and u is a farmer in w', u' is a donkey in w', and u owns u' in w'.

Exercise 3

On the model of (97), compute the satisfaction condition for the sentence *Usually, if a boy sees a helicopter, he talks about it with a friend.*

This completes our formulation of the satisfaction conditions for English LFs. Now we have to define truth. Following Heim, we are going to depart slightly from the classical definition of truth in order to accommodate the fact that certain utterances are context dependent and may fail to be true or false if uttered in an inappropriate context. To see this, consider the following example:

(98)   John likes him_3.

This sentence contains a free pronoun. Its felicity depends on whether the context supplies us with an appropriate referent for the pronoun him_3, say, in the form of a gesture of indication by the illocutionary agent. We can then analyze (98) as follows. First, in order for this sentence to have a truth value, the context must specify a referent for him_3. If it does, the sentence is true if John likes that person and false if he doesn't. If the context fails to specify a suitable referent, then the sentence is uninterpretable (i.e., neither true nor false). We can express this more precisely as follows. Let us assume that a context c specifies a possibly partial sequence $c+$ such that $c+_n$, if defined, is the individual pointed at (or otherwise indicated) in context c in connection with the pronoun with index n. We can then define felicity relative to a context c (in symbols, F_c) and truth relative to a context c in a world w (in symbols, $T_{c,w}$) as follows:

(99)   *Felicity:* $F_c(\phi)$ (i.e., ϕ is felicitous relative to c) iff for every variable x_i free in ϕ, $c+_i$ is defined.

(100)   *Truth:* For any ϕ and any c such that $F_c(\phi)$, and any world w:
   i. $T_{c,w}(\phi)$ (i.e., ϕ is true in w relative to c) iff for some assignment a, $Sat_{w,a}(\phi)$ and for any variable x_i free in ϕ, $a_i = c+_i$.
   ii.   It is not the case that $T_{c,w}(\phi)$ (i.e., ϕ is false in w relative to c) iff there is no assignment a such that $Sat_{w,a}(\phi)$ and for every variable x_i free in ϕ, $a_i = c_i$.

These definitions formally capture the idea sketched above that sentences have definite truth conditions only relative to a context in which they can be felicitously uttered (i.e., where all the relevant information is supplied).

Before concluding this section, we shall briefly discuss Heim's approach to definites. The question she considers is whether definites too might be nonquantificational in nature. This would make definite and indefinite NPs pleasingly symmetric. Let us see how such an idea might be pursued. We have argued that indefinites generally introduce something new into the discourse, and we have tried to capture this with the Novelty Condition. By the same token, one might say that definites generally pick out something that is already familiar. A possible way of capturing this idea, in first approximation, is to analyze definites as free variables whose value has to be given by the context. Consider the following example:

(101)   [Every man]$_i$ likes [the woman]$_j$.

Assume that the definite in (101 is translated as a free variable, so that the reading we get can be expressed by the following English formula:

(102)   [every$_i$ [man$_i$] [t$_i$ likes x$_j$]]

For this sentence to be felicitous, the context would have to supply a suitable referent (i.e., a woman) for x$_j$. So the sentence would be felicitous only if the context supplies a particular woman, and it would be true iff every man likes that woman This seems a plausible approximation to the meaning of (101).

To get this idea to work we need to make two basic assumptions. First, we need to assume that the descriptive content of the definite is presupposed in a context where a sentence like (101) is uttered felicitously. Presuppositions in this sense can be taken to be a component of the conversational background—that is, the set of knowledge, beliefs, assumptions, and so on shared by the illocutionary agents.[20] Among the things presupposed in uttering (101), there must be the information that the value of x$_j$ is a woman. It is this kind of knowledge that an illocutionary agent exploits when he or she utters (and/or interprets) a definite description. Second, the index associated with a definite description must not be accidentally caught by an unselective binder. In other words, we must prevent (101) from getting the LF in (103):

(103)   [every$_{i,j}$ [man$_i$] [t$_i$ likes x$_j$]]

The truth conditions of formula (103) are totally wrong for (101). We can avoid deriving (103) by stipulating that definites are exempted from Quantifier Indexing: the index of a definite is never copied onto a quantifier.

This would work as far as cases like (101) are concerned. But Heim notes that this line of thought would get us in trouble in connection with examples like (104):

(104)   Every man$_i$ likes [the woman he$_i$ marries]$_j$.

If we translate the definite as a free variable here, then we wouldn't get the value of *the woman* to vary with respect to each man. And trying to say that the index j in cases like these undergoes Quantifier Indexing also yields the wrong truth conditions, as the reader can easily check. Note that these cases work rather nicely on the traditional Russellian analysis of definite descriptions. Thus, within the present setup a unified treatment of indefinites and definites as free variables appears to be problematic. This issue is addressed in Heim 1982, chapter 3, and we shall discuss it further below, in section 1.7.3 and in chapter 4.

This concludes our exposition of Heim 1982, chapter 2, which is an incarnation of the first soul of DRT. Our semantics has taken the form of a direct interpretation of LF-structures. Let us now see what it would take to give an indirect semantics, in the form of a translation of LF-structures into a logic.

1.6.3 Semantics via Translation

It may be useful to have a formal language (without the complexities of things like relative clauses, agreement, etc., which abound in natural language) where the kinds of anaphoric relations that we have been investigating can be expressed directly. Among other applications, such a language could be used to provide convenient means for specifying the semantics of English, much in the same way Intensional Logic is used in Montague Grammar. A formal language of this sort was designed by Kamp (1981) and has been used in many different variants in much subsequent work. Here I will present one such variant designed to fit well with Heim's (1982, chapter 2) theory.[21] I will call this language DRT_K ('K' for Kamp).

The basic vocabulary of DRT_K is constituted by a set VAR of variables, a set $CONS_n$ of n-place predicates, and the logical connectives '$\Rightarrow_\forall$', '$\Rightarrow_{always}$', and '$\neg$'. There are two types of formulae in DRT_K, namely *Discourse Representation Structures (DRSs)* and *Conditions (C's)*. DRSs are used to represent the content of a complete discourse and consist of a domain and a condition. A DRS H has the form $x_{i_1}, \ldots, x_{i_n}[\phi]$, where ϕ is a condition and $x_{i_1}, \ldots, x_{i_n}$ is a (possibly null) sequence of variables. Such variables constitute the local domain of the DRS. The local domain of a DRS H is indicated as d(H). Conditions are clauses that specify the actual content of a DRS, the internal articulation of a discourse. They are defined recursively as follows:

(105)   i.   If $\beta \in \text{CONS}_n$ and $x_{i_1}, \ldots, x_{i_n} \in \text{VAR}$, then $\beta(x_{i_1}, \ldots, x_{i_n}) \in C$ (Conditions of this sort are called "atomic.")
        ii.   If $\phi, \Psi \in C, \phi \wedge \Psi \in C$
        iii. If $K_1, K_2 \in \text{DRS}$, then $K_1 \Rightarrow_\forall K_2, K_1 \Rightarrow_{\text{always}} K_2, \neg K_1 \in C$

In DRT_K, existential quantification is expressed by formulae of the form $x_{i_1}, \ldots, x_{i_n}[\phi]$. Intuitively, a formula of the form $x_{i_1}, \ldots, x_{i_n}[\phi]$ is true iff there exists a way of finding values for $x_{i_1}, \ldots, x_{i_n}$ that make ϕ true. This corresponds to an LF-structure of the form $[_S \exists_{i_1, \ldots, i_1} \phi]$. Universal quantification is expressed by formulae of the form $[K_1 \Rightarrow_\forall K_2]$. Intuitively such formula is true if every way of finding values for the variables in the local domain of K_1 that verifies the condition in K_1 provides us with a way of also verifying K_2. Formulae of the form $[K_1 \Rightarrow_{\text{always}} K_2]$ express a modalized universal quantification and are used to represent constructions with adverbs of quantification.

Let us illustrate how this language works by showing how some English sentences will be expressed in it. Each example sentence in (106) is viewed as a complete discourse; each sentence is accompanied by one of its standard first-order representations and the DRS that would correspond to it.

(106)   a.   Every man likes a woman.
        a'. $\forall x[\text{man}(x) \rightarrow \exists y[\text{woman}(y) \wedge \text{like}(x,y)]]$
        a''. $[x[\text{man}(x)] \Rightarrow_\forall y[\text{woman}(y) \wedge \text{like}(x,y)]]$ (wide-scope *every*)
        b.   Every man likes a woman.
        b'. $\exists y[\text{woman}(y) \wedge \forall x[\text{man}(x) \rightarrow \text{like}(x,y)]]$
        b''. $y[\text{woman}(y) \wedge x[\text{man}(x)] \Rightarrow_\forall [\text{like}(x,y)]]$ (wide-scope *a*)
        c.   A man walked in. He was wearing a hat. Every woman greeted him.
        c'. $\exists x \exists y[\text{man}(x) \wedge \text{walk-in}(x) \wedge \text{hat}(y) \wedge \text{wear}(x,y) \wedge \forall y[\text{woman}(y) \rightarrow \text{greet}(y,x)]]$
        c''. $x,y[\text{man}(x) \wedge \text{walk-in}(x) \wedge \text{hat}(y) \wedge \text{wear}(x,y) \wedge z[\text{woman}(z)] \Rightarrow_\forall [\text{greet}(z,x)]]$
        d.   Every man who has a donkey beats it.
        d'. $\forall x \forall y[[\text{man}(x) \wedge \text{donkey}(y) \wedge \text{has}(x,y)] \rightarrow \text{beat}(x,y)]$
        d''. $[x,y[\text{man}(x) \wedge \text{donkey}(y) \wedge \text{has}(x,y)] \Rightarrow_\forall [\text{beat}(x,y)]]$
        e.   If a man owns a donkey he always beats it.
        e'. $\forall x \forall y \square[[\text{man}(x) \wedge \text{donkey}(y) \wedge \text{has}(x,y)] \rightarrow \text{beat}(x,y)]$
        e''. $[x,y[\text{man}(x) \wedge \text{donkey}(y) \wedge \text{has}(x,y)] \Rightarrow_{\text{always}} [\text{beat}(x,y)]]$

This language can also be displayed in a sort of "flowchart" format. The conversion to this format is accomplished by performing three easy steps on a DRS:

(107)   i.   Write each bracket as a box.
         ii.   Write each variable on a bracket inside the box, near the top.
         iii.   Replace conjunction by a carriage return.

I illustrate how this works by showing what (106a) and (106d) look like in flowchart format:

(108)   Every man likes a woman.

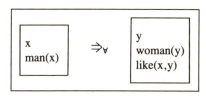

Every man who has a donkey beats it.

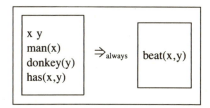

This flowchart notation is the one adopted in Kamp 1981. I will switch back and forth between linear and flowchart notations as needed. I will also occasionally refer to the brackets in the linear notation as ''boxes.''

It should be apparent that one can specify a simple Tarski-style semantics for DRT_K. Once the semantics for DRT_K is established, the semantics for English can take the form of a compositional translation of LF into DRT_K. The evident homomorphism between the LF-structures generated by Heim's construal rules and the formal language of DRT_K should make it intuitively clear that such a mapping will be easy to formulate. In the appendix to this chapter, I give both the semantics for DRT_K and the mapping from LF into DRT_K.

Where does this leave us? Do we gain anything from the approach developed in the present section? The answer is not univocal. On the one hand we could reason that one shouldn't multiply levels unnecessarily, and that the present semantics via translation does precisely that. On the other hand, it can be replied that it is usually convenient to have a formal language that wears its truth conditions on its sleeves, so to speak (as much of the complexity of natural language syntax has been eliminated). Such a language provides us with a convenient way to write out these truth conditions, and it can be equipped with a proof theory that will facilitate computing entailments and the like. The fact remains that in the setup we have chosen the mapping into DRT_K is in principle dispensable.

Kamp (1981) tries to make a case that the level of DRS_K is in fact an essential aspect of meaning, a necessary intermediate link between syntax and truth conditions. Generally, in theories of natural language we can claim to have a case in favor of the existence of a certain structure whenever we crucially need to appeal to properties of that structure in order to explain something. In Kamp 1981 and in most of the work it generated, there is no level of LF. Surface structures are directly mapped into DRSs. On this basis one could claim the following. Accessibility, viewed as a structural property of DRSs (see the appendix for the relevant definitions), determines when a pronoun can be anaphorically linked to an indefinite antecedent: this is possible only when the variable corresponding to the indefinite occurs in a DRS accessible from the one where the pronoun occurs. Of course, one can state this condition on anaphora in other forms as well. For example, in (19) above we stated it using structural properties of surface structures. But it is only at the level of DRSs that it becomes clear that the relevant relation is the manifestation of a natural notion of scope. It is only at that level that one sees why this relation is what it is. This would constitute an argument in favor of the necessity of a level such as the one that DRT_K provides.

However, it is clear that such argument has force only if we directly map surface structures into DRT_K. What emerges from our discussion of Heim's approach is that if one accepts a level of LF—that is, a syntactic level at which surface structures are disambiguated—the line of argumentation we have just sketched loses much of its bite. As we saw, it is possible to provide a set of construal rules yielding LFs that have essentially the same semantics as DRSs. Since an account of accessibility follows from that semantics, it remains to be seen in what sense a level of DRSs as such crucially enters in characterizing possible anaphoric links.[22]

1.7 THE SECOND SOUL OF DISCOURSE REPRESENTATION THEORY

The fundamental idea underlying the second way of implementing DRT is that one can simplify the construal component considerably by using a notion of meaning that is richer than the classical one. In the classical view the meaning of a sentence ϕ is its content, that is, its truth conditions. Depending on whether one is dealing with extensional or intensional contexts, truth conditions can be represented by satisfaction sets (i.e., the set of assignments that satisfy a formula ϕ) or by sets of worlds (i.e., the sets of worlds in which ϕ is true). An alternative view, explicitly articulated by, for instance, Stalnaker (1978) and Lewis (1979), is that the equation 'meaning = content' is not quite complete. According to this view, meaningfulness also needs to encompass the way in which expressions can modify the contexts in which they are used. Each expression has a certain potential for changing the contexts in which it can be used appropriately. In any concrete communicative situation, illocutionary agents will share a certain amount of information, pertaining, for example, to which language is being used, who the speaker is, what beliefs are held in common, and so on. This shared information provides the context for the utterance. Utterances constantly update their contexts by altering the information shared by the illocutionary agents. Suppose, for example, we are talking about tomorrow's weather and we wonder how cold it is going to be. This means that in the futures compatible with what we believe, the temperature may vary. In some such futures it is 50°F, in some it is 55°F, and so on. Imagine that at this point, I read in the newspaper forecast that tomorrow's temperature is going to be in the upper 60s, and I convey that information to you. This changes the shared information by ruling out some of the alternatives previously left open. In particular, if the information is successfully passed along from me to you, our common set of beliefs shrinks. Some of the futures that previously were held to be possible are no longer held to be such.

What I just presented is a sketchy summary of Stalnaker's and Lewis's views on context change. I will for the most part leave it in this impressionistic form, without trying to explore further the foundational issues it raises. Following the lead of Heim and others,[23] I will proceed by setting up interpretation procedures for natural languages that are inspired by such view and study their empirical consequences. In particular, in this section I will discuss Heim's own version of dynamic semantics, which uses the concept of 'file'.

1.7.1 File Change Semantics

The metaphor that File Change Semantics (FCS henceforth) builds on is that in processing a discourse one sets up files where information is stored. Adding a piece of information to a system of files involves updating it. Suppose, for example, that we know Pavarotti was murdered. We do not know, however, whether he was murdered by one or more people, whether his murderers are male or female, and so on. We can represent our information state by means of a file that looks like this:

(109)   a. Someone$_i$ killed Pavarotti.
        b. f: {⟨w,a⟩: a$_i$ killed Pavarotti in w}

If we know (109a), we know that our world is among those where one or more individuals have killed Pavarotti. In any such world, there must be individuals that would make 'Someone$_i$ killed Pavarotti' true. Thus, the file f associated with (109a) must minimally determine a set of world–assignment pairs ⟨w,a⟩ such that a$_i$ killed Pavarotti in w, as illustrated in (109b). We do not know which of the worlds in (109b) we are in and we don't know which individuals do in fact make 'Someone$_i$ killed Pavarotti' true. We only know that for some assignment a, our world must be in (109b). The set in (109b) represents our information state, the set of alternatives that are open if (109a) is taken to be a fact. Suppose, now, we find evidence that the murderer is Italian (or that the murderers are). This means that f gets updated as follows:

(110)   a. He$_i$ is Italian.
        b. f': {⟨w,a⟩ : a$_i$ killed Pavarotti and a$_i$ is Italian in w}

Adding (110a) to (109a) takes us from f to f'. Intuitively, we add the information ___ *is Italian* to the i'th file card, which narrows down the set of alternatives from those that were previously available.

So the meaning of *He$_i$ is Italian* can be represented as a function from files into files. In our example, such function maps the file in (109b) into (110b). That is,

(111) f + He$_i$ is Italian = f'

As the notation indicates, adding 'He$_i$ is Italian' to f results in f'. To know the definition of the function ' + He$_i$ is Italian' is to know the meaning of *He$_i$ is Italian*. Consequently our semantics should define for each sentence S a function $+S$ from files to files. Since files represent contexts, $+S$ can be taken to be a formal rendering of the concept 'context change potential'. Our task in what follows is to give a semantics of (the relevant portions of) English in terms of context change potentials and see what consequences this has for anaphora.

To start, we can simplify things a bit by disregarding for now the world component of a file. That is, instead of representing the contexts associated with a file in terms of world–assignment pairs, we will represent them just as sets of assignments. This is harmless as long as we stick to extensional contexts. And we can, in fact, make the point we want to make by limiting ourself to extensional contexts. Once the basic mechanism of context change potentials is understood, it will be easy to bring intensionality back into the picture. So in the remainder of this section, we will illustrate our semantics by means of an extensional first-order model $\langle U, Ext \rangle$, were U is a domain of individuals and Ext assigns to the constants an (extensional) value of the appropriate type.

Examples (110) and (111) tell us what the function ' $+ He_i$ is Italian' does in one specific case. However, it is not hard to derive a general definition of ' $+ He_i$ is Italian' from them. For any file f, let $Sat(f)$ be its satisfaction set. We can then say the following:

(112)   For any file f: $f + He_i$ is Italian $= f'$, where
         $Sat(f') = Sat(f) \cap \{a: a_i$ is Italian$\}$

In other words, whenever we process He_i is Italian in f we exclude from f's satisfaction set those assignments that are incompatible with the information being added. The general form of (112) for an arbitrary atomic sentence $\beta(x_{i_1}, \ldots, x_{i_n})$ is the following:

(113) $f + \beta(x_{i_1}, \ldots, x_{i_n}) = f'$, where
         $Sat(f') = Sat(f) \cap \{a: \langle a_{i_1}, \ldots, a_{i_n} \rangle \in Ext(\beta)\}$

We can view (113) as the first step in the recursive definition of $+S$ for an atomic S.

The next step would be to consider coordinated structures. Suppose, for example, that we increment the information associated with He_i is Italian with, say, He_i is blond. In other words, suppose we are dealing with a discourse of the following form:

(114) He_i is Italian. He_i is also blond.

The discourse in (114) forms (in the terminology of the previous section) a molecular formula whose components are He_i is Italian and He_i is blond. We know what their individual context change potentials are, and we now want to determine the context change potential of (114) as a whole. A natural way of doing so is the following:

(115) $f + [He_i$ is Italian. He_i is also blond$]$
         $= (f + He_i$ is Italian$) + He_i$ is blond

In other words, we proceed incrementally, by first adding the first sentence to f, then the second. This means that we first exclude from the satisfaction set of f assignments incompatible with 'He_i is Italian'. Then we exclude from the result those incompatible with 'He$_i$ is blond'. We can generalize from this case to any molecular structure:

(116)   If S is a molecular formula composed of $S_1, \ldots, S_n$, then $f + S$
        $= (f + S_1) + \ldots + S_n$

The next case to consider is that of indefinites. We want to make use of the idea that indefinites introduce something new (i.e., they introduce a new file card), while definites do not (i.e., they merely update an existing file card). But in order to do so, we must be able to retrieve from a file its "active" file cards. Accordingly, we will say that for any file f, $D(f)$ is its domain, where $D(f)$ is just a set of indices. Intuitively, $D(f)$ are the indices of the file cards (i.e., indefinites) that are active in f. So for example, if we process *Someone$_i$ killed Pavarotti* relative to an initial file f, this will make the i'th file card active in the resulting file (i.e., i will be added to the domain of f). We will also want to make sure that i isn't already active in f, in order to capture the idea that indefinites create *new* discourse referents.

It is intuitively plausible to maintain that if a certain file card i is not active in a file f, then that file says nothing about i. Files cannot carry information about discourse referents that are not active. This can be formally expressed in terms of the following condition:

(117)   For any file f and any assignment a and b, if n $\notin D(f)$ and a $\approx_n$
        b, then a $\in$ Sat(f) iff b $\in$ Sat(f), where a $\approx_n$ b is to be read as "a
        differs from b at most on n."

Condition (117) says that if n is not in the domain of a file f and a and b differ at most on what they assign to n, then a is in the file's satisfaction set just in case b is, which captures the fact that f does not say anything about n.

As is evident from the informal considerations above, adding a domain to files enables us to state more precisely the condition that governs the differential behavior of definites and indefinites. In particular, we can restate the Novelty Condition (along with the familiarity condition on definites) as follows.

(118)   *Novelty/Familiarity Condition (NFC):* If S is uttered in f, then for
        every NP$_i$ in S it must be the case that
        i.   if NP$_i$ is indefinite, i $\notin D(f)$, and
        ii.   if NP$_i$ is definite, i $\in D(f)$.

Given that files are made up of satisfaction sets and file domains, context change potentials will, in general, manipulate both. They will activate and deactivate file cards as well as add information to them. Thus, how a sentence affects the domain of a file must be added to the definition of context change potential. Accordingly, we need to modify (113) above along the following lines:

(119) $f + \beta(x_{i_1}, \ldots, x_{i_n}) = f'$ where
         $\text{Sat}(f') = \text{Sat}(f) \cap \{a: \langle a_{i_1}, \ldots, a_{i_n} \rangle \in \text{Ext}(\beta)\}$ and
         $D(f') = D(f) \cup \{i_1, \ldots, i_n\}$

According to (119), in processing an atomic sentence we intersect the satisfaction set of the file with that of the sentence and add to the file domain the indices of the variables occurring in the atomic sentence. Let us see how this works by means of a couple of examples. Imagine again adding *He_i is Italian* to an arbitrary file:

(120)   a. $f + \text{He}_i$ is Italian
         b. $i \in D(f)$

Since *he_i* is definite, this will only work if i is an active card in f (i.e., if we already have some information about it), which is what (120b) states. We then update f by eliminating the assignments incompatible with *he_i*'s being Italian and we add i to the domain of f. But since, by the NFC, i must already be in $D(f)$, the domain of the file will in fact remain unchanged.

Imagine instead adding to a different file f_1 something like (109a), repeated here as (121a):

(121)   a. Someone_i killed Pavarotti.
         b. [someone_i [t_i killed Pavarotti]]

The LF of (121a) will be as in (121b) (ignoring the rule of Existential Closure). Formula (121b) is a molecular one. So we proceed sequentially by first adding *someone_i* to f_1 and then adding [t_i killed Pavarotti] to the result. The indefinite determiner *some,* we assume, makes no contribution (aside from signaling indefiniteness). Thus we are left with processing *one_i*, which is an atomic formula, where *one* counts as the predicate and the index i as the variable. We first check that i is not in $D(f_1)$, as *someone* is indefinite. Then we add i to $D(f_1)$ along with the information that i is a person (which is recorded in the satisfaction set). At this point, we go on with [t_i killed Pavarotti], which will add to the file the information that i killed Pavarotti. This is how indefinites introduce new file cards.

It should be noted that if we were to add [t_i killed Pavarotti] directly to

f_1, under the assumption that i $\notin$ $D(f_1)$, the result would be infelicitous, because the trace t_i is definite and requires that i already be in the domain of the file. However, *someone$_i$* adds i to the file domain, thereby creating a felicitous context for [t_i killed Pavarotti]. This shows that felicity conditions project nicely in the present approach, which can thus be seen to have general applications regarding the problem of presupposition projections. It has been observed in the literature (cf. Soames 1989 for an overview) that a conjunction has the same presuppositions as each of its conjuncts, *unless* the first conjunct entails the presuppositions of the second. We observe that the same holds of the requirement that the index of a definite be familiar; being a felicity condition, this requirement can be regarded as a presupposition. So for example, the conjunction in (122a) has the same presupposition as (122b) in isolation, namely that i must be familiar.

(122)   a. Mary entered the room and saw him$_i$.
        b. Mary saw him$_i$.

In this sense, the conjunction in (122a) inherits the felicity condition of (122b). But if we embed (122a) in a conjunction like (123), the presupposition is filtered out:

(123)   Someone$_i$ was waiting in the room. Mary entered and saw him$_i$.

Discourse (123) does not require that i be familiar, while its component (122a) does. This is so because the presence of *someone$_i$* introduces the index we need and thus entails that that index is familiar. What is interesting in this connection is that this is a consequence of the way in which FCS is set up. It simply follows from the fact that the Novelty/Familiarity Condition is checked incrementally at each step going from left to right. So the initial context is modified by the first sentence alone, and it is only in the resulting context that we check whether the presuppositions of the second sentence are satisfied. In short, the first conjunct sets up the context for the second. This procedure links the projection properties of conjoined structures to their meaning in an interesting way.[24]

Our discussion so far has given us a rough outline of how FCS works in some basic cases. It may be appropriate, before moving on to more complicated cases, to give an indication of how FCS determines truth conditions. For any sentence S, we can define the truth of S relative to a file f in terms of $+S$ as follows:

(124)   S is true relative to f iff Sat($f + S$) $\neq \varnothing$.

Intuitively, we say that S is true in a context f iff the satisfaction set we obtain by adding S to f is non-empty (i.e., if adding S to f doesn't turn f into a false file). This presupposes in turn that the satisfaction set of f is non-empty (i.e., that the file encodes true information and the addition of S is truth preserving).[25] Defining truth conditions in terms of context change potentials shows that we do not lose the classical notion of meaning in our new dynamic setup; we merely enrich it.

It can be shown that the definition in (124) works well (at least for the cases considered so far) in the sense that it assigns to sentences the intuitively correct truth conditions. In particular, it can be shown that the truth conditions associated with, say, (125a) by definition (124) are equivalent to those of (125b), in spite of the fact that indefinites are treated like free variables (see the appendix for a proof).

(125)   a. [A woman]$_i$ walked in.
         b. There is a woman that walked in.

An immediate consequence of this fact is that text-level Existential Closure becomes superfluous. At no point in computing the truth conditions of sentences like (125a) do we need to appeal to it. We see here the payoff of a principled departure from the classical notion of meaning.

1.7.2 Quantificational Structures in File Change Semantics

It is now time to look at quantificational structures. We will limit our attention here to quantificational NPs of the form *every N* and will discuss them mostly informally. This should suffice as an illustration of how FCS works for quantifiers in general. (In the appendix, we give the details of the relevant formal definitions.)

Consider a simple sentence like (126):

(126)   a. Every man is snoring.
         b. [every man$_i$ [t$_i$ is snoring]]

Let us assume that the tripartite structure in (126b) is the LF associated with (126a). This structure is derived from (126a) via QR and Quantifier Construal. It is made up of the quantifier *every* and two atomic formulae, 'man$_i$' and [t$_i$ is snoring], where the former is the restriction of *every* and the latter its nuclear scope. We want to determine the file change potential of this sentence, and we want to do so compositionally by means of the file change potentials of its components.

Here is the idea. We start with the satisfaction set of the original file, namely Sat(f), and test the assignments in Sat(f) one by one. For each a in Sat(f), we test whether every way of turning a into an assignment that satisfies the restriction also results in an assignment that satisfies the scope. To do that, we first compute 'f + man$_i$'. Then we check whether every assignment b identical to a (except possibly with respect to what a assigns to i) that is in Sat(f + man$_i$) is also in ((f + man$_i$) + t$_i$ is snoring). If a passes this test, we keep it in the satisfaction set of the derived file; else we discard it.

To illustrate further, let us imagine evaluating (126b) relative to a file f_Ω such that Sat(f_Ω) is the set of all possible assignments Ω. This file represents total lack of information. Let us call it the *total* file. For each a in Ω, we check whether every a$'$ identical to a except that a$'_i$ is a man is such that a$'_i$ is in Sat((f) + man$_i$) + [t$_i$ is snoring]). If every a$'$ passes this test, we keep a in Sat(f + (126b)); else we throw it out. Now, if we are in a situation where every man snores, then every a in Ω will pass the test, and thus we will have that Sat(f + (126b)) = Sat(f) = Ω. If we are in a situation where some man doesn't snore, no a in Sat(f) will pass the test and we will have that Sat(f + (126b) = $\varnothing$. So in this case we either get the original satisfaction set or the empty set. This won't always be the case, though. Consider the discourse constituted by (127a–b) below:

(127)   a. [A man]$_1$ walked in.
          b. [Every kid]$_2$ saw him$_1$.
          c. Two men, John and Bill, walked in. Every kid saw John but not Bill.

Imagine evaluating first (127a) relative to f_Ω, and assume we are in the situation described in (127c). This will get us from Ω to a set of assignments A = Sat(f_Ω + (127a)) such that for every a in A either a$_1$ = John or a$_1$ = Bill (for these are the two men that walk in). Then we proceed to evaluating (127b). Since every kid saw just John, all the assignments such that a$_1$ = Bill will be discarded.

Notice that computing Sat(f + [every S$_1$ S$_2$]) involves setting up two auxiliary files, namely first f + S$_1$ and then ((f + S$_1$) + S$_2$). At each step, we must make sure that the Novelty/Familiarity Condition is respected. So, in particular, in (127) we must have that 1 $\notin$ D(f_Ω), 1 $\in$ D((f_Ω) + (127a)), and 2 $\notin$ D((f_Ω) + (127a)). But the cards that are introduced in the auxiliary files are not kept active in the domain of the resulting file, because in general we cannot refer to the NPs associated with the auxiliary files of a universal:

(128)   *Every man$_i$ is snoring. Mary heard him$_i$.

While the procedure outlined above appears to be on the right track, it needs to be slightly modified for cases like the following:

(129) a. Every boy loves a cat.
       b. every [boy$_i$] [a cat$_j$ [t$_i$ loves t$_j$]]

Formula (129b) is the LF of (129a); the bold brackets mark the restriction and the scope of *every*. The condition on universals informally stated above requires that every assignment in 'f + boy$_i$' must also be in ((f + boy$_i$) + a cat$_j$ [t$_i$ loves t$_j$]). But this won't capture the truth conditions of sentences like (129a), because for an assignment a to be in Sat(f + boy$_i$) it suffices that a$_i$ is a boy, regardless of what a assigns to j. In general, a$_j$ needn't be a cat (which is what our present truth conditions would require). What we want is that for every a such that a$_i$ is a boy, there is a b identical to a on index i, such that b$_j$ is a cat that b$_i$ loves. So, what we want is the satisfaction of the following requirement:

(130) Consider every a in Sat(f). Now take every b that keeps constant what a assigns to the file cards active in f. For any such b that is in Sat(f + boy$_i$), there must be a c such that c is equal to b on the indices in D(f + boy$_i$) and c is in Sat((f + boy$_i$) + a cat$_j$ [t$_i$ loves t$_j$]).

The effect of this requirement is to build the nuclear-scope-level rule of Existential Closure into the file change potential of a universal. This is the formal rendering of the familiar idea that something of the form [every S$_1$ S$_2$] is true just in case every way of satisfying S$_1$ can be turned into a way of satisfying S$_2$.

A definition along these lines will assign the truth conditions we want to donkey sentences. Let us see how this works by means of an example. Consider (131):

(131) a. Every student$_i$ that had a problem$_j$ discussed it$_j$ with a professor$_k$.
       b. [every [student$_i$ that [a problem$_j$ [t$_i$ had t$_j$]]] [a professor$_k$ [t$_i$ discussed it$_j$ with t$_k$]]

Relative to a file f, (131b) (i.e., the LF of (131a)) will be true iff for every a in Sat(f + [student$_i$ that [a problem$_j$ [t$_i$ had t$_j$]]]) (where i and j must be new relative to D(f)), there is a b that keeps constant the values assigned by a to i and j such that b is in Sat((f + [student$_i$ that [a problem$_j$ [t$_i$ had t$_j$]]]) + [a professor$_k$ [t$_i$ discussed it$_j$ with t$_k$]]). This means that for every way of assigning a value for i and j such that i is a student and j a problem that i has, there must be a way of finding a value for k such that i is a student, j a problem that i has, and k a professor, and i discusses j with k.

Notice that the present semantics, besides assigning the desired truth conditions and anaphoric possibilities to donkey sentences, also enables us to dispense with Quantifier Indexing and Existential Closure of the nuclear scope. Quantifier Indexing is superfluous because file domains keep track of what NPs are being quantified over. Existential Closure of the nuclear scope is superfluous because it is now built into the context change potential of universal structures.

The semantics of other quantificational determiners like *no, most,* and so forth can be given in a parallel manner. Similarly for the semantics of negation. The semantics for adverbs of quantification is a modalized version of the semantics for determiners, which involves going back to regarding the content of a file as a set of world–assignment pairs, rather than as a set of assignments.

The net outcome of FCS is a considerable simplification of the construal component, at the cost of an arguably more complex semantics. In the first incarnation of DRT we considered, we had more complicated rules of construal and a simple Tarski-style semantics. Now we have a fancier, more dynamic semantics and a simpler LF. The issue boils down very clearly to where it is better to have the action. Is it more natural to have Existential Closure in the syntax or to have it in the semantics, as part of the definition of how various expressions can change the context? The answer is not obvious. Heim tries to make a case for FCS which rests primarily on the treatment of definites. Let us briefly look at it.

1.7.3 Definites in File Change Semantics

The theory of definites sketched within the first version of DRT was based on the idea that, in general, definites are free variables whose value is fixed by the context. More specifically, in the case of definite descriptions it was also assumed that the content of the description is presupposed. This view ran into problems in connection with sentences like the following:

(132) a. Everyone$_i$ who sees [the man with the red mustache]$_j$ insults him$_j$.

  b. Everyone$_i$ who sees [the man that betrayed him$_i$]$_j$ insults him$_j$.

In (132a) we don't want j to be bound by *everyone.* If that was allowed, (132a) would get the reading in (133a):

(133) a. $\forall_{i,j}$ [i sees j] [i insults j]

b. Presupposition: j is a man with a red mustache
c. $\forall_i$ [i sees j] [i insults j]

Given the presupposition in (133b), formula (133a) is felicitous only in a context which individuates a particular man with a red mustache. But in this context (133a) wouldn't make sense. What we want is (133c).

However, for (132b) something different is needed. Consider (134):

(134)   a. $\forall_i$ [i sees j] [i insults j]
         b. Presupposition: j is a man that betrayed i
         c. $\forall_{i,j}$ [i sees j and j is a man that betrayed i] [i insults j]

Formula (134a) and presupposition (134b) are what we get if we apply to (132b) the same reasoning we employed with (132a). But it is unclear how to interpret the presupposition in (134b). This presupposition would call for a context with a particular individual who has betrayed somebody. Be that as it may, formula (134a) seems to constitute the wrong meaning for (132b). What we want is something more like (134c), where the index of the definite is bound by the universal quantifier and the content of the presupposition has been ''accommodated'' in its restriction. So it would seem that different kinds of definite descriptions should be treated differently. And the question is whether there is anything systematic that can be said about this.

FCS uses a mechanism for dealing with familiarity different from the one developed in section 1.6. Familiarity is no longer a ''formal'' property of LF but a felicity condition on contexts, that is, a presupposition of sorts. And FCS seems to have potential in dealing with the problem of presupposition projection. So it is worth exploring whether we can make progress on the problem of definites by exploiting the FCS machinery.

The first thing to do, in this connection, is to try to be more explicit on the nature of presuppositions. Following Stalnaker, let us regard presuppositions as, roughly, what speakers take as their common base of knowledge, beliefs, assumptions, and the like. This common ground can be represented as a set of worlds. A presupposition is a proposition entailed by the common ground.

In what form can a Stalnaker-style view of presuppositions be implemented in FCS? Presuppositions are what is entailed by the common ground. A file represents, in a way, a common ground. So we need a notion of a file entailing a sentence. In order to get at such a notion, we need to put intensionality back into our model. We can do so by going back to the view (sketched in (109)) that the content of a file f, instead of being a set of assignments

Sat(f), is a set C(f) of world–assignment pairs. Or, equivalently, we can assume that the function Sat is world indexed; that is, for any world w, Sat$_w$(f) is the set of assignments associated with f in w.[26] We can then define entailment as follows:

(135)   a.   A file f *entails* a file f' iff for any w and any a, if a $\in$ Sat$_w$(f), then there exists a b such that b agrees with a on D(f) and b $\in$ Sat$_w$(f').

   b.   A file f entails a sentence S iff f entails f + S.   (Heim 1987, p. 41)

This is a rather straightforward variation on (one of) the standard notions of entailment.

At this point we can build into the Novelty/Familiarity Condition given in (118) the idea that the content of a description must be presupposed:

(136)   *Extended Novelty/Familiarity Condition (NFC):* If S is uttered in f, then for every NP$_i$ in S it must be the case that
   i.   if NP$_i$ is indefinite, i $\notin$ D(f), and
   ii.   if NP$_i$ is definite, i $\in$ D(f) and f entails NP$_i$.

Here we have extended the NFC by adding a final clause to it which makes explicit the requirement that the content of a definite description must be presupposed.

Now, the examples discussed in (132) are cases where it is unclear whether the presupposition associated with the definite (i.e., the Extended NFC) is met. This raises the general issue of how to deal with situations where presuppositions may be violated. A possible line one might want to follow in this connection (proposed in Lewis 1979) is to assume that cooperative speakers first try to fix the context. Only if this turns out to be impossible does communication break down (and the sentence turn out to be infelicitous). Let us illustrate what is involved by means of an example. Imagine that we are talking to Pavarotti, who, for all we know, may or may not have a car. At some point he says, "My car is parked outside." It is clear that at the moment this sentence is uttered, its presupposition—namely that Pavarotti has a car—is not satisfied (in the sense of being taken for granted by the illocutionary agents). Yet the sentence is felicitous. A possible explanation is that we accommodate the presupposition; that is, we modify the common ground by adding to it the information that Pavarotti has a car, and we then process the sentence relative to this modified common ground. Since the information that Pavarotti has a car does not conflict with any known fact and is not otherwise controversial, the accommodation can successfully be carried through without giving rise to failure or deviancy.

Let us now turn to the theory of definites embodied in the Extended NFC. As the example just given illustrates, there are going to be plenty of contexts in which a definite is not familiar (in the sense of there being an active file card for it in the current file). A familiarity-based theory of definites is forced to deal with these cases in terms of accommodation: it must introduce a file card for the definite and then interpret the definite relative to this modified file. With this in mind, let us reexamine the problematic examples in (132), repeated here.

(132)   a. Everyone$_i$ who sees [the man with the red mustache]$_j$ insults him$_j$.
         b. Everyone$_i$ who sees [the man that betrayed him$_i$]$_j$ insults him$_j$.

Suppose that (132a) is interpreted relative to a file f that does not contain any information on a specific man with a red mustache. In this case, we introduce in f the information that such a man exists (and is in some relevant sense unique) and then process (132a) relative to the new file thus produced. The net result is that (132a) is interpreted as something like 'There is a (unique) man with a red mustache, and everyone who sees him insults him'. This gives reasonably adequate truth conditions for (132a). They are, in fact, the standard Russellian truth conditions for this sentence. They do not arise, however, directly from the meaning of *the,* as on Russell's approach, but indirectly via accommodation. To the extent that f makes it easy or hard to accommodate the relevant information, the sentence will be easy or hard to make sense of.

Consider next (132b). Assume that we are interpreting this sentence relative to a file f that contains no active file card j. In order to meet the Extended NFC we must accommodate. Suppose we modify f so as to make it entail 'j betrayed i'. If we did this by introducing a file card for i, too, we could not interpret *everyone$_i$* as binding that i (*everyone$_i$* requires that i be novel). We could try to accommodate in some other way, without introducing in f a file card for i, for example by entering the information that j betrays everyone. Then we could go on and interpret (130b), which would end up saying that everyone who sees this universal traitor insults him. But presumably the common ground contains other information that rules out the existence of such a universal traitor. That such a character should exist is, after all, highly unlikely. So this type of accommodation is rejected, as it clashes with other assumptions in the common ground. At this point, what options do we have?

The only seemingly plausible alternative is to accommodate the information 'j betrays i' not in f but in the auxiliary files that we used to set up in evaluating the restriction of *every*. Recall that to evaluate a formula of the form [every ϕ Ψ], we first compute $f + \phi$ and we then compute $(f + \phi)$ + Ψ. These auxiliary files are discarded in the end. What must be going on in the case at hand, therefore, is that we accommodate 'i betrays j' as part of the setting up of the auxiliary file $f + \phi$. The first kind of accommodation, which we have considered and rejected, is "global" in the sense that it modifies the original context. This second type of accommodation is more "local" in that it modifies only the auxiliary files that we set up in evaluating the universal.

For further illustration, let us consider the LF of (130b):

(137)   every [one$_i$ who [t$_i$ sees x$_j$]] [t$_i$ insults him$_j$]

Here the brackets in boldface indicate the restriction and the scope of *every*. In (137), we are treating the definite [the man that betrayed him$_i$]$_j$ as a free variable (as on our previous, static theory). Let us for a minute represent files using directly logical forms (rather than their content). The two kinds of accommodations we are comparing correspond to the following two LFs:

(138)   a. *Global Accommodation:*
          [man that betrayed him$_i$]$_j$
          every [one$_i$ [t$_i$ sees x$_j$]] [t$_i$ insults him$_j$]
         b. *Local Accommodation:*
          every [one$_i$ [man that betrayed him$_i$]$_j$ [t$_i$ sees x$_j$]] [t$_i$ insults him$_j$]

The LF in (138b) results in the right truth conditions. *Every* is free to quantify over both i and j, since the first occurrence of j, being accommodated, qualifies as "new" (while x$_j$ becomes "old" relative to the accommodated material). The effect of this kind of accommodation, where the presupposed material is entered in the restriction of *every,* is that of "filtering out" the presupposition. This filtering is due to the fact that global accommodation is not viable, since "it doesn't make sense"—that is, it clashes with assumptions that are presumed to be part of the common ground.

This is the line to which the familiarity-based theory of definites appears to be committed. Novel definites must be accommodated. One first tries to accommodate globally by changing the context in which the whole sentence is being processed. If assumptions present in the common ground make that impossible, one tries to accommodate locally in the auxiliary files that are being set up in evaluating the various operators.[27]

Where does this leave us with respect to FCS, vis-à-vis an approach that employs construal rules and a standard static semantics? Do we now have an argument in favor of the former, as Heim (1982, chapter 3) suggests? The situation is far from clear, One could argue that in the static theory it appears somewhat arbitrary whether the index of a definite is allowed to undergo Quantifier Indexing or not. In FCS, per contra, we are able to relate the behavior of indefinites to a general theory of presupposition projection. And, to the extent that we have reasonably strong intuitions as to when global accommodation would clash with assumptions that are likely to be in the common ground, we can claim to be able to predict *when* indefinites will end up being quantified over by operators. But while such claim may be true, it is not obvious that it can be construed as an argument supporting the File Change machinery. Suppose we take accommodation to be a syntactic operation on Logical Forms. That is, taking literally what we did in (138), let us assume that accommodation is actually an operation that copies chunks of LFs. Then it would seem that we can reproduce our reasoning without resorting at all to any kind of dynamic semantics. All we need is a notion of common ground and the observation that, given plausible assumptions as to what can be part of it, something like (138a) is likely to be uninterpretable, while (138b) will generally make perfectly good sense. So if we are willing to syntacticize accommodation, by viewing it essentially as a further rule of construal, we are left with no empirical argument in favor of FCS.[28]

1.8 SUMMARY

In the present chapter we have identified the main empirical properties of what has come to be known as donkey anaphora—properties which set it aside from c-command anaphora on the one hand and from other kinds of discourse anaphora on the other. We have then introduced DRT as a way of dealing with it and considered some preliminary evidence as to why such a framework might be successful. We have seen that the assumptions that are constitutive of classical DRT can be implemented in two ways. One way is to map S-structures into representations that are easy to interpret by familiar techniques. This involves setting up the right construal rules (i.e., the right set of transformations). The second way involves a principled shift of perspective in the semantics, namely toward viewing meaning as context change. There clearly is a trade-off between these two approaches. This trade-off involves deciding at which level one keeps track of new and old indices and where one does perform Existential Closure. So far, we have not been able to find evidence that strongly supports one approach over the other. I do believe, however, that such evidence can indeed be found; the next chapters are devoted to this task.

APPENDIX

I The Semantics of DRT_K and the Mapping from LF into DRT_K

DEFINITION I. Accessibility relative to DRT_K. If $K = x_1 \ldots x_n [K_1]$, $K = \neg K_1$ or $K = K_1 \Rightarrow_Q K_2$, we say that K is *immediately accessible* from K_1 and K_1 is immediately accessible from K_2. We also say that each DRS is immediately accessible from itself. We then define accessibility in general as follows: K is *accessible* from K' iff there is a sequence of DRSs $\langle K,K_1, \ldots , K_n,K' \rangle$ such that each element in the sequence is immediately accessible from the next one.

We also say that the *accessible domain* of a DRS K is the set of all variables in the local domain of all the DRSs accessible from K (i.e., $U_i\ d(K_i)$ for each K_i accessible from K). For any DRS K, an occurrence of a variable x_i is *free in K* iff x_i does not occur in the accessible domain of the minimal DRS containing x_i.

Example
a. If John has a monkey and every boy has a cow, he is happy.
b. $[_{K_0}\ x[_{K_1}\ monkey(x) \wedge has(j,x) \wedge y[_{K_2}\ boy(y)] \Rightarrow_\forall z[_{K_3}\ cow(z) \wedge has(y,z)]]$ $[_{K_4}\ happy(j)]]$
c. Set of accessible DRSs from each sub-DRS in (a):
   K_0, K_1, K_4 are accessible from K_4
   K_0, K_1, K_2, K_3 are accessible from K_3
   K_0, K_1, K_2 are accessible from K_2
   K_0, K_1 are accessible from K_1
   K_0 is accessible from K_0

Exercise 4

Consider the following discourse:

> Some student doesn't have a problem. If a student who has a problem talks to every professor who has a son, he will find it helpful.

Draw a possible DRS for this discourse and determine for each sub-DRS in it what DRSs are accessible from it.

In giving the semantics for DRT_K, Kamp (1981) uses partial embedding functions. We will use a semantics which is closer to the one we introduced in section 1.6.2. The semantics we will adopt is fully equivalent to Kamp's as far as donkey sentences are concerned.

As in section 1.6.2, we take models to be triples of the form $\langle W,A,Int \rangle$. Assignments are sequences of elements of A. As before, we define first what it is for an assignment a to satisfy a DRT_K formula ξ in a world w (in symbols, $Sat_{w,a}(\xi)$). Then we define felicity relative to a context c and truth in w relative to c.

DEFINITION 2. Satisfaction for DRT_K.

   i. If ξ is a DRS of the form $x_{i_1}, \ldots, x_{i_n}[\phi]$, then $Sat_{w,a}(\xi)$ iff there is a b $\approx_{\{i_1, \ldots, i_n\}}$ a such that $Sat_{w,b}(\phi)$.

   ii. If ξ is an atomic condition of the form $\beta(\alpha_{i_1}, \ldots, a_{i_n})$, then $Sat_{w,a}(\xi)$ iff $\langle a_{i_1}, \ldots, a_{i_n} \rangle \in Int(\beta)(w)$.

   iii. If ξ is a condition of the form $\phi_1 \wedge \ldots \wedge \phi_n$, then $Sat_{w,a}(\xi)$ iff $Sat_{w,a}(\phi_1), \ldots,$ and $Sat_{w,a}(\phi_n)$.

   iv. If ξ is a condition of the form $\neg K$, $Sat_{w,a}(\xi)$ iff it is not the case that $Sat_{w,a}(K)$.

   v. If ξ is a condition of the form $K_1 \Rightarrow_\forall K_2$, then $Sat_{w,a}(\xi)$ iff for every $b \approx_{d(K_1)}$ a, if $Sat_{w,b}(K_1)$, then $Sat_{w,b}(K_2)$.

   vi. If ξ is a condition of the form $K_1 \Rightarrow_{always} K_2$, then $Sat_{w,a}(\xi)$ iff $Sat_{w,b}(K_2)$ for every w' and every b such that $- b \approx_{d(K_1)} a - w R w' \qquad - Sat_{w,b}(K_1)$

We say that a DRS K is *felicitous* relative to a context c iff for any variable x_{i_k} free in K, $c +_{i_k}$ is defined. If K is felicitous relative to c, we say that K is *true* in a world w iff there is an assignment a such that $Sat_{w,a}(K)$ and for any variable x_{i_k} free in K, $a_{i_k} = c +_{i_k}$.

Exercise 5

Give the DRSs and compute the truth conditions of (a) *Every woman loves him* and (b) *Always, if a man likes every dog, he is crazy.*

For any LF-structure ∂, let $Tr(\partial)$ be the translation of ∂ into DRT_K. Tr is given a recursive definition below. In this definition, the terms 'atomic', 'molecular', and 'operator-headed formula' are used as characterizations of LF-structures, as per definition (86) in section 1.6.2.

DEFINITION 3. Translation of LFs into DRT_K.

   i. If ∂ is an atomic formula consisting of a predicate β and variables $\alpha_{i_1}, \ldots, \alpha_{i_n}$, $Tr(\partial) = \beta(\alpha_{i_1}, \ldots, \alpha_{i_n})$.

   ii. If ∂ is a molecular formula consisting of the formulae $\partial_1, \ldots, \partial_n$, then $Tr(\partial) = Tr(\partial_1) \wedge \ldots \wedge Tr(\partial_n)$.

   iii. If ∂ is an operator-headed formula of the form $[not\ \partial']$, then $Tr(\partial) = \neg Tr(\partial')$.

   iv. If ∂ is an operator-headed formula of the form $\exists_{i_1, \ldots, i_n} \partial'$, then $Tr(\partial) = x_{i_1}, \ldots, x_{i_n}[Tr(\partial')]$.

   v. If ∂ is an operator-headed formula of the form $[every_{i_1, \ldots, i_n} \partial_1 \partial_2]$, then $Tr(\partial) = x_{i_1}, \ldots, x_{i_n}[Tr(\partial_1)] \Rightarrow_\forall Tr(\partial_2)$.

   vi. If ∂ is an operator-headed formula of the form $[always_{i_1, \ldots, i_n} \partial_1 \partial_2]$, then $Tr(\partial) = x_{i_1}, \ldots, x_{i_n}[Tr(\partial_1)] \Rightarrow_{always} Tr(\partial_2)$.

Exercise 6

Give the LF of the sentence *Mostly, if a boy sees a donkey, he tells every farmer.* Then translate the LF into DRT_K, showing each step in the translation process.

II Definitions and Results in FCS

DEFINITION 1. The function $+S$ in an intensional setting.

For any file f, assignment a, and world w:

  i. If S is atomic, with predicate β and variables $\alpha_{i_1}, \ldots, \alpha_{i_n}$, then
     $Sat_w(f + S) = Sat_w(f) \cap \{a: \langle a_{i_1}, \ldots, a_{i_n} \rangle \in Int(\beta)(w)\}$
     $D(f + S) = D(f) \cup \{i_1, \ldots, i_n\}$

  ii. If S is molecular, with $S_1, \ldots, S_n$ as its components, then
     $Sat_w(f + S) = Sat_w((f + S_1) + \ldots + S_n)$
     $D(f + S) = D((f + S_1) + \ldots + S_n)$

  iii. If S is the negation of S', then
     $Sat_w(f + S) = \{a \in Sat_w(f):$ there is no $b =_{D(f)} a$ such that $b \in Sat_w(f + S')\}$
     $D(f + S) = D(f)$

  iv. If S is a universally quantified formula with S_1 as restriction and S_2 as scope, then
     $Sat_w(f + S) = \{a \in Sat_w(f):$ for every $b =_{D(f)} a$ such that $b \in Sat_w(f + S_1)$, there is a $c =_{D(f+S_1)} b$ such that $c \in Sat_w((f + S_1) + S_2)\}$
     $D(f + S) = D(f)$

For the semantics of [no $S_1 S_2$], change *every* in (iv) to *no;* for the semantics of [most $S_1 S_2$], change *every* in (iv) to *most;* etc.

  v. If $S = $ [always $S_1 S_2$], then
     $Sat_w(f + S) = \{a \in Sat_w(f):$ for every w' such that w R w' and every $b =_{D(f)} a$ such that $b \in Sat_{w'}(f + S_1)$, there is a $c =_{D(f+S_1)} b$ such that $c \in Sat_{w'}((f + S_1) + S_2)\}$
     $D(f + S) = D(f)$

The semantics for other adverbs of quantification is similar.

Exercise 7

Consider the following:

  (a) [Every person who had [a car]₅]₃ drove it₅ to a conference with him₄.

Give the LF of this sentence. Let S_1 and S_2 be the restriction and scope of *every* in this LF. Then imagine evaluating the sentence relative to a file f. Give the conditions that $D(f)$ and $D(f + S_1)$ have to satisfy for $f + $ (a) to be defined. Finally, assuming that $D(f) = \{4,5\}$, compute $D(f + S_1)$ and $D((f + S_1) + S_2)$.

THEOREM. The following sentences from section 1.7.1 have the same truth conditions:

(125)   a.   [A woman]$_i$ walked in.

         b.   There is a woman that walked in.

PROOF. We need to show two things, namely,

   i. (125a) $\Rightarrow$ (125b)

  ii. (125b) $\Rightarrow$ (125a)

To show (i) is straightforward, by contraposition. If there is no woman that walks in, then we won't be able to find any u such that a_i = u. Sat(f + (125a)) must therefore be empty.

     To show (ii), let us assume that (125b) is true. Let u be a woman that walked in. Now pick an arbitrary assignment a in Sat(f) and change it to an assignment b identical to a, except that b_i = u. Notice that since [a woman]$_i$ is indefinite it must be the case that i $\notin$ D(f). Hence, by condition (117), it follows that b is in Sat(f) iff a is. And since, by hypothesis, a is in Sat(f) b will also be. Thus we have that b must also be in Sat(f + (125a)), since by construction b_i is a woman that walked in. $\square$

2   Dynamic Binding

2.1 INTRODUCTION

In chapter 1 we have considered a static and a dynamic version of DRT and discussed why DRT (however implemented) sheds interesting light on non-c-command anaphora. There are, however, a number of problems that either version of classical DRT leaves open. In the present chapter, I would like to discuss these problems and argue that their solution calls for a dynamic approach, albeit one which is somewhat different from that considered in the previous chapter.[1] I will call this approach the *Dynamic Binding* approach.

I will begin by raising three issues in an impressionistic form. They are the following:

(1)   a. Are the truth conditions we have assigned to donkey sentences generally right?

          b. Are determiners really unselective binders, as classical DRT maintains?

          c. How does the treatment of NPs in classical DRT square with the theory of generalized quantifiers?

I will argue that the answer to (1a–b) is No. This will lead us to abandon some of the basic assumptions of classical DRT and develop an approach where generalized quantifiers play a more direct and central role than they do in classical DRT. The approach we will pursue also calls for a principled integration of some of the tenets of DRT with the idea that pronouns can at times be descriptions in disguise. The questions in (1) are not only interesting in their own right but also because, if I am right, they provide us with empirical arguments in favor of a principled enrichment of semantics in the direction of a dynamic treatment of pronoun binding, over an approach that employs transformations on Logical Forms.

The rest of this introduction is devoted to making clearer the issues raised in (1).

2.1.1 Two Readings of Donkey Sentences

In classical DRT, donkey sentences such as (2a) are analyzed as in (2b), following Geach's (1962) suggestions:

(2)   a. Every man that has a donkey beats it.

          b. every$_{x,y}$ [x is a man $\wedge$ y is a donkey $\wedge$ x has y] [x beats y]

In this way, indefinites in the restriction of *every* systematically get universal force. While such analysis seems to work well in many cases, there is also a significant set of examples that do not fit smoothly into this mold. Consider (3):

(3)   a. Yesterday, every person who had a credit card paid his bill with it.   (R. Cooper)
       b. Every person who has a dime will put it in the meter. (Pelletier and Schubert 1989)
       c. Every person who submitted a paper had it rejected once.

Analyzing these sentences along Geachean lines, as we did for (2), gives the wrong results. For example, in the case of (3b) it would wrongly require that people empty their pockets of all their dimes. In a situation where people put just one of their dimes into the parking meter, (3b) is predicted to be false by the analysis we have so far adopted. This clashes frontally with our intuitions. The truth conditions of (3b) are roughly the following:

(4)   Every person who has a dime will put in the meter one of his/her dimes.

The interesting fact here is that the indefinites in the restriction of *every* to which the pronouns are anaphorically related appear to have existential force. Accordingly, let us call this type of reading ∃-reading (or *existential reading*) in contrast with the ∀-reading (or *universal reading*) exemplified by (2b).

∃-readings appear to be widespread and systematic. For example, it should be noted that they show up with determiners and adverbs of quantification of any kind, as the following examples illustrate:

(5)   a. Most women that have a dime will put it in the meter.
       b. Usually, if a man has a nice hat, he wears it to church.

Notice also that these sentences in no way carry a uniqueness presupposition (as Kadmon 1990 would have it). For example, sentence (5a) does not exclude from consideration women that have more than one dime. Moreover, similar phenomena arise also with plurals, as the following illustrates:

(6)   Most people that have two dimes handy will put them in the toll machine.

Sentence (6) has exactly the same characteristics as the previous examples with singular indefinites, namely, it does not exclude from consideration people that have more than two dimes, nor does it force them to put all of their pairs of dimes in the toll machine.

In fact, even sentences like the classical (2a), which prima facie seem to be most naturally analyzable in terms of a ∀-reading, turn out to allow quite clearly for ∃-readings, in suitable contexts. The following example (which I owe to P. Casalegno) illustrates this:

(7)   The farmers of Ithaca, N.Y., are stressed out. They fight constantly with each other. Eventually, they decide to go to the local psychotherapist. Her recommendation is that every farmer who has a donkey should beat it, and channel his/her aggressiveness in a way which, while still morally questionable, is arguably less dangerous from a social point of view. The farmers of Ithaca follow this recommendation and things indeed improve.

Clearly, if we utter (3a) in the context described in (7) we say something true, and yet no farmer must beat all of his poor donkeys. Nor are we limiting ourselves to a consideration of farmers that own just one donkey.

Thus, we seem to have come upon a wholly general and pervasive phenomenon—so pervasive as to make it quite mysterious why this phenomenon has remained at the margin of the discussion for so long.[2] As a matter of fact, one might be tempted to take ∃-readings as basic and regard ∀-readings as an epiphenomenon. The basis for this might be the observation that ∀-readings are stronger, in the sense that they entail the corresponding ∃-readings. When this situation arises, one can try to get by with assigning the weaker reading to the relevant construction and argue that the stronger one arises in suitable contexts via Gricean mechanisms. This strategy has been successfully applied in some other cases, such as the inclusive vs. exclusive interpretation of 'or'.

However, this strategy won't work for donkey sentences, because of examples of the following kind, due to Heim (p.c.):

(8)   Every man who owned a slave owned his offspring.

The point here is that just a single pair ⟨a,b⟩ such that a owns b but not b's offspring would be sufficient to falsify (8). If the only reading that the semantic system assigns to (8) were the existential one, it would be hard to account for our intuition that a single exceptional owner–slave pair would falsify the sentence. This suggests that ∀-readings, too, must be present as part of the semantics of sentences like (8) and cannot always be explained using Gricean maxims.

There are some regularities in the distribution of ∃- vs. ∀-readings, which has been studied extensively by Kanazawa (1993). For example, downward entailing quantifiers and existential quantifiers appear to favor ∃-readings:

(9)   a. No father who has a teenage son lends him the car on week-
        days.   (Rooth 1987)
        b. At least two boys who borrowed a book from me returned it on
        time.   (Kanazawa 1993)

Sentence (9a) does not say that no father lends his car on weekdays to all
his sons, but that he doesn't lend it to *any* of them (i.e., the presence of a
single father–son pair $\langle u, u' \rangle$ such that u lends the car on weekdays to u'
suffices to make (9a) false). Similarly, (9b) doesn't require that two boys
return all of their books on time. However, contrary to what is claimed in,
e.g., Chierchia 1992a, the preference for ∃-readings we see in sentences like
(9) seems to be just a tendency. There are sentences isomorphic to (9) that
appear to have a ∀-reading:

(10)   a. No one who has an umbrella leaves it home on a day like
        this.   (Kanazawa 1993)
        b. At least one boy who had an apple for breakfast didn't give it to
        his best friend.   (van der Does 1993).

In testing your intuitions concerning (10a), imagine finding out that u is a
person and u' an umbrella owned and left home by u. Does this suffice to
make (10a) false? Not if u carried along another one of his umbrellas. This
intuition is inconsistent with an ∃-reading of (10a). If (10a) had only an
∃-reading, the existence of just one exceptional person–umbrella pair would
suffice to make the sentence false. As regards (10b), if every boy gave an
apple to his best friend, (10b) would be false (even if a few boys kept a second
apple for themselves). This intuition is only consistent with a ∀-reading of
(10b).

    On the basis of these considerations I will assume that both ∃-readings
and ∀-readings are generally available, with some sentences favoring one
over the other. I will focus on how these readings are obtained, without
saying anything as to why certain contexts favor certain readings. If it turns
out that the tendencies just mentioned (and others observed in the literature)
do have a systematic explanation, so much the better. For the time being, I
will assume that the distribution of readings in donkey sentences parallels
what happens with, say, quantifier scope. For sentences that contain multiple
quantifiers, the grammar generates all possible scopings, but some such scopings may be hard or impossible to get, for a variety of reasons (such as the
nature of the common ground, processing factors, etc.). While this may well
not be the last word on these matters, I see no alternative to it, given our

current level of understanding of the phenomena (but cf. Kanazawa 1993 for an interesting attempt at predicting a more constrained distribution of ∀- vs. ∃-readings, which I think is consistent with the line I will be taking).

To summarize so far, we have seen that classical DRT, which assigns only ∀-readings to donkey sentences, goes wrong with a significant class of cases. Besides ∀-readings, donkey sentences appear to have also ∃-readings. ∃-readings are by no means a marginal phenomenon, and the theory has to reflect this fact. The question is how. In addressing this question, I will proceed as follows. First I will put ∀-readings aside and focus on how to modify classical DRT so as to get ∃-readings. Subsequently (in section 2.5) I will reconsider ∀-readings and propose a way of obtaining them.

2.1.2 Proportions and Unselectivity

If we analyze *most* on a par with *every* as done in DRT, we run into what has come to be known as the proportion problem:[3]

(11)   a. Most farmers that have a donkey beat it.
       b. most$_{x,y}$ [farmer(x) $\wedge$ donkey(y) $\wedge$ x owns y] [x beats y]

If we interpret the logical form in (11b) along the lines discussed in chapter 1, we get wrong results. A formula like (11b) would be true just in case most of the pairs that satisfy the antecedent satisfy the consequent. But the truth conditions we obtained in this way are not right. Imagine a situation with nine farmers that own one donkey each and don't beat it and one farmer that owns fifty donkeys and beats them all. On the analysis we have just given (11a) is expected to be true in this situation (for the majority of *pairs* that satisfy the restriction satisfy the scope). But this conflicts with our intuitions: in the situation I have just described it is plainly false that most farmers that own a donkey beat it.

The problem seems to stem from the fact that *most* in (11b) is taken to quantify over pairs. As *most* is assumed to be an unselective binder, it quantifies symmetrically over all variables free in its scope. In contrast with this prediction, (11a) seems to amount to a quantification over donkey-owning farmers; that is, *most* in (11a) appears to quantify asymmetrically over the variable that corresponds to the head noun. This casts doubt on the idea that determiners are unselective binders.

A similar point can be made for other quantifiers as well:

(12)   a. At least two men who have a donkey beat it.
       b. at least two$_{x,y}$ [farmer(x) $\wedge$ donkey(y) $\wedge$ x owns y] [x beats y]

Clearly, if (12b) is construed as a quantification over pairs, we get the wrong truth conditions for (12a). Problems of a related nature also arise with conditionals. Consider:

(13)   Usually, if a farmer owns a donkey, he beats it.

It seems that on its most prominent reading, (13) would be false in the situation described for (11) above. This suggests that the most prominent reading of (13) is one where we quantify asymmetrically over the subject (i.e., over donkey-owning farmers). In other words, (13) seems to have the same truth conditions as (11a).

This is not the whole story on conditionals, however. There are interesting differences between relative clauses and *if/when*-clauses with respect to this issue, differences which have been discussed widely in the literature (cf. note 3). In sentences like (11a), what one quantifies over is completely determined structurally by the head of the NP. (11a) simply has no reading on which we count pairs rather than farmers. Things are different for *if/when*-clauses. We know that *if/when*-clauses must occupy the restriction of a (possibly null) adverb of quantification, but which of the indefinites that occur in them is actually being quantified over will vary from case to case. Take the following examples:

(14)   a. If a village is inhabited by a painter, it is usually pretty. (Kadmon 1990)
         $\Rightarrow$ most$_x$ [x is a village inhabited by a painter] [x is pretty]
         b. If a woman has a son with a man, she usually keeps in touch with him.   (I. Heim)
         $\Rightarrow$ most$_{x,y}$ [man(x) $\wedge$ woman(y) $\wedge$ x has a son with y] [x keeps in touch with y]
         c. In this department, when a student gives a paper to a professor, she expects her to comment on it promptly.
         $\Rightarrow$ most$_{x,y,z}$ [student(x) $\wedge$ professor(y) $\wedge$ paper(z) $\wedge$ x gives z to y] [x expects y to comment on z promptly]

For each of these examples I have given the logical form that expresses what I take to be the dominant reading. To begin, consider (14a). Imagine we are sampling a region with ten villages inhabited by painters. Of these, eight are inhabited by two painters and are pretty. The other two are ugly. One of the ugly ones is inhabited by just one painter. The other is the site of a famous local art fair and is inhabited by twenty painters. In this scenario it seems to be true that if a painter lives in a village, the village is usually pretty. But again, the majority of village–painter pairs that satisfy the antecedent do not satisfy the consequent. We seem to understand (14a) as involving a quantification over villages that are inhabited by painters; that is, we are quantifying over the indefinite in object position. This type of reading is sometimes referred to as the "object-asymmetric" reading.

Consider next (14b). Here we seem to quantify over woman–man pairs (not over woman–man–son triplets). Imagine that we are considering a population of twenty couples with children. Of these couples, eighteen have one child and do not keep in touch, while two have fifteen children each and do keep in touch. Relative to this sample, sentence (14b) would quite clearly be false. Yet, if we were counting triplets it should be true, as the reader can easily check. So in this case we seem to quantify over the subject and the indefinite in the PP adjunct.

In (14c) finally, we seem to quantify over student–professor–paper triplets (i.e., all of the indefinites). The reader ought to be able to construct suitable scenarios to test this intuition.

What emerges from these considerations is that adverbs of quantification do not seem to be as unselective either as they prima facie appear, in that they can selectively exempt from binding some of the NPs in their restriction. They have more freedom in this respect than determiners.

The factor that seems to influence most directly which indefinites are selected by the adverb of quantification appears to be what the *topic* is, that is, the theme-rheme structure of the discourse. Consider the following example:

(15)   Dolphins are truly remarkable. When a trainer trains a dolphin, she usually makes it do incredible things.

Here we are talking about dolphins. The second sentence in (15) is true iff most dolphins that are properly trained do incredible things. The presence of one dumb dolphin that was trained by scores of trainers and fails to perform doesn't make (15) false. Thus in (15) we are not quantifying over trainer–dolphin pairs (or, for that matter, over trainers). We are quantifying over dolphins, which, as the context makes clear, are the topic of the discourse. Notice what happens, though, if we change the topic.

(16)   Trainers from here are absolutely remarkable with all sort of animals. If a trainer from here trains a dolphin, she usually makes it do incredible things.

In this context, the second sentence in (16) (which is structurally identical to the second sentence in (15)) would be true iff most trainers from here that train a dolphin make it do wonderful things. The presence of one trainer who is unsuccessful with scores of dolphins wouldn't affect the truth of (16). So what the adverb selects for quantification seems to be a function of what is taken to be the sentence topic.

The idea that adverbs of quantification select the topic is corroborated by the observation made by Rooth (1985) and others that focal stress influences what one takes to be the target of a quantificational adverb. For example, while the most natural reading of (14a) out of the blue is the object-asymmetric one, focal stress can change things:

(17)   If A VILLAGE is inhabited by a painter, it is usually pretty (while if a city is, it is dirty and ugly).

I use capitals to indicate focal stress. Sentence (17) is most naturally construed as being about painters and their habitat. So to check its truth we would count painters rather than villages. The unstressed part is what we quantify over, that is, the topic or theme. This is consistent with the fact that contrastive stress often signals what is new in a discourse, that is, the rheme or "comment."

To summarize, the main observations about proportions seem to be the following. Quantificational determiners bind only the variable associated with their head nouns. The evaluation of a sentence containing an NP like *most men that own a donkey* requires counting donkey-owning men, not man–donkey pairs. Adverbs of quantification restricted by a *when/if*-clause are more flexible. They do not necessarily bind all of the indefinites in their restriction. Rather, they are free to associate with (i.e., directly bind) one or more or possibly all of the indefinites present in their restriction. Which indefinites are selected by a quantificational adverb is a function of the theme-rheme structure of the sentence. The indefinites that end up bound by the adverb constitute in some sense what the sentence is about, that is, the theme or topic of discourse. Classical DRT does not predict this distribution of readings. Instead, it wrongly predicts (in fact, it is designed to predict) that every quantificational element (be it a determiner or an adverb) uniformly binds all the indefinites in its restriction.

2.1.3 Discourse Representation Theory and Generalized Quantifiers

In the theory of generalized quantifiers, NP denotations are analyzed as sets of sets and determiners as relations between sets. Some standard examples are the following:

(18)   a. every man $\Rightarrow$ {X : MAN $\subseteq$ X}   (where MAN is the set of men)
        a'. every(X,Y) = X $\subseteq$ Y
        b. a man $\Rightarrow$ {X : MAN $\cap$ X $\neq$ $\varnothing$}
        b'. a(X,Y) = X $\cap$ Y $\neq$ $\varnothing$
        c. no man $\Rightarrow$ {X : MAN $\cap$ X = $\varnothing$}
        c'. no(X,Y) = X $\cap$ Y = $\varnothing$

It has also been noted that the domain of quantification changes constantly in discourse; sometimes two occurrences of the same quantifier in one sentence may be associated with different domains. The following is an example by L. Rizzi:

(19)   a. A panel for an award (where different disciplines, including lin-
            guistics, are represented) has to select the winner among the
            applicants (who are also from different disciplines). Now is the
            time for the panel to deliberate by voting.
        b. Every linguist voted for a linguist.

The natural interpretation of (19b) against the background of (19a) is that every linguist on the panel voted for a linguist not on the panel. On every other choice of domain, sentence (19b) would be false. Thus the two quantifiers in (19b) are associated with different domains. Considerations such as these have led, e.g., Westerståhl (1988) to view determiner meanings as functions D from domains U to binary relations D_U over subsets of U. While agreeing with Westerståhl on this score, I will generally omit making explicit the relativization of generalized quantifiers to a domain U (except when it makes a difference).

Many important empirical properties of NPs have been studied based on the assumption that they denote generalized quantifiers. A case in point is the discovery of *conservativity* as a universal characteristic of determiner meanings, where conservativity is defined as follows:[4]

(20)   D(X)(Y) $\Leftrightarrow$ D(X)(X $\wedge$ Y)

I assume here that (i) D is a function from sets into sets of sets, (ii) the interpretation of D(X)(Y) is $[\![Y]\!] \in [\![D(X)]\!]$, and (iii) in this context '$\wedge$' is interpreted as set intersection. Another simple and well-known application of the theory of generalized quantifiers is the treatment of NP coordination. Under the hypothesis that NPs denote generalized quantifiers, coordinate structures such as those in (21a) can be readily interpreted by means of set intersection, as shown in (21b).

(21)   a. Professor Jones, every student, and a lecturer were present.
         b. [[Professor Jones]] ∩ [[every student]] ∩ [[a lecturer]]

These ideas can be integrated into a very general theory of constituent coordination that extends Boolean operators to every category, bypassing the problems that accounts based on, for example, a syntactic transformation of conjunction reduction run into.[5]

How does this line of inquiry fit with DRT? It is not obvious. In DRT,
indefinites are assimilated to free variables, while universally quantified NPs
are split into two components. In an NP like *every man,* the common noun
part contributes essentially a free variable, while the determiner is viewed
as an unselective binder that binds not only the variable associated with
the common noun but also other indefinites that the NP may contain. Now,
the very heart of the generalized quantifier approach is the idea that all
NPs get (or can get) a uniform denotation. The question is whether this uni-
formity can be at all achieved within DRT. Let us see how this could be
done.

We can easily raise the type of NP denotations to that of sets of sets in
simple cases. For example, *a man* could be analyzed as follows:

(22)   a. {X : x is a man and x is in X}
         b. $\lambda P [man(x) \wedge P(x)]$ (using Montague's IL)

The set term in (19a) (or (19b)) will denote a set of sets relative to a value
assignment to the free variable x which occurs in it. The problem comes
when we try to give the same analysis to universally quantified NPs:

(23)   a. every man ⇒ {P : for every x, if x is a man, then x ∈ P}
         b. every man who has a donkey ⇒ {R : for every ⟨x, y⟩, if x is a
            man, y a donkey and x has y, then ⟨x,y⟩ ∈ R}
         c. every man who lent a book to a student ⇒ a set of three-place
            relations. . . .

This example should clearly illustrate the nature of the problem. A universal
NP will have to be a generalized quantifier of varying adicity, depending on
how many indefinites occur free in its left argument. Now, it is not clear
how to obtain this result in an elegant way, but, more to the point, it wouldn't
help us much with coordination. Consider:

(24)   [NP [NP Every farmer who keeps an animal in a barn] and [NP everyone
         who has a pet]] must feed it.

Here we are coordinating two universal NPs. The first one contains two indefinites (hence, according to the hypothesis sketched above, it should be a set of three-place relations). The second NP contains only one indefinite (and hence should be a set of two-place relations). As the two NPs are of different types, our simple analysis in terms of generalized Boolean operators is not available to us. So what do we do, assuming we don't want to go back to conjunction reduction?

I use coordination facts merely to illustrate what I take to be a general and simple issue. The treatment of important semantic phenomena calls for a system of higher-order meanings. Classical DRT with its flat tripartite structures is a first-order system. Its only non-lexical category is that of sentences. This is a limitation that needs to be overcome. The question is how this can best be done.

2.1.4 The Plan

We have now identified three areas where DRT seems to run into empirical and conceptual problems. Our objective is to remedy this situation by (i) focusing on how $\exists$-readings should be obtained, (ii) trying to get proportions right, and (iii) studying how generalized quantifiers (and, more generally, higher-order meanings) can be part of the picture. In doing this we would like to see whether we come across new considerations that favor one of the two souls of DRT over the other. I will first make a proposal in the spirit of the first soul—one that employs construal and accommodation rules—in an attempt to push that line as far as it will go. I will then indicate what I take to be some shortcomings of this approach. Having done so, I will develop an alternative which does away with construal rules in favor of a dynamic notion of meaning. My proposal is closely related to File Change Semantics and to other work in the same spirit but is most directly based on Groenendijk and Stokhof 1990. I will argue that this alternative doesn't suffer from the shortcomings of the former approach. Finally, I will discuss how my proposal can be supplemented so as to obtain not only $\exists$-readings but also $\forall$-readings for donkey sentences.

2.2 EXTENSIONS OF CLASSICAL DRT

Our initial strategy in pursuing the goals outlined in section 2.1 will be quite conservative.[6] We shall stick as much as possible to the assumptions of classical DRT. In particular, we shall maintain the view that quantification is basically unselective and explore what is to be added to the construal component in order to get the facts right. Throughout this section we will, accordingly, assume a classical Tarskian semantics.

2.2.1 A New Set of Construal Rules

Let us tackle the proportion problem by considering the case of quantificational determiners. We need to ensure that they only bind the variable associated with the head noun. As a first step toward this goal, let us assume that determiners are automatically coindexed with their head (where the index of the head is projected to its maximal projection). For example:

(25)   a. Most men that have a dime put it in a meter.
        $\Rightarrow$ $[_{NP_i}$ most$_i$ $[_{N'}$men$_i$ that have a dime$_j$]] $[t_i$ put it$_j$ in a meter$_k$]
        b. [[most$_i$ $\exists$[men$_i$ that have a dime$_j$]] $\exists[t_i$ put it in a meter$_k$]]

The structure in (25a) to the right of the arrow represents the stage of the derivation after QR has applied. Since we would like NPs to be constituents at LF (so as to be able to formulate, e.g., rules of NP conjunction), we must exempt quantificational determiners from undergoing Quantifier Construal. Moreover, we want to close existentially both the material in the restriction and that in the scope of the quantificational determiner. This gives us (25b). The idea is that the existential quantifiers in the restriction and scope of (25b) ought to bind the indefinites they respectively c-command. In this way, the quantifier *most* winds up binding only the index it carries by construction (i.e., the one associated with the head noun). We thus get quantification over dime-owning men (rather than man–dime pairs). However, even before working the details out any further, we can already see a difficulty here. How can the pronoun *it* in the scope of (25b) be anaphoric to *a dime?* If *a dime* is existentially closed, it will be inaccessible to the pronoun *it* and hence an anaphoric link between the two ought to be impossible. We have to remedy this. One way of doing so is to accommodate the material in the restriction into the scope, by adjoining the former to the latter (before $\exists$-Closure). Applying this idea to (25a), we get (26a):

(26)   a. [most$_i$ [men$_i$ that have a dime$_j$]] [[men$_i$ that have a dime$_j$][t$_i$ put it in a meter$_k$]]
        b. *Accommodation:* [Det N'] IP $\Rightarrow$ [Det N'] [N' IP]

A general formulation of the rule is given in (26b). It takes the N' of an NP in IP-adjoined position and Chomsky-adjoins it onto the IP (leaving a copy behind). At this point, we can apply $\exists$-closure to both the restriction and the scope. The result is as follows:

(27)   a. [most$_i$ $\exists$[men$_i$ that have a dime$_j$]] $\exists$[[men$_i$ that have a dime$_j$][t$_i$ put it$_j$ in a meter$_k$]]

b. $\exists$-*Closure (partial):* [Det N'][N' IP] $\Rightarrow$ [Det $\exists$N'] $\exists$[N' IP]

c. [most$_i$ $\exists_j$[men$_i$ that have a dime$_j$]] $\exists_{j,k}$[[men$_i$ that have a dime$_j$][t$_i$ put it$_j$ in a meter$_k$]]

The rule of $\exists$-Closure can be formulated in first approximation as in (27b). At this point Quantifier Indexing applies, mapping (27a) into (27c). In the formulation of Quantifier Indexing, we drop the stipulation that indices on the head of an NP count as "indefinite," so that, for example, the index on *men* in (27a) is not copied onto '$\exists$'.

There are a couple of things that should be noted. The first is that obviously we still need text-level Existential Closure for simple sentences like *A man walked in; he was wearing a hat.* Thus in (27) we are adding an extra environment to Existential Closure as previously formulated in 1.6 (which is why (27b) is a partial formulation of $\exists$-Closure). The second thing to note is that the rules exemplified in (26)–(27) must be crucially restricted to *quantificational* NPs. This can easily be seen with examples of the following kind:

(28)   Every man who has a house that has a lawn must mow it regularly.

We will leave the details to the reader to work out, but it should be intuitively clear that our procedure would make *a lawn* inaccessible to the pronoun *it,* unless we stipulate that (26)–(27) do not apply to indefinite NPs like *a house that has a lawn.*

Let us turn now to the case of *if/when*-clauses, for which a more flexible approach is needed. To begin with, we can assume that quantificational structures are created in the usual manner by Quantifier Construal:

(29)   If a painter lives in a village it is usually pretty.
        $\Rightarrow$ usually [if a painter lives in a village][it is pretty]

Suppose that instead of automatically copying the indices of indefinites onto the closest available binder, we say that an adverb of quantification (Q-adverb) can be indexed freely with one or more indefinites in its c-command domain. For reasons that will become clear shortly, instead of copying the index of indefinites onto a Q-adverb, we assume that this operation, which precedes and feeds Accommodation and $\exists$-Closure, adds a second index to indefinites. For example:

(30)   *Q-Adverb Indexing:* usually$_k$[if a painter$_{i,k}$ lives in a village$_j$][it$_j$ is pretty]

The indexing in (30) is going to correspond to the subject-asymmetric reading of (29). The reason for doing things this way is that it allows us to keep Accommodation and ∃-Closure basically as they are. In example (30), we first copy the restriction onto the scope and then ∃-Closure applies to both restriction and scope as before, yielding:

(31)   Accommodation: usually$_k$ [if a painter$_{i,k}$ lives in a village$_j$][if a paint-er$_{i,k}$ lives in a village$_j$][it$_j$ is pretty]]

(32)   ∃-Closure: usually$_k$ ∃[if a painter$_{i,k}$ lives in a village$_j$] ∃[[if a paint-er$_{i,k}$ lives in a village$_j$][it$_j$ is pretty]]

The result undergoes Quantifier Indexing. We stipulate that only the first index on an indefinite counts for Quantifier Indexing, while the second does not. So in the case of (31)–(32) we get:

(33)   Quantifier Indexing: usually$_k$ ∃$_{i,j}$[if a painter$_{i,k}$ lives in a village$_j$] ∃$_{i,j}$[[if a painter$_{i,k}$ lives in a village$_j$][it$_j$ is pretty]]

It now remains to be specified how the double indexing is interpreted. This is done by means of the following satisfaction condition:

(34)   An assignment a satisfies *painter*$_{i,k}$ iff a_i is a painter and $a_i = a_k$.

So essentially, the double indexing introduces into the satisfaction condition an equation of the form given in (34). This means that (31)–(32) is assigned the following truth conditions:

(35)   Most a_k's such that for some painter a_i that lives in a village a_j, $a_i = a_k$, are such that a_k is identical to some painter that lives in a pretty village.

Sentence (35) says that most painters who live in a village live in a pretty one, which gives us the right truth conditions for the subject-asymmetric reading of (29). In a sense, this method allows Q-adverbs to freely "rebind" indefinites in their restriction.

To summarize, our revision of DRT leads us to the following set of ordered rules:

(36)   i. Quantifier Construal
         ii. Adverb Indexing (which adds a second index to indefinites)
        iii. Accommodation
         iv. ∃-Closure (with three distinct environments: the text, and the restriction and scope of operators)

v. Quantifier Indexing (which indexes only ∃ and applies only to the first index of indefinites)

2.2.2 Discussion

At a descriptive level the theory sketched above meets the goals we identified. First, determiners are no longer unselective. They now bind only the argument associated with their head. Q-adverbs are also no longer completely unselective; they are free to choose the arguments they quantify over. Second, the readings on donkey-type dependencies we get are the existential ones. And third, we can maintain a completely standard interpretation of determiners and NPs as generalized quantifiers. For example:

(37)   a. $[\![_{NP_i} \text{ most}_i [_{N'} \text{men}_i \text{ that have a dime}_j]]\!] = [\![\text{most}]\!](\{u: [\![_{N'} \text{men}_i \text{ that have a dime}_j]\!]\})$

   b. $[\![\text{most}]\!](X) = \{Y: |X \cap Y| > |X \cap Y^-|\}$

Here we see that N's are interpreted as sets (by abstracting over the index of the head) and determiners as functions from sets into generalized quantifiers.

However, there are reasons to be dissatisfied with this approach. The first stems from the observation that we had to employ a complex set of obligatory, deterministic construal rules that apply selectively to only some determiners (the quantificational ones). Current syntactic theory tells us that such rules are impossible. Consider, for example, Accommodation, which copies an N' onto a higher IP to the right. Under the view that traces are copies of the dislocated material (revived in Chomsky 1992), this operation can be viewed as an instance of Move α, but one that has none of the familiar characteristics of movement (it doesn't move a head or a maximal projection, it is not triggered by morphological properties of the phrase, etc.). At present, it is not clear how the characteristics of these rules could be related to more general properties of LF. A natural alternative is to build these operations as part of the lexical meaning of the relevant determiners (along the lines explored within FCS). But it is hard to see how to do that (and get the facts right) if we stick to the simple Tarski-style semantics that we have adopted here.

A second consideration has to do with the fact that not only does the approach of section 2.2.1 fail to conform to what is generally known about the syntax of LF, it also fails to conform to what is known about semantics. Consider our rule of accommodation again. The uncontroversial cases of presupposition accommodation are exemplified by simple processes like, say, the following: Pavarotti, of whom we don't know whether he has a car, tells us, "My car is parked outside." Here, rather than blocking, we infer that he has a car and accommodate this information in the common ground. This process has roughly the following properties: (i) it is triggered by a presupposition mismatch and hence follows semantic interpretation; (ii) consequently, there is a clear intuition that an inferential process, however semiconscious, is taking place. Contrast this with the interpretation of the pronoun *it* in *Most farmers that have a donkey beat it*. Here the claim is that a similar inferential process, triggered by the intention to be able to interpret the pronoun, should be taking place. But this is not at all confirmed by our intuitions. The anaphoric dependencies under consideration appear to be totally unmarked and easy to interpret. In fact, the rule as stated is completely automatic and precedes semantic interpretation.

These difficulties are of a conceptual nature. But there are also empirical problems having to do with coordination. One of our goals was to arrive at a simple Boolean semantics for NP coordination in structures of the following kind:

(38)   [Every boy who has a dog and every girl who has a cat] must feed it.

The problem is that the NP in (38) does not meet the structural description for our accommodation rule. And if we can't accommodate, we can't interpret the pronoun *it* in (38) and we predict that such anaphoric link should be impossible, contrary to facts. Notice also that if we try to extend Accommodation to (38), it is far from clear how to do so in a way that would make sense. The pronoun *it* should wind up syntactically bound by *a dog* and *a cat* at the same time, which seems incoherent. Thus the theory of section 2.2.1 seems to crash rather badly with respect to one of the desiderata. While it allows for an interpretation of NPs as generalized quantifiers, it does not naturally extend to coordinated NPs.

We have explored at some length the possibility of dealing with the problems laid out at the outset of this chapter in terms of construal rules. One could certainly conceive of many different variants of this approach in a similar vein. And it is likely that if one is liberal enough in allowing construction-specific stipulations, descriptive adequacy can be attained. We know that by using an arbitrarily complex set of transformational operations we can describe virtually any linguistic phenomenon. The question we want to ask is whether our understanding of the syntactic and semantic properties of Logical Form is thereby enhanced. As things stand now, I don't see that that is the case. I am motivated, therefore, to look at approaches that eschew construal rules in favor of a more elaborate semantics, in the spirit of FCS.

2.3 A NEW DYNAMIC APPROACH

Our objective in the present section is to elaborate the ideas embodied in the second soul of DRT (exemplified by FCS) by developing a higher-order system of meanings within which the descriptive goals singled out at the beginning of this chapter can be satisfactorily attained. In the process, we will recast some of the proposals made in section 2.2 in a dynamic framework; consequently, it should be possible for the reader to use the approach considered there (and dismissed) as a guide to the new one developed here.

In FCS, sentence meaning is represented as a function from files to files. We could take this type of function as the basic building block for a system of higher types. However, I prefer to proceed differently and recast the dynamics in a version of Montague's Intentional Logic (IL). My preference is guided by practical reasons. IL is a formal system familiar to linguists and has come to constitute a convenient lingua franca in semantics. Its use might facilitate the incorporation into dynamic semantics of previous work couched in Montague-style semantics. At any rate, it should be kept in mind that a great variety of dynamic systems are currently being explored which employ different techniques and notations. While there might be important differences among them, from my current point of view (aimed at finding out whether the dynamic approach as a whole has substantial empirical support) I am inclined to regard such differences as "in-house" disagreements, to be dealt with at some later stage.

2.3.1 Reviewing Montague's Intentional Logic

Let us begin by reviewing Montague's IL.[7] Basic types in IL are e (for 'entity') and t (for 'truth value'). Expressions of type e are singular terms, while expressions of type t are well-formed formulae. Complex types have the form $\langle a,b \rangle$, where a,b are themselves types. An expression of type $\langle a,b \rangle$ is something that combines with an a to yield a b. Some important extensional types are the following:

(39) | *Type* | *Example* | *Explanation* |
|---|---|---|
| $\langle e,t \rangle$ | run | One-place predicate. Combines with a singular expression to yield a formula. |

$\langle e,\langle e,t\rangle\rangle$	love	Two-place predicate. Combines with a singular term to yield a one-place predicate.
$\langle\langle e,t\rangle,t\rangle$	every (man)	Generalized quantifier. Combines with a one-place predicate to give a formula.
$\langle\langle e,t\rangle,\langle\langle e,t\rangle,t\rangle\rangle$	every	Determiner. Combines with a one-place predicate to give a generalized quantifier.

Each extensional type a has an intensional correlate $\langle s,a\rangle$. An expression of type $\langle s,a\rangle$ will have as its semantic value an intension, where the latter is viewed as a function from a set of parameters into an extensional object (of type a). IL has variables and possibly constants of any type (including the intensional ones). The formulae (i.e., expressions of type t) are closed under the usual connectives (i.e., $\rightarrow$, $\leftrightarrow$, $\neg$, $\wedge$, $\vee$) and quantifiers. The quantifiers can bind variables of any type. The λ-abstractor is also available and works in the usual manner: if α is a variable of type a and β an expression of type b, $\lambda\alpha[\beta]$ is an expression of type $\langle a,b\rangle$. Montague's IL has also a stock of modal operators, but to simplify things, we will leave them aside for now. (This limitation will be overcome in chapter 4.) Finally, we have the "cap" operator ' $^\wedge$ ' and the "cup" operator ' $^\vee$ ', which enable us to switch back and forth between extensions and intensions. If β is of type a, $^\wedge\beta$ is of type $\langle s,a\rangle$ and denotes β's intension. If β is of type $\langle s,a\rangle$ instead, $^\vee\beta$ is of type a and denotes β's extension at the parameter at which it is being considered.

So far this is just as in Montague's IL. We now come to the one innovation I want to propose, as far as syntax is concerned. We introduce a distinguished set of variables of type e, called *discourse markers* (*DM*).[8] While ordinary variables function in the way familiar from classical logic, discourse markers are going to behave "dynamically": if x_i is a discourse marker, a quantifier of the form Qx_i' will be able to bind beyond its syntactic scope in circumstances to be specified shortly. I will use x_i, y_i, . . . for discourse markers and v_i, u_i, . . . for static variables. Semantically, to determine the value of variables and discourse markers, we will have two distinct assignment functions. An assignment function g to ordinary variables will map a variable of type a into something of type a. An assignment ω to discourse markers assigns to them individuals of type e. In symbols:

(40)   a. $[\![v_i]\!]^{g,\omega} = g(v_i)$ b. $[\![x_i]\!]^{g,\omega} = \omega(x_i)$

where '$[\![\ \ ]\!]^{g,\omega}$' is the interpretation function relative to the assignments g and ω (and is also implicitly relativized to a model M).

We said that we are going to leave aside modalities for the time being, which will enable us to disregard possible worlds and times. Given this, how are we going to represent intensions? If we disregard worlds and times, what are the parameters on which extensions may depend? The only candidates left are the assignments to variables. In particular, we choose to use assignments to discourse markers for the role that worlds play in Montague's IL. This gives us an—admittedly inadequate—characterization of intensions, one which will suffice only for extensional contexts. Propositional content will be represented by sets of assignments, which is similar to what we did in introducing FCS, where files were represented by sets of assignments.

Given this change, the semantic domains are going to be defined as follows:

(41)   For each type a, D_a are the denotations of entities of type a.
        a. D_e = U (where U is the domain of individuals)
        b. D_t = {0,1} (where '0' represents falsehood and '1' truth)
        c. $D_{\langle a,b \rangle} = D_b{}^{D_a}$ (the sets of all functions from D_a into D_b)
        d. $D_{\langle s,a \rangle} = D_a{}^{\Omega}$ (where Ω is the set of all possible assignments to DMs)

By (41d), $D_{\langle s,t \rangle}$ (i.e., the set of "propositions") will be $\{0,1\}^{\Omega}$, which is the set of all possible sets of assignments. (Throughout, I take the liberty of switching back and forth between sets and the corresponding characteristic functions.)

The interpretation function $[\![\ \ ]\!]^{g,\omega}$ (for a given model M = $\langle U,F \rangle$, where U is a set and F an interpretation of the constants) will associate with every expression β of type a a member $[\![\beta]\!]^{g,\omega}$ of D_a relative to a g and an ω. The definition of the interpretation function is completely standard and proceeds just as for Montague's IL, with the exception of the cap and cup operators, whose semantics is as follows.

(42)   a. $[\![^{\wedge}\alpha]\!]^{g,\omega} = \lambda\omega'. [\![\alpha]\!]^{g,\omega'}$. That is, $[\![^{\wedge}\alpha]\!]^{g,\omega}$ is that function h in $D_a{}^{\Omega}$ such that for any $\omega' \in \Omega$, $h(\omega') = [\![\alpha]\!]^{g,\omega'}$.
        b. $[\![^{\vee}\alpha]\!]^{g,\omega} = [\![\alpha]\!]^{g,\omega}(\omega)$.

It might be best to see what this semantics involves by working through a simple example:

(43) $[\![^{\wedge}love(j,x)]\!]^{g,\omega} = \lambda\omega'.[\![love(j,x)]\!]^{g,\omega'} = \{\omega': John loves \omega'(x)\}$

We compute here the proposition associated with (the translation of) a simple sentence like *John loves x*. (43) is written using the so-called relational notation, according to which 'love(j,x)' stands for 'love(x)(j)'. As is easy to see, the expression '$^\wedge$love(j,x)' comes out as denoting the (characteristic function of the) set of cases that make the formula 'love(j,x)' true, that is, the satisfaction set associated with it.[9]

This completes our review of the fundamentals of our version of Montague's IL, in which our new dynamic semantics (based most directly on Groenendijk and Stokhof 1990) will be couched. The only two differences compared to Montague's IL are the introduction of discourse markers and the use of assignments to discourse markers as semantic parameters over which the cap operator abstracts. Strictly speaking, the absence of times and worlds makes the system extensional, even though it retains an intensional flavor because of the presence of Montague's cap operator.[10]

Exercise 1

   (a) What happens if we have a formula with both static and dynamic variables? Compute $[\![^\wedge\text{love}(u,x)]\!]^{g,\omega}$.
   (b) Give the semantic value of $^\wedge$bald(j).
   (c) Show that $[\![^\vee{}^\wedge\alpha]\!]^{g,\omega} = [\![\alpha]\!]^{g,\omega}$.

I now turn to giving an informal idea of how the dynamics will be restructured with respect to FCS. We will then see how to formalize this idea within IL as modified here.

2.3.2 The Idea in Informal Terms

Typically, sentences introduce new discourse referents and deactivate old ones, thereby constraining the way discourse unfolds. This aspect of context change can be represented in IL along the following lines. Let S' be the standard translation into IL of a sentence S. The formula [S' $\wedge$ p] conjoins S' with a propositional variable which can be filled by adding information to S in any possible way. Metaphorically speaking, we add to S' a hook onto which incoming information can be hung. In this sense, [S' $\wedge$ p] can be viewed as a representation of the options one has available as a consequence of uttering S in the initial context—that is, as the context change potential of S.[11] Formulae of the form [S' $\wedge$ p] become the unit in terms of which our semantic recursion will be expressed. More specifically, a discourse, which in simple cases is built up by adding sentences one by one, will involve integrating the corresponding context change potentials. Let us see how this can be done. Suppose we utter S_1 followed by S_2. Their respective meanings, represented by $[S_1' \wedge p]$ and $[S_2' \wedge p]$, must now be put together. How? A simple way is by means of an operation of the following kind:

(44) $[S_1' \wedge p] + [S_2' \wedge p] = [S_1' \wedge S_2' \wedge p]$

We substitute the meaning of S_2 for the variable over possible continuations present in the meaning of S_1. The result is a new context change potential that contains its own slot into which new, incoming discourse can be accommodated.

To see this more concretely, take a simple sentence containing an indefinite like *A man walked in*. Its representation in IL (ignoring tense) will be as follows:

(45) $\exists x[\text{man(x)} \wedge \underline{\text{walk-in(x)}} \wedge p]$

The underlined portion of the formula in (45) is the standard translation of *A man walked in,* while 'p' is the variable over possible continuations inserted in accordance with our model of context change potentials. Note that the scope of '$\exists x$' in (45) includes p; that is, it extends over the slot that is going to be filled by new pieces of discourse. This is a way of representing Karttunen's insight that indefinites, unlike other NPs, set up discourse referents that can be used in subsequent text. So, for example, having uttered *A man walked in,* we can go on with *He was tall,* whose context change potential is [tall(x) $\wedge$ p]. By composing the latter with (45) on the basis of rule (44), the variable corresponding to the pronoun *he* winds up being bound by the quantifier corresponding to the NP *a man*.

(46) $\exists x[\text{man(x)} \wedge \text{walk(x)} \wedge p] + [\text{tall(x)} \wedge p] = \exists x[\text{man(x)} \wedge \text{walk(x)} \wedge \text{tall(x)} \wedge p]$

So on the present view, in a discourse like *A man walked in. He was tall,* the pronoun *he* is semantically bound by the indefinite *a man,* without being in the syntactic scope of the latter. We have here a rather simple reconstruction of Karttunen's notion of "active discourse referent," one that is compatible with the classical idea that indefinites are existentially quantified terms.

The semantics I have just sketched lends itself straightforwardly to a compositional, Montague-style interpretive procedure. In classical Montague semantics, formulae are interpreted in terms of their truth conditions, and the semantic values of their components are given on the basis of what they contribute to the truth conditions. This is implemented by assigning the logical type t to sentences like *A man runs*, the type $\langle e,t \rangle$ to predicates like *man* or *run*, the type $\langle\langle e,t \rangle,\langle\langle e,t \rangle, t \rangle\rangle$ to determiners like *a*. Under such a type assignment, *a* combines first with *man*, forming *a(man)*, and the result combines with *run*, forming *a(man)(run)*. This procedure can be varied in a number of ways (e.g., it can be intensionalized), but the variations are all going to be informed by the same basic methodology. Now, our proposal is that the value of sentences be specified in terms of context change potentials, rather than in terms of truth conditions. Hence, the value of subsentential units must be what they contribute to context change potentials. To make things more concrete, let *cc* be the type of context change potentials. This replaces *t* as the type of sentence translations. As an automatic consequence of this, the type of predicates has to be changed to $\langle e,cc \rangle$, that is, the type of functions from individuals to context change potentials. Let us call things of this type *dynamic predicates*. Dynamic predicates will be like ordinary predicates with the addition of a placeholder for subsequent discourse. For example:

(47)   a. man $\Rightarrow$ λx [man(x) $\wedge$ p]
         b. run $\Rightarrow$ λx [run(x) $\wedge$ p]

The static portion of this way of translating predicates is underlined. Extending this further, determiners can be viewed as functions that take a pair of dynamic predicates and return a context change potential (which means that their type will be $\langle\langle e,cc \rangle\langle\langle e,cc \rangle,cc \rangle\rangle$). Accordingly, the meaning of *a* can be taken to be roughly as follows:

(48) λPλQ $\exists$y [P(y) $\triangle$ Q(y)]

P and Q in (48) are variables of type $\langle e,cc \rangle$, and '$\triangle$' is the operation for conjoining context change potentials defined in (44) (previously notated as '+'). Putting this together we get the following:

(49)   a man $\Rightarrow$ a(man)
        = λPλQ $\exists$y [P(y) $\triangle$ Q(y)] (λx [man(x) $\wedge$ p])
        = λQ $\exists$y [λx [man(x) $\wedge$ p](y) $\triangle$ Q(y)]   (by λ-conversion)
        = λQ $\exists$y [[man(y) $\wedge$ p] $\triangle$ Q(y)]   (by definition (44))

The reduced translation of *a man* in (49) is of type $\langle\langle e,cc \rangle,cc \rangle$ and can be thought of as a dynamic generalized quantifier. *A man* can be further combined with a predicate like *run*, yielding (50):

(50)   A man runs $\Rightarrow$ a(man)(run)
        = λQ $\exists$y [[man(y) $\wedge$ p] $\triangle$ Q(y)] (λx [run(x) $\wedge$ p])

$$= \exists y \, [[\text{man}(y) \wedge p] \mathbin{\triangle} \lambda x \, [\text{run}(x) \wedge p](y)] \quad \text{(by λ-conversion)}$$
$$= \exists y \, [[\text{man}(y) \wedge p] \mathbin{\triangle} [\text{run}(y) \wedge p]] \quad \text{(by λ-conversion)}$$
$$= \exists y \, [\text{man}(y) \wedge \text{run}(y) \wedge p] \quad \text{(by definition (44))}$$

The last step in the reduction of the meaning of *A man runs* is a consequence of the definition of '$\triangle$'. This is a simple illustration of how the context change potential of this sentence can be compositionally derived. Notice that the ordinary way of translating *A man runs* is, in a way, still part of the new translation. But the presence of placeholders allows us to handle binding across sentences.

2.3.3 The Logic of Context Change

Assuming that the truth-conditional content of a sentence S is adequately represented by its translation ϕ into IL, how can we formalize S's context change potential in IL? In the previous section we suggested that the context change potential associated with ϕ should determine, relative to a context, the cases that remain open after uttering ϕ. What are the cases that remain open after processing ϕ? Evidently all those compatible with ϕ, namely λp $[\phi \wedge \check{\,}p]$. This λ-expression is of type $\langle\langle s,t\rangle,t\rangle$. It denotes a (characteristic function of a) set of propositions, namely, those compatible with ϕ—the possible continuations of ϕ in the context ω. From now on, I will use the term *Context Change Potential* (*CCP*) for functions of this type. I will abbreviate $\langle\langle s,t\rangle,t\rangle$ as cc and $\lambda p[\phi \wedge \check{\,}p]$ as '$\uparrow \phi$'. The "up-arrow" can be viewed as an operator mapping the ordinary, static value of a formula into the corresponding CCP. It attaches the slot for subsequent discourse to formulae.

(51) $\uparrow : t \to cc$ (where $cc = \langle\langle s,t\rangle,t\rangle$)
         $\uparrow \phi = \lambda p \, [\phi \wedge \check{\,}p]$

A CCP $\uparrow \phi$ corresponds to what we expressed as '$+\phi$' in FCS. It may be useful to consider a few concrete examples of CCPs. Take a simple sentence like (52a) below. Assuming that the pronoun in (52a) is translated as a discourse marker, say 'x_j', the "static" meaning of (52a) will be as in (52b), while its dynamic counterpart will be as in (52c).

(52)   a. He$_j$ runs.
         b. $\text{run}(x_j)$
         c. $\uparrow \text{run}(x_j) = \lambda p \, [\text{run}(x_j) \wedge \check{\,}p]$

Exercise 2

Compute the value of $[\![\lambda p[\mathrm{run}(x_1) \wedge {}^{\vee}p]]\!]^{g,\omega}$.

The CCP associated with sentence (52a) works as follows: it checks whether the current case ω satisfies the condition associated with (52a), that is, whether ω satisfies 'run(x_3)'; if it does (i.e., if $\omega(x_3)$(runs), any proposition containing ω will constitute a possible continuation for (52a). If it doesn't, then there is no way to go on. Formally, $[\![\lambda p[\mathrm{run}(x_1) \wedge {}^{\vee}p]]\!]^{g,\omega}$ will be the set of all propositions that contain ω, if ω verifies 'run(x_3)', or else the empty set. Subsequent discourse narrows this set down further. But of course, if the set is empty (because the current assignment falsifies the sentence), there is nothing to narrow down. It should be noted that in a way, the CCPs of formulae like (52a) do not really change the input context ω; rather, they test it. They check whether the input context has certain properties. If it does, that context is passed on; otherwise it is rejected. Following Groenendijk and Stokhof (1991), we will call CCPs that have such property *tests*.

Let us consider next the CCP of a sentence with indefinites, like (53a) below. This is given in (53b). (We will see shortly how (53a) can be compositionally mapped onto (53b). Again, we disregard tense for simplicity.)

(53)   a. A man ran.
        b. $\lambda p \exists x_1[\mathrm{man}(x_1) \wedge \mathrm{run}(x_1) \wedge {}^{\vee}p]$

It may be useful to compute the denotation associated with (53b). I will only present some of the key steps in the computation. I use boldface letters for individuals of the appropriate type. If g or ω is an assignment, by $g[\alpha/\mathbf{u}]$ and $\omega[\alpha/\mathbf{u}]$ I refer to assignments identical to g and ω respectively, except that the value of α is $\mathbf{u}$. (Remember that here, and throughout, I take the liberty of representing characteristic functions in terms of the corresponding sets when convenient.)

(54) $[\![\lambda p \exists x_1[\mathrm{man}(x_1) \wedge \mathrm{run}(x_1) \wedge {}^{\vee}p]]\!]^{g,\omega}$ is a function that maps a proposition p into true iff it makes true '$\exists x[\mathrm{man}(x_1) \wedge \mathrm{run}(x_1) \wedge {}^{\vee}p]$'. Formulated as a set:
$\{\mathbf{p}: [\![\exists x[\mathrm{man}(x_1) \wedge \mathrm{run}(x_1) \wedge {}^{\vee}p]]\!]^{g[p/\mathbf{p}],\omega} = 1\}$ is the set of those $\mathbf{p}$ such that for some e '[man(x_1) $\wedge$ run(x_1) $\wedge$ ${}^{\vee}p$]' is true (where p is $\mathbf{p}$ and e is x_1); that is:
$\{\mathbf{p}:$ for some e $[\![\mathrm{man}(x_1) \wedge \mathrm{run}(x_1) \wedge {}^{\vee}p]]\!]^{g[p/\mathbf{p}],\omega[x_1/e]}\}$ is the set of those $\mathbf{p}$ such that for some e which is a running man $\mathbf{p}(\omega[e/x_1]) = 1$; or, viewing propositions as sets of assignments:
$\{\mathbf{p}:$ for some e which is a man and runs $\omega[x_1/e] \in \mathbf{p}\}$

What emerges is that the denotation of '$\lambda p \exists x[man(x_1) \wedge run(x_1) \wedge \check{}p]$' consists of all the propositions **p** containing a case $\omega[x_1/e]$ which is just like the input case ω except that the value of x_1 is reset to a running man. Thus the CCP in (53b) actually changes the input context. The discourse marker x_1 now becomes an "address," or "file card," associated with a running man. So some CCPs test whether the input context has certain properties. Others actually change the input context by imposing conditions on a certain discourse marker (which corresponds to opening a new file card).

We now have a way of associating CCPs with formulae. The question arises whether it is possible to compositionally retrieve out of a CCP its truth-conditional content. The question can also be formulated as asking under what conditions a CCP is "true." The answer is rather straightforward: a CCP can be said to be true in a given context iff it admits possible continuations in that context (i.e., iff it is non-empty). A CCP that, instead, incorporates a condition that doesn't hold relative to an initial assignment c yields the empty set in c. The simplest way of expressing this in IL is by noting that if a CCP is non-empty, it must contain the set Ω of all possible assignments (i.e., the tautologous proposition). This is so because the CCP associated with a formula ϕ is defined as the set of propositions compatible with ϕ, and the tautologous proposition is compatible with all and only the true formulae. So if a formula ϕ is true (relative to ω), the tautologous proposition will be compatible with it. We can exploit this fact to formulate a *truth* or *assertion operator,* which we will denote as '$\downarrow$'. Let T be any tautology so that $\hat{}T$ will denote the set of all possible cases (i.e., $[\![\hat{}T]\!]^{g,\omega} = \Omega$). We then define '$\downarrow$' as follows:

(55) $\downarrow A = A(\hat{}T)$

The expression '$\downarrow A$' can be read as "A is true." In FCS this corresponds to the definition of truth for files. The rationale behind using this notation is that '$\downarrow$' provides us with a kind of inverse of '$\uparrow$'. In a sense, '$\uparrow$' maps a proposition into the corresponding CCP, whereas '$\downarrow$' maps a CCP into the corresponding static proposition (by filling in its slot with something uninformative, like a tautology). So the $\downarrow$-operator enables us to talk of the truth conditions associated with (or the propositional content of) a CCP. An easy computation reveals that for any formula ϕ, $\downarrow \uparrow \phi$ is the same thing as ϕ. Interestingly, the identity does not hold in the other direction. That is to say, $\uparrow \downarrow A \neq A$. We will provide relevant examples below.

Exercise 3

Show that $\downarrow \uparrow \phi = \phi$.

The idea we are pursuing is that sentences are interpreted in terms of CCPs. Complex sentences and discourses are formed by putting their constituent sentences together by means of the various connectives and quantifiers. Accordingly, we will want to define the CCP of complex sentences and discourses compositionally, in terms of the CCPs associated with their components. In FCS, this corresponds to defining the file change potential of complex sentences in terms of the file change potentials of their components. In the present setup, it amounts to defining logical operations like conjunction, disjunction, and so forth on CCPs. These definitions can be given quite elegantly as follows.

(56)   The Logic of CCPs
    i. $A \mathrel{\underline{\wedge}} B = \lambda p[A(^\wedge B(p))]$
    ii. $\underline{\neg} A = \uparrow \neg \downarrow A$
    iii. $A \mathrel{\underline{\vee}} B = \underline{\neg} [\underline{\neg} A \mathrel{\underline{\wedge}} \underline{\neg} B]$
    iv. $A \mathrel{\underline{\rightarrow}} B = \underline{\neg} A \mathrel{\underline{\vee}} [A \mathrel{\underline{\wedge}} B]$[12]
    v. $\underline{\exists} x A = \lambda p \underline{\exists} x [A(p)]$
    vi. $\underline{\forall} x A = \underline{\neg} \underline{\exists} x \underline{\neg} A$

The notational convention I am adopting should be transparent. If 'O' is a standard connective or quantifier, '$\underline{O}$' is its counterpart as defined over CCPs. To discuss in detail the technical aspects of these definitions goes beyond what we are set to do here. However, in the remainder of this section we will go over some of their properties that are of direct relevance to our concerns.

Clause (56i) defines conjunction, which is viewed as a kind of function composition. It corresponds to the operation of discourse sequencing discussed in the previous section. If we utter S followed by S' in an input context ω, ω is first modified by S, then the result is further modified by S'. However, in our formal reconstruction, S and S' are associated with the sets of their possible continuations. They do not apply directly to the input context but determine how the discourse can go on relative to this input context. So we must make sure that S' is among the possible continuations of S and then take the set of possible continuations of the result. We do this in three steps. First we apply S', the second conjunct, to a propositional variable p. Then we apply the first conjunct S to the result; this amounts to checking whether

S' can be a possible continuation of S. And finally we reabstract over the propositional variable originally introduced, thereby getting at the alternatives that remain open after processing S followed by S'. We will shortly see a concrete example.

A kind of function composition is also what is used in (56v) to define existential quantification over CCPs. Existentially quantifying over a CCP A amounts to applying A to an arbitrary proposition p, doing ordinary existential quantification, and then reabstracting over p. As we saw from example (53), this will generally induce a resetting of the initial context. The effect of defining conjunction and existential quantification as function compositions is that the semantic scope of an existential quantifier will extend into a conjunct that lies outside its syntactic scope. In other words, the formulae in (57) will be equivalent.

(57) $[\underline{\exists}x\ A] \mathbin{\triangle} B\ =\ \underline{\exists}x\ [A \mathbin{\triangle} B]$

Perhaps the best way to see this is by means of an example. Consider the CCP in (58a) below. Its propositional content could be expressed as 'Some man walks in'. Next consider the CCP function in (58b), which would correspond to a proposition like 'He is blond'.

(58)   a. $\underline{\exists}x_1\ [\lambda p\ [man(x_1) \wedge walk\text{-}in\ (x_1) \wedge {}^{\vee}p]]$
        b. $\lambda p[blond(x_1) \wedge {}^{\vee}p]$

Imagine conjoining (58a) with (58b), as in (59a) below. Clearly the occurrence of x_1 in the second conjunct is not in the syntactic scope of $\underline{\exists}x_1$. Yet, if we apply the definitions of $\underline{\exists}$ and $\triangle$, the occurrence of x_1 in the second conjunct ends up being bound. The steps of the derivation are shown in (50b–h). This illustrates the general validity of the equivalence in (57).

(59)   a. $\underline{\exists}x_1\ [\lambda p\ [man(x_1) \wedge walk\text{-}in(x_1) \wedge {}^{\vee}p]] \mathbin{\triangle} \lambda p[blond(x_1) \wedge {}^{\vee}p]$
        b. $\lambda p\ [\underline{\exists}x_1\ [man(x_1) \wedge walk\text{-}in\ (x_1) \wedge {}^{\vee}p]] \mathbin{\triangle} \lambda p[blond(x_1) \wedge {}^{\vee}p]$
           def. of $\underline{\exists}$, (56v)
        c. $\lambda q[\lambda p\ \underline{\exists}x_1\ [man(x_1) \wedge walk\text{-}in(x_1) \wedge {}^{\vee}p]({}^{\wedge}[\lambda p[blond(x_1) \wedge {}^{\vee}p]$
           $(q)])]$ def. $\triangle$, (56i)
        d. $\lambda q[\lambda p\ \underline{\exists}x_1\ [man(x_1) \wedge\ walk\text{-}in(x_1) \wedge\ {}^{\vee}p]({}^{\wedge}[blond(x_1) \wedge$
           ${}^{\vee}q])]$ (λ-conv.)
        e. $\lambda q\ \underline{\exists}x_1\ [man(x_1) \wedge walk\text{-}in(x_1) \wedge {}^{\vee}{}^{\wedge}[blond(x_1) \wedge {}^{\vee}q]]$
           (λ-conv.)
        f. $\lambda q\ \underline{\exists}x_1\ [man(x_1) \wedge walk\text{-}in(x_1) \wedge blond(x_1) \wedge {}^{\vee}q]$
           (${}^{\vee}{}^{\wedge}$-cancellation)
        g. $\underline{\exists}x_1 \uparrow [max(x_1) \wedge walk\text{-}in(x_1) \wedge blond(x_1)]$ def. of $\underline{\exists}$, (56v)
           (from right to left)

Of particular interest is the step that takes us from (59d) to (59e). Here a discourse marker that is not in the scope of any quantifier lands, via λ-conversion, in the scope of a quantifier. This has all the appearances of an improper λ-conversion, where a free variable gets accidentally bound. But that is not the case here. The relevant occurrence of x_1 is in the scope of the ^-operator. The ^-operator as we saw, is an unselective abstractor: by abstracting over cases, it abstracts over all the discourse markers in its scope, and thus effectively binds them. Consequently, the last occurrence of x_1 in (59d) qualifies as a bound occurrence, which makes the conversion to (59e) sound.

It may be useful to contrast the treatment of conjunction and existential quantification with the treatment of negation. It is a priori conceivable to treat negation as a sort of composition as well. This would mean adopting the definition in (60a) instead of the one in (56ii), repeated here as (60b).

(60)   a. $\neg A = \lambda p\ [\neg A(p)]$
        b. $\underline{\neg}A = \uparrow \neg \downarrow A$

How do we choose between these alternatives? Truth-conditionally both definitions yield the same results. Let us illustrate this by means of an example. Consider a sentence like *John smokes*. The corresponding CCP would be $\lambda p[\text{smoke}(j) \wedge \ {}^{\vee}p]$. Its negation according to definition (60a) is given in (61a), while its negation according to definition (60b) is given in (61b). We can see that the corresponding truth conditions, (given in (61a$'$) and (61b$'$) respectively), boil down to the same thing.

(61)   a. $\lambda p\ \neg[\text{smoke}(j) \wedge \ {}^{\vee}p]$
        a$'$. $\downarrow \lambda p\ \neg[\text{smoke}(j) \wedge \ {}^{\vee}p] = \lambda p\ \neg[\text{smoke}(j) \wedge \ {}^{\vee}p](^{\wedge}T) = \neg \text{smoke}(j)$
        b. $\uparrow \neg \downarrow \lambda p[\text{smoke}(j) \wedge \ {}^{\vee}p] = \lambda p[\neg \text{smoke}(j) \wedge \ {}^{\vee}p]$
        b$'$. $\downarrow \lambda p[\neg \text{smoke}(j) \wedge \ {}^{\vee}p] = \lambda p[\neg \text{smoke}(j) \wedge \ {}^{\vee}p](^{\wedge}T) = \neg \text{smoke}(j)$

Even though the truth-conditional import of these negated CCPs is indistinguishable, their dynamics are very different from one another. Looking at the CCP in (61a) (i.e., the one obtained via the definition in (60a)), we see that here negation includes admissible continuations in its scope. This is in contrast with what happens in (61b) (i.e., the CCP obtained via the definition in (60b)). Here admissible continuations fall outside of the scope of negation. To see the importance of this difference, imagine continuing the discourse in question as shown in (62a).

(62)   a. John doesn't smoke. He drinks.
        b. [¬ λp [smoke(j) ∧ ˇp]] △ λp[drink(j) ∧ ˇp]
           (i) λp ¬[smoke(j) ∧ ˇp] △ λp[drink(j) ∧ ˇp]
                (by 60a)
           (ii) λp ¬[smoke(j) ∧ drink(j) ∧ ˇp]
                (by def. of △ (56i))

The semantics for (62a) is given in (62b). Now, by adopting the definition of negation given in (60a), (62b) reduces to (62b.ii), whose truth-conditional import is the following:

(63)   ↓ λp ¬[smoke(j) ∧ drink(j) ∧ ˇp] = ¬[smoke(j) ∧ drink(j)]

But this does not correctly characterize the content of (62a). Formula (63) says that *John smokes* and *John drinks* are not both true (which does not exclude that John smokes, however). The problem is the following. By defining negation as composition, we make [¬A] ∧ B equivalent to ¬[A ∧ B] (just as [∃xA] △ B is equivalent to ∃x[A △ B]). But notice that the proposition associated with [¬A] entails the one associated with ¬[A ∧ B]. So ¬A by itself already contains the information conveyed by ¬[A ∧ B]. Clearly, there would be no point in adding B to ¬A if the result we get is ¬[A ∧ B], as the latter is less informative than the former. Adding a new piece of information should increase the information we already have. The fact that negation cannot be understood as composition is an immediate consequence of this truism.

    This provides us with a clear reason for adopting the definition of negation given in (61b). According to this definition, negating a CCP A involves first extracting the corresponding proposition, then negating it and taking the possible continuations of the result.

Exercise 4

Show that in [¬∃₁ [λp [man(x₁) ∧ walk-in(x₁) ∧ ˇp]]] △ λp[blond(x₁) ∧ ˇp] the last occurrence of x₁ is unbound.

One consequence of doing things this way is that negations of CCPs are all tests: they do not change the input context but merely check whether it has a certain property. Consequently a quantifier inside a negated CCP will be "closed off" or "deactivated": it will be unable to bind discourse markers in subsequent discourse. This reflects the impossibility of the anaphoric link in (64):

(64)   *It is not the case that a manᵢ walked in. Heᵢ was blond.

What emerges from this discussion of negation is that it follows from very simple facts about information growth that negation cannot involve composition, and that as a consequence, negated CCPs must be tests. In fact, the above considerations extend to all operators that, in some sense, "contain" negation, viz. the downward entailing operators of Ladusaw (1979). Thus for example, the fact that the anaphoric link in (65) is impossible can be imputed to the fact that *no man* is defined as '$\neg\exists x[man(x_i)]$'.

(65)   *No man$_i$ walked in. He$_i$ was wearing a hat.

If no man walked in, it certainly is the case that no man walked in wearing a hat. The semantic scope of *no man* must be limited to its syntactic one, or else there would be no way to add further information to a sentence containing *no*. This leads to the following elementary principle:

(66)   *Principle of Informativeness:* Downward entailing operators are tests.

This principle is not peculiar to the present framework, but is implicitly operative in any version of DRT/FCS.[13] We are merely stating it explicitly here.

We now turn to discussing the definition of '$\veebar$' and '$\forall$'. The definition of '$\veebar$' and '$\forall$' simply mimics one of the standard ways in which these elements are defined in first-order logic. The important thing to notice, in this connection, is that since the definition of '$\veebar$' and '$\forall$' involves negation, and since negation turns any CCP it operates on into a test, it follows that disjunctive and universal CCPs will also be tests. Any active quantifier they may contain will be closed off and hence unable to bind outside its syntactic scope. Rather than working through this formally, I'll simply give some natural language analogues along with a schematic characterization of their logical form as an illustration.

(67)   a.   *John has a new car$_i$ or Mary has it$_i$.
              $[\exists xA \veebar B]$
         b.   *Either John is home or he went out to get a coke$_i$. It$_i$ is sugar-free.
              $[A \veebar \exists xB] \wedge C$
         c.   *Every student$_i$ came to the party. He$_i$ had fun.
              $[\forall x B] \wedge C$

All these anaphoric links (putting aside any "specific" interpretation of the indefinites) are ill-formed. If the respective logical forms of the formulae in

(67) are as indicated, none of the quantifiers will be able to reach outside of their syntactic scope, in virtue of the presence of negation in the definition of $\underline{\vee}$ and $\underline{\forall}$.

The last item we should discuss is implication. In classical first-order logic 'ϕ → ψ' is usually defined as '¬ϕ $\vee$ ψ'. If we were to adopt a parallel definition here, implication would inherit all the features of disjunction: implications would be tests. Moreover, both the antecedent and the consequent of an implication would be turned into tests. This would prevent any quantifier in the antecedent from binding a discourse marker in the consequent. Yet such binding is precisely what seems to be going on in donkey anaphora. This suggests that we should seek an alternative characterization of implication. The one proposed in (56iv) exploits the schema 'A → B = ¬A $\vee$ [A $\wedge$ B]'. Truth-conditionally, '¬ϕ $\vee$ ψ' and '¬ϕ $\vee$ [ϕ $\wedge$ ψ]' are equivalent. But their dynamic counterparts are not. Using conjunction has the effect that quantifiers active in the antecedent will be able to bind discourse markers in the consequent. Suppose, for example, we give a canonical translation into IL of *Every man that has a donkey beats it,* using $\underline{\forall}$ and $\underline{\rightarrow}$. This is shown in (68a) below. The antecedent corresponds to *man that has a donkey* and the consequent to *beats it.* The discourse marker corresponding to the pronoun is not in the syntactic scope of the quantifier corresponding to *a donkey.* By applying the definitions of $\underline{\forall}$ and $\underline{\rightarrow}$, (68a) winds up saying that for every x, either x is not a donkey-owning man or x is a man that has a donkey and beats it. Use of dynamic conjunction in the consequent enables *a donkey* to semantically bind *it.* So (68a) is provably equivalent to (68b) (cf. the appendix to this chapter, part II).

(68)   a. $\underline{\forall}$x [λp[man (x) $\wedge$ ∃y [donkey(y) $\wedge$ has(x,y) $\wedge$ ˇp]] $\underline{\rightarrow}$ λp [beat(x,y) $\wedge$ ˇp]]

        b. ↑ ∀x[[man (x) $\wedge$ ∃y [donkey(y) $\wedge$ has (x,y)]] → ∃y [donkey (y) $\wedge$ has(x,y) $\wedge$ beat(x,y)]]

Thus the definition of '→' adopted here delivers the ∃-reading of donkey sentences.

There is one further remark worth making. It concerns the fact noted above that while ' ↓ ' followed by ' ↑ ' cancels out (i.e., ↓ ↑ ϕ = ϕ), this doesn't hold in the other direction (i.e., ↑ ↓ A ≠ A). By now, it isn't hard to see why this is so. As usual, let us work through an example. Consider (69):

(69)   a. λp ∃x[man(x) $\wedge$ ˇp]

        b. ↑ ↓ λp ∃x[man(x) $\wedge$ ˇp]

In order to check whether (69a) is the same as (69b) we need to reduce the latter. This is done in (70).

(70)   a. $\uparrow \lambda p \; \exists x[man(x) \wedge \, {}^{\vee}p]({}^{\wedge}T)$ (def. of $\downarrow$)
        b. $\uparrow \exists x[man(x) \wedge \, {}^{\vee \wedge}T]$ (λ-red.)
        c. $\uparrow \exists x[man(x)]$ (${}^{\vee \wedge}$-canc., taut.)
        d. $\lambda p[\exists x[man(x)] \wedge \, {}^{\vee}p]$

At this point we observe that while (69a) and (69b) are truth-conditionally equivalent, they differ in binding potential. This is due to the fact that the placeholder p for subsequent discourse is in fact in the scope of $\exists x$ in (69a) but not in (70d). So, we see that a $\uparrow \downarrow$ sequence "closes off" a CCP A, by deactivating any active quantifier that may be present in A.

In this section, we have familiarized ourselves with the way in which IL can be used to spell out context change potentials and their logic. CCPs have been defined as functions determining the set of possible continuations of a formula. Such functions introduce a placeholder into which subsequent discourse is going to be placed. The logic of CCPs determines quite elegantly how complex CCPs are compositionally built up from simpler CCPs. We also have seen that formulae that are truth-conditionally equivalent can be made dynamic in nonequivalent ways. The fundamental law of the logic of CCPs is the equivalence in (57); in a way all of its other properties are a consequence of this equivalence. It may be worth pointing out that the logic of CCPs is not just something specifically designed to deal with anaphora. It is a version of the dynamic logic for programming languages.[14] A program can be expressed by a formula whose meaning is viewed as a transition between states. When a program is run in an initial state ω, it leads to a new state ω'. States can be represented as assignments to the variables of the program. The intuitive analogy with the view of meaning we are exploring is evident. While this need not be of direct relevance to linguistics, it does show that the dynamic perspective on semantics has a wider range of motivations than one might initially think.

Exercise 5

Are the following formulae equivalent?
(a) i. A   ii. $\neg \neg A$
(b) i. $[\uparrow \phi \; \triangle \; \uparrow \psi]$ ii. $\uparrow [\phi \wedge \psi]$
(c) i. $\underline{\forall} x \, [\uparrow \phi \Rightarrow \uparrow \psi]$ ii. $\uparrow \forall x[\phi \rightarrow \psi]$

2.3.4 Compositional Logical Forms for English

We can use our modified IL to set up a Montague-style compositional translation procedure that maps sentences into the corresponding CCPs. This can be done quite simply by replacing Montague's type t with cc:[15]

(71)   *Basic Principle of Dynamic Interpretation:*
$$t \rightarrow cc$$

Let us see what consequences this move has, beginning with the interpretation of lexical items. Take an extensional transitive verb like *love*. It is a two-place relation, whose type in Montague's type theory is $\langle e, \langle e, t, \rangle \rangle$. Principle (71) tells us to replace it with something of type $\langle e, \langle e, cc \rangle \rangle$, which we can obtain by extending ' ↑ ' so as to apply to relations in the manner indicated in (72a). The same principle applied to the case of a common noun like *woman* yields (72b).

(72)   a. love $\Rightarrow$ ↑ love $= \lambda u \lambda v$ ↑ love(v,u) $= \lambda u \lambda v \, \lambda p \, [\text{love}(v,u) \wedge$ ˇp][16]
        b. woman $\Rightarrow$ ↑ woman $= \lambda u$ ↑ woman(u)

Consider next the case of determiners. In Montague grammar (and in generalized quantifier theory) they are viewed as relations between properties. Thus in the present framework they will be viewed, in some sense, as relations between the dynamic counterpart of properties. This is illustrated in (73).

(73) $a_1 \Rightarrow \lambda P \lambda Q \, \exists x_1 \, [\text{ˇ}P(x_1) \, \Delta \, \text{ˇ}Q(x_1)]$ (P,Q of type $\langle s, \langle e, cc \rangle \rangle$)
        $\text{every}_2 \Rightarrow \lambda P \lambda Q \underline{\forall} x_2 \, [\text{ˇ}P(x_2) \rightarrow \text{ˇ}Q(x_2)]$

It is clear that this is just the standard semantics for determiners, with the types adjusted so as to yield CCPs in the end. P and Q in (73) range over the dynamic counterparts of properties whose type ($\langle s, \langle e, cc \rangle \rangle$) I will abbreviate as *dp* (for "dynamic properties"). Determiners map pairs of dynamic properties into CCPs. I assume that determiners have the same index as the NP node that dominates them.

At this point, the interpretive procedure is completely determined. In each subtree of the form $[_o \alpha \, \beta]$ we will find a function and an argument, and the interpretation of the mother is simply obtained by applying the function to the argument. NPs in QR'ed position are interpreted via λ-abstraction; that is, $[_S NP_i S] \Rightarrow NP(\text{^}\lambda v_i S)$. This is all standard. The following is a simple example:

(74)   a. Every man loves a woman.
        b. One possible LF for (a):
        [a woman$_1$ every man$_2$ [t$_2$ loves t$_1$]]

c. Translation of (b):

$a_1(\char`^\uparrow woman)(\char`^\lambda u_1 [every_2(\char`^\uparrow man)(\char`^\lambda u_2 \uparrow love(u_2,u_1))])$

d. Reduced version of (c):

$\lambda p\ \exists x_1[woman(x_1) \wedge \forall x_2[man(x_2) \rightarrow love(x_2,x_1)] \wedge \,\check{}p]$

Exercise 6

Show the steps of the reduction from (74c) to (74d).

Observe that the placeholder p is in the scope of $\exists x_1$ but not in the scope of $\forall x_2$. Thus *a woman* will be able to bind discourse markers in subsequent discourse but *every man* will not. This corresponds to the observation that universals in general cannot bind outside of their syntactic scope, but existentials can. In the particular example at hand, extension of the scope of *a woman* beyond its syntactic scope is expected to be possible only on the wide-scope reading (where there is a particular woman that every man loves). If *a woman* were construed to have narrow scope with respect to *every man*, it would be closed off, since the quantifier *every* creates tests.

This illustrates how a completely straightforward interpretive procedure can be devised. The assignment of a meaning to subsentential units is done following the usual method of looking at the contribution of these units to sentence meaning. The only substantive differences is that sentence meaning is now viewed in terms of context change potential rather than in terms of truth conditions (principle (71)). Notice in particular that existential and universal NPs, while differing in their binding potential just the way they do in DRT/FCS, are assigned a uniform semantic type, namely $\langle dp, cc \rangle$. In other words, an NP maps a dynamic property into a CCP, in a way that parallels their treatment as generalized quantifiers (viewed as a mapping from a property/set into a truth value). We will refer to NP denotations of type $\langle dp,cc \rangle$ as *dynamic generalized quantifiers*. This treatment of NPs is going to facilitate dealing with phenomena where they behave uniformly (without wiping out the differences between them). For example, it paves the way for a treatment of cross-categorial operators like conjunction and disjunction along the lines of Partee and Rooth 1983. In particular, NP conjunction can be defined in the usual manner:

(75)   a. $NP_1 \triangle NP_2 = \lambda P [NP_1(P) \triangle NP_2(P)]$

b. every boy that has a dog and every girl that has a cat $\Rightarrow$
    $\lambda P[\forall x\ [\,\underline{\uparrow} boy (x) \triangle \exists y\ [\,\uparrow dog (y) \triangle \ \uparrow has(x,y)] \Rightarrow \check{}P(x)] \triangle$
    $\forall x\ [\,\underline{\uparrow} girl(x) \triangle \exists y\ [\,\uparrow cat (y) \triangle \ \uparrow has(x,y)] \Rightarrow \check{}P(x)]]$

This approach to coordination assigns to a sentence like (76a) the reading (76b).

(76)   a. Every boy that has a dog and every girl that has a cat will beat it

        b. $[\forall x [\uparrow boy(x) \vartriangle \exists y [\uparrow dog(y) \vartriangle \uparrow has(x,y)] \rightarrow \uparrow beat(x,y)] \vartriangle$
         $\underline{\forall}x [\uparrow girl(x) \vartriangle \underline{\exists}y [\uparrow cat(y) \vartriangle \uparrow has(x,y)] \rightarrow \uparrow beat(x,y)]]$

Here the pronoun *it* receives the intuitively correct interpretation. It may be worth noticing that there are structurally similar sentences that appear to be marginal, for example:

(77)   a. ??Every boy that has a dog and a woman will beat it.
        b. $[\underline{\forall}x [\uparrow boy(x) \vartriangle \exists y [\uparrow dog(y) \vartriangle \uparrow has(x,y)] \rightarrow$
            $\uparrow beat(x,y)] \vartriangle \underline{\exists}y [\uparrow woman(x) \vartriangle \uparrow beat(x,y)]]$

The reading our approach assigns to (77a) is (77b). Notice that while the last occurrence of y in the first conjunct is dynamically bound, the one in the second conjunct is not, which might explain the strangeness of (77a). This indicates that the present approach allows us to generalize in the right direction the analysis of coordination, which seemed intractable in an approach based on construal rules. However, a detailed treatment of coordination in a dynamic setting will have to be deferred to some other occasion.

Exercise 7

Give the LF for *Every man who has a donkey beats it* and its node-by-node translation into IL.

Clearly, our revised version of IL provides the basis for a compositional semantics of the anaphoric dependencies under discussion. It might also be worth pointing out that given how the logic of CCPs is set up, the present approach is subject to the same scopal restrictions as classical DRT: an indefinite will be able to bind a pronoun if it is accessible to it. Notice, finally, that in the resulting system, quantification is inherently asymmetric. If we want to visualize this, we can point to the fact that while in classical DRT/ FCS the form of quantification is $Q(\phi,\psi)$, where Q binds all variables free in ϕ, in the present framework the form of quantification is $D(\lambda x\phi)(\lambda x\psi)$, where what one quantifies over is the argument corresponding to x. This notation clearly marks the asymmetric character of the quantificational force of determiners in our approach. Thus no problem with proportions is likely to arise. But to actually show this, we must discuss *most* and other determiners.

2.3.5 Dynamic Conservativity

A (dynamic) determiner is a relation between (dynamic) properties. In the previous section we have given the semantics of *a* and *every*. It is possible to arrive at a general characterization of *all* dynamic determiners? In trying to address this question, we should bear in mind that static determiners have general properties, such as conservativity (repeated here from (20) above under (78a)), that have a natural dynamic counterpart (like (78b)):

(78) a. *Static Conservativity:* $D(X)(Y) \leftrightarrow D(X)(X \wedge Y)$
        where X, Y are sets and '$\wedge$' is interpreted as intersection.
      b. *Dynamic Conservativity:* $D(P)(Q) \leftrightarrow D(P)(P \triangle Q)$
        where P,Q are dynamic properties and $\triangle$ is generalized dynamic conjunction.

We would want a way of characterizing dynamic determiners that makes properties like conservativity fall out. I will illustrate how to achieve this by reformulating the semantics for *every* in a way that generalizes to all quantificational determiners (i.e., *no, most, both,* etc.).

As a first step in this direction, let us consider the following equation:

(79) every (man that has a donkey) (beat it)
      = every (man that has a donkey) (has a donkey <u>and</u> beat it)

On the assumption that the underlined "and" in (79) is dynamic, the indefinite *a donkey* will be able to bind the pronoun *it,* which is just what one would want. However, in order to turn the schema in (79) into a well-formed definition, the *every* on the left-hand side of ' = ' must be different from the one on the right, as the former is to be defined in terms of the latter. More specifically, we want the *every* on the left of ' = ' to have the same type as dynamic *a*. Hence, it should relate two dynamic properties. The *every* on the right of ' = ', on the other hand, can just be taken to be the ordinary *every,* analyzed in accordance with the theory of generalized quantifiers as a relation among sets. We assume, that is, that *every* $(X)(Y) = X \subseteq Y$. This in turn entails that the arguments of *every* on the right of ' = ' are sets, while, generally speaking, in a dynamic setting predicates are interpreted as dynamic properties. However, we can always extract from dynamic properties the sets that constitute their extensions. After all, dynamic properties are really just sets with an additional slot for continuations, which can be wiped out by means of the $\downarrow$-operator. So we can begin to turn the schema in (79) into a proper definition by restating its right-hand side as follows:

(80)   every (λx $\downarrow$ [x is a farmer that owns a donkey])(λx $\downarrow$ [x is a farmer that owns a donkey and x beats it])

The $\downarrow$-operator transforms dynamic properties into sets, but this will happen only after the restriction and the scope of *every* have been dynamically conjoined. Consequently, any indefinite occurring in the restriction will have a chance to bind any indefinite occurring in the scope.

There is one step missing in order for us to arrive at the definition we are looking for. We should recall that we want sentences to denote context change potentials, as these are our basic building blocks. So we want to put back into (80) the slot that we had taken out to be able to use the familiar meaning of *every*. The $\uparrow$-operator serves this purpose. We can then at last write out the following definition:

(81)   every' (man that has a donkey) (beat it) =
       $\uparrow$ every (λx $\downarrow$ [x is a farmer that owns a donkey])(λx $\downarrow$ [x is a farmer that owns a donkey and x beats it])

The functor *every'* is the dynamic counterpart of static *every* and defined in terms of the latter. It maps pairs of dynamic properties into context change potentials (just like *a*).

The meaning of *every* we have just defined is clearly equivalent to the one defined in the previous section (in terms of '$\forall$' and '$\rightarrow$'). But there is one interesting difference (and advantage) compared to our previous definition. The schema in (81) generalizes to *all* so-called quantificational determiners (*no, most, less than n*, etc.). Such a generalization is given in (82a):

(82)   a. $D'(P)(Q) = \uparrow D(\downarrow P)(\downarrow [P \triangle Q])$
          where:
            i. P and Q are of type $\langle s,\langle e,cc\rangle\rangle$ and D is a static determiner
            ii. $\downarrow P = \lambda x \downarrow \check{}P(x)$
            iii. $P \triangle Q = \hat{}\lambda x \downarrow [\check{}P(x) \triangle \check{}Q(x)]$
        b. $\lambda P\lambda Q\exists x [P(x) \triangle Q(x)]$

We assume that all quantificational determiners are defined by the schema in (82a), while indefinite determiners are treated according to the model of *a* in (82b).[17] This gives us a fully general characterization of dynamic determiners that fixes their truth-conditional content with the help of their static counterparts. Every quantificational determiner will be internally dynamic (i.e., indefinites in the left argument will be able to bind into the right argument) but externally static (i.e., indefinites in either argument of a quantificational determiner will not be able to bind beyond the syntactic scope of the determiner). Indefinites will instead be both internally and externally dynamic. The difference in the treatment of indefinites vs. quantificational determiners corresponds to the DR-theoretic assumption that indefinites "introduce discourse referents" or "set up file cards," while quantificational determiners do not. Quantificational determiners introduce "box splitting" or set up "temporary files." The assumption that indefinites are special is what the present theory has in common with DRT; this assumption is no more and no less stipulative here than it is in DRT. But in the present theory all determiners and NPs come up naturally as having a uniform type and the proportion problem does not arise. A sentence like *Most men that have a donkey beat it* is assigned by (82a) the truth conditions 'Most men that have a donkey are men that have a donkey and beat it' (cf. the appendix, part IV).

In concluding this section, it might be interesting to contrast the present approach with the one explored in section 2.2. There, equivalences like the one in (79) were obtained by means of an actual copying rule; here they are obtained by a condition on the lexical meaning of determiners. While as a copying rule the condition in question appeared to be quite ad hoc and led to descriptive difficulties, as a semantic definition it enables us to immediately derive conservativity, an independently observable property of determiners (cf. the appendix, part III). In fact, it can be argued that definition (82a) is just how the conservativity constraint should be stated in a dynamic setting.

2.4 ADVERBS OF QUANTIFICATION AND EXISTENTIAL DISCLOSURE

It is now time to turn to adverbs of quantification (Q-adverbs) and *if/when*-clauses. This is a complex topic that we will need to address both here and in the next chapter (and even so, we will hardly be able to cover all the relevant issues). I will first argue that Q-adverbs can bind both eventualities and ordinary objects. Then I will make a specific proposal as to how this happens. Finally I will discuss a number of possible extensions.

2.4.1 Quantification over Events

It is unquestionable that some *if/when*-clauses involve a quantification over eventlike entities:

(83)   a. When Pavarotti sings, I am always happy.
        b. If John is in town, he usually visits us.

Any plausible analysis of the truth conditions of the sentences in (83) seems to involve a quantification over eventualities or situations. For example, a possible analysis of (83a) could go as follows:

(84)   a. Events:
          Every event which is a singing by Pavarotti overlaps with an
          eventuality in which I am happy.
        b. Situations:
          Every minimal situation in which Pavarotti sings is part of a
          situation in which I am happy.

A possible way to implement an analysis like the one in (84a) is to adopt some version of Davidson's idea that verbs have an extra argument slot for events.[18] The event argument is what adverbials (and tense) are, in general, taken to modify and what Q-adverbs can quantify over. An analysis along the lines of (84b) requires instead the development of a situation-based semantics.[19] A possible way to do so is by assuming that worlds are made up of situations, ordered by a part-of relation. It is over the minimal elements relative to this ordering (i.e., the part-of relation) that Q-adverbs operate.

Quite clearly, choosing between these alternatives (each of which has many variants) is not something that can be done just on the basis of the phenomena we are dealing with in the present work, for the role of events and situations in semantics is pervasive. Moreover, I have not so far come across crucial evidence that would force one to prefer one of the approaches in (84) over the other. I will basically follow the Davidsonian line here, for that involves a less radical departure from standard assumptions and can be more readily incorporated in the general semantic framework we have been developing. However, when appropriate, I will switch from "event-talk" to "situation-talk," on the assumption that a situation-based semantics is also compatible with our framework.[20]

On the Davidsonian approach, the truth conditions of a simple sentence like (85a) would be expressed roughly as in (85b):

(85)   a. Pavarotti sings.
        b. $\exists e\ [\text{sing (Pavarotti, e)}]$[21]

As usual, I am disregarding tense. Formula (85b) says that there is a singing by Pavarotti. The extra argument of a verb can be an event (as in 85b)) or a state, depending on the aspectual class of the verb (and the structure of the

VP).[22] The dynamic version of (85b) (i.e., the CCP associated with (85a)) is obtained as usual by inserting in (85b) a slot for admissible continuations.

(86) $\lambda p \exists e$ [sing(Pavarotti, e) $\wedge$ ˘p]

The event argument, besides being existentially closed as in (86), can also be quantified over by a Q-adverb (we will see shortly how this happens). So the reduced translation of (83a), according to the semantics for Q-adverbs, will be something like:

(87) $\forall e$ [sing(Pavarotti,e)] [$\exists e'$ [overlap (e,e') $\wedge$ happy(I,e')]]

The underlined part relates the singing event to the state of happiness. I assume that this link comes about in virtue of whatever mechanism deals with tense sequencing in discourse. It is quite generally assumed that each sentence introduces an eventuality, and that this eventuality is systematically related to the eventuality previously introduced in ways which depend on the tense and aspect of the sentences involved. The principles that govern this process are complex. My strategy will simply be that of introducing case by case the links between events that are called for in the relevant representations, without being explicit as to how exactly they come about. I believe that several of the current approaches to tense in discourse can be worked into the present framework. And in fact, it may be possible to improve on current theories by exploiting a dynamic setup (cf. Muskens 1990, van Eynde 1992 for discussion). But I will not engage in such an attempt here, as that would constitute too much of a departure from our main topic.

Once we allow for Q-quantification to operate on eventualities at all, the question arises as to whether this suffices, that is, whether we can maintain that Q-adverbs quantify always and uniformly over eventualities. The key to this question has to do, I think, with sentences like the following ((88a) is repeated from section 2.1):

(88)   a. When a painter lives in a village, it is usually pretty.
        b. A 'u' usually follows a 'q'. (M. Rooth)

As we have seen, these sentences have various readings. Sentence (88a) can be understood as quantifying over painters or over villages, and sentence (88b) as quantifying over occurrences of 'u' or of 'q'. How can we get these different readings by quantifying solely over eventualities? Here is a possibility, suggested by Heim (1990). We can analyze the sentences in (88) along the following lines:

(89)   a. Every minimal situation s that contains a village inhabited by a painter is a situation where the village in s is pretty.

b. Every minimal situation s which contains a 'u' is part of a situation where the 'u' in s follows a 'q'.

Sentence (89a) is a possible analysis the object-asymmetric reading of (88a), and (89b) is one of the subject-asymmetric reading of (88b). I have switched here to situation-talk, as that illustrates perhaps more vividly what the intent of this proposal is. When we want to identify an indefinite *a N* as the "theme" or "topic," we look at minimal situations, each of which contains exactly one such N. For example, in (89a) we look at minimal situations containing a village inhabited by a painter. How many such minimal situations are there? Clearly, as many as there are villages inhabited by painters. For (88a) to be true on the object-asymmetric reading, most situations s of this type have to be such that the village in s is pretty. To get the subject-asymmetric reading of (88a), we must look instead at minimal situations containing painters who live in a village. And so on. Now consider what is involved in developing a compositional semantics capable of delivering readings of this sort. First, we have to identify at LF the NPs we want to quantify over. Second, we have to quantify over minimal situations containing an "instance" of such indefinites. In order to do so, if indefinites are existentially quantified NPs, we have to get from them to the corresponding property, so that we can identify their instances. Moreover, to be workable, this analysis has to be coupled with an adequate treatment of the descriptions 'the village in s' or 'the painter in s'.

Assuming that this can be done satisfactorily, we can then ask whether the result is in any way different from having Q-adverbs quantify over both individuals and eventualities. Hardly, it would seem.[23] On the situational approach just sketched, the kind of situation we need to get an asymmetric reading must be in a one–one correspondence with the individuals we quantify over in the objectual approach. But this means that on the situational approach as well we must have what amounts to objectual quantification. Moreover, on both approaches, we need a mechanism to single out the NPs that act as themes or topics. So the two approaches appear to be isomorphic. In what follows, I will assume that Q-adverbs can quantify over both individuals and eventualities and will focus on how NPs can be singled out as themes. This will avoid getting us into the details of a situation-based semantics. The reader who prefers a uniform quantification over situations should have no difficulty translating my proposal, along the lines sketched above.

2.4.2 Topic Selection

The descriptive generalization we arrived at in section 2.1 was that Q-adverbs form tripartite structures where *if/when*-clauses, if present, provide the restriction. Moreover, Q-adverbs can select one or more or possibly all of the indefinites in an *if/when*-clause as "topics" or "themes," that is, as what is actually quantified over. As a guide to the approach we will adopt, let us review briefly what we proposed in section 2.2. Consider the following sentence:

(90)   a. Always, when a cat has blue eyes, it meows.
        b. Always$_i$ $\exists_j$ [when a cat$_{j,i}$ has blue eyes] $\exists_j$ [a cat$_{j,i}$ has blue eyes it$_j$ meows]

The LF in (90b) is derived as follows. First $\exists$-Closure applies to both restriction and scope; then the adverb is coindexed with an indefinite selected as theme. Third, Accommodation copies the restriction onto the scope. Doubly indexed indefinites like *cat*$_{j,i}$ are interpreted as 'x_j is a cat and $x_j = x_i$'. So (90b) says that most i's that are identical to blue-eyed cats are identical to blue-eyed cats that are intelligent. Now we are prepared to develop an approach based on the same idea, but arguably simpler. In the present setup, indefinites are existentially quantified terms. So in order to get them to be bound by Q-adverbs, we will need a rule of 'Existential *Dis*closure' (ED). The term (and the corresponding operation) are due to Dekker (1990a). ED is a compositional semantic operation that achieves the same effect as the double indexing of indefinites in (90b).

Before giving the definition of ED, I will illustrate what I mean by means of an example. The CCPs of the *when*-clause and of the main clause in (90), according to our assumptions, will be (91a) and (91b) respectively:

(91)   a. a cat has blue eyes $\Rightarrow$ $\lambda p \exists x$ [cat(x) $\wedge$ has-blue-eyes(x) $\wedge$ ˇp]
        b. it is intelligent $\Rightarrow$ λp [intelligent(x) $\wedge$ ˇp]

We want to wipe out the existential quantifier in (91a) so as to obtain something that the Q-adverb can bind. It turns out that the open character of indefinites enables us to do so compositionally. We can define an operation which, so to speak, replaces '$\exists$' with a 'λ', turning a CCP into a (dynamic) property that can act as the restriction for *every*. Informally, the operation that does the trick involves adding an equation of the form 'x = u' to (91a), so that we obtain the following:

(92) $\exists x \uparrow [cat(x) \wedge$ has blue eyes $(x)] \vartriangle \uparrow x = u$
        $= \lambda p \exists x [cat(x) \wedge$ has blue eyes $(x) \wedge x = u \wedge \,^\vee p]$

In this way, we introduce a free variable 'u' in the *when*-clause, which can be bound by a Q-adverb. In a generalized quantifier framework, we abstract over u in (92), obtaining a property that can act as the left argument of the determiner function. The result of abstracting over u is:

(93)   a. $\lambda u \lambda p \exists x [cat(x) \wedge$ has-blue-eyes$(x) \wedge x = u \wedge \,^\vee p]$
        b. $\lambda x \uparrow [cat(x) \wedge$ has-blue-eyes$(x)]$

The dynamic property in (93a) is equivalent to (93b). At this point, having obtained the desired restriction, there are no obstacles to our interpreting *always* just like *every*, which gives us:

(94)   every$'(\,^\wedge \lambda x \uparrow [cat(x) \wedge$ has-blue-eyes$(x)])(\,^\wedge \lambda x \uparrow$ intelligent $(x))$

This yields precisely the truth conditions we want for (90a).[24]

What is the basic idea, then? Simply this: Q-adverbs are (modalized versions of) determiner meanings: *always* is just (a modalized counterpart of) *every*, *usually* of *most*, *never* of *no*, etc. However, determiners come with heads that wholly determine their restriction. Q-adverbs do not. They may lack a structurally projected restriction altogether (as in *John always bugs me*). Or if they have one, what they bind is left to various discourse factors to determine, as part of topic selection. Topic selection is cast simply as a form of abstraction. The framework we have adopted enables us to abstract over variables that are existentially quantified, because of the open character of existentially quantified NPs.

In general, Existential Disclosure can be defined as follows:

(95)   Existential Disclosure (ED): For any discourse marker α_n and CCP A,
        $\underline{\lambda \alpha_n} A = \lambda u(A \vartriangle \uparrow \alpha_n = u]$

This operation only yields the intended results if A contains some active quantifiers. It doesn't work if A contains only closed ones. Consider, for example, the following variant of (90a).

(96)   *When every cat$_i$ has blue eyes, it$_i$ is usually$_i$ intelligent.

The CCP of the *when*-clause, according to the procedure set up in Section 2.3.2, would be:

(97)   a. $\lambda p[\forall x_i \ [cat(x_i) \wedge has\text{-}blue\text{-}eyes(x_i)] \wedge \check{\ }p]$
         b. $\lambda u_i \lambda p[\forall x_i \ [cat(x_i) \wedge has\text{-}blue\text{-}eyes(x_i)] \wedge x_i = u_i \wedge \check{\ }p]$
         c. Most u's that are identical to $\underline{x}_i$ and such that every cat has blue eyes are intelligent.

The universal quantifier cannot reach into subsequent discourse. The variable p in (97) is not in the scope of '$\forall$'. Consequently, if we add an equation of the form '$x_i = u_i$' to (97a), it will not be bound by '$\forall$', as (97b) illustrates. Moreover, the resulting property in (97b) is not a good restriction for a quantifier like *usually*. Quantifiers of that sort in natural language presuppose that in principle more than one individual can satisfy their restriction. This is attested by the oddity of sentences like *Usually when John dies, he dies happily*. Since it is part of the common ground that one dies only once, the quantifier *usually* plays no role in this sentence. We might dub this the "contentfulness presupposition."[25] The situation with (97b) is similar. Such a property can only be satisfied by the value of x_i. Hence, as a restriction to a quantifier like *usually,* it will violate the contentfulness presupposition. If we use (97b) as a restriction, we get the truth conditions in (97c), where it is clear that the quantifier *most* is completely superfluous.

     This shows that by its very nature, Existential Disclosure works only for CCPs that contain indefinites. So we no longer need to stipulate that a Q-adverb must be coindexed with an indefinite. We can freely assign indices to Q-adverbs. If some index does not correspond to an indefinite in the restriction, its disclosure will make the quantifier superfluous and the resulting sentence will therefore be deviant.

     It is also clear from the way Existential Disclosure is defined that if more than one indefinite is present, we are free to choose any one of them as a topic, since we are free to pick any variable. We can implement this by assuming the following:

(98)   Q-Adverb Indexing:
         Q-adverbs can be indexed freely.

This replaces our previous rule of Q-Adverb Indexing (and does away with the double indexing of indefinites; cf. section 2.2.1 above). An indefinite coindexed with a Q-adverb is disclosed. So, for example, in the case of (99a), we can choose either the subject (obtaining the subject-asymmetric reading, given in (99a′)) or the object (obtaining the object-asymmetric one, given in (99b–b′)).

(99)   a. Usually$_i$ [when a painter$_i$ lives in a village$_j$] [it$_j$ is pretty].
    a′. most′($^\wedge\lambda x_i$ [↑ painter′(x$_i$) △ ∃x$_j$ [↑ village′(x$_j$) △ ↑ live in′-(x$_i$,x$_j$)]])($^\wedge\lambda x_i$ ↑ pretty′(x$_j$))
    b. Usually$_j$ [when a painter$_i$ lives in a village$_j$] [it$_j$ is pretty].
    b′. most′($^\wedge\lambda x_j$ [↑ village′(x$_j$) △ ∃x$_i$ [↑ painter′(x$_i$)△ ↑ live in′(x$_i$,x$_j$)]])($^\wedge\lambda x_j$ ↑ pretty′(x$_j$))

Notice that the abstraction on the second argument in (99a′) is seemingly vacuous. This vacuity, however, is only apparent, since *most′*(A)(B) is interpreted as *most′*(A)(A △ B), where the second argument is a genuine property. The interpretation of the sentence will thus be 'Most painters that live in a village are such that the village (they live in) is pretty'.[26]

Exercise 8

Show the equivalence of (a) ↓ EVERY′($^\wedge\lambda x_i$∃x$_i$ ↑ man(x$_i$))($^\wedge\lambda x_i$ ↑ tall(x$_i$)) and (b) ∀u[man(u)↦ tall(u)].

It is also possible for a Q-adverb to select more than one indefinite, as in the following case:

(100)   a. Always$_{i,j}$ [if a woman$_i$ has a child$_k$ with a man$_j$][she$_i$ keeps in touch with him$_j$].
    b. ∀ x$_i$x$_j$∃x$_k$[↑ woman′(x$_i$)△ ↑ man′(x$_j$)△ ↑ child′(x$_k$)△ ↑ has(x$_i$,x$_k$,x$_j$)][↑ keep-in-touch-with′(x$_i$,x$_j$)]

If we abstract on both NPs in (100a), the Q-adverb must be interpreted as a dyadic quantifier. This illustrates an interesting general point, namely that the adicity of Q-adverbs must be flexible. Since in principle there is no constraint on the number of indefinites that can be selected as topic, Q-adverbs must be allowed to have adicity n, for any n. Determiners are monadic; that is, in a static setting, they are relations between properties (extensionally, sets). Polyadic (static) quantifiers are relations between n-place relations (extensionally, sets of n-tuples). And n-place quantifiers can be made dynamic in exactly the same way as their 1-ary counterparts. (See the appendix, part V, for details.)[27]

The view that emerges is the following. There is a process of topic selection that determines which NPs within an *if/when*-clause are chosen as main topics. This process is semantically interpreted as Existential Disclosure. Q-adverbs are (modalized) polyadic counterparts of determiners. I assume that in interpreting *if*/*when*-clauses, one freely selects a number of topics and freely assigns an adicity to the Q-adverb. If the number of topics and the adicity of the adverb do not match, the resulting structure will be uninterpretable and therefore be discarded.

In classical DRT, Q-adverbs are unselective: they bind all the variables accessible to them. Technically, this was implemented as a quantification over assignments. In the present framework, there is no unselective binding.[28] What looks like it is an epiphenomenon which results from the iterative application of Existential Disclosure to all the NPs in an *if*/*when*-clause. Q-adverbs are not in construction with a head. They are quantificational elements whose restriction is determined by discourse factors. As any number of arguments can be selected as topics, Q-adverbs turn out to be semantically polyadic counterparts of determiners.

There are several issues concerning Q-adverbs that need to be fleshed out further. In the following subsection, I will briefly address some of them.

2.4.3 Further Developments and Open Issues

Consider a sentence of the following sort, with the indexing given:

(101)   a. Usually$_i$ [if an Italian$_i$ is tall] [an American$_i$ is blond].
         b. most$'($^$\lambda x_i[\uparrow$ Italian$'(x_i) \triangle \uparrow$ tall$'(x_i)][$^$\lambda x_i[\uparrow$ American$(x_i) \triangle \uparrow$ blond $(x_i)])$

No independent constraint rules out this form of indexing.[29] Consequently, ED will apply, yielding a reading that says that most tall Italians are, in fact, blond Americans. But obviously, (101) lacks such a reading. In order to rule it out, we must appeal to the Novelty Condition, which therefore seems to be another feature that the present theory must inherit from classical DRT. In the next chapter we will see, however, that under closer scrutiny the Novelty Condition turns out to be dispensable.

In section 2.4.1 we have shown that in some cases Q-adverbs can bind the event argument. We now know which mechanism is responsible for this. Consider again example (83), whose LF is (102a).

(102)   a. Always$_e[_e$when Pavarotti sings $[_s$I am happy]
         b. Pavarotti sings $\Rightarrow \lambda p \exists e$ [sing(Pavarotti, e) $\wedge$ ˇp]
         c. I am always happy $\Rightarrow \lambda p \exists s$ [happy(I,s) $\wedge$ ˇp]

Here the Q-adverb simply selects the index of the event variable associated with the *when*-clause (which, we may assume, is syntactically instantiated in some component of the tense and aspect system). ED then applies in the usual manner.

Another prominent feature of Q-adverbs we have discussed is the fact that there may not be an overt restriction. In cases where there is not, we can assume that tripartite structures are formed by splitting or partitioning the main clause. For example, (103a) can be analyzed as in (103b):

(103)   a. A dog usually barks.
         b. [usually$_i$ [a dog$_i$][t$_i$ barks]]

At this stage, we might assume that the LF in (103b) is obtained by moving the subject out of the main clause and sister-adjoining the Q-adverb to the result. We will discuss the splitting algorithm further in the next chapter. For now it is more important to see how structures like (103a) may be interpreted. We have so far assumed that indices on Q-adverbs mark what gets disclosed. But ED is only defined on CCPs, while in (103b) we have an NP denotation. The simplest assumption in cases like these might be that such an NP is applied to a contextually supplied variable, thereby yielding a CCP, which then undergoes disclosure in the usual manner. The outcome is the following:

(104)   most(^λx$_i$ [$\uparrow$ dog(x$_i$) $\triangle$ $\uparrow$ C(x$_i$)])(^λx$_i$[$\uparrow$ bark(x$_i$)])

This says that most contextually relevant dogs (e.g., hungry ones) bark. In a sense, it is as if there is always a null *when*-clause present in sentences of this sort. Of course, sentences such as (104), being generic, are strongly modalized. But spelling out what is involved in this modalization, would take us too far afield.[30]

In appropriate contexts, it is also possible to have Q-adverbs with no structural restriction of any kind:

(105)   a. Usually$_e$ [$_e$John smokes].
         b. most(^λe $\uparrow$ C(e))(^λe[$\uparrow$ smoke(j,e)])

Sentence (105) is interpreted as saying that most contextually relevant eventualities (e.g., after-dinner scenarios, or instances of John waking up etc.) are eventualities in which John smokes.

We mentioned at several stages that focal structure seems to correlate with how a sentence is partitioned. For example, we have seen earlier in this chapter that the following sentences tend to have different readings depending on what is focused (where '[$_F$]' indicates focal stress):

(106)   a. When a trainer from here trains [$_F$a dolphin], she makes it do wonderful things.

    b. When [$_F$ a trainer from here] trains a dolphin, she makes it do
       wonderful things.
    c. A 'u' usually follows [$_F$a 'q'].
    b. [$_F$ A 'u'] usually follows a 'q'.

Sentence (106a) tends to be understood as quantifying over trainers, and
(106b) as quantifying over dolphins. Sentence (106c) quantifies over occurrences of 'u', and sentence (106b) over occurrences of 'q'. The generalization
that emerges seems clear. Everything else being equal, what the Q-adverb
selects does not bear focal stress. Focal stress falls either within the scope
or within those portions of the restriction that are nonthematic. This makes
sense. Stress tends to fall on what is new, that is, rhematic parts. Consider,
for example, a cleft sentence like (107):

(107)   It is John who did that.

Here, prominence tends to go on *John*. Assigning any other prominence is
odd (everything else being equal). I think that whatever governs mappings
between syntactic structure and unmarked prominence patterns in structures
like (107) must also be at work in structures like (106).

    There has been much progress recently in our understanding of focus, and
there have been interesting attempts to relate the phenomena in (106) to
theories of focus (e.g., Krifka 1992, Rooth 1985, 1992). Our approach is
compatible with several aspects of these proposals.[31] However, I do not think
it is possible to view the formation of tripartite quantificational structures as
an immediate manifestation of focal structure. Some aspects of the splitting
process appear to have little to do with focus. For example, the fact that
material in a left-adjoined *if/when*-clause is part of the restriction seems to
be purely structural. Also purely structural appears to be the partitioning of
(108b).

(108)   a. Computers usually route this plane.
       b. Italians usually know this recipe.

Sentence (108) can be understood either as saying that it is a property of
computers in general that they route this plane (where *usually* selects the
subject) or as saying that it is a property of this plane that there are computers
that route it (where *usually* selects the object). Sentence (108b) has only the
correspondent of the first reading, namely that it is a property of Italians in
general that they know this recipe. There is no way to get (108b) to mean
that it is a property of this recipe that there are Italians who know it, no

matter what we do with focal stress. What the Q-adverb selects in the case of (108b) does not seem to be in any way determined by focus. The contrast in (108) seems to have to do with the different kinds of predicates in (108), viz. the fact that *route* is stage-level while *know* is individual-level in Carlson's (1977) sense.[32] These considerations support the view that topic selection by a Q-adverb must be couched in structural terms which are at least partly independent from focal structure, the way we are doing it here.

In this discussion of Q-adverbs, I am leaving out many important details (some of which will be discussed in chapter 3). But even so, the general picture should be reasonably clear. Tripartite structures are formed as in DRT (leaving open the possibility that when an overt restriction is absent, the restriction position may be occupied by material moved out of the main clause). Q-adverbs select any number of indefinites (as their "topics" or "themes") by being coindexed with them. Indefinites coindexed with a Q-adverb undergo ED. In (109), we summarize the relevant processes:

(109)   a. *Q-Adverb Construal:* Sister-adjoin a Q-adverb to a suitable restriction (i.e., a *when*-clause if present, or else material moved out of the main clause)

   b. *Q-Adverb Indexing:* Freely index the Q-adverb.

   c. $\text{ADV}_{i_1,\ldots,i_n}$ [X] [Y] $\Rightarrow$ ADV ($\underline{\lambda}\ x_{i_1},\ldots,\underline{\lambda}x_{i_j} X$) ($\underline{\lambda}\ x_{i_1},\ldots,\underline{\lambda}x_{i_j} Y$) where $\underline{\lambda}$ is ED as defined in (95). If X is not a CCP, make it into one by using variables of appropriate type.

All construal rules (other than those in (109)) are eliminated. The main innovation resides in the use of ED. We have seen in section 2.2 that classical DRT and its descendants need a number of existential closure rules that apply to a disjoint set of environments (the nuclear scope, the text, the restriction). On the present approach we have one rule—namely ED—that applies freely in a uniform environment (the arguments of a Q-adverb). By switching perspective, we have achieved greater unity. This, I submit, constitutes a further empirical argument in favor of going dynamic. However, before fully taking stock, we need to say something as to how ∀-readings fit into this general picture.

2.5 ∀-READINGS: A PRELIMINARY ACCOUNT

The basic empirical generalization we have reached in sec. 2.1 is that both ∃-readings and ∀-readings are generally available in donkey anaphora contexts, even though sometimes only one of them will be salient, due to idiosyncratic, poorly understood properties of the context. The question we need to address, albeit we can do so here only in a somewhat speculative way, is how ∀-readings come about.

2.5.1 Are Determiners Ambiguous?

A hypothesis that immediately comes to mind is that the availability of ∀-readings next to ∃-readings is simply a matter of lexical ambiguity. Quantificational determiners like *every* and *most* might have two interpretations, where one assigns existential force to indefinites in the restriction (the one we have studied so far) while the second assigns universal force to them. This second interpretation would assign to (110a) the truth conditions in (110b):

(110) a. Most men who have a donkey beat it.
       b. For <u>most</u> x such that x is a man who has a donkey, for <u>every</u>
          donkey x has, x beats it.

An analysis of ∀-readings along these lines (originally formulated in Root 1986 and Rooth 1987) involves splitting the quantificational force of a determiner into two components, represented by the underlined portions of (110b). The first component binds the variable supplied by the head of the NP; its quantificational force depends on the lexical meaning of the determiner. The second component, by contrast, is fixed for every determiner and binds universally the indefinites in the restriction. It is fairly easy to reproduce this approach, which can be varied in a number of ways, within our framework. For example, Groenendijk and Stokhof (1990) propose a natural alternative to our way of defining implication that yields the strong truth conditions for donkey sentences, namely:

(111) $A \rightarrow_\forall B = \neg[A \triangle \neg B]$

The definition incorporates the claim that *every* way of verifying A leads to a way of verifying B. It can be shown that if implication is analyzed as in (111), (112a) and (112b) become equivalent:

(112) a. $[\exists xA] \rightarrow_\forall B$ b. $\underline{\forall}x[A \rightarrow_\forall B]$

Accordingly, a donkey sentence such as (113a) becomes equivalent to (113b).

(113) a. $\forall x\ [\lambda p[man(x) \wedge \exists y\ [donkey(y) \wedge has(x,y) \wedge \check{}p]] \rightarrow_\forall \lambda p$
          $[beat(x,y) \wedge \check{}p]]$
       b. $\uparrow \forall x\forall y[[man(x) \wedge donkey(y) \wedge has(x,y)]] \rightarrow beat(x,y)]$
          (cf. Groenendijk and Stokhof 1990)

Thus, by changing very slightly the definition of implication, we can get either the $\exists$-reading or the $\forall$-reading of donkey sentences. This approach can be generalized to all determiners by using the following schema:

(114) $D'(P)(Q) = \uparrow D(\downarrow P)(\downarrow [P \rightarrow_\forall Q])$

Although I have no knockdown argument against it, there are several reasons which make me skeptical as to the ultimate viability of the ambiguity hypothesis. In what follows, I will point out three of them. The first is a simplicity consideration. Any determiner that has the structure in (110) turns out *not* to be dynamically conservative in the sense of definition (78b), repeated here as (115a):

(115)   a. $D(P)(Q) = D(P)(P \wedge Q])$
         b. $\downarrow \forall x[\check{}P(x) \rightarrow_\forall \uparrow [\downarrow \check{}Q(x) \leftrightarrow \downarrow \check{}Q'(x)]] \rightarrow [\downarrow D(P)(Q) \leftrightarrow \downarrow D(P)(Q')]$

If, for example, we analyze *every* as in (110), it is clear that 'Every person who has a dime will put it in the meter' does not come out equivalent to 'Every person who has a dime is a person who has a dime and puts it in the meter', for the former entails that every dime owned by everyone is put in the meter, while the latter does not. There are arguably ways of defining dynamic conservativity suitable to determiners with $\forall$-readings. For example, Kanazawa (1993) proposes (115b), which for cases that involve no Dynamic Binding can be shown to reduce to static conservativity (just like (115a) does). However, in my opinion, a definition like (115b) is formally and conceptually more complex than definition (115a). Hence, if there were a principled way of obtaining $\forall$-readings that enabled us to stick to the simpler definition, it would be preferable.

The second argument against the lexical ambiguity hypothesis is more empirical in nature (if somewhat speculative). The availability of $\forall$-readings, in addition to $\exists$-readings, for determiners like *every* is presumably universal. If this availability was a matter of lexical ambiguity, one would expect there to be languages where the ambiguity is resolved. That is, one would expect to find languages where, say, the *every* which has the $\exists$-reading and the one which has the $\forall$-reading are realized as different words or morphemes. I am not aware of any language where this is so. This is surprising if the availability of these two types of readings is to be ascribed to a genuine case of lexical ambiguity.

The third point I would like to make concerns the architecture of the system. We saw above that DRT comes with a notion of scope (namely, accessibility) that Dynamic Binding inherits. A pronoun α can be dynamically bound by an antecedent β only if α is accessible to β. However, it was pointed out in chapter 1 that anaphora across inaccessible domains is also possible under certain circumstances. Thus besides Dynamic Binding, we need a second device to deal with anaphora across inaccessible domains. The E-type strategy, where pronouns are assimilated to descriptions whose content is contextually supplied, appears to be well suited for this role. Now, if the E-type strategy is generally available, nothing will prevent it from also being available in donkey anaphora contexts. Suppose, then, that the latter strategy, when used in donkey anaphora contexts, is responsible for ∀-readings. This would clearly account for the systematic availability of such readings in a way that is more explanatory than simply positing a putative, universal lexical ambiguity.

In view of these considerations, I will now investigate the hypothesis that the E-type strategy is responsible for ∀-readings of donkey sentences.

2.5.2 The E-Type Strategy Reconsidered

It is generally agreed upon that pronouns can either be bound or have contextually specified values. But of course this does not imply that pronouns are ambiguous. The situation is just as with variables in logic, which can have free and bound uses without being ambiguous. To flesh this out further, the defining characteristic of pronouns is that they have no inherent semantic content. Their content is provided in essentially two ways: via semantic binding (in the appropriate configurations) or via contextually available information. The E-type strategy, I believe, is part of the second way of individuating the content of pronouns; it is a strategy to retrieve through the context the value of unbound pronouns. More specifically, the linguistic and extralinguistic context can supply descriptions which can be exploited to reconstruct the intended value of a pronoun. In a way, the present work as a whole is simply an attempt to spell out a bit further the traditional claim that pronouns can be bound or free, by arguing on the one hand that binding is not only static (under c-command), but also dynamic and by arguing on the other hand that interpreting free pronouns through the context has its own systematicity (embodied in the E-type strategy). In talking below of E-type strategy and E-type pronouns we are merely recognizing the undeniable existence of semantically unbound pronouns and exploring some regularities in their interpretation.

In this section, I will sketch a very simple approach to E-type pronouns that borrows from various proposals put forth in the literature.[33] Let us begin by reconsidering a sample of the typical cases of anaphora across inaccessible domains discussed in chapter 1:

(116)   a. Every man except John gave his paycheck$_i$ to his wife. John gave it$_i$ to his mistress.   (L. Karttunen)
        b. Morrill Hall doesn't have a bathroom$_i$ or it$_i$ is in a funny place. (B. H. Partee)
        c. It is not true that John doesn't have a car$_i$. It$_i$ is parked outside.
        d. John doesn't have a car$_i$ anymore. He sold it$_i$ last month.

Now let us adopt the view that E-type pronouns are functions from individuals to individuals, where the nature of the function is contextually specified. To see what is involved, let us examine how the interpretation of the sentences in (116) can be specified:

(117)   a. Every man except John put his paycheck in the bank. John gave f(John) to his mistress.
           f: a function from individuals into their paychecks
        b. Either Morrill Hall doesn't have a bathroom or f(Morrill Hall) is in a funny place.
           f: a function from places into bathrooms located in those places
        c. It is not true that John doesn't have a car. f(John) is parked outside.
           f: a function from people into their cars
        d. John doesn't have a car anymore. He sold f(John) last month.
           f: a function from people into the car they used to have

What governs the use of E-type pronouns is simply the fact that in certain contexts, such as those in (116), functions from individuals into individuals become salient in the common ground and can be used in interpreting the pronouns.

To be a little more explicit, let us assume that pronouns in general will denote n-place functional variables from entities into entities. The case where $n = 0$ can be identified with the case where pronouns are simply entity-level variables. This amounts to saying that in a sense, pronouns (like verbs, prepositions, etc.) come with different adicities. If the adicity of a pronoun is zero, that is, if it is a genuine entity-level variable, an entity (singular or plural depending on the pronoun's morphological marking) must be supplied as its value. And this can be done either via binding or by retrieving a characterization of the relevant entity from the context. When the adicity of a pronoun is equal to or greater than one, a function and suitable arguments must be retrieved from the context. This is what happens in (117). As we will see in chapter 4, the idea just sketched fits well within a general theory of definites that views them as ways of characterizing individuals in terms of identifying properties that possibly have some contextual parameters.

Under the present view, the interpretation of pronouns will be governed by whether they are argument taking or not, plus general principles of type coherence. In particular, 0-place pronouns, being of type e, can be taken directly as arguments by predicates. One- (or more-) place functional pronouns cannot. They must first be applied to some suitable argument.[34]

Now, when pronouns are interpreted functionally, they seem to have a particular semantic property, namely that of being unmarked as to whether the value of the function is singular or plural. To see this, let us take a second look at, say, (117b). Suppose that after having uttered (117b), we find out that Morrill Hall has two bathrooms and they are both in funny places. Have we uttered a falsehood then? Or have we uttered something we are now unable to interpret against the scenario that turned out to obtain? It seems to me that the answer to both questions is No. I think we would have no special difficulty in recognizing the sentence as true under the envisaged circumstances. Of course, if we knew beforehand that Morrill Hall had two bathrooms, the use of the singular in (117b) would constitute an uncooperative way to convey the relevant information. Still, the fact that we wouldn't regard (117b) as ungrammatical goes to show that the choice of number in the case under discussion is not a hardwired semantic constraint but rather something that reveals the unmarked expectation of the speaker, or possibly just his lack of interest in cardinality issues.

A similar phenomenon can be observed with overt definites. Contrast (118a) with (118b):

(118)   a. The task was hard.
         b. Every policeman must report on the task assigned to him.

The definite description in (118a) has a strong uniqueness presupposition. If there is more than one salient task around, we won't know how to interpret (118a). Notice that the definite in (118a) does not denote a function of a linguistically supplied argument. Per contrast, the definite in (118b) does. It denotes a function from policemen into tasks assigned to them. And the sentence still seems perfectly interpretable also if some policeman is assigned more than one task. In that case, we understand that the policeman has to make a report on all his tasks.

Yet another kind of definite that behaves this way are free relatives, as the following example illustrates.

(119)   What I see on my plate (namely two overcooked carrots) looks
disgusting.

The free relative in (119) is morphologically singular but can clearly denote
a plural entity. We thus conclude that when pronouns (and, perhaps, definites
in general) are interpreted functionally, their number is morphologically singular but can be semantically neutral.

To summarize so far, we have argued that pronouns can denote functions
with contextually supplied domains and ranges, and that when they do they
are neutral as to whether their values are entities or groups. These functional
readings of pronouns are what is responsible for the interpretation of pronouns
that are semantically unbound (i.e., for anaphoric links that span across
inaccessible domains). Now, if pronouns can be functional in cases of anaphora across inaccessible domains, there should be no reason to expect the
unavailability of such interpretation in donkey anaphora contexts. Thus, next
to the interpretation studied so far, a sentence like (120a) will have the
interpretation in (120b).

(120)   a. Every man who has a donkey$_i$ beats it$_i$.
b. $\forall x$ [[man(x) $\wedge$ $\exists y$ [donkey(y) $\wedge$ has (x,y)]] $\rightarrow$ beat(x,f(x))]
c. f: a function from men into the donkey (or donkeys) they own.

In formula (120b) I am ignoring the dynamics, as it is irrelevant here (a
practice I will follow throughout). The functional interpretation of the donkey
pronoun in (120a) is made possible by the fact that the subject noun phrase
brings to salience a function from men into their donkeys. As argued above,
such function is number neutral in that it can have a plural entity (i.e., the
maximal set of donkeys owned by each man) as its value for some argument.[35] On this interpretation, (120a) literally means that every man beats
the donkey or donkeys he owns. But this is just the $\forall$-reading of sentence
(120a). Thus the E-type strategy, under the present construal, delivers us
$\forall$-readings of donkey sentences for free.

To explore the potential of this line of analysis further, consider now a
more complicated case, namely (76a) above, repeated here:

(121)   Every boy that has a dog and every girl that has a cat will beat it.

This sentence also has a strong reading (which, in fact, is its prominent one).
How does it come about on the present approach? Well, the first NP in (121)
makes salient a function from boys into dogs, while the second NP brings to
prominence a function from girls into cats. The pronoun *it* can then be inter-

preted as the union of these two functions. Such a function will map x into x's dogs if x is a boy; it will map x into x's cat if x is a girl. Accordingly, the logical form of (121) will be as follows:

(122)   a. $\lambda P[\forall x \ [boy(x) \wedge \exists y \ [dog(y) \wedge has(x,y)] \rightarrow \ ^{\vee}P(x)] \wedge$
$\forall x \ [girl(x) \wedge \exists y \ [cat(y) \wedge has(x,y)] \rightarrow \ ^{\vee}P(x)]](^{\wedge}\lambda z[beat$
$(z,f(z))])$

   b. $[\forall x \ [boy(x) \wedge \exists y \ [dog(y) \wedge has(x,y)] \rightarrow beat(x,f(x))] \wedge$
$\forall x \ [girl(x) \wedge \exists y \ [cat(y) \wedge has(x,y)] \rightarrow beat(x,f(x))]]$

This kind of example is very hard to handle for theories of E-type anaphora that try to reconstruct the antecedent of the pronoun by means of copying rules (like Neale 1990 or Heim 1990).

It is perhaps worth emphasizing once more that I am *not* arguing in favor of locating the ambiguity between ∃- and ∀-readings in pronouns rather than in determiners. Pronouns, like variables, are not ambiguous but rather have bound and free uses. The E-type strategy is a theory of how free pronouns are interpreted. If the hypothesis just sketched is correct, the apparent ambiguity in the interpretation of donkey pronouns would actually make sense.

Let us summarize the main steps of our argumentation. Besides semantic binding (whether dynamic or not) the content of pronouns can also be contextually supplied. Sentences like those in (116) show that the context can supply interpretations of a functional nature; that is, pronouns can sometimes be interpreted as functions. We have also observed that such functions appear to allow (maximal) plural entities as values. But if this is so, there is nothing to prevent functional interpretations from occurring in donkey anaphora contexts, where the argument of the function is bound by a c-commanding antecedent. This inexorably yields ∀-interpretations. The alternative to this hypothesis is to posit a semantic ambiguity in the interpretation of determiners. But positing an ambiguity explains nothing, while on the present approach we have at least the beginning of an explanation of why donkey pronouns appear to have the readings they do.

2.5.3 Limits of the E-Type Strategy

Almost every author who has written on anaphora has taken a kind of all-or-nothing stand: either pronouns (in non-c-command anaphora) are *all* dynamically bound variables or they are *all* descriptions in disguise. This is understandable. It looks like a straightforward application of Occam's razor. Everything else being equal, if you can get by with one technique, why should you resort to a second one? Once one assumes that E-type anaphora exists, one needs to be able to state why it is not possible to get away with this mechanism alone. I will now give some reasons as to why I think that E-type anaphora cannot do without Dynamic Binding.

My first point is that the simple version of the E-type strategy we have sketched above is incapable by itself of accounting for both ∀- and ∃-readings of donkey sentences. We might of course modify it in such a way that it can produce both readings. Here is one way of doing so. It is possible to assume that functional pronouns do not have to be understood as functions into maximal groups but can be interpreted as choice functions that arbitrarily select one of the possible values. We can then stipulate that when this happens such functions are interpreted as being existentially quantified. Accordingly, a sentence like (123a) will be interpreted as (123b):

(123)   a. Every man that has a donkey beats it.
         b. $\exists f \forall x\ [[\text{man}(x) \land \exists y\ [\text{donkey}(y) \land \text{has}(x,y)]] \rightarrow \text{beat}(x, f(x))]$
         c. f: a function from men into one of their donkeys

Formula (123b), under the interpretation of the function given in (123c), is equivalent to the ∃-reading of (123a). Lappin and Francez (1993) make a proposal along these lines. But unlike our proposal, this *is* perfectly analogous to having two interpretations of determiners. It merely shifts the locus of the ambiguity from determiners to pronouns. Hence it has little explanatory value.

A second difficulty for a treatment of non-c-command anaphora based solely on the E-type strategy has to do with the fact that the phenomena involved do not appear to be homogeneous. In particular, we have observed that pure donkey anaphora appears to be governed by an accessibility constraint and is no more sensitive to pragmatic factors than ordinary c-command anaphora. On the approach I am advocating, there are good reasons for this. Dynamic Binding comes with a notion of scope, completely independent of pragmatic factors. At the same time, it cannot deal with functional readings of pronouns (such as those exemplified by paycheck sentences) or, more generally, with anaphora across inaccessible domains, which appear to be highly sensitive to pragmatic factors. By contrast, the E-type strategy is pragmatically driven. It is, in fact, just a way to articulate a strategy of content retrieval through contextual information. It deals easily with the functional interpretation of pronouns. But it has hardly anything to say about the insensitivity of accessibility to pragmatics. If there was only one strategy, this clustering of properties would remain mysterious. Such a strategy could perhaps deal well with one class of cases but would require a set of additional hypotheses to deal with the other.

Finally, there is also an empirical reason why I think that the E-type strategy alone cannot be sufficient. DRT and any DRT derivative, including Dynamic Binding, is primarily designed to account for facts like the following:

(124) a. John saw a dog $\Rightarrow \exists x[dog(x) \wedge saw(j,x)]$
       b. John saw a dog. It was black $\Rightarrow \exists x[dog(x) \wedge saw(j,x) \wedge black(x)]$
       c. When a dog is black, it is always mean $\Rightarrow \forall x[[dog(x) \wedge black(j,x)] \rightarrow mean(x)]$

Without Dynamic Binding, we have to argue that the pronouns in (124) are descriptions in disguise. Consider now the following set of facts:

(125) a. John walked in $\Rightarrow \exists e [walk\text{-}in(e,j)]$
       b. John walked in. He turned on the light.
          $\exists e [walk\text{-}in(e,j) \wedge \exists e' [e<e' \wedge t.o.t.l.(e,j)]$
       c. When John walks in, he always turns on the light $\Rightarrow \forall e[walk\text{-}in(e,j) \rightarrow \exists e' [e<e' \wedge t.o.t.l(e',j)]]$

Clearly the pattern in (125) is fully parallel to the one in (124).[36] In particular, example (125a) shows that in simple sentences the event variable is understood as being existentially quantified over, just like the indefinite in (124a). Sentence (125b) shows that the scope of an existentially quantified event variable must extend beyond its c-command domain, just like the one associated with an indefinite (cf. (124b)). Finally, sentence (125c) shows that an event variable in the presence of a quantificational adverb picks up from it its quantificational force, just like indefinites do (cf. (124c)). No one, as far as I know, has worked out or even proposed an analysis of the pattern in (125) in terms of descriptions in disguise. And there are reasons to believe, at present, that there would be difficulties in trying to do so. For example, we have seen that uniqueness presuppositions are not systematically present in donkey-type dependencies. In fact, we were forced to adopt a number-neutral characterization of E-type pronouns. If we were to apply this characterization to (125) we would make patently wrong predictions, for (125b) reports about a single walking event.

So DRT and all its derivatives (including the Dynamic Binding approach) currently have no viable alternative as far as (125) is concerned. Of course we could say that the hypothesis that existential quantification is "open-ended" applies only to event-talk (as, e.g., Neale 1990 does). But why would that be so? Shouldn't and wouldn't any reasonable account of (125) extend to talk of ordinary individuals as well? To put it differently, what we need to account for (124) is no more than what we need to account for (125). If, as it seems, DRT is necessary to deal with intrasentential event anaphora, then such an account will inevitably extend to anaphora in general.

These considerations lend support, in my opinion, to the view that the E-type strategy by itself cannot take over the ground of Dynamic Binding. It may be useful, at this point, to summarize the main characteristics of the two interpretive strategies:

(126) *Dynamic Binding:*
    a. Subject to accessibility
    b. Insensitive to pragmatic factors
    c. Responsible for $\exists$-readings in donkey anaphora contexts
    d. Not subject to uniqueness or, in the case of groups, maximality presuppositions (though they can be present if triggered by independent mechanisms, such as, e.g., scalar implicatures)

    E-Type Strategy:
    a. Not subject to accessibility
    b. Sensitive to pragmatic factors
    c. Responsible for $\forall$-readings in donkey anaphora contexts
    d. Subject to uniqueness/maximality presuppositions

It is important to bear in mind that this clustering of properties is by no means accidental. It follows directly from the way in which the two strategies are defined.

2.6 SUMMARY AND CONCLUSIONS

In the present chapter we have considered some important problems that classical DRT leaves open (excess of unselectivity, proportions, NP meanings). Our primary concern was whether in addressing these problems we could find evidence that would help us choose between what we have identified as the two souls of DRT. Therefore we have first tried to solve the problems at hand by modifying and expanding the set of construal rules of (the static version of) classical DRT, but we have seen that the results were unsatisfactory. We have then modified and expanded our original dynamic semantics, with arguably greater success. The system of Dynamic Binding developed here has several things in common with classical DRT, while at the same time differing from it in important respects. Below I list these commonalities and differences:

(127)   *Commonalities between DRT and Dynamic Binding:*
    a. Quantificational structures are tripartite
    b. Indefinites are "open," other determiners are "closed"
    c. *If/when*-clauses form the restriction of quantificational structures, where the quantificational element is a (possibly null) adverb of quantification
    d. Accessibility

(128)   *Differences between (static) DRT and Dynamic Binding:*
    a. Rules of construal vs. "fancier" meanings
    b. Indefinites as free variables vs. indefinites as existentially quantified terms
    c. Existential Closure vs. Existential Disclosure
    d. A higher-order system of meanings

It seems to me that Dynamic Binding has enough in common with DRT to make it legitimate to regard the former as a version of the latter. Still, the differences that obtain between the two are important and, I claim, favor Dynamic Binding over its predecessors. In a nutshell, what are the advantages that Dynamic Binding has to offer? I can see fundamentally three:

(129)   *Claimed Advantages of Dynamic Binding over DRT:*
    a. Existential Disclosure is superior to Existential Closure
    b. No need for accommodation
    c. Account of NP coordination

Let me briefly elaborate on these points. Concerning (129a), classical DRT is empirically inadequate: it gives rise to the proportion problem and remains silent on $\exists$-readings. The variations on classical DRT we have considered are empirically adequate (at least as far as proportions are concerned), but unequivocally need more stipulations than Dynamic Binding needs. In particular, Existential Closure has to apply to three disjoint and unrelated environments (restriction of quantifiers, scope of quantifiers, the text level), while Existential Disclosure applies to just one environment (the domain of Q-adverbs). Moreover, classical DRT needs to stipulate an accommodation rule to make potential antecedents accessible after they have been incorrectly deactivated by Existential Closure (point 129b)). Accommodation is inherently costly and in the required form cannot be related to more general properties of LF. Dynamic Binding replaces accommodation by a characterization of the lexical meaning of determiners that is just a statement of the conservative character of determiners.[37] Finally, the static DRT-based approach seems to have empirical difficulties with NP coordination that the dynamic approach avoids.

The Dynamic Binding approach is couched in a variant of Montague's IL. Probably FCS can be turned into a higher-order system of meanings as well and be used for similar purposes. As far as I can see, the differences between these two ways of proceeding are essentially technical—but this remains to be worked out.

The Dynamic Binding approach does not affect the traditional view that aside from semantic binding, a pronoun can retrieve its antecedent directly from the context. The E-type strategy is viewed here as an instance of the latter mechanism. A very simple version of such strategy permits us to derive ∀-readings and helps explain the apparent ambiguity with ∃-readings in donkey sentences. The viability of our approach to E-type anaphora needs to be put in the context of a more general theory of definites. Chapter 4 will be devoted to this task. We have also given some reasons why donkey dependencies cannot in general be viewed as E-type dependencies.

So we seem to have made some progress in our exploration of the trade-offs between "complicating the syntax" and "complicating the semantics." On the basis of the above considerations, I conclude that an approach that exploits a richer notion of meaning sheds more insight on the nature of the phenomena under discussion than one based on construal rules. This is a case where a choice of this sort is not just grounded on abstract methodological preconceptions.

APPENDIX

I. The Syntax and Semantics of the Revised Version of Intensional Logic

The set TYPE of types is defined as follows:

(1)   The set of TYPE of types is the smallest set such that:
       i. $e, t \in$ TYPE
       ii. If $a, b \in$ TYPE, $\langle a, b \rangle$, $\langle s, a \rangle \in$ TYPE

(2)   For each $a \in$ TYPE, the set ME_a of well-formed expressions of type a is the smallest set such that:
       i. $\text{DM} \subseteq \text{Var}_e$, where DM is the set of 'discourse markers'
       ii. $\text{Var}_a, \text{Cons}_a \subseteq \text{ME}_a$
       iii. If $\beta \in \text{ME}_{\langle a, b \rangle}$ and $\alpha \in \text{ME}_a$, $\beta(\alpha) \in \text{ME}_b$
       iv. If $\alpha \in \text{Var}_a$ and $\beta \in \text{ME}_b$, $\lambda \alpha[\beta] \in \text{ME}_{\langle a, b \rangle}$

v. If $\phi, \psi \in ME_t$, and $\alpha \in Var_a$, then $\neg\phi$, $[\phi \wedge \psi]$, $[\phi \vee \psi]$, $\exists\alpha\phi$, $\forall\alpha\phi$ are all in ME_t

vi. If $\beta \in ME_a$, $^\wedge\beta \in ME_{\langle s,a\rangle}$

vii. If $\beta \in ME_{\langle s,a\rangle}$, $^\vee\beta \in ME_a$

Let U be a domain of individuals and Ω be the set of DM-assignments (i.e., $\Omega = U^{DM}$). For any type a, the set D_a of denotations of type a (relative to U) is defined as follows:

(3)   i. $D_e = U$ ii. $D_t = \{0,1\}$
        iii. $D_{\langle a,b\rangle} = D_b{}^{D_a}$ iv. $D_{\langle s,a\rangle} = D_a{}^{\Omega}$

A model M is a pair of the form $\langle U,F\rangle$, where U is a set of individuals and for any $a \in$ TYPE and $\alpha \in Cons_a$, $F(\alpha) \in D_a$. Let g be an assignment to the variables that are not discourse markers (i.e., for any type a and any member α of $Var_a - DM$, $g(\alpha) \in D_a$). For any assignment g and any DM-assignment ω, the interpretation function $[\![\ ]\!]^{g,\omega}$ is defined as follows (relative to a model M):

(4)   i. If $\alpha \in DM$, $[\![\alpha]\!]^{g,\omega} = \omega(\alpha)$

        ii. If $\alpha \in Var_a - DM$, $[\![\alpha]\!]^{g,\omega} = g(\alpha)$

        iii. If $\alpha \in Cons_a$, $[\![\alpha]\!]^{g,\omega} = F(\alpha)$

        iv. $[\![\beta(\alpha)]\!]^{g,\omega} = [\![\beta]\!]^{g,\omega}([\![\alpha]\!]^{g,\omega})$

        v. $[\![\neg\phi]\!]^{g,\omega} = 1$ iff $[\![\phi]\!]^{g,\omega} = 0$,   etc.

        vi. If $\alpha \in DM$, $[\![\forall\alpha\phi]\!]^{g,\omega} = 1$ iff for every $e \in U$, $[\![\phi]\!]^{g,\omega[\alpha/e]} = 1$, where $\omega[\alpha/e]$ is identical to ω except that $\omega(\alpha) = e$
        If $\alpha \in Var_a - DM$, $[\![\forall\alpha\phi]\!]^{g,\omega} = 1$ iff for every $e \in D_a$, $[\![\phi]\!]^{g[\alpha/e],\omega} = 1$

        vii. If $\alpha \in DM$, $[\![\exists\alpha\phi]\!]^{g,\omega} = 1$ iff for some $e \in U$, $[\![\phi]\!]^{g,\omega[\alpha/e]} = 1$, where $\omega[\alpha/e]$ is identical to ω except that $\omega(\alpha) = e$
        If $\alpha \in Var_a - DM$, $[\![\exists\alpha\phi]\!]^{g,\omega} = 1$ iff for some $e \in D_a$, $[\![\phi]\!]^{g[\alpha/e],\omega} = 1$

        viii. If $\alpha \in DM$, $[\![\lambda\alpha\beta]\!]^{g,\omega} = \lambda e \in U.[\![\beta]\!]^{g,\omega[\alpha/e]}$ (i.e., $[\![\lambda\alpha\beta]\!]^{g,\omega}$ is that function h from U into D_b (where b is the type of β) such that for any $e \in U$, $h(e) = [\![\beta]\!]^{g,\omega[\alpha/e]}$).
        If $\alpha \in Var_a - DM$, $[\![\lambda\alpha\beta]\!]^{g,\omega} = \lambda e \in D_a. [\![\beta]\!]^{g[\alpha/e],\omega}$.

        ix. $[\![^\wedge\alpha]\!]^{g,\omega} = \lambda\omega'. [\![\alpha]\!]^{g,\omega'}$ (i.e., $[\![^\wedge\alpha]\!]^{g,\omega}$ is that function h in $D_a{}^{\Omega}$ such that for any $\omega' \in \Omega$, $h(\omega') = [\![\alpha]\!]^{g,\omega'}$).

        x. $[\![^\vee\alpha]\!]^{g,\omega} = [\![\alpha]\!]^{g,\omega} (\omega)$.

II. Example

We want to show the equivalence of (5a) and (5b):

(5)   a. $\forall x [\lambda p[man(x) \wedge \exists y [donkey(y) \wedge has(x,y) \wedge {}^\vee p]] \xrightarrow{} \lambda p [beat(x,y) \wedge {}^\vee p]]$

        b. $\uparrow \forall x[[man(x) \wedge \exists y [donkey(y) \wedge has(x,y)]] \to \exists y [donkey(y) \wedge has(x,y) \wedge beat(x,y)]]$

In order to do so, let us first prove the identity in (6):

(6) $\forall x \uparrow \phi = \uparrow \forall x \phi$

PROOF:

  a. $\forall x \uparrow \phi$
  b. $\neg \exists x \neg \uparrow \phi$ (def. of $\forall$)
  c. $\neg \exists x \uparrow \neg \downarrow \uparrow \phi$ (def. of $\neg$)
  d. $\neg \exists x \uparrow \neg \phi$ ($\downarrow \uparrow$-canc.)
  e. $\neg \exists x [\lambda p [\neg \phi \wedge \check{}p]]$ (def. of $\uparrow$)
  f. $\neg \lambda p \exists x [\neg \phi \wedge \check{}p]$ (def of $\exists$)
  g. $\uparrow \neg \downarrow \lambda p \exists x [\neg \phi \wedge \check{}p]$ (def. of $\neg$)
  h. $\uparrow \neg \exists x \neg \phi$ (def. of $\downarrow$, λ-conv., $\check{}\hat{}$-canc., taut.)
  i. $\uparrow \forall x \phi$ (taut.)

Let us now proceed to show the equivalence in (5). As a first step we apply the definition of $A \to B$ as $A \veebar [A \triangle B]$. This takes us from (5a) to (7). I indicate under the relevant formulae what counts as A and what as B in (7).

(7) $\forall x [\neg \lambda p[man(x) \wedge \exists y [donkey(y) \wedge has(x,y) \wedge \check{}p]] \veebar$

               $\neg A$

$[\lambda p[man (x) \wedge \exists y [donkey(y) \wedge has(x,y) \wedge \check{}p]] \triangle \lambda p [beat(x,y) \wedge \check{}p]]$

      $[A$ $\triangle$ $B]$

The next set of reductions applies successively the definitions of $\neg$, $\triangle$, and $\veebar$ until we obtain in the body of the formula something of the form '$\uparrow \phi$', where ϕ is an ordinary first-order formula:

(8)   a. $\forall x [\neg \lambda p[man(x) \wedge \exists y [donkey(y) \wedge has(x,y) \wedge \check{}p]] \veebar \lambda p[man(x) \wedge \exists y [donkey(y) \wedge has(x,y) \wedge beat(x,y) \wedge \check{}p]]]$ (def. of $\triangle$)
  b. $\forall x [\lambda p[\neg [man(x) \wedge \exists y [donkey(y) \wedge has(x,y)]] \wedge \check{}p] \veebar \lambda p[man(x) \wedge \exists y [donkey(y) \wedge has(x,y) \wedge beat(x,y) \wedge \check{}p]]]$ (def. of $\neg$)
  c. $\forall x \neg [\neg \lambda p[\neg [man(x) \wedge \exists y [donkey(y) \wedge has(x,y)]] \wedge \check{}p] \triangle \neg [\lambda p[man(x) \wedge \exists y [donkey(y) \wedge has(x,y) \wedge beat(x,y) \wedge \check{}p]]]]$ (def. of $\veebar$)
  d. $\forall x \neg [\lambda p[\neg \neg [man(x) \wedge \exists y [donkey(y) \wedge has(x,y)]] \wedge \check{}p] \triangle \lambda p \neg [man(x) \wedge \exists y [donkey(y) \wedge has(x,y) \wedge beat(x,y)]] \wedge \check{}p]$ (def. of $\neg$)
  e. $\forall x \neg [\lambda p[man(x) \wedge \exists y [donkey(y) \wedge has(x,y)]] \wedge \check{}p] \triangle \lambda p \neg [man(x) \wedge \exists y [donkey(y) \wedge has(x,y) \wedge beat(x,y)]] \wedge \check{}p]$ (taut.)
  f. $\forall x \neg [\lambda p[man(x) \wedge \exists y [donkey(y) \wedge has(x,y)] \wedge \neg [man(x) \wedge \exists y [donkey(y) \wedge has(x,y) \wedge beat(x,y)]] \wedge \check{}p]$ (def. of $\triangle$)
  i. $\forall x \lambda p[\neg [man(x) \wedge \exists y [donkey(y) \wedge has(x,y)] \wedge \neg [man(x) \wedge \exists y[donkey(y) \wedge has(x,y) \wedge beat(x,y)]]] \wedge \check{}p]$ (def. of $\neg$)

j. ∀x ↑¬[man(x) ∧ ∃y [donkey(y) ∧ has(x,y)] ∧ ¬[man(x) ∧ ∃y [don-
key(y) ∧ has(x,y) ∧ beat(x,y)]]]   (def. of ' ↑ ')

Now the first-order formula embedded under ' ↑ ' has the following form:
¬[ξ ∧ ψ ∧ ¬ [ξ ∧ ζ]], where ξ = man(x), ψ = ∃y [donkey(y) ∧ has(x,y)] and
ζ = ∃y[donkey(y) ∧ has(x,y) ∧ beat(x,y)]. A formula of the form ¬[ξ ∧ ψ ∧ ¬
[ξ ∧ ζ]] is logically equivalent to [[ξ ∧ ψ] → ζ]. It follows that (8j) is equivalent
to (9):

(9)   ∀x ↑ [[man(x) ∧ ∃y [donkey(y) ∧ has(x,y)]] → ∃y [donkey(y) ∧ has(x,y)
          ∧ beat(x,y)]]

By (2) this is the same as (10):

(10)   ↑ ∀x[[man(x) ∧ ∃y [donkey(y) ∧ has(x,y)]] → ∃y [donkey(y) ∧ has(x,y)
          ∧ beat(x,y)]]

This establishes the result.

III. Conservativity

Let a dynamic determiner D′ be defined as follows:

DEFINITION 1. D′ (P)(Q) = ↑ D(λu ↓ ˇP(u))(λu ↓ [ˇP(u) ∆ ˇQ(u)]) (= (65))
We want to show that D′ satisfies *Dynamic Conservativity*, where Dynamic Conservativity is defined as follows:

DEFINITION 2. D′(P)(Q) = D′(P)(P ∆ Q), where P ∆ Q = ^λu [ˇP(u) ∆ ˇQ(u)]

We assume that the free variables in P are disjoint from the set of active quantifiers
in Q (see Groenendijk and Stokhof 1991 for a general discussion of this restriction).
    We start by noticing that if a *cc* A meets the constraint just mentioned, the
following holds:

THEOREM 1. A = A ∆ A (Groenendijk and Stokhof 1991)
We can now proceed with our derivation. All the following formulae are equivalent:
a. D′(P)(P ∆ Q)
b. D′(P)(^λv[ˇP(v) ∆ ˇQ(v)])   (def. of P ∆ Q)
c. ↑ D(λu ↓ ˇP(u))(λu ↓ [ˇP(u) ∆ ˇ^λv[ˇP(v) ∆   (DEFINITION 1)
   ˇQ(v)](u)])
d. ↑ D(λu ↓ ˇP(u))(λu ↓ [ˇP(u) ∆ [P(u) ∆ ˇQ(u)]])   (ˇ^-canc., λ-conv.)
e. ↑ D(λu ↓ ˇP(u))(λu ↓ [ˇP(u) ∆ ˇP(u) ∆ ˇQ(u)])   (Associativity of ∆)
f. ↑ D(λu ↓ ˇP(u))(λu ↓ [ˇP(u) ∆ ˇQ(u)])   (THEOREM 1)
g. D′(P)(Q)   (DEFINITION 1)

This establishes the result. Notice that we make no assumptions as to the nature of D. So Dynamic Conservativity does not presuppose Static Conservativity.

IV. Three Examples of Determiners Generated by DEFINITION I

i.   *Every*

every$'$(P)(Q) $= \uparrow [\downarrow P \subseteq \downarrow [P \vartriangle Q]]$

Example:

a. Every man who has a donkey beats it

b. P $=$ $^\wedge\lambda u\lambda p$ [man(u) $\wedge$ $\exists$y[donkey(y) $\wedge$ has(u,y) $\wedge$ $^\vee$p]]

c. Q $=$ $^\wedge\lambda u\lambda p$[beat(u,y) $\wedge$ $^\vee$p]

d. $\downarrow$ P $= \lambda v \downarrow [^{\vee\wedge}\lambda u\lambda p$ [man(u) $\wedge$ $\exists$y[donkey(y) $\wedge$ has(u,y) $\wedge$ $^\vee$p]](v)]
  $= \lambda v$[man(v) $\wedge$ $\exists$y[donkey(y) $\wedge$ has(v,y)]]

e. $\downarrow$ [P $\vartriangle$ Q] $= \downarrow [^\wedge\lambda u\lambda p$ [man(u) $\wedge$ $\exists$y[donkey(y) $\wedge$ has(u,y) $\wedge$ $^\vee$p]] $\vartriangle$ $^\vee\lambda u\lambda p$[beat(u,y) $\wedge$ $^\vee$p]]
  $= \lambda u$[man(u) $\wedge$ $\exists$y[donkey(y) $\wedge$ has(u,y) $\wedge$ beat(u,y)]]

f. $\uparrow [\downarrow P \subseteq \downarrow [P \vartriangle Q]] = \uparrow [\lambda v$[man(v) $\wedge$ $\exists$y[donkey(y) $\wedge$ has(v,y)]] $\subseteq \lambda v$[man(v) $\wedge$ $\exists$y[donkey(y) $\wedge$ has(v,y) $\wedge$ beat(v,y)]]]

ii.   *Most*

Static *most:* most(X)(Y) $= |X \cap Y| > |X \cap Y^-|$

where for any set X, $|X|$ is the cardinality of X (i.e., the number of elements of X).

Dynamic *most:* most$'$(P)(Q) $= \uparrow [\downarrow P \cap \downarrow [P \vartriangle Q]| > |\downarrow P \cap \downarrow [P \vartriangle Q]^-|$

Example:

a. Most men that have a donkey beat it.

b. P $=$ as in (i.b)

c. Q $=$ as in (i.c)

d. $\downarrow$ P $=$ as in (i.d)

e. $\downarrow$ [P $\vartriangle$ Q] $=$ as in (i.e)

f. $\uparrow | \downarrow P \cap \downarrow [P \vartriangle Q] | > |\downarrow P \cap \downarrow [P \vartriangle Q]^-| = \uparrow [| \lambda v$[man(v) $\wedge$ $\exists$y[donkey(y) $\wedge$ has(v,y)]] $\cap \lambda v$[man(v) $\wedge$ $\exists$y[donkey(y) $\wedge$ has(v,y) $\wedge$ beat(v,y)]]| $> |\lambda v$[man(v) $\wedge$ $\exists$y[donkey(y) $\wedge$ has(v,y)]] $\cap \lambda v$[man(v) $\wedge$ $\exists$y[donkey(y) $\wedge$ has(v,y) $\wedge$ beat(v,y)]]$^-$|]

   Interpreting set intersection as conjunction and set complementation as negation, we reduce the λ-terms in (f) as follows:

g. $\uparrow |\lambda v$[man(v) $\wedge$ $\exists$y[donkey(y) $\wedge$ has(v,y) $\wedge$ beat(v,y)]| $> |\lambda v$[man(v) $\wedge$ $\exists$y[donkey(y) $\wedge$ has(v,y)] $\wedge$ $\neg\exists$y[donkey(y) $\wedge$ has(v,y) $\wedge$ beat(v,y)]|

iii. *No*

no$'$(P)(Q) $= \uparrow (\downarrow P \cap \downarrow [P \vartriangle Q] = \emptyset)$

Example:

a. No man who has a donkey beats it.

b. $\uparrow [\lambda v[\text{man}(v) \wedge \exists y[\text{donkey}(y) \wedge \text{has}(v,y)]] \cap \lambda v[\text{man}(v) \wedge \exists y[\text{don-key}(y) \wedge \text{has}(v,y) \wedge \text{beat}(v,y)]] = \emptyset]$

V. Polyadic Quantification

Let D_n be a static n-place determiner. Its dynamic counterpart $D_n{}^+$ is defined as follows:

DEFINITION 3. $D_n + (R)(K) = \uparrow D_n(\downarrow R)(\downarrow R \vartriangle K])$
where R and K are of type $\langle s, \langle e, \ldots \langle e,cc \rangle \ldots \rangle$ and

$$\overset{\text{n- times}}{\downarrow R = \lambda u_1, \ldots ,\lambda u_n \downarrow [\check{}R(u_1). \ldots (u_n)]}$$
$$\downarrow [R \wedge K] = \hat{}\lambda u_1, \ldots ,\lambda u_n \downarrow [\check{}R(u_1). \ldots (u_n) \vartriangle \check{}K(u_1). \ldots (u_n)]$$

Solutions to Selected Exercises

Exercise 1

(a) $[\![\hat{}\text{love}(u,x)]\!]^{g,\omega} = \lambda \omega'. [\![\text{love }(u,x)]\!]^{g,\omega'} = \{\omega' : g(u) \text{ love } \omega'(x)\}$

(b) $[\![\hat{}\text{bald}(j)]\!]^{g,w} = \lambda \omega'.[\![\text{bald}(j)]\!]^{g,\omega}$, where

$\lambda \omega'.[\![\text{bald}(j)]\!]^{g,\omega'}$
$= \Omega$, if $[\![\text{bald}(j)]\!]^{g,\omega} = 1$
$= \emptyset$, otherwise

(c) $[\![\check{}\hat{}\alpha]\!]^{g,\omega} = [\![\hat{}\alpha]\!]^{g,\omega}(\omega) = \lambda \omega'.[\![\alpha]\!]^{g,\omega'} (\omega) = [\![\alpha]\!]^{g,\omega}$

Exercise 3

Proof:

a.	$\downarrow \uparrow \phi$	(assumption)
b.	$\downarrow \lambda p[\phi \wedge \check{}p]$	(Def. of $\uparrow$)
c.	$\lambda p[\phi \wedge \check{}p](\hat{}T)$	(def. of $\downarrow$)
d.	$[\phi \wedge \check{}\hat{}T]$	(λ-conv.)
e.	$\phi \wedge T$	($\check{}\hat{}$-canc.)
f.	ϕ	(taut.)

Exercise 4

Let us proceed by first reducing the left-hand part of the formula:

a.	$\neg \exists x_1 [\lambda p [\text{man}(x_1) \wedge \text{walk-in}(x_1) \wedge \check{}p]]$	
b.	$\uparrow \neg \downarrow \exists x_1 [\lambda p [\text{man}(x_1) \wedge \text{walk-in}(x_1) \wedge \check{}p]]$	def. of $\neg$)
c.	$\uparrow \neg \downarrow \lambda p[\exists x_1[\text{man}(x_1) \wedge \text{walk-in}(x_1) \wedge \check{}p]]$	(def. of $\exists$)
d.	$\uparrow \neg\lambda p[\exists x_1[\text{man}(x_1) \wedge \text{walk-in}(x_1) \wedge \check{}p](\hat{}T)]$	(def. of $\downarrow$)
d.	$\uparrow \neg[\exists x_1[\text{man}(x_1) \wedge \text{walk-in}(x_1) \wedge T]$	(λ-conv.)
		($\check{}\hat{}$-canc.)
e.	$\uparrow \neg\exists x_1[\text{man}(x_1) \wedge \text{walk-in}(x_1)]$	(taut.)
f.	$\lambda p[\neg\exists x_1[\text{man}(x_1) \wedge \text{walk-in}(x_1)] \wedge \check{}p]$	(def. of $\uparrow$)

Now the last occurrence of 'p' in (f) is not in the scope of $\exists x_1$; hence, if a possible continuation of (f) will contain 'x_1', it will not be bound.

Exercise 6

The task was to show the steps in the reduction of (74c) in the text, repeated here:

    a. a_1(ˆ ↑ woman)(ˆλu_1 <u>every$_2$ (ˆ ↑ man)(ˆλu_2 ↑ love$'(u_2,u_1)$)</u>)

We proceed by reducing first the underlined portion of (a):

    b. every$_2$(ˆ ↑ man)(ˆλu_2 ↑ love$'(u_2,u_1)$)

    c. every$_2$(ˆ$\lambda u \lambda p$[man(u) $\wedge$ ˇp])(ˆ$\lambda u_2 \lambda p$[love$'(u_2,u_1)$ $\wedge$ ˇp])   (def. of ↑ [twice])

    d. $\lambda P \lambda Q \forall x_2[\text{ˇ}P(x_2)] \rightarrow$ ˇ$Q(x_2)$](ˆ$\lambda u \lambda p$[man(u) $\wedge$ ˇp])(ˆ$\lambda u_2 \lambda p$ [love$'(u_2,u_1)$])
       (def. of every$_2$)

    e. $\underline{\forall} x_2[$ˇˆ$\lambda u \lambda p$ [man(u) $\wedge$ ˇp]$(x_2) \rightarrow$ ˇˆ$\lambda u_2 \lambda p$[love$'(u_2,u_1)$](x_2)]   (λ-conv.
      [twice])

    f. $\underline{\forall} x_2[\lambda u \lambda p$ [man(u) $\wedge$ ˇp]$(x_2) \rightarrow \lambda u_2 \lambda p$ [love$'(u_2,u_1)$](x_2)]   (ˇˆ-canc. [twice])

    g. $\underline{\forall} x_2[\lambda p$ [man(x_2) $\wedge$ ˇp] $\rightarrow \lambda p$ [love$'(x_2,u_1)$]]   (λ-conv. [twice])

    h. ↑ $\forall x_2$[man$(x_2) \rightarrow$ love$'(x_2,u_1)$]   (def. of $\underline{\forall}$, $\rightarrow$, ↑)

By substituting (h) for the underlined portion in (a), we get (i):

    i. a_1(ˆ ↑ woman)(ˆ$\lambda u_1 \lambda p$ [$\forall x_2$[man$(x_2) \rightarrow$ love$'(x_2,u_1)$] $\wedge$ ˇp])

Through steps parallel to (b)–(h), (i) reduces to (j):

    j. $\lambda p \exists x_1$[woman(x_1) $\wedge$ $\forall x_2$[man$(x_2) \rightarrow$ love$'(x_2,x_1)$] $\wedge$ ˇp]

Exercise 8

The task was to show the equivalence of (a) and (b):

    a. ↓ EVERY$'$(ˆ$\underline{\lambda} x_i \underline{\exists} x_i$ ↑ man(x_i))(ˆ$\underline{\lambda} x_i$ ↑ tall(x_i))

    b. $\forall u$[man(u) $\rightarrow$ tall(u)]

We proceed as follows:

    c. ↓ ↑ [↓ ˆλx_i $\underline{\exists} x_i$ ↑ man(x_i) $\subseteq$ ↓ [ˆ$\underline{\lambda} x_i \underline{\exists} x_i$ ↑ man(x_i) $\triangle$ ˆλx_i ↑ tall(x_i)]]
      (from (a), def. of EVERY$'$ [cf. iv in Appendix to this chapter])

    d. [↓ $\underline{\lambda} x_i \underline{\exists} x_i$ ↑ man(x_i) $\subseteq$ ↓ [ˆ$\underline{\lambda}$ $x_i \underline{\exists} x_i$ ↑ man(x_i) $\triangle$ ˆ$\underline{\lambda} x_i$ ↑ tall(x_i)]]   (↓
      ↑-canc.)

    e. [↓ ˆ$\lambda u_i \underline{\exists} x_i$ ↑ man(x_i) $\triangle$ ↑ x_i = u_i $\subseteq$ ↓ [ˆ$\lambda u_i \underline{\exists} x_i$ ↑ man(x_i) $\triangle$ ↑ x_i = u_i
      $\triangle$ ˆλu_i ↑ tall(x_i) $\triangle$ ↑ x_i = u_i]]   (def. of λ)

    f. [↓ ˆ$\lambda u_i \underline{\exists} x_i$ ↑ man(x_i) $\triangle$ ↑ x_i = u_i $\subseteq$ ↓ [ˆ$\lambda u_i \underline{\exists} x_i$ ↑ man(x_i) $\triangle$ ↑ x_i = u_i
      $\triangle$ ↑ tall(x_i) $\triangle$ ↑ x_i = u_i]]   (def. of $\triangle$)

    g. [↓ ˆ$\lambda u_i \underline{\exists} x_i$ ↑ man(x_i) $\triangle$ ↑ x_i = u_i $\subseteq$ ↓ [ˆ$\lambda u_i \underline{\exists} x_i$ ↑ man(x_i) $\triangle$ ↑ tall(x_i)
      $\triangle$ ↑ x_i = u_i]]   (taut.)

    h. [$\lambda u_i \exists x_i$[man(x_i) $\wedge$ x_i = u_i] $\subseteq$ [$\lambda u_i \exists x_i$[man(x_i) $\wedge$ tall(x_i) $\wedge$ x_i = u_i]]   (def.
      of ↓)

    i. [λu [man(u)] $\subseteq \lambda u$[man(u) $\wedge$ tall(u)]]   (taut.)

    j. [λu [man(u)] $\subseteq \lambda u$[tall(u)]]   (set theory)

This is equivalent to (b) above.

3   Extensions: Reconstruction, Topicalization, and Crossover

3.1 INTRODUCTION

In this chapter, I will explore how Dynamic Binding deals with a set of facts that have not received much attention in the literature. These have to do with backwards dependencies involving both right- and left-adjoined *if/when*-clauses, as well as other kinds of adjuncts. Up to now we have followed classical DRT in maintaining that indefinites in an *if*-clause are accessible to pronouns in the main clause, but not vice versa. There are, however, cases where this does not hold; for example:

(1)   a. If it is overcooked, a hamburger usually doesn't taste good.
          b. A hamburger usually doesn't taste good if it is overcooked.

In (1a) the subject of the main clause antecedes a pronoun in a left-adjoined *if*-clause. In (1b), it antecedes a pronoun in a right-adjoined *if*-clause. Note also that when it is right adjoined, the *if*-clause is still understood as being part of the restriction of the quantificational adverb. Plainly, we need a way of incorporating within the restriction material internal to the main clause. Understanding what is going on will lead us to some very fundamental issues having to do with the binding theory and crossover phenomena. I will argue that the proper treatment of sentences such as those in (1) not only calls for a dynamic approach to meaning, but actually provides arguments of a novel kind in its favor.

This chapter is organized as follows. In the rest of this section, I will present the relevant data. In section 3.2, I will outline my proposal in an informal way. In section 3.3, I will discuss the formal underpinnings of what was proposed in section 3.2 and consider some of its consequences. Finally, in section 3.4, I will extend my proposal further to yet another set of facts.

I will begin by considering two related sets of data. The first concerns backwards anaphoric dependencies into left-adjoined *if/when*-clauses. The second concerns right-adjoined *if/when*-clauses. It turns out that these dependencies display a number of prima facie puzzling features.

3.1.1 Left-Adjoined *If/When*-Clauses

In describing the data that follow, I will use XP^a to mark a constituent XP which contains a donkey antecedent and XP^p to mark a constituent that contains a donkey pronoun. Let us now consider what patterns of backwards dependencies one finds in left-adjoined *if/when*-clauses. A first thing to note is that the number of such dependencies is not limited to one. The following sentences all appear to be well-formed on the intended reading:

(2)   [if/when NP^p VP^p] [NP^a VP^a]
    a. If he$_i$ consider it$_j$ too difficult, a teacher$_i$ won't adopt a textbook$_j$.
    b. If she$_i$ finds it$_j$ spectacular, a photographer$_i$ takes many pictures of a landscape$_j$.
    c. If it$_i$ enters his$_j$ territory, a pirate$_j$ usually attacks a ship$_i$.

Notice that there doesn't seem to be any obvious restriction as to the main clause position of the antecedents. They can be in subject or object position, as well as embedded within an NP (as in *many pictures of a landscape* in (2b)). Notice also that the anaphoric dependencies can be crossing (as in (2a,b)) or nested (as in (2c)).

Interestingly, one also finds "mixed" patterns, where donkey pronouns and antecedents appear together in the *if/when*-clause:

(3)   [if/when NP^p VP^a] [NP^a VP^p]
    a. When it$_i$ spots a mouse$_j$, a cat$_i$ attacks it$_j$.
    b. If he$_i$ lies to a student$_j$, a teacher$_i$ loses his$_j$ trust.

Here a donkey pronoun in the *if/when*-clause is anteceded by material in the main clause, while at the same time there is a dependency going in the opposite direction (i.e., the VP-internal argument in the *if/when*-clause antecedes a donkey pronoun in the main clause). The pronoun–antecedent order in the *if/when*-clause doesn't seem to matter, as the following examples show:

(4)   [if/when NP^a VP^p] [NP^a VP^p]
    a. If a boy$_i$ lies to her$_j$, a girl$_j$ won't trust him$_i$ anymore.
    b. When a foreigner$_i$ asks him$_j$ for directions, [a person from Milan]$_j$ replies to him$_i$ with courtesy (while somebody from Rome doesn't always).

Here we have an indefinite in the subject position of an *if/when*-clause anteceding a donkey pronoun in the main clause, while at the same time material in the main clause antecedes a donkey pronoun in the *if/when*-clause. Surprisingly, however, the pronoun–antecedent order in the *main* clause does make a difference:

(5)   *[if/when NP^p VP^a] [NP^p VP^a]
    a. *If she$_i$ lies to a boy$_j$, he$_j$ won't trust a girl$_i$ anymore.
    b. *When he$_i$ spots a ship$_j$, it$_j$ is attacked by a pirate$_i$.

The contrast in grammaticality between (2)–(4) and (5) is quite striking. If the order in the main clause is [NP^p VP^a], changing the pronoun–antecedent order in the *if/when*-clause doesn't restore grammaticality:

(6)   *[if/when NP^a VP^p] [NP^p VP^a]
       a.   *If a boy$_i$ lies to her$_j$, he$_i$ loses a girlfriend$_j$.
       b.   *When a cat$_i$ spots it$_j$, it$_i$ attacks a mouse$_j$.

These examples are still considerably degraded, relative to (2)–(4).[1] Thus we find a systematic gap in the paradigm of backwards dependencies: there can't be a pronoun in the subject position of the main clause.

    These observations can be summarized as follows:

(7)   *Paradigm of Backwards Donkey Dependencies:*
       [if/when NP^p VP^p] [**NP^a VP^a**]
       [if/when NP^a VP^p] [**NP^a VP^p**]
       [if/when NP^p VP^a] [**NP^a VP^p**]
       *[if/when NP^p VP^a] [**NP^p VP^a**]
       *[if/when NP^a VP^p] [**NP^p VP$_a$**]

It should be emphasized that the gap in (7) is not a ban against pronouns in subject position of the main clause as such, for these are allowed in standard donkey sentences (e.g., *If a farmer$_i$ owns a donkey$_j$, he$_i$ beats it$_j$*). Nor can such a gap be imputed to some general prohibition against a VP-internal indefinite in the main clause anteceding a pronoun in the *if/when*-clause, for that is also possible, as evidenced by the examples in (2). It appears to be the combination of a pronoun in the subject position of the main clause with the presence of backwards dependencies that results in ungrammaticality. The generalization can be stated in the following terms:

(8)   *Pronominal Subject Constraint:* No NP in the *if/when*-clause can antecede a pronoun in the subject position of the main clause if there is a dependency going backwards from the main clause to the *if/ when*-clause.

The nature of this constraint is prima facie quite mysterious. It doesn't lend itself readily to some kind of functional or processing explanation. And our intuitions about it appear to be fairly solid and systematic (in spite of the low frequency of occurrence of these constructions). This is the kind of data that raises serious issues of learnability. If this constraint doesn't follow from general principles, it is hard to see how a native speaker could ever come to have the relevant intuitions.

3.1.2 Right-Adjoined *If/When*-Clauses

It is worth contrasting the data in the previous section with corresponding sentences involving right-adjoined *if/when*-clauses. Here, too, we find cases of backwards and forward anaphora. Consider the following examples:

(9) $[NP^a\ VP^a\ [if\ NP^p\ VP^p]]$
        a. A painter$_i$ is inspired by a village$_j$ if she$_i$ finds it$_j$ picturesque.
        $[NP^a\ VP^p\ [if\ NP^p\ VP^a]]$
        b. A painter$_i$ will rent it$_j$ if she$_i$ finds a cottage$_j$ picturesque.
        $[NP^a\ VP^p\ [if\ NP^a\ VP^p]]$
        c. A rich, capricious person$_i$ will buy it$_j$ right away if a nice car$_j$ impresses him$_i$.

From (9a), we see that indefinites can antecede pronouns in right-adjoined *if/when*-clauses, either from the subject position or from a VP-interal position. From (9b–c), we see that anaphora can simultaneously go in both directions with right-adjoined *if/when*-clauses, just as with left-adjoined ones.[2] However, there are certain anaphoric links that are also ill-formed when right-adjoined *if/when*-clauses are involved. In particular, a pronoun in subject position cannot be bound by an indefinite in a right-adjoined clause. The following examples illustrate this:

(10)   a.   *He$_i$ is happy when a man$_i$ sings.
        b.   When a man$_i$ sings he$_i$ is happy.

The restriction exemplified in (10a) differs from the Pronominal Subject Constraint in that while the latter is operative only in the presence of backward dependencies, the restriction in (10a) is operative regardless of the presence or absence of other dependencies. The ungrammaticality of sentences like (10a) has been previously observed in the literature (for example in Reinhart 1976, 1983a,b) and, unlike the Pronominal Subject Constraint, has a natural explanation within current approaches to binding. The explanation is phrased in terms of Principle C of the binding theory, under the assumption that the right-adjoined *if/when*-clauses are in a position where they are c-commanded by the matrix subject. This would be so if, for example, the *if/when*-clause were attached either to I′ or lower:

(11)   a.

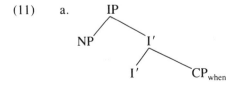

b.
```
        IP
      /    \
    NP      I′
           /  \
          I    TP
              /  \
            TP   CP_when
```

TP (= Tense Phrase) in (11b) is assumed to be a functional head intermediate between the outermost one (here IP, which would correspond to Subject Agreement in, e.g., Chomsky 1992) and VP. To avoid having to write this extra structure every time, I will adopt (11a) (but nothing hinges on this; see Iatridou 1991 for relevant discussion). If adjunction to a position c-commanded by the subject is the only option for right-adjoined *if/when*-clauses, then the ungrammaticality of (11a) can be accounted for in terms of the principle requiring pronouns not to both precede and c-command their antecedents (i.e., Principle C of the binding theory). That is, (10a) is ungrammatical for the same reasons for which *He_i likes every man_i* is ungrammatical.[3]

So the main issue in need of an account, as far as right-adjoined *if/when*-clauses are concerned, is how the anaphoric links in (9) come about. Given our current assumptions (i.e., material in the restriction is accessible to the nuclear scope, but not vice versa), it is not clear how their interpretation is to be obtained.

3.2. THE PROPOSAL

I will argue that a rather straightforward extension of Dynamic Binding as formulated in chapter 2 provides us with a simple account of the data considered in the previous section. First I will review our basic assumptions concerning Dynamic Binding. Then I will discuss right-adjoined and left-adjoined *if/when*-clauses in turn. In the present section, I will give a largely informal presentation of the main idea. In subsequent sections, I will flesh out in more detail how this main idea is to be implemented and what its major syntactic and semantic consequences are. The technical details can be found in the appendix to this chapter.

3.2.1 Background

Let us begin by reviewing our main assumptions so far. Expressions are interpreted dynamically in terms of their context change potential. Indefinites set up 'discourse referents' whose semantic scope extends beyond their c-command domain, while other NPs do not. Indefinites are viewed as "open-ended," existentially quantified terms.

A basic tenet of DRT is that a left-adjoined *if/when*-clause is generally part of the restriction of a quantificational adverb (Q-adverb). A Q-adverb can bind the situation variable introduced by the *if/when*-clause or one or more of the indefinites that occur in it. Even though indefinites are interpreted as being existentially quantified, their open character enables them to behave as variables when embedded under Q-adverbs. Technically, this is achieved through an operation of Existential Disclosure (ED) that turns indefinites into variables in the restriction of a Q-adverb. This is the opposite of what happens in classical DRT, where indefinites are assimilated to free variables and undergo an operation of Existential Closure ($\exists$-closure) in certain environments. In the previous chapter, I argued that an approach based on ED offers some advantages over classical DRT. In particular, $\exists$-closure has to apply to a disjunctively specified set of environments, while ED applies (freely) to indefinites in the domain of a Q-adverb. I assume that ED is marked at LF by indexing Q-adverbs. Here are some examples, repeated from chapter 2.

(12)   a. When John is in the bathtub, he usually sings.
        a.' usually$_s$ [$_{CP_s}$ when John is in the bathtub] [he sings]
        b. If a painter lives in a village, it is usually pretty.
        b'. usually$_j$ [a painter$_j$ lives in a village$_i$] [it$_i$ is pretty]
        b". usually$_i$ [a painter$_j$ lives in a village$_i$] [it$_i$ is pretty]

The LF in (12a') represents the reading where we quantify over situations in which John is in the bathtub. This is the only plausible reading for (12a) as there are no indefinites in it. The LF in (12b) represents the subject-asymmetric reading of (12b) (i.e., 'Most painters that live in a village live in a pretty one'), while (12b") represents its object-asymmetric reading (i.e., 'Most villages inhabited by a painter are pretty').

This, in its barest outline, is the approach developed in chapter 2. We will now proceed to flesh it out some more in light of the evidence discussed above.

3.2.2 The Logical Form of Tripartite Structures

So far we have assumed that Q-adverbs give rise at LF to tripartite structures of the form shown in (13), where 'Re' is the restriction and 'Sc' the scope.

(13)   XP

                ADV   Re   Sc

However, if we take LF as being determined by X' theory and if we assume binary branching, then (13) is not viable as a LF representation. Two possible alternatives might be the following:

(14)   a.

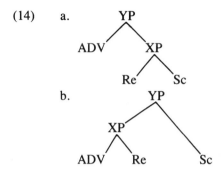

But both of these structures appear to be problematic. For one thing, it is not obvious how to interpret (14a) compositionally. The constituent XP in (14a) includes both the restriction and the scope. But they can be interpreted as such only relative to the Q-adverb, which is not part of XP. In other terms, the Q-adverb is a relation and its arguments cannot be interpreted qua arguments without it, just as in *John loves Mary, John . . . Mary* cannot be interpreted without *loves*. Special interpretive procedures can always be devised, but it would be interesting to see whether this is avoidable. As far as (14b) is concerned, it is not clear how to obtain it syntactically, given current assumptions about movement. At S-structure, the Q-adverb is generally part of the main clause. So its position at LF must be obtained by raising it to a higher position after "spell-out" (i.e., after the operation that maps syntactic representations into phonetic ones). But this would result in a movement of the following kind:

(15)   a.

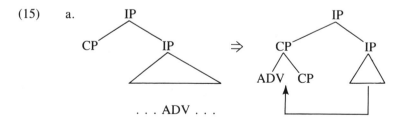

It is not clear how to obtain a structure of this sort on the basis of standard assumptions about movement, as ADV winds up adjoined to a position which is too low in the tree. Again, we can devise some mechanism that accomplishes the task, but it might be worthwhile to try to avoid doing so, at least as an initial strategy.

In view of this situation, I propose to adopt the following format for structures involving Q-adverbs:

(16)

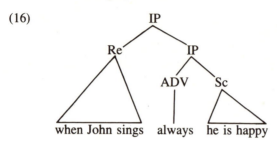

The assumption here is that wherever it may be at S-structure, at LF a Q-adverb selects its scope by adjoining to it. The scope of the adverb is simply its c-command domain (at LF). This is consistent with standard assumptions about movement and yields structures that are amenable to a rather straightforward compositional interpretation. The adverb is simply interpreted as a relation that combines with its relata one at a time (much as in *John loves Mary*, we interpret *love Mary* first and then apply the result to *John*). Furthermore, on the basis of the LF in (16), we can define the restriction of a Q-adverb as what c-commands the adverb locally (i.e., from within the same maximal projection). Nothing essential in how the semantics works changes under these new assumptions. All we have done is regularize the relevant LFs a bit, by making them consistent with X′-theoretic assumptions.[4] (See the Appendix, part I, for details.)

The present hypothesis has another desirable consequence: we can altogether dispense with the Novelty Condition, thereby simplifying the theory further. There were essentially two kinds of sentences that in classical DRT were used to motivate the Novelty Condition, namely:

(17)   a. An Italian$_i$ was tall. An American$_i$ was blond.
        b. If an Italian$_i$ is tall, an American$_i$ is usually blond.
        c.

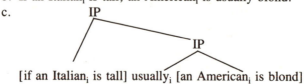

[if an Italian$_i$ is tall] usually$_i$ [an American$_i$ is blond]

On a Dynamic Binding approach, (17a) was never a problem. Indefinites are existentially quantified, and *an American$_i$* would introduce a new quantifier that resets the context so that the values of the two indefinites (even if coindexed) would be independent of each other. Under our new proposal, (17b) also ceases to be a problem. The structure of (17b) at LF will be (17c). Here *an American* is coindexed with a c-commanding chain formed by *an Italian* and the adverb *usually,* which jointly act as its binder. Hence we have a bound R-expression, which is ruled out by Principle C. So the problematic indexing turns out to be excluded by the binding theory.[5] Under the new assumptions, there is no way for an indefinite in the restriction to get cobound with an indefinite in the scope. The effects of the Novelty Condition are derivable, and an independent constraint to deal with them is no longer called for.

3.2.3 The Syntax and Semantics of Right-Adjoined *If/When*-Clauses

The new tripartite structures discussed in the previous section are straightforward to construct for left-adjoined *if/when*-clauses. It suffices to adjoin the adverb to the main clause. The interesting question now becomes whether tripartite structures of this kind can also be constructed for right-adjoined *if/ when*-clauses. This relates to what Diesing (1992) calls "clause splitting" or "partitioning." My proposal owes much to hers, even though it differs from it in nontrivial ways.[6] In showing how tripartite structures are to be constructed and interpreted in the case of right-adjoined *if/when*-clauses I will proceed inductively, by looking at examples in order of increasing complexity. Consider first the following simple case:

(18)   a. A cat$_j$ usually$_j$ meows if it$_j$ is hungry.
        b.

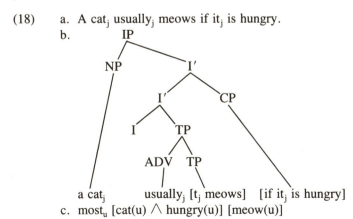

        c. most$_u$ [cat(u) $\wedge$ hungry(u)] [meow(u)]

Suppose that at LF the Q-adverb is adjoined to TP (which, in this case, might also be its S-structure position). Its scope is thus set to TP. The *if*-clause and the subject NP are external to the scope of *usually* and locally c-command it. We can therefore take them as jointly forming the restriction. They are interpretively integrated as shown in (18c).

We can restate what is going on in the following terms. Besides admitting tripartite structures of the form in (19a), we will also admit tripartite structures of the form in (19b):

(19)   a.

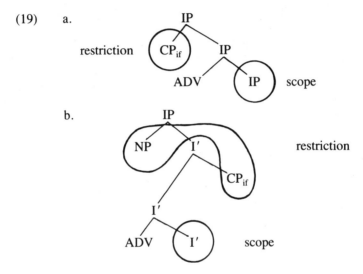

The structure in (19b) differs from the one in (19a) in two ways: (i) the *if/when*-clause occurs to the right; (ii) besides the *if/when*-clause, there is other material that locally c-commands the Q-adverb and its scope. Whether an *if/when*-clause occurs to the right or to the left doesn't affect the way it is interpreted. And the other material outside the scope can easily be semantically incorporated in the restriction, together with the *if/when*-clause.

In structures like (18b), we want to integrate NPs coming from the main clause (in this case, the subject) together with the right-adjoined *if/when*-clause. The most straightforward way to do so is by shifting the type of NPs to that of formulae and then simply conjoining the NP in question with the *if/when*-clause. It is trivial to devise a suitable type-shifting mechanism that achieves that (cf. the appendix, part II).[7] We turn the NP *a cat* into a formula which we then conjoin (dynamically) with the *if/when*-clause. Since we use

Dynamic Binding, the NP *a cat* will bind the pronoun *it* in the *if*-clause. The result undergoes Existential Disclosure, just like before, and provides us with the restriction for the Q-adverb.

The nodes in the sequence ⟨a cat$_i$, usually$_i$, t$_i$⟩ in (18b) are coindexed, and each item c-commands the items to its right. They therefore form a chain. In this chain, *usually* is the operator, *a cat* determines the range (= restriction), and t$_i$ is the variable bound by the operator. The *if*-clause is a modifier of the restriction (much as a relative clause is in quantified NPs like *every boy that John met,* where *boy* is the restriction of *every* and *that John met* modifies *boy*).

We assume that in general the Q-adverb is completely free to select its scope, by adjoining to it at LF. Certain choices may, however, result in structures that are uninterpretable or otherwise deviant. For example, if in (18b) we were to adjoin *usually* to the top IP, the Q-adverb would be left without a restriction and the resulting structure would be uninterpretable.

Let us now show that the splitting algorithm just outlined works also with more challenging examples. Consider:

(20)   a. A computer usually routes a plane$_i$, if it$_i$ is modern.
        b.

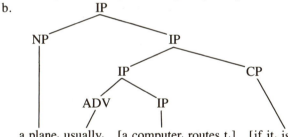

         a plane$_i$ usually$_i$ [a computer$_j$ routes t$_i$]   [if it$_i$ is modern]
        c. most u [plane(u) $\wedge$ modern(u)] $\exists$v[computer(v) $\wedge$ route(v,u)]

Sentence (20a) has many interpretations. The pragmatically most plausible one says roughly that most modern planes are routed by a computer. In order to obtain this reading, we must select the scope in such a way that the subject is included in it. This can be done by adjoining *usually* to IP at LF. Having done that, we must extrapose the *if*-clause to a position where it c-commands *usually,* for we want the *if*-clause to be in the restriction. Finally, we pull the object NP out of the scope and adjoin it to IP, where it is incorporated in the restriction. All this (which is obtained using Move α in familiar ways) results in the desired interpretation, viz. (20c).

Our splitting algorithm may, of course, generate structures that are some-

how deviant and hence ruled out by the other, independent features of
the theory. Suppose, for example, that we were to adjoin the object NP
in (20a) to a position where it does not c-command the (extraposed) CP.
In other words, suppose we end up with a structure of the following
type:

(21)

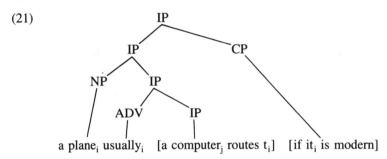

a plane$_i$ usually$_i$ [a computer$_j$ routes t$_i$] [if it$_i$ is modern]

In this case, *a plane* wouldn't be able to antecede the pronoun *it*, for the
following reasons. First, *a plane* does not c-command *it* and hence cannot
statically bind it. Second, the pronoun *it* is not accessible to the indefinite,
for the binder closest to *a plane* under this analysis is *usually*, which does
not c-command the pronoun *it*, and hence Dynamic Binding is also impossible.

It is perhaps worthwhile to reiterate that however the scope is selected,
the *if/when*-clause must always end up in the restriction of a Q-adverb.[8] In
the present terms, wherever we adjoin the Q-adverb, we want the *if/when*-
clause (if present) to locally c-command it. Some version of this configurational requirement is assumed within every variety of DRT. One way to go
is to assign to *if/when*-clauses a semantic type incompatible with their being
included in the scope of a Q-adverb (or in a structure that lacks a Q-adverb
altogether). We might, for example, assume that *if/when*-clauses are interpreted as propositions. Since they are not root sentences, in order for them
to be interpreted their meaning must be integrated with the meaning of the
main clause. And for that to happen there has to be a suitable operator (i.e.,
a Q-adverb) in their immediate environment. While the details need to be
worked out further, an approach along these lines appears prima facie plausible.[9]

The splitting algorithm just developed can handle, without additional stipulations, cases where one antecedent is in the main clause and one in the *if/
when*-clause, as in the following variation on (96) above:

(22)   a. A painter$_i$ usually rents it$_j$ if she$_i$ finds a cottage$_j$ picturesque.
        b.

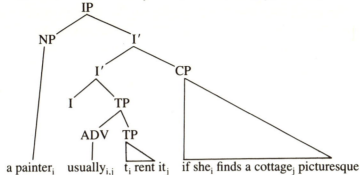

a painter$_i$ usually$_{i,j}$ t$_i$ rent it$_j$ if she$_i$ finds a cottage$_j$ picturesque

This structure turns out to be rather straightforward. The Q-adverb is adjoined to TP. In this way, the subject and the *if*-clause are incorporated in the restriction. The Q-adverb then discloses the subject in the main clause and the object in the *if*-clause.

As is evident from these examples, I am assuming that quantificational NPs can be left in situ. Actually, what we have so far could be modified as to make it compatible with the assumption, often found in the literature, that quantificational NPs are always scoped by moving them to an A′-position. But I really see no need to do so. Nothing in the syntax forces NPs to move to an A′-position at LF. In general, it is assumed that quantificational NPs must move in order to be interpretable—that is, for semantic reasons. This, however, is not quite true. We know since the publication of Montague 1973 that quantificational NPs can be interpreted in situ. If one doesn't like Montague's way of doing so, there are other, more recent approaches (involving for example, type-shifting) that are rather elegant. In fact, in some cases (including the present one) it seems that forcing NPs to raise leads to a more complicated semantics. For these reasons, I will maintain that Quantifier Raising (QR) is completely optional. If a quantificational NP doesn't move, its scope will still be defined as what it c-commands. Thus a sentence like, say, (23a) below has several well-formed LFs. One is (23a) itself. In this case the subject will have wide scope over the object.

(23)   a. [$_{IP}$ a technician [$_{I'}$ inspected every plane]]
        b. [every plane$_i$ [$_{IP}$ a technician$_j$ inspected t$_i$]]

Another well-formed LF for the sentence in question will be (23b), where the object has scope over the subject. And so on. This approach, based on good old Occam's principle "Do not do things you don't have to do," also has the advantage of being compatible with Montague's treatment of intensional verbs, which to my knowledge has no viable alternative to this date.[10]

As a further case, consider the following:

(24)   a. A teacher usually won't adopt a textbook if he finds it too difficult.

    b.

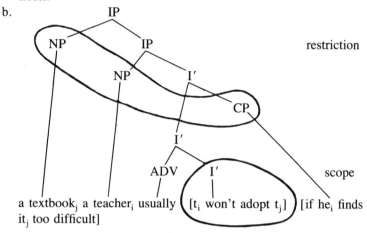

Here we adjoin the Q-adverb to I′ and move the object out of the scope. So we wind up with two NPs besides the *if*-clause in the restriction.

In general, we build up logical forms of the type given in (25a), which are interpreted as schematically indicated in (25b):

(25)   a. $[NP_1, \ldots, NP_n [ADV \; XP] \; CP]$
        b. $ADV \; ([NP_1 \wedge \ldots \wedge NP_n \wedge CP_{if}], XP)$

Hence, by adopting the tripartite structures sketched in the previous section and adapting Dynamic Binding accordingly, we can handle right-adjoined *if*/*when*-clauses in a simple way. (See the appendix, part III, for technical details.)

To summarize so far, the (possibly null) Q-adverb freely selects its scope by adjoining to it at LF. The restriction is what locally c-commands the Q-adverb. Ordinary types of movement (NP preposing, extraposition) concur in creating the intended LF. With this much in mind, we now turn to a consideration of backwards anaphora involving left-adjoined *if/when*-clauses.

3.2.4 Fronted Adjuncts and Principle C

To see what problems are involved in dealing with backwards anaphora in left-adjoined *if/when*-clauses, let us consider a simple example:

(26)   When it$_i$ is hungry, a cat$_i$ usually meows.

Suppose that we start out with a structure like the following:

(27)   a.

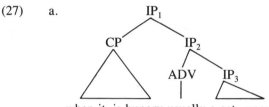

when it$_i$ is hungry usually a cat$_i$ meows
    b. [$_{IP_1}$ when it$_i$ is hungry [a cat$_i$ [$_{IP_2}$ usually$_i$ [t$_i$ meows]]]]
    c. [a cat$_i$ [$_{IP_1}$ when it$_i$ is hungry [$_{IP_2}$ usually$_i$ [t$_i$ meows]]]]

In order to bring *cat* into the restriction we have to raise it. But if we adjoin it to IP$_2$, as shown in (27b), *a cat* will fail to c-command (or be accessible to) the pronoun in the *when*-clause. If we adjoin it to IP$_1$, as shown in (27c), it will be able to antecede *it,* but the resulting structure is expected to be a Weak Crossover (WCO) violation. We could, of course, stipulate that generic indefinites are exempted from Weak Crossover. But that would be a very boring move. And it would probably not help anyway. For suppose that something makes WCO irrelevant to the structures under consideration. Suppose that NPs can be scoped to a position where they c-command pronouns in a left-adjoined *if/when*-clause. What would then be the reason for the Pronominal Subject Constraint? We would be completely in the dark as to why precisely the pattern in (7) should arise.

It is appropriate at this point to discuss briefly what assumptions I will be making concerning Weak Crossover. I will assume here a very simpleminded approach to it, based on Leftness along the lines of Jacobson 1977 and Chomsky 1976:

(28)   a. * *Leftness:* * Q$_i$ [. . . pro$_i$ . . . t$_i$ . . .],   where ⟨Q$_i$ . . . t$_i$ . . .⟩
            is an A′-chain
        b. Quantificational NPs must be novel.

Arguably, (28a) can be viewed as a novelty condition on nonpronominal NPs. Such NPs must be novel in their c-command domain, where novelty is formally construed as the requirement that their traces not be co-bound to a pronoun on their left at LF. So for example, in (27c) we have a chain ⟨a cat$_i$, usually$_i$, t$_i$⟩ whose tail is co-bound with the pronoun *it,* in violation of WCO. It is conceivable that (28) may be derived from something more general. If that turns out to be the case, so much the better. At present, I do not see how to draw such connection. In particular, I do not see how what we need can be derived in terms of the Bijection Principle (see Koopman and Sportiche 1982), for reasons that will become apparent in the course of this chapter.

This formulation of WCO is generally thought to be beset by severe problems. So a brief excursus is needed to give an indication of how I think such problems should be dealt with. I will briefly mention two families of issues that have been discussed in the literature. One has to do with sentences like the following, discussed in Higginbotham 1980, 1983:

(29)   a. Some musician$_i$ will play [every piece you want him$_i$ to]$_j$.
        b. [some musician$_i$ [every piece you want him$_i$ to]$_j$ [t$_i$ will play t$_j$]]

The problem is that if the object in (29) must be assigned scope, the pronoun *him* winds up in a position where Leftness is violated. Yet sentence (29) is perfectly grammatical. There are two ways to go in this situation. We can complicate the definition of Leftness (e.g., along the lines discussed in Higginbotham's work). Or we can give up the idea that QR is obligatory. The second line is the one we have chosen here. In a theory like ours, where NPs have the option of being interpreted in situ, (29a) can be assigned the intended interpretation without scoping the object out, and hence we can stick to a simpler characterization of Leftness.[11]

The second set of problems has to do with the fact that (28) appears not to stand much of a chance for holding up crosslinguistically, in view of the variety of word orders one finds in the languages of the world. For example, a complicated debate is currently taking place concerning the interaction of WCO and scrambling, for languages that have both. There is a great deal of disagreement as to what the facts are, and I will not try to take a stand on the matter. A related issue concerns what one would expect to happen in languages with different basic word orders, like, say, VOS languages. This in turn depends on what WCO phenomenology one finds in these languages and what the right analysis of the VOS order turns out to be. Suppose, for example, that the order of the base is universally SVO (as Kayne 1993 proposes) and that other orders are derived via movement. Then one could try to generalize (28) so as to make it sensitive to the underlying order in VOS languages. Alternatively, one could imagine that whatever is responsible for the position of the subject in VOS languages also forces QR to adjoin quantifiers to the right. In this case, we could simply use the mirror image of (28) for VOS languages. In order words, the position of the subject, the landing site for QR, Leftness, and possibly more would all be subsumed under the same parameter. The fact of the matter is that at present we just do not know what the correct answer to these questions is. However, it is by no means obvious to me that an approach based on Leftness is going to be inherently more problematic in dealing with crosslinguistic variation than a purely hierarchical one.

Going back to our main topic, it is clear that if we adopt Leftness, there is no way of bringing the antecedent into the restriction in structures like (27) by raising it. However, there is an alternative analysis for left-adjoined *if/when*-clauses. We have seen that they can be generated within IP. If that is so, then they can presumably also be fronted from that IP-internal position. In other words, a left-adjoined *if/when*-clause, besides being base generated in that position, could also be topicalized from an IP-internal position. This would result in structures of roughly the following kind:

(30)

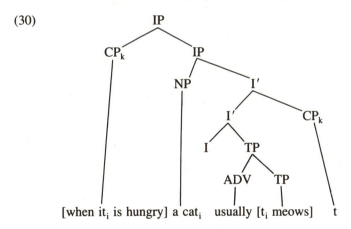

This structure opens up a new possibility: that of interpreting the left-adjoined *when*-clause relative to its "base" position.[12] Let us say, for the time being, that a *when*-clause like the one in (30) can be *reconstructed* back into the IP-internal position and that it is the reconstructed structure that gets interpreted:

(31)

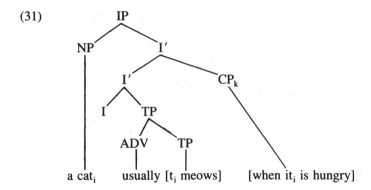

a cat$_i$ usually [t$_i$ meows]   [when it$_i$ is hungry]

In (31) we have a right-adjoined *when*-clause, which we know how to interpret. Both the NP *a cat* and the *when*-clause are in the restriction of *usually*. The pronoun is to the right of the trace it is co-bound with; hence no WCO violation ensures. All our problems just disappear.

We must of course understand better what exactly is meant by "reconstruction" here. But let us hold that off for a moment and explore some of the consequences of the view just sketched. For the time being, I use "reconstruction" as a purely descriptive label for the process that enables us to treat a left-adjoined *when*-clause as if it was in its original site. I will get to a more thorough discussion of reconstruction in the next section.

There is an immediate consequence of this analysis. If reconstruction is the only way in which backwards dependencies in left-adjoined clauses can be obtained, then the Pronominal Subject Constraint is just a straightforward Principle C effect. Consider some of the typical manifestations of such a constraint, like the sentences in (32) (a variant of those in (5) and (6)):

(32)   a.   *If she$_i$ lies to a boy$_j$, he$_j$ usually won't trust a girl$_i$ anymore.
        b.   *If a boy$_i$ lies to her$_j$, he$_i$ usually loses a girlfriend$_j$.

Since these constructions involve backwards dependencies, it must be assumed that they are fronted from an IP-internal position and their semantics has to be done in terms of the following structures:

(33)   a.   [he$_j$ [won't trust a girl$_i$ anymore if she$_i$ lies to a boy$_j$]]
        b.   [he$_i$ [loses a girlfriend$_j$ if a boy$_i$ lies to her$_j$]]

The structures in (33) clearly constitute a flat violation of Principle C. The Pronominal Subject Constraint singles out exactly the cases where we have a pronoun in the subject position of the main clause. But such pronouns will inexorably end up c-commanding their antecedents at the reconstructed level; whence the ungrammaticality. A seemingly bizarre gap in the paradigm of backwards anaphora is accounted for in terms of a very basic principle of grammar.

Nothing prevents a left-adjoined *if/when*-clause from being generated to the left (without being topicalized from an IP-internal position). In such a case a donkey antecedent in the *if*-clause will be able to bind a pronoun in the subject position of the main clause. This is what happens with "ordinary" donkey anaphora like the following:

(34)

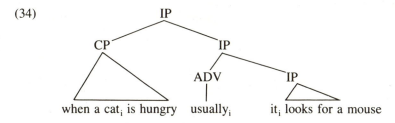

when a cat$_i$ is hungry   usually$_i$ it$_i$ looks for a mouse

But then, there is no way that material in the main clause can possibly antecede material in the *if/when*-clause. The reconstruction option is not available; if it was, Principle C would immediately kick in, ruling the sentence out. And raising of an NP in the main clause to a position where it is accessible to a pronoun in the *if*-clause will be ruled out by whatever takes care of WCO effects.

To summarize so far, my proposal admits two possibilities, which are schematically listed in (35):

(35)   *Case (i)*. Left-adjoined *if/when*-clauses are topicalized from an IP-internal position.
Consequences:
→ Backwards dependencies are possible via reconstruction.
→ There cannot be a pronoun in the subject position of the main clause anteceded by an NP in the *if/when*-clause.
Case (ii). If/when-clauses are directly adjoined to the left.
Consequences:
→ Backwards dependencies are impossible (no reconstruction, WCO effects).
→ A pronoun in the subject position of the main clause can be anteceded by an NP in the *if/when*-clause.

The main advantages of this way of looking at the phenomena under consideration are three:

(36)   a. We do not have to exempt indefinites from WCO.
       b. We have a unitary mechanism to interpret both left-adjoined and right-adjoined *if/when*-clauses.
       c. We reduce the Pronominal Subject Constraint to a principle of core grammar.

It should be noted that these consequences do not depend on the particular approach to donkey anaphora I am pursuing. In particular, they do not depend on Dynamic Binding at all. Any reasonable way of dealing with donkey anaphora can be married to the ideas schematically illustrated in (35). However, I think that Dynamic Binding becomes relevant once we try to make explicit what is meant by "reconstruction." To this I now turn.

3.3 RECONSTRUCTION

So far I've been using the term "reconstruction" as a purely descriptive label to refer to processes whereby dislocated material behaves as if it was in its original site. In this section, I would like to be more explicit as to the nature of the processes under discussion. This will lead us to delve more deeply into the syntax of *if/when*-clauses and its relation to topicalization and to the binding theory.

In particular, I would like to compare two main views of reconstruction (each of which has several variants). One view is that the process happens at LF: the moved constituent ends up being put back in the trace position (or ends up having a copy in the trace position) *prior to* truth-conditional interpretation. Chomsky 1992 is one of the latest examples of this kind of approach. The other is to view reconstruction as *part of* the truth-conditional interpretation. That is, the moved constituent is interpreted as if it was in the position of the trace, without an actual syntactic reconstruction. These two strategies are not necessarily mutually exclusive. It is at least conceivable that a syntactic approach might be justified for certain constructions and an interpretive one for other constructions. This is indeed what I will end up proposing.

I will start by fleshing out these two approaches a bit more and indicating what I believe is involved in choosing between them. One thing they have in common is that neither of them has a *rule* of reconstruction. Rather, they try to use independently needed mechanisms, which I take to be a desirable goal. Let us see first how we could pursue the more syntactic approach in connection with the problem under consideration, by building on Chomsky's (1992) proposals. Chomsky has suggested going back to the view that moved phrases leave an identical copy behind. He argues that the presence of this copy in the base position enables one to deal with binding-theoretic and interpretive issues in an arguably elegant way, without a need for an independent syntactic process of reconstruction. If we adopt the copy theory of traces and assume that left-adjoined *if/when*-clauses might actually be fronted from an IP-internal position, the structure of a sentence like (37a) would look roughly as in (37b):

(37)   a. When it is hungry, a cat meows.
        b. [when it is hungry] [a cat meows [when it is hungry]]

We then have to ensure that the lower *when*-clause is not "spelled out," while the upper one is. Conversely, we have to ensure that the upper *when*-clause is ignored at LF (maybe by deleting it), while the lower one is "semantically active," as it were. It is not altogether obvious how to achieve this. One way to go is to assume a general principle according to which only the head of a chain undergoes spell-out. We could then assume that the elements of an A'-chain can be freely deleted up to recoverability at LF (after spell-out). This process would apply to A'-dependencies involving no *wh*-operator. (A'-dependencies involving a *wh*-operator would be dealt with in the manner suggested by Chomsky.) On the basis of these assumptions, at LF we would have:

(38)   ~~[when it is hungry]~~ [a cat meows [when it is hungry]]

The structure in (38) is what is semantically interpreted. The effects discussed in the previous section would then follow directly.

    While this approach has many appealing features, if it can be made precise, it is not clear that it is right for the problem at hand. Suppose that left-adjoined *if/when*-clauses are not moved but directly generated in a left-adjoined position and linked to an IP-internal position by means of an operator–variable construction. Suppose, in other words, that the right analysis of the relevant cases is along the lines of the analysis of topicalization proposed by Chomsky (1977) and schematically summarized in (39a):

(39)   a. $TOP_i \ [_{CP} \ O_i \ \ldots \ t_i \ \ldots \ ]$
        b. $John_i \ [O_i \ Bill \ likes \ t_i]$
        c. $[when \ it_i \ is \ hungry]_k \ O_k \ [a \ cat_i \ meows \ t_k]$

The operator in (30a,b,c) might either be directly generated in CP-adjoined position and linked to an IP-internal empty category, or it might be moved from within the IP. In either case, we would *not* expect t_i to be a copy of the *when*-clause, for the *when*-clause would never have been in the trace position to begin with. Consequently, an approach to reconstruction based on the copy theory of traces would not be available in the case at hand. One might try to rework the theory of operator dependencies so that operator-bound variables always end up being copies of the antecedents of operators (even when no movement is involved). But I will not try to do so here. I will stick to the more traditional theory of operator–variable constructions, while at the same time following Chomsky (1992) for *wh*-movement.

Is the analysis of topics given in (39), or one of its derivatives, compatible with the account sketched in the previous section? Yes, under two assumptions. First, we need to be able to interpret a dislocated constituent as if it was in the trace position. Second, we need to formulate the binding theory using the notion of *chain*.

The latter is an idea that has been around for a while in various forms and has been extensively studied by Barss (1986). To see, in a preliminary form, what is involved, consider one of the ungrammatical examples under discussion namely (32a) repeated her as (60a):

(40)   a.   *If she$_i$ lies to a boy$_j$, he$_j$ usually will not trust a girl$_i$.
        b.   [if she$_i$ lies to a boy$_j$]$_k$ O$_k$ [he$_j$ usually will not trust a girl$_i$ t$_k$]

In (40b), $\langle$[if she$_i$ lies to a boy$_j$]$_k$, O$_k$, t$_k\rangle$ forms a chain. The pronoun *he$_j$* in the main clause c-commands t_k, the tail of the chain. We want to say that in virtue of this, *he$_j$* qualifies as a potential antecedent for material contained in the chain as a whole. Thus, it is as if *he$_j$* c-commanded *a boy$_j$*, and this is what gives rise to a Principle C violation. Something along these lines is a fairly natural option in any framework that has chains (including one that, like Minimalism, only admits interface conditions).

The interpretive part of an analysis like the one in (39) is even more straightforward. Simply assume that the operator in structures like (39a) is (interpreted as) a λ-abstractor. So, for example, a sentence like (39b) is interpreted as in (41):

(41) λx_i [like(Bill, x$_i$)] (John) = like(Bill, John)

Clearly, this way of interpreting topicalized structures does not expand the inventory of interpretive rules, for they are going to include λ-conversion (or something that amounts to it) in anyone's theory. The interpretation of (39c) proceeds in the same manner:

(42)   λp [a cat$_i$ usually meows when p] (it$_i$ is hungry)
         = [a cat$_i$ usually meows when it$_i$ is hungry]

However, (42) has an interesting twist to it. Notice that in (42) a pronoun which is free before the conversion gets bound after the conversion. The standard (static) semantics for variable binding would not validate the conversion in (42). So this option would not be available to us in a plain static setting. What is needed is a semantics where formulae are interpreted as functions over assignments, which is precisely what we have in a dynamic setting.

Now, I believe there is evidence that at least some left-adjoined *if/when*-clauses must indeed be base-generated topics linked via an operator to an IP-internal position. This means that the approach in (39) must be the correct one for such constructions. To the extent that such an approach needs Dynamic Binding to work, it provides new empirical support for it. In what follows I will first discuss in what way exactly the approach in (39) might need Dynamic Binding. Then I turn to the evidence in favor of (39).

3.3.1 The Role of Dynamic Binding in a Theory of Reconstruction

In order to see in what way exactly the approach in (39) involves Dynamic Binding, it might be worthwhile to go through an example in some detail. The sentence we want to interpret compositionally is (43a), on the Logical Form in (43b), using the interpretive schema in (43c):

(43)   a. If it$_i$ is hungry, a cat$_i$ usually meows.
         b. [if it$_i$ is hungry]$_k$ O$_k$ [a cat$_i$ usually$_i$[t$_i$ meows] t$_k$]
         c. XP O$_k$ IP ⇒ λx$_k$ [IP] (XP)

Let us begin by giving the interpretation of the relevant parts of (43a), according to our assumptions so far:

(44)   a. [if it$_i$ is hungry]$_k$ ⇒ ↑ hungry(x$_i$)
         b. [a cat$_i$ usually meows [$_{CP}$ t$_k$]] ⇒ MOST (ˆλx$_i$ [↑ cat(x$_i$) Δ ˘H])
            (ˆ$\underline{λ}$ x$_i$ ↑ meow(x$_i$))

In (44a) we see the interpretation of the *if*-clause, in (44b) the interpretation of the main clause. Note that the main clause contains a Q-adverb that induces splitting into a restriction and scope. The restriction is made up of the subject *a cat* (which undergoes Disclosure) and the CP trace, that is, a variable ranging over the intension of CPs (which in the present setup are Context Change Potentials). The scope is, essentially, the material in the VP. Now, by applying the interpretive schema in (43c), we get:

(45)   a. λ H [MOST$'$ ($^\wedge\lambda$ x_i [$\uparrow$ cat(x_i) Δ $^\vee$H]) ($^\wedge\underline{\lambda}x_i$ $\uparrow$ meow(x_i))] ($^\wedge$ $\uparrow$ hungry(x_i))
       b. MOST$'$ ($^\wedge\lambda x_i$ [$\uparrow$ cat(x_i) Δ $\uparrow$ hungry(x_i)]) ($^\wedge\underline{\lambda}$ x_i $\uparrow$ meow(x_i))

Formula (45a) reduces to (45b) by λ-conversion and $^\vee\,^\wedge$-cancellation. Since '$^\wedge$' abstracts over assignments to discourse markers, the conversion in (45) is valid. If the syntactic analysis of topicalization as an operator–variable dependency is independently supported, we have here evidence of a novel kind in favor of Dynamic Binding, for the latter provides us with a natural semantics for operator–variable syntactic dependencies that enables us to do away with a rule of reconstruction.

The claim I just made calls for more careful scrutiny perhaps. Dynamic Binding as construed here involves two components: (i) the abstraction over assignments and (ii) the interpretation of sentences as CCPs. The first component is realized by suitably defining '$^\wedge$'; the second, by inserting a "hook" for subsequent discourse in the interpretation of sentences. We saw in chapter 2 that the second component crucially needs the first in order to do its job. Now, as should be clear from (45), our semantics for topicalization only employs the first component. If in (45) we drop all the $\uparrow$-operators, the conversion from (45a) to (45b) stays valid, thanks to how '$^\wedge$' is defined and used. Hence we don't really need the full-fledged apparatus of Dynamic Binding to deal with reconstruction. We merely need the possibility of abstracting over assignments, which in principle can be independently adopted.[13] But then, isn't the claim that we have found new evidence in favor of Dynamic Binding overstated?

This is a legitimate doubt. It is indeed possible to use IL as redefined here to provide a semantic treatment of reconstruction without committing oneself to a full-fledged dynamics. Some researchers might want to pursue such a line. Still, I think there is a clear sense in which a semantic treatment of reconstruction does provide support for a dynamic perspective. Suppose for the sake of argument that the evidence in favor of a semantic treatment of reconstruction along the lines discussed above is indeed convincing. If we start out from an ordinary, static semantics, in order to accommodate reconstruction we have to endow our machinery with facilities that enable us to manipulate sets of assignments. If we start out from a dynamic standpoint, we already have all we need. In fact, the dynamic perspective is independently motivated. If the argumentation in chapters 1 and 2 is on the right track, Dynamic Binding constitutes the best available theory of donkey type dependencies. We now note that this independently needed machinery gives us for free a semantic treatment of reconstruction. In other words, If Dynamic Binding is right, phenomena like semantic reconstruction are just what one would expect to find. Finding in actuality what an independently motivated abstract system leads one to expect does constitute new confirming evidence in its favor, if anything does. Be that as it may, we will also see, in sections 3.4.3 and 3.4.4 below, that this perspective has empirical payoffs beyond reconstruction which crucially depend on the second component of Dynamic Binding as well (i.e., on the interpretation of sentences as CCPs).

Being clearer now about the way in which Dynamic Binding relates to a semantic treatment of reconstruction, we turn to a discussion of the empirical evidence in favor of such a treatment.

3.3.2 On the Syntax of If/When-Clauses

In this section we will show that there are at least three cases where *if/ when*-clauses display connectivity (that is, "reconstruction") effects while at the same time arguably being generated directly in their surface position. They are cleft sentences, *if/when*-clauses adjoined to questions, and *if/then*-clauses. I will first discuss these constructions informally, then sketch a formal analysis. Since in all these cases, the *if/when*-clauses at no level are in the position of the gap, the copy theory of traces is of no help in dealing with connectivity. Unless we are willing to posit what amounts to an actual rule of syntactic reconstruction, we have to resort to an interpretive approach.

3.3.2.1 Clefts

If/when-clauses can be clefted (cf. Collins 1989, Iatridou 1991):

(46)   a. It is when Pavarotti sings that I get a headache.
        b. It is if John arrives late that we will be in trouble.

The general consensus for some time now has been that in clefts the focused element is generated directly in its surface position and linked to an IP-internal gap in the *that*-clause via an operator. The structure of clefts is similar to that of relative clauses, and the arguments that have been put forth in favor of an operator movement analysis of relatives carry over to clefts. For example, one reason for favoring an operator movement analysis over, say, a deletion (or head movement) analysis of externally headed relatives is that the case marking of the head is generally independent of the case of the gap. On a deletion or head movement analysis, this would require special stipulations, while on an operator movement analysis it is to be expected. The same is true of the focus phrase in clefts. I will not try to be any more specific as to the exact analysis of clefts, as this would take us too far afield, and simply adopt a structure along the lines of Chomsky 1977, schematically represented below:

(47)   [it is XP$_i$ O$_i$[. . . t$_i$ . . .]]

Now we note that clefted *if/when*-clauses behave exactly like left-adjoined ones with respect to backwards anaphora. For instance:

(48)   a.   It is if he considers it too difficult that a teacher won't adopt a textbook.
        b.   It is [if he considers it too difficult]$_k$ O$_k$ [that a teacher won't adopt a textbook t$_k$]
        c.   *It is if he spots a ship that is attacked by a pirate.

In fact, the whole set of phenomena considered in section 3.1 can be reproduced using cleft sentences. Even though I am not offering an explicit syntax and semantics for these constructions here, it seems to me that what they show is fairly clear. Sentence (48a,b) shows that we must be able to interpretively reconstruct the *if*-clause in the gap position in order to make the indefinites accessible to the pronouns anaphoric to them. Sentence (48c) shows that Principle C effects are present here, too.

3.3.2.2 CP-Adjoined If/When-Clauses

The next construction I would like to consider are cases of *if/when*-clauses adjoined to questions, such as the following:

(49)   a. If John comes, what will we do?
        b. When John arrives, who will take care of him?
        c. Bill wonders if John comes, who will entertain him.

Presumably, we don't want to say that the *if/when*-clauses in (49) are extracted from an IP-internal position, for extraction out of questions is generally banned. Yet, the kinds of *if/when*-clauses in (49) are also subject to the Pronominal Subject Constraint:

(50)   a.   If he$_i$ finds it$_j$ difficult, will a teacher$_i$ adopt a textbook$_j$?
        b.   *If he$_j$ lies to a girl$_i$, will she$_i$ trust a boy$_j$?
        c.   When it$_i$ is hungry, how dangerous is a tiger$_i$?
        d.   *When it$_i$ sees a mouse$_j$, can it$_j$ run away from a cat$_i$?

This means that these constructions display Principle C effects. We have another typical connectivity effect: these kinds of *if/when*-clauses appear to be directly generated to the left, as far as their locational properties are concerned, while semantically and for binding theoretic purposes, they behave as if they where IP internal.

This observation as well points toward an operator–variable analysis of this construction, schematically represented as follows:

(51)   [[if John comes]$_k$ O$_k$ [who will entertain him e$_k$]]

where the operator O$_k$ is assumed to be base generated in the position indicated and coindexed with an empty category (unlike what happens with clefts, where the operator undergoes movement). Since the operator is directly generated external to the *wh*-phrase, it will not be subject to whatever conditions govern movement dependencies. At the same time, the *if*-clause can be semantically interpreted as if it was in the gap position (using λ-conversion), and the binding theory can treat it as if it was in the gap position as well (using the notion of chain). This is, of course, just a first approximation. We will try to make the structure in (51) more explicit shortly.

3.3.2.3 If-Then-*Clauses*

The third kind of relevant construction is represented by *if/then*-clauses, studied by Collins (1989) and Iatridou (1991). Collins and Iatridou discuss contrasts of the following kind:

(52)   a.   How did every boy say that if his mother comes the car will be fixed?
        b.   *How did every boy say that if his mother comes then the car will be fixed?

The examples in (52) show that long extraction across a left-adjoined *if*-clause is possible only if no *then* intervenes. As Collins and Iatridou argue, this contrast suggests that the presence of *then* introduces an extra barrier. One can assume that in structures like (52a), the *if*-clause is simply adjoined to IP (whether based generated or moved), hence no barrier intervenes to block extraction. In structures like (52b), on the other hand, a functional category separates the antecedent from the consequent, preventing extraction from the latter. We will try shortly to be more explicit as to the nature of this functional category. Meanwhile, we may note that if *if/then*-clauses are islands for extraction, we presumably do not want to say that the protasis (*if*-clause) originates inside the apodosis (main clause introduced by *then*) and is extracted out of it. For otherwise it would be mysterious why a *wh*-word (like *how* in (52)) could not follow the same extraction path, whatever that may be.

Now, *if*/*then*-clauses behave in the same way as other *if*-clauses with respect to anaphora. Specifically, backwards anaphora into a left-adjoined *if*/*then*-clause is possible and subject to the Pronominal Subject Constraint:

(53)   a.   If it$_i$ is hungry, then a cat$_i$ meows.
        b.   If he$_i$ finds it$_j$ too difficult, then a teacher$_i$ won't adopt a text-book$_j$.
        c.   *If a mouse$_i$ sees it$_j$, then it$_i$ runs away from a cat$_j$.

In terms of the analysis proposed in section 3.2, the ungrammaticality of (53c) is a Principle C effect. This in turn entails that there must be a chain linking the *if*-clause to an IP-internal position, albeit not one which is created by movement. So here, too, we may adopt an analysis along the following lines:

(54)   [if it is hungry]$_k$ O$_k$[then a cat meows e$_k$]

The operator in (54) is generated in clause-initial position and linked to a base-generated empty category within the clause (as for the constructions in section 3.3.2.2 above).

In conclusion, there appears to be evidence that several kinds of left-adjoined *if*-clauses form structures of the following kind:

(55)   [CP$_i$ O$_i$ [. . . e$_i$ . . .]] $\Rightarrow$ λe$_i$[. . . e$_i$ . . .](CP)

The gap in such a structure can arise via movement or be a base-generated empty category. The interpretation of this structure proceeds uniformly as shown. Furthermore, we need a formulation of the binding theory whereby whatever c-commands e$_i$ also c-commands CP$_i$. In the next section we will try to spell out some of the details. But note that the general point just made does not appear to be bound to specific theoretical assumptions in a crucial manner; thus it would presumably stand even if the more detailed proposals below turned out to be wrong.

3.3.3 Topicalization and Recursive CPs

One way of making the analysis just sketched more precise is through a version of the 'Recursive Comp' analysis of topicalization, such as the one recently proposed by Authier (1992) and Watanabe (1992), among others.

According to such an analysis, an embedded topic like (56a) would have the structure given in (56b):

(56) a. Mary claims that beans John doesn't like.
      b. $[_{CP_1}$ that $[_{CP_2}$ beans$_i$ O$_i$ $[_{IP}$ John doesn't like t$_i$]]

The structure in (56b) involves a recursive CP, where *that* occupies the head position of CP_1, the topic phrase *beans* is adjoined to CP_2, and the operator O_i is fronted into the Spec of CP_2. It is also assumed that the head of CP_2 is occupied by a null [+WH] head.

This structure, which accounts nicely for the position of embedded topics in sentences like (56a), seems to run into a word order problem in cases of the following sort (from Watanabe 1992):

(57) a. ?I wonder to whom this book we should give.
      b. *I wonder this book to whom we should give.

The ungrammaticality of (57b) is expected. Given that the Spec of CP_2 is occupied by the *wh*-phrase, the topic cannot be extracted. What is unexpected is the relative improvement of (57a) relative to (57b). Both sentences should be equally ungrammatical for the same reasons (i.e., given that in (57a) the Spec of CP_2 is occupied by the operator, extraction of the *wh*-phrase should be banned). I assume that the observed contrast is due to the fact that English also marginally allows IP-adjoined topics. The reason why (57a) is not so bad might be that the topic *this book* is adjoined to IP. This is a marked option in English, as attested by the somewhat degraded character of (57a), and may be forced here by the fact that *wonder* selects a [+WH] Comp, which requires a *wh*-phrase in its Spec, as suggested in slightly different terms by Authier and Watanabe. Hence, if one tries to topicalize within an embedded question, the only possibility that doesn't violate constraints on movement and selectional requirements is adjunction to IP.

A recursive Comp analysis can be extended in a natural way to *if-then* conditionals. As a first approximation we might analyze *if-then* conditionals as follows:

(58) a. Mary believes that if it is hungry, then a dog barks.
      b. $[_{CP_1}$ [that $[_{CP_2}$ if it is hungry $[_{C'}$ then O$_i$ $[_{IP}$ a dog barks e$_i$]]]]

In this structure *that* is in CP_1 while *then* is analyzed as a C_2^0, that is, as a complementizer that heads the inner CP. The operator O is base generated in a position adjoined to IP. This analysis accounts immediately for a number of properties of these constructions. In particular, since the Spec position of

CP_2 is occupied by the *if*-clause, no movement out of it will be possible. Moreover, the fact that the presence of *then* in C_2^0 requires an *if*-clause to its immediate left (cf. the ungrammaticality of **Then Mary will leave if John comes*) can be accounted for in terms of Spec-Head agreement (i.e., *then* requires an *if*-clause in its Spec). While these appear to be welcome results, there are, however, some aspects of the behavior of *then*-clauses that do not follow from the analysis in (58b). For one thing, *then* can also occur independently of an *if*-clause:

(59)   a. John walked in. Then he walked out.
        b. Mary walked in. John then walked out.

The meaning of *then* in these uses appears to be related to its meaning when it occurs in construction with *if*-clauses. For example, in (59b) a possible interpretation of the second sentence might be that as a consequence of Mary's walking in, John walked out. Similarly, in conditionals the apodosis is viewed as a consequence of the protasis. This relatedness of meaning does not seem to be accidental and might be captured by trying to somehow relate the two instances of *then,* which does not happen on the analysis in (58b). A second aspect of the behavior of *if*/*then*-clauses that does not follow from (58b) can be seen by looking at the following pattern:

(60)   a. John said that if Mary is at home, she will help him.
        b. If Mary is at home, John said that Mary will help him.
        c. John said that if Mary is at home, then she will help him.
        d. If Mary is at home, then John said that she will help him.

Sentence (60b) has a reading which is equivalent to (60a). On this reading the conditional is construed as modifying the embedded clause. An analogous construal is impossible in (60d); that is, (60d) has no reading in which it is equivalent to (60c). This shows that when *then* occurs clause initially in construction with an *if*-clause, it limits the scope of the latter to the next clause down. On the analysis in (58b) this is unexpected. For what would prevent the operator O in (58b) from being linked to a more embedded clause? It is not obvious. So what the analysis in (58b) misses is the strictly local character of the *if*/*then*-construction.

A way of minimally modifying (58b) that would accommodate these facts might be the following. First, we can assume that *then* is a pronominal element (a 'pro-sentence') that can freely occur in adjoined position, somewhere within IP. It is not necessary for our purposes to establish where exactly *then* may be adjoined. We just note that since it can occur after the subject (cf. (59b)), adjunction to a site internal to IP (where it is c-commanded by the subject) must be possible. For simplicity's sake, let's assume that this site is I′:

(61)   [John [$_{I'}$ then [$_{I'}$ left]]]

Suppose next that there is a C^0 head that carries agreement features, analogous maybe to those associated with *wh*-movement, requiring the presence of a conditional in its Spec position. Let us call these features CN (for 'conditional'). We might assume that CN requires an overt morphological support (by analogy to what happens with, say, *do* in English) and that this support is provided by incorporating *then*—that is, a semantically compatible head—into C^0 via head-movement. This would result in a structure of the following kind:

(62)   a. [[if it barks]$_k$ [[CN]$_k$ [a dog then usually barks]]]

        b. [[if it barks]$_k$ [then$_k$ [a dog t$_k$ usually barks]]]
        c. $\lambda\ p_k\ \text{most}_x\ [\text{dog}(x) \wedge p_k]\ [\text{bark}(x)]\ (\text{bark}(x))$

In (62a) the conditional is coindexed with its head via Spec-Head agreement. *Then* raises into C^0 and amalgamates with the agreement features of C^0, leaving a trace behind. As a consequence, we have a link between the *if*-clause and an IP-internal position. This is the link we want for interpretive and binding theoretic purposes. In (62c) I give a schematic indication of how such structure is to be interpreted.

The analysis just sketched preserves the good aspects of the previous one, while at the same time accounting for the local character of the relevant relation in terms of the properties of head movement. In particular, presumably adverbials are somehow licenced by elements within Infl (see, e.g., Travis 1988). In order for *then* to climb a long distance (as on the intended reading of (61d)), it would have to pass through inflectional elements other than those that license it, which any reasonable definition of head movement will rule out. This is still pretty vague, but the basic idea should be clear.[14]

We can extend these considerations to an analysis of the cases where *if/ then*-clauses are adjoined to questions:

(63)   a. If John comes, then who will entertain him:
        b. [$_{CP_1}$ [if John comes]$_k$ then$_k$ [$_{CP_2}$ who$_i$ [WH] [t$_i$ t$_k$ will entertain him]]]

As illustrated in (63b), here the head of the inner Comp is occupied by a
WH-feature which triggers *wh*-movement into its Spec. The head of the outer
Comp is occupied at D-structure by the CN agreement features which, in
turn, trigger incorporation of *then*. This means that *then* first incorporates
into C_1^0 and then moves further into the higher C_2^0 (see Roberts 1991 for
technical details on this kind of "excorporation"). It is plausible to maintain
that this is allowed in virtue of the fact that CN and WH are sufficiently
different as heads so as not to interfere with each other (with respect to, e.g.,
minimality considerations; cf. Rizzi 1990). Notice that while the present
analysis predicts the ungrammaticality of (60d) on a reading equivalent to
(60c) (repeated here as (64a) and (64b) respectively), it also predicts the
grammaticality of (64c):

(64)   a. John said that if Mary is at home, then she will help him.
         b. If Mary is at home, then John said that she will help him.
         c. If Mary is at home, John said that then she will help him.
         d. John said that [$_{IP}$ if Mary is at home [$_{IP}$ then [she will help him]]]

The structure in (64d) constitutes the source of (64c). In (64d) the *if*-clause
is base generated in IP-adjoined position, and so is *then*. Since there is no
[+CN] Comp, *then* does not undergo incorporation and remains as an adverbial pro-sentence. Under these circumstances, the *if*-clause, which constitutes
the antecedent of *then,* can be fronted to the root clause, resulting in (64c).

This analysis has a further welcome consequence, which has to do with
yet another property of *if-then*-clauses, namely the fact that the structures
exemplified in (63) cannot occur in embedded position.:

(65)   *Mary wonders if John comes, then who will entertain him.

This restriction follows from the fact that the head position of the outer CP
is occupied by *then,* which, not being a *wh*-element, cannot satisfy the selectional requirements of *wonder*-type verbs. And the WH-features in the inner
CP cannot raise into the outer one, the head position being already taken.

Consider finally the ungrammaticality of the following sentence and contrast it with the grammatical (58a) above, repeated here as (66b):

(66)   a.   *Mary believes that if John comes, then who will entertain him.
         b.   Mary believes that if it is hungry, then a dog barks.

Sentence (66a) would require three embedded CPs (one to host *that,* one to
host *then,* and one for [+WH]). We know on independent grounds that a
recursion of depth three of embedded CPs is impossible (cf. the parallel

constraint that obtains on VP shells). Watanabe (1992) offers some considerations as to why this might be so.

Let us turn now to an analysis of *if*-clauses adjoined to CPs without *then*, like (67a):

(67)   a.   I wonder if John comes, who will entertain him.
        b.   *If John comes, I wonder who will entertain him.
        c.   *If Mary leaves, every boy$_i$ wonders who will help him$_i$.
              (Collins 1989)

As the examples in (67) directly show, such sentences share some but not all of the properties of *if-then*-clauses. In particular, they share with *if-then*-clauses the strict locality conditions that prevent (67b,c) from having a "downstairs" interpretation. Thus, for example, (67b) has no reading equivalent to (67a). At the same time, the construction in question can occur in embedded position (contrast (67a) with (65)). This latter fact suggests an analysis along the following lines:

(68)   [$_{CP_1}$ if John comes O$_i$ [$_{CP_2}$ who will e$_i$ entertain him]]

In this structure, the *if*-clause is directly generated in Spec of CP$_1$. The head position of CP$_1$ is empty. Consequently it does not require that any morphologically overt material move into it. At the same time, the WH-head of CP$_2$ can move into it and thereby satisfy the selectional requirements of *wonder* (this is fully parallel to what Watanabe (1992) proposes for *regret*-type verbs). I assume that the *if*-clause is linked via an operator to an empty category base generated internally to IP. Within the present set of assumptions, it seems plausible to maintain that this empty category is a null counterpart of *then*. In virtue of its pronominal nature, the empty category needs to be identified under conditions of strict locality, and the operator coindexed with the *if*-clause seems to provide us with a suitable way to do so. Thus we are in the presence here of a kind of A'-bound *pro,* a construction studied extensively by Cinque (1990).

It should be noted that besides *if*-clauses, other kinds of CP-external adjuncts are also admitted (while CP-external *arguments* in English appear to be more marginal):

(69)   a.   For our country, who wouldn't be willing to give his life?
        b.   *Our country, who doesn't like t?
        c.   With so little money, how far do you think you can go?
        d.   *So little money, who gave t to you?

As the examples make clear, these kinds of CP-external adjuncts do not appear to be subject to the same kinds of locality conditions (i.e., essentially, clause-boundedness) as the *if*-clauses exemplified in (67). This suggests that we are dealing with a somewhat different construction here, whose analysis I must leave open at this point.

Before leaving this topic, I should point out one final important prediction that the present analysis makes. Backwards anaphora is only possible out of topicalized *if/when*-clauses. Topicalization creates islands for extraction. Hence, we expect extraction out of an *if/when*-clause containing cataphoric elements to be impossible, Now, prima facie it would seem that this prediction is not so clearly borne out, in view of examples of the following kind:

(70)   ?How did you say that if it$_i$ is hungry a dog$_i$ behaves t?

In (70) we have a topicalized *if*-clause (as shown by the presence of backwards anaphora) out of which we have extracted a *wh*-phrase. Though not perfect, (70) does not seem to be altogether impossible. However, the *if*-clause in (70) might be a parenthetical adjunct, in which case all bets are off, given the poorly understood character of parentheticals. So we must look for cases where a parenthetical interpretation is impossible. If we do so, here is what we find:

(71)   a.   *How did [every cat owner]$_i$ say that if it$_j$ attacks his$_i$ cat a dog$_j$ would be punished t?
         b.   ?How did [everyone]$_i$ say that if [his$_i$ cat]$_j$ meows too loudly it$_j$ would be punished t?
         c.   *To which scholastic board did every teacher$_i$ say that if he$_j$ disrupts his$_i$ class a student$_j$ shall be reported t?
         d.   ?To which scholastic board did every teacher$_i$ say that if a student$_j$ disrupts his$_i$ class he$_j$ shall be reported t?

Sentence like (71a) and (71c) seem to be systematically worse than sentences like (71b) and (71d).[15] This is what we would expect. In (71b) and (71d) there is no backwards anaphora. Hence the *if*-clause can simply be IP-adjoined, and extraction across it is therefore possible. In (71a) and (71c), by contrast, we do have backwards anaphora, which is only possible if the *if*-clause is topicalized. Hence extraction is impossible.

Thus, in conclusion, this analysis seems to predict to a considerable degree the behavior of a wide variety of *if*-clauses, while relating it to a general proposal on the structure of topicalization. Notice in particular that if I am on the right track regarding the structure of *if-then*-clauses, then the IP-internal empty category is a trace of *then*. Hence it would seem that the copy theory of traces (which might well be right for, say, *wh*-dependencies) could not even in principle play a role in explaining the fact that for interpretive and binding theoretic purposes the *if*-clause behaves as if it was within IP. If the analysis sketched out above turns out to be correct, then the proposal of an interpretive reconstruction coupled with a formulation of the binding theory in terms of the notion of chain has no viable alternative, as far as I can see.[16]

3.3.4 Chain Binding and Antireconstruction

The binding theory is the object of intense investigation and much controversy. Within the limits of the present work, I can only give an indication of the general direction in which the data considered above seem to point.

Our objective is to formulate a version of the binding theory that exploits the notion of chain. The one I will adopt is a variant of what Barss (1986) proposes. In Barss's approach, the notion of c-command is replaced by the notion of accessibility sequence. An accessibility sequence is a path of nodes that connects the bindee to its potential binder. For a binding relationship to be well-formed, the path that connects binder and bindee must meet certain structural requirements. Consider, for example, a simple case like the following:

(72)   a. John thinks that Bill loves himself.
        b.

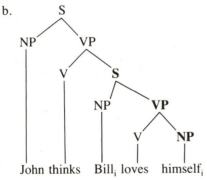

In (72a) the embedded subject is the antecedent of the reflexive pronoun *himself*. The accessibility sequence is indicated in boldface in (72b) (to simplify things, I am reverting here to a notation that predates functional categories). The top of the sequence immediately dominates the binder, the bottom immediately dominates the bindee. Basically, for an accessibility sequence to be well-formed, each node in the sequence must immediately dominate its predecessor. This is very similar to how "slash categories" work in GPSG and its derivatives.

Notice that the path that connects *himself* to the top S node also forms a well-formed accessibility sequence (since each node in it immediately dominates its predecessor). Yet *John* cannot antecede the reflexive. Observe, however, that the path connecting *John* and *himself* is not minimal, given that it contains a proper subpath that connects *himself* to another potential antecedent, namely *Bill*. We may assume that reflexives can be connected to their binders only via minimal accessibility sequences. Much work on the definition of a minimal binding domain (i.e., governing category) can be recast in these terms.

So far the notion of accessibility sequence is a straightforward notational variant of c-command. However, it lends itself to extensions that can deal with some considerably harder cases. Consider:

(73)   a. A picture of himself$_i$ John$_i$ would never give t$_i$ me.
        b.

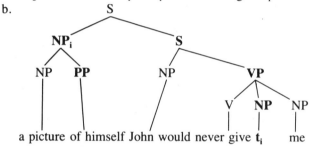

The accessibility path we want is marked in boldface in (73b). It is obtained by taking two accessibility paths that are related to each other via the links of a chain. Starting from the anaphor we go up the tree. Once we reach NP$_i$, we have the option of going to the corresponding trace t$_i$ and resuming the path upwards from there. In other words, each link of a well-formed accessibility sequence must either immediately dominate its predecessor or form a chain with it. This enables us to extend the coverage of the binding theory to cases like (73a), for which standard c-command doesn't work. In cases like these we will say, following Barss, that the antecedent *chain-binds* the reflexive.

This approach has further consequences. Consider the following:

(74)   [Pictures of himself]$_i$ John said t$_i$ that Bill should never have taken t$_i$'.

In (74) both *John* and *Bill* can antecede the reflexive. On an approach based on chain accessibility, this is to be expected. We go up the tree starting from the reflexive. Once we reach the NP *pictures of himself,* we can go to a trace of the chain which that NP is part of and resume from there. If we pick the lowest trace t_i' and go up from there, we find *Bill* as the closest possible antecedent; if we go to the intermediate trace t_i and resume from there, we find *John* as an antecedent. In either case, we can form a chain accessibility sequence which is minimal in the relevant sense.

I am ignoring here several complications that are not directly relevant to our present concerns. Basically, as far as I can see, an approach that employs chain accessibility, such as Barss's, gives us exactly what we want for the case at hand. Below I give a sketch of the formal definitions.

(75) I. *The Binding Theory*
      a. A reflexive must be minimally bound.
      b. A nonreflexive pronoun must be minimally free.
      c. An R-expression must be free.

  II. *Chain Binding*
      a. α binds β relative to a chain accessibility sequence Δ iff α and β are coindexed and Δ connects β to α. α minimally binds β relative to Δ iff α binds β relative to Δ and for no Δ' and no α', Δ' connects β to α' and $\Delta' \subseteq \Delta$.
      b. Δ is a chain accessibility sequence that connects β to α iff Δ is a sequence of nodes $\langle\beta_1, \ldots, \beta_n\rangle$, where (i) $\beta_i = \beta$; (ii) $\beta_n =$ the mother of α, and (iii) for each i, $1 \leq i \leq n$, either β_{i+1} immediately dominates β_i or $\langle\beta_i, \beta_{i+1}\rangle$ are a link in a CHAIN.
      c. A CHAIN $\langle\beta_1, \ldots, \beta n\rangle$ is a sequence of nodes sharing the same θ-role such that for any i, $1 \leq i \leq n$, β_i c-commands and is coindexed with β_{i+1}.[17]

A few comments on some consequences of these definitions are called for. First, Barss assumes that these conditions apply at S-structure. But nothing in the approach just sketched forces this to be so. Nothing would change in what I have proposed if we assume the binding theory to be an interface (i.e., LF) condition. Second, Chomsky (1992) has shown that by adopting the copy theory of traces, some of the effects studied by Barss can be dealt with in terms of the more traditional notion of c-command. While the copy theory of traces might well be right, we have seen that there are reconstruction effects concerning structures that do not involve movement but, arguably, operator–variable constructions. If this is so, then a formulation of the binding theory that uses the notion of chain still seems to be called for. Finally, Barss explicitly excludes Principle C from the purview of chain binding (and deals with it in terms of an obviation condition), in view of certain cases that require some discussion, to which I turn next.

We have argued that the data considered in the present chapter strongly support the need to define Principle C in terms of chain binding. The same has been observed for other adjuncts. For example:

(76)   a.   *Next to a man$_i$, he$_i$ saw a snake.
        a'. *[next to a man$_i$]$_k$ [he$_i$ saw a snake e$_k$]
        b.   *Without a friend$_i$, he$_i$ is lost.
        b'. *[without a friend$_i$]$_k$ [he$_i$ is lost t$_k$]

The ungrammaticality of these examples can be attributed to Principle C, under the assumptions that they are topicalized from an IP-internal position and that Principle C is defined in terms of chain binding. Speas (1990) argues that some nonclausal adjuncts do not display Principle C effects. For example:

(77)   (??) On Rosa$_i$'s birthday, she$_i$ should take it easy.

Speas finds (77) grammatical. I disagree with her judgment. For me examples like (77) are very marginal at best. Be that as it may, it can be shown that even if coreference between *Rosa* and *she* is acceptable, it cannot be attributed to a relaxation of Principle C. For suppose that these two NPs could be coindexed. Then we would expect that a quantifier in the left-dislocated adjunct could bind a pronoun in the subject position. This, however, appears to be impossible.

(78)   *On everyone$_i$'s birthday, he$_i$ misbehaves.

Note that this cannot be attributed to the fact that *everyone* is in a position where it cannot have scope over the whole S; the following example shows that it can:

(79)   a. On everyone's birthday, someone misbehaves.
        b. [everyone$_i$ [on t$_i$'s birthday]] [someone$_j$ [t$_j$ misbehaves]]

Sentence (79a) has the reading given in (79b). Thus, if *everyone* and the subject were allowed to bear the same index, nothing would prevent (78) above from being grammatical. Such coindexing must be disallowed, and Principle C, under the construal adopted here, does precisely that.

There are, however, other cases that have been argued to show that Principle C does not apply to dislocated constituents. Van Riemsdijk and Williams (1981) discuss contrasts like the following:

(80)   a.   *He$_i$ hung those pictures that John$_i$ took himself.
        b.   [Which pictures that John$_i$ took]$_k$ did he$_i$ hang t$_k$ himself?

Clearly (80b) is much better than (80a). Van Riemsdijk and Williams call this phenomenon ''antireconstruction'' and attribute it to the depth of embedding: if an NP is deeply embedded in a dislocated constituent, it fails to undergo reconstruction, or at any rate is not subject to Principle C. On an approach that uses chain binding for the binding theory as whole, like the one I am adopting, how are we are going to deal with this? There are (at least) three options, which I will briefly sketch.

Lebeaux (1988), in his interesting discussion of antireconstruction, notices that the relevant NP in sentences like (80a) is contained within a relative clause. He proposes that relative clauses are inserted in the tree by a generalized transformation, which can take place after *wh*-movement. This enables material contained within this kind of adjunct to be exempted from the binding theory. For example, under a copy theory of traces, the copy would not contain the material in the adjunct and hence that material would not be ''seen'' by conditions that are sensitive to properties of traces.

Lebeaux's approach is consistent with the general line we are taking here. However, it predicts an argument/adjunct asymmetry that I find very tenuous at best. Compare (80b), reported here as (81a), with (81b):

(81)   a.   [Which pictures that John$_i$ took]$_k$ did he$_i$ hang t$_k$ himself?
        b.   [Which claim that Judge Thomas$_i$ harassed his employees] did he$_i$ resent the most?

Since the NP *Judge Thomas* occurs within an argument, it must be syntactically projected before *wh*-movement, according to Lebeaux. Hence it should undergo reconstruction (or whatever subsumes its effects) and be subject to Principle C. Accordingly, it is expected that (81b) should be ungrammatical or at least considerably worse than (81a). But for most speakers there is hardly any contrast between the sentences in (81).

A somewhat different, though related, approach is presented by Heycock (1992). She argues that the relevant notion is that of ''referentiality.'' The *wh*-phrases in (81) are arguably referential, in contrast with the following:

(82)   How many stories about Diana$_i$ did she$_i$ invent herself?

Heycock claims that sentences like (82) are systematically worse than sentences like (81). She proposes that referential phrases undergo reconstruction (or whatever subsumes its effects under the copy theory of traces), while nonreferential ones do not. She argues that this follows from the semantics of the relevant phrases, in interaction with other, independently needed assumptions. While I find Heycock's discussion thought-provoking, my judgments do not support the presence of a sufficiently systematic contrast between (81) and (82). Also, I am not sure that the relevant notion of "referentiality" can be made semantically precise. At any rate, even if I am wrong in my analysis of the data and if the relevant notion of referentiality can be spelled out, I believe that Heycock's solution would be compatible with what I am proposing.

Currently I am inclined to attribute antireconstruction effects to a different property of grammar. As pointed out in chapter 1, Principle C prevents an R-expression from being coindexed with (and hence bound by) another NP. But it does not prevent coreference. Coreference must be treated in some other way, such as, for example, Reinhart's (1983a,b) Non-Coreference rule, which states roughly that two NPs not bearing the same index should not be understood as coreferential if a reflexive (i.e., explicitly bound variable) is allowed in the same structural configuration. Consider in this light the above examples, say (81a), repeated here again:

(81a)   [Which pictures that John$_i$ took]$_k$ did he$_j$ hang t$_k$ himself?

Under our analysis, Principle C prevents *John* and *he* from being coindexed. Hence, on the basis of Reinhart's rule, they should not be coreferential *if* there is a structurally isomorphic alternative which allows a reflexive pronoun in one of the two relevant positions. The question is whether such an alternative exists. It appears that this is not so, for both of the following are ungrammatical:

(83)   a.   *Which picture that himself took did John hang on the wall?
        b.   *Which picture that John took did himself hang on the wall?

Since a (non-emphatic) reflexive in either position is disallowed, Reinhart's rule predicts that the two NPs in (81a) can be interpreted as coreferential, modulo pragmatic plausibility. Contrast this with what happens with examples like (76a), repeated here as (84a):

(84)   a.   *Next to a man$_i$, he$_i$ saw a snake.
        b.   ??Next to John$_i$, he$_i$ saw a snake.
        c.   Next to himself, John saw a snake.

If we are right, the ungrammaticality of (84a) is to be attributed to Principle C. Such a principle also prevents *John* and *he* from being coindexed in (84b). Now, here there is an isomorphic alternative where a reflexive is allowed, namely (84c). Hence, Reinhart's Non-Coreference rule predicts that interpreting *John* and *he* as coreferential in (84b) should be considerably harder than in (81a), which indeed is the case. Perhaps this is all there is to say about antireconstruction.

It thus appears that a simple and general formulation of all binding theoretic principles in terms of chain binding is possible. Antireconstruction effects raise a number of interesting issues, but at present at least, they appear to be consistent with the general line adopted here.

3.3.5 Summary

Before going on, it might be useful to present in schematic form the structures we have arrived at for various kinds of *if*/*when*-clauses, along with their interpretation.

(85)   *Right-Adjoined If/When-Clauses*

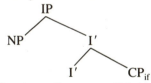

Example: A cat usually meows if it is hungry.
S-structure and LF (in this case they coincide):

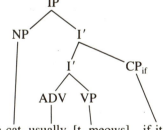

a cat$_i$ usually$_i$ [t$_i$ meows]   if it$_i$ is hungry
Interpretation: usually$_i$ ([cat(x$_i$) $\wedge$ hungry(x$_i$)], [meows(x$_i$)])

(86)   *Left-Adjoined If/When-Clauses* (not linked to an IP-internal position)

IP
CP$_{if}$ IP

Example: If a cat meows, it is usually hungry.

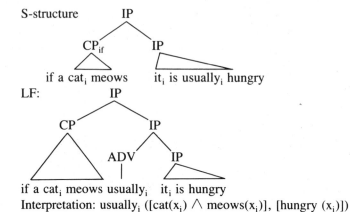

S-structure

if a cat$_i$ meows   it$_i$ is usually$_i$ hungry

LF:

if a cat$_i$ meows usually$_i$ it$_i$ is hungry

Interpretation: usually$_i$ ([cat(x_i) $\wedge$ meows(x_i)], [hungry (x_i)])

(87) *Topicalized If/When-Clauses*

    a. [$_{CP_1}$ that [$_{CP_2}$ if-clause [$_{CP_2}$ O [$_{IP}$ . . .]]]]
       This structure involves operator movement.
       Example: (John said that) if it is hungry, a cat meows.

    b. [$_{CP_1}$ if-clause [$_{CP_2}$ O [$_{CP_2}$ WH [$_{IP}$ . . .]]]]
       In this structure there is no operator movement.
       Example: If it is hungry, how does a cat behave?

    c. [$_{CP_1}$ if-clause then$_i$ ([$_{CP_2}$ WH) [$_{IP}$ t$_i$ . . .]]]
       Example: i. If it is hungry, then how does a cat be-
             have?   (with CP$_2$)
           ii. If it is hungry, then a cat usually meows. (without
            CP$_2$)

       In this structure there is head movement of *then*.

3.4 SOME RELATED CONSTRUCTIONS

We have limited ourself so far to consideration of *if/when*-clauses and don-key-type dependencies. But there are other types of binding that raise similar issues. Consider, for example, the following pattern:

(88)   a.   When he$_i$ is tired, no student$_i$ does well.
      b.   ??When he$_i$ is tired, I interrogate no student$_i$.
      c.   I interrogate no student$_i$ when he is tired.

In (88a), we have a quantificational NP *no student* binding a pronoun in a left-adjoined *when*-clause. This link appears to be acceptable. However, the acceptability of the link in question decreases sharply if the quantificational NP is VP-internal, as in (88b). If the adjunct is right-adjoined instead, as in

(88c), a VP-internal NP (as well as, of course, an NP in subject position) can antecede a pronoun occurring in the adjunct. Facts of this sort have received a fair amount of attention in the literature, especially thanks to the work of T. Reinhart (1976, 1983a,b). Here are some further examples, taken from Reinhart's work, that involve other kinds of adjuncts:

(89)   a.   Near his$_i$ child's crib, nobody$_i$ would keep matches.
        b.   ??Near his$_i$ child's crib, you should give nobody$_i$ matches.
        c.   You should give nobody$_i$ matches near his$_i$ child's crib.

These judgments have to be taken contrastively, as usual. While there is a great degree of variability as to how acceptable one finds sentences like (89b) in isolation, no speaker I have checked with denies that a contrast exists. Reinhart argues that these facts are to be explained in terms of c-command at S-structure. Her account has been widely challenged, however, on the basis of various kinds of counterevidence. And at any rate, it is interesting to see what alternatives there are to Reinhart's proposal in an approach that only admits interface conditions. I will argue that within the present setup Reinhart's generalization can be explained in an interesting manner.

To begin with, notice that in certain respects, the above kinds of structures exhibit exactly the same problems we have been discussing. For how is a quantificational NP to reach into a left-adjoined adjunct of any kind? If we think of such move in terms of QR, there are only two options, illustrated in (90).

(90)   a. Near his$_i$ child's crib, nobody$_i$ would keep matches.
        b. [near his$_i$ child's crib] [nobody$_i$ [t$_i$ would keep matches]]
        c. [nobody$_i$ [near his$_i$ child's crib] [t$_i$ would keep matches]]

Either we scope the subject NP at the level of the lowest S, as in (90b), but then it is unclear how it can bind the pronoun. Or we scope it at the topmost S, as in (90c), but that should result in a WCO violation. This is exactly the problem we were facing in connection with backwards donkey anaphora.

However, Reinhart's examples display a subject/nonsubject asymmetry that backwards donkey anaphora does not. As we saw, contrary to what happens in (88)–(89), a VP-internal object can antecede a pronoun in a left-adjoined *if/when*-clause. Here is a further example:

(91)   If it$_i$ is well done, I always enjoy a spaghetti western$_i$.

So the issues we face can be summarized as follows:

(92)   a. How does a quantificational NP bind into a preposed adjunct
             without violating WCO?
         b. Why do quantificational NPs display a subject/nonsubject asym-
             metry when binding into a left-adjoined phrase, while indefinites
             do not?

As far as (92a) is concerned, it is obviously very tempting to deal with it in
exactly the same terms as with left-adjoined *if/when*-clauses. Suppose that
left-adjoined phrases are topicalized and their interpretation proceeds by λ-
converting the topic into its IP-internal position. In this way, we can get a
pronoun in a left-adjoined phrase to be bound without giving rise to a WCO
violation.

(93)   a. [near his$_i$ child's crib] O_k [nobody$_i$ keeps matches t_k]
         b. $\lambda \alpha_k$ [nobody$_i$ keeps matches α_k] (next to his$_i$ crib)
             = [nobody$_i$ keeps matches next to his$_i$ crib]

The structure of the relevant sentences is as illustrated in (93a), and they
are interpreted as in (93b). On the basis of this analysis, we would expect
left-adjoined modifiers to display strong Principle C effects, and, as noted
above for (76), repeated here, they do:

(76)   a. *Next to a man$_i$, he$_i$ saw a snake.
         b. *Without a friend$_i$, he$_i$ is lost.

The ungrammaticality of (75) suggests that adjuncts of this kind do not have
the option of being base generated in left-adjoined position. They are always
moved out of (or linked to) an IP-internal position.

While this seems to work rather well (and indeed is a prediction of the
theory we are pursuing), we still lack an account of subject/nonsubject asymmetries. The analysis of, for example, (89b), repeated here as (94a), should
proceed in exactly the same way as illustrated in (93):

(94)   a. ??Near his$_i$ child's crib you should give nobody matches.
         b. [near his$_i$ child's crib]$_k$ O_k [you should give nobody$_i$ matches
             t_k]
         c. $\lambda \alpha_k$ [you should give nobody$_i$ matches α_k] (near his$_i$ child's
             crib)

In principle, "lowering" (i.e., λ-converting) the fronted adjunct into its base
position shouldn't be any harder here than it is for (93a). And yet (94a) is

considerably worse. To find a clue as to why this might be so, let us compare the structures of the counterparts of the relevant sentences where the adjunct is in its base position.

(95)   a.

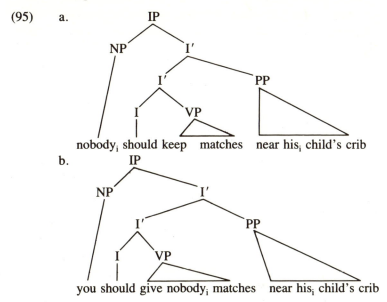

The key difference is clearly in the lower position of the potential binder of the pronoun in (95b) relative to (95a), which Reinhart tried to exploit directly using c-command at S-structure. There might be an alternative way, however, to build on her insight within our set of assumptions. Recall, in particular, that our splitting algorithm maintains QR to be optional. This has an interesting consequence with respect to the structures in (95). In (95a), since the subject c-commands the adjunct, there is no need to resort to QR in order to get the pronoun to be bound by the subject (cf. the appendix, part V). In (95b), however, since the adjunct is arguably higher up in the tree than the VP-internal material, we will have to use QR in order to bind the pronoun. While we can interpret (95a) directly off its S-structure, so to speak, we will need scoping in order to interpret (95b). In particular, in (95a) we interpret the I'-constituent as λx_i [x_i *should keep matches near his_i child's crib*]. This property is predicated of the subject, which will thereby automatically bind the pronoun. To interpret (95b) we need instead to interpret first the open sentence, [*you should give t_i matches near his_i crib*], and then quantify *nobody_i* into it. Now, the same considerations apply of course to the cases where the adjunct is fronted, like (89a) and (89b), since we are assuming that these are interpreted in just the same way as their counter-parts in (95) (the only difference being that in (89a–b) the adjunct has to be λ-ed back into its original position). Here are the relevant structures.

(96)   a.

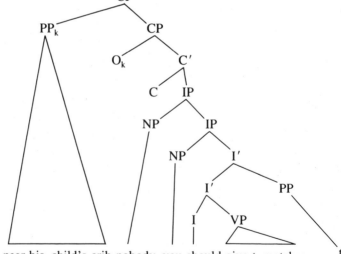

near his$_i$ child's crib   nobody$_i$ should keep   matches   t$_k$

a′. λ α$_k$ [nobody$_i$ should keep matches α$_k$] (near his$_i$ child's crib)

b.

near his$_i$ child's crib nobody$_i$ you should give t$_i$ matches   t$_k$

b′. λ α [nobody (λ x$_i$ you should give x$_i$ matches α$_k$] (near his$_i$ child's crib)

In (96a), λ-converting the fronted adjunct in its IP-internal position makes it accessible to the quantifier, even if the latter is not QR'ed. The subject is high enough to bind into the adjunct, also without QR. In (96b), λ-converting the fronted adjunct back in will not make it accessible to the object, unless we scope it out at a level where it can bind material in the adjunct. We might conjecture, therefore, that QR, as it were, blocks reconstruction. Descriptively, we can say that QR prevents a left-dislocated adjunct from being reconstructed in its original site. If this is so, then there is no way for a pronoun in a left-adjoined adjunct to be bound by a VP-internal NP.

Now, given that we don't have a syntactic process of reconstruction, the intended generalization cannot quite be stated as I just did. It must be stated in semantic terms, as a constraint on λ-conversion. Something has to make the conversion in (96b′) invalid. What can it be? We have pointed out several times that the apparatus of dynamic semantics is crucial to making the relevant λ-conversions proper. If instead we were to use a static semantics in (96b′), there would be no compositional way to perform such an operation. Suppose now that for some reason QR blocks dynamic interpretation. Suppose, in other words, that the semantics of QR is static. This is easy to obtain, for we can always retrieve from a Context Change Potential its static counterpart (by plugging in the variable into which possible continuations can be hooked). It would then follow that in (96a′), where QR is not necessary, we would be able to λ-convert the preposed adjunct into its original position. But in (96b′) this conversion would be blocked, because QR is necessary yet requires a static semantics which does not validate the conversion in question. In this way, Reinhart's generalization would be accounted for.

What we need can be stated as follows:

(97)   *Dynamic Blocking:*
         a. The semantics of QR is static.
         b. $\mathrm{NP}_i\ [\mathrm{S}] \Rightarrow\ \downarrow \mathrm{NP}'(\char"02E6\lambda\ x_i\ \downarrow\ \mathrm{S}')$
            where NP′ and S′ result from replacing all variables of type $\langle s,a \rangle$ occuring in the translations of NP and S, respectively, with variables of type a (and adjusting types accordingly).

I will try to explain informally what Dynamic Blocking does and why it is formulated in this way, referring to the appendix, part IV, for more details. Essentially, Dynamic Blocking stipulates an incompatibility between quantifying-in and dynamic interpretation. It limits the availability of dynamic semantics to structures that do not involve quantifying-in. Semantically speaking, this stipulation can be straightforwardly implemented. Recall that Dynamic Binding has two components: (i) the abstraction over assignments to discourse markers and (ii) the interpretation of sentences as CCPs. Our objective is to eliminate (i), in order to account for Reinhart's generalization. But in the present setting, this cannot be done without also eliminating (ii), since (ii) (i.e., the possibility of defining CCPs) depends on (i). The shutting off of (i) and (ii) is done in two steps. First, we eliminate all variables of type $\langle s,a \rangle$ from the relevant formulae. Since, the abstraction operator creates expressions of type $\langle s,a \rangle$, once variables of that type are eliminated, its use will be severely limited. But in order to eliminate it altogether, we also need to eliminate functions that take arguments of type $\langle s,a \rangle$ (such as dynamic generalized quantifiers). This is what the second step accomplishes. By means of the $\downarrow$-operator, which takes us from dynamic meanings to their truth-conditional content, we wipe out the place-holders in terms of which CCPs are defined. These two steps jointly prevent us from effectively using abstraction over assignments, and hence disactivate completely the dynamics. Thus the effect of Dynamic Blocking is that of making the interpretation of QR that of a familiar, Montague-style quantifying-in rule. (See the appendix for an example.)

This approach has an immediate consequence. Consider sentences involving indefinites, such as (91) above, repeated here as (98a):

(98)   a. If it$_i$ is well done, I always enjoy a spaghetti western$_i$.
        b.

c. $\lambda \alpha_k [\forall x [\text{spaghetti-western}(x) \wedge \alpha_k] [\text{I enjoy } x]] (\hat{}\text{well-done}(x))$
    $= \forall x [\text{spaghetti-western}(x) \wedge \text{well-done}(x)] [\text{I enjoy } x]$

The LF of (98a) is given schematically in (98b). The part below the dotted line is the tripartite structure induced by the quantificational adverb. For the object to be understood as part of the restriction (and thus be able to antecede the pronoun in the *if*-clause), it must be adjoined as shown. But this adjunction is not interpreted as quantifying-in. It is interpreted as ∃-Disclosure. Thus Dynamic Binding is not blocked, and the conversion in (98c), which schematically indicates how the LF in (98b) is interpreted, is valid. By stating Dynamic Blocking as a semantic constraint on quantifying-in, we immediately derive the asymmetry in the behavior of indefinites vis-à-vis quantificational NPs.

We may wonder what could be the intuitive rationale behind Dynamic Blocking. I think that an answer may be found in the model of information flow Dynamic Binding assumes. Dynamic Binding is rooted in the idea that each sentence sets up a context for the next one. This process inherently follows the way in which on-line, left-to-right processing takes place. Under the assumption that topicalized constituents are interpreted in their original position, these do not disturb the sequential process that leads to the incrementation of the context. Quantifying-in, however, is designed for the specific purpose of overriding the linear (in English, left-to-right) order in which quantifiers are semantically processed. Dynamic Binding does not tolerate this tampering with its standard on-line way of setting up contexts. Hence the incompatibility of quantifying-in and Dynamic Binding. I realize, of course, that this is vague and speculative. Still, there might be something to it, even if our current understanding prevents us from spelling these ideas out more precisely.

It should also be clear at this point why an approach to Weak Crossover based on Bijectivity must be replaced by one based on Leftness. In examples like Reinhart's *You should give nobody$_i$ matches near his$_i$ child's crib*, under the present assumptions we have a clear violation of Bijectivity, for *nobody* (or its trace) does not c-command *his*, and hence we have a quantifier locally binding two variables. If we exempt adjuncts from the Bijection Principle (as suggested in unpublished work by T. Stowell), then we get in trouble with left-adjoined adjuncts. In a sentence like **If a pirate spots it$_i$, a ship$_i$ is attacked by him*, nothing would prevent *a ship* from raising to a position where it could bind the pronoun *it*, and we would lose our Principle C–based explanation of the Pronominal Subject Constraint.

So we are led to deal with Reinhart's generalization (i.e., a subject/ nonsubject asymmetry that concerns quantificational NPs) in terms of a principle of Dynamic Blocking—a principle for which we have tried to offer some intuitive justification. But clearly, no amount of rhetoric on the rationale of Dynamic Blocking can hide the fact that so far it only accounts for Reinhart's generalization. We have an empirical phenomenon and we have posited a "principle" designed to take care of it. If this were all there was to it, it is not clear that one could claim to have made any substantive progress, in spite of the fact that within our set of assumptions, Dynamic Blocking comes rather naturally. However, as it turns out, the empirical coverage of Dynamic Blocking extends, perhaps surprisingly, well beyond the data we have used to motivate it. In particular, there are at least four unrelated phenomena that fall right into place if we assume Dynamic Blocking. These will now be presented in turn.

3.4.1 An Argument/Adjunct Asymmetry

It has sometimes been observed that Reinhart's generalization does not hold in unqualified form, in view of contrasts of the following kind:[18]

(99)   a.   ??Near its$_i$ stable, John beat every donkey$_i$.
        b.   To its$_i$ author, John returned every paper$_i$.

(100)   a.   ??After his$_i$ interview, John introduced the chairman to every job candidate$_i$.
        b.   To his$_i$ future boss, John introduced every newcomer$_i$.

Sentences (99a) and (100a) are rather marginal, as one would expect on the basis of Reinhart's generalization. Sentences (99b) and (100b), though, are considerably better. This comes as a surprise. However, there is an obvious difference between the (a)- and the (b)-sentences, namely the status of the fronted constituents: these are adjuncts in the former, arguments in the latter. Even though it is plausible that this difference has something to do with the contrast in grammaticality judgments, it is not clear exactly how. On the present account, a simple answer to this puzzle is available. The relevant constructions involve double object verbs. According to many authors, in this type of construction the object asymmetrically c-commands the indirect object. For example, Jacobson (1987) and Larson (1988) propose that the structure of the VP in a sentence like (99b) would be:

(101)   [returned [$_{VP}$ every paper [[$_V$ t] to its$_i$ author]]]

The trace $[_V \ t]$ is left behind by the verb, which is raised to a higher V-position. In this structure, the indirect object comes in before (i.e., lower than) the direct object. Thus the direct object can bind pronouns within the indirect object without being QR'ed. Accordingly, λ-conversion of the topicalized indirect object into its original position will be possible (i.e., it won't be blocked by QR). Hence the (b)-sentences in (99)–(100) are indeed predicted to be grammatical. In the (a)-sentences, however, the pronoun is contained in an adjunct, which is arguably higher up than VP-internal arguments. Hence our story applies in its usual manner: binding of pronouns within the adjunct from within the VP requires QR, which blocks Dynamic Binding (and λ-conversion).[19]

Notice that the present approach also predicts the following sentences to be degraded:

(102)   a. ??His$_i$ exam John returned to every student$_i$
        b. ??His$_i$ boss John introduced to every newcomer$_i$.

This is so because the fronted argument is the higher of the two. The lower argument can bind material in the upper one only via QR. So there must be QR involved in the interpretation of (102a–b), which will trigger Dynamic Blocking. Indeed, I find that the actual judgments support this prediction. As far as I know, the contrasts in (99)–(102) are unaccounted for in current theories.

3.4.2 Disambiguating Effects of Preposed Adjuncts

Consider sentence (103a):

(103)   a. A book by Eco was assigned to every student.
        b. every student$_i$ [a book by Eco was assigned to t$_i$]

Clearly, (103a) has a reading according to which *every student* has wide scope relative to *a book,* a reading represented by the LF in (103b). Now let us add to (103a) a left-adjoined modifier containing a pronoun bound by *a book:*

(104)   Since it$_j$ was interesting, a book$_j$ by Eco was assigned to every student.

Here it becomes impossible to construe *every student* as having scope over *a book.* Why? According to our analysis, left-adjoined modifiers are topics linked via an operator to an IP-internal position, while QR adjoins NPs to

IP. Here are the options we have in order to get *every student* to have wide scope:

(105)   a. [since it was interesting]$_k$ O$_k$ [every student$_i$ [a book by Eco was assigned to t$_i$ t$_k$]]
         b. [every student$_i$ [$_{CP}$ [since it was interesting]$_k$ O$_k$ [a book by Eco was assigned to t$_i$ t$_k$]]

In (105a), QR adjoins *every student* to IP. As usual, this blocks dynamic interpretation, making it impossible to convert the preposed adjunct to a position where it would be accessible to *a book*. In (105b), QR adjoins *every student* externally to the topic (i.e., given our analysis of topics, to CP). This would not interfere with Dynamic Binding, but we may assume it is disallowed by the local character of QR (cf. May 1985).

If, on the other hand, *every student* does not undergo QR, we have a structure of the following sort:

(106)   [since it was interesting]$_k$ O$_k$ [a book by Eco was assigned to every student t$_k$]

In (106), as we know, the preposed adjunct can be converted within the scope of the subject NP. This forces the wide-scope reading of *a book*. So the disambiguating effect of a preposed adjunct (with backwards anaphora into it) is predicted.

3.4.3 Asymmetries with Preposed Adjuncts Involving Non-C-Command Anaphora

A subject/nonsubject asymmetry similar to the one discussed by Reinhart can also be observed in cases of non-c-command anaphora.[20] Consider the following contrast:

(107)   a.   Near it$_i$, every man who had [a donkey]$_i$ put a bale of hay.
         b.   *Near it$_i$, John saw every man who had [a donkey]$_i$

Sentences like (107b) appear to be systematically worse than sentences like (107a), even though we are not dealing here with c-command anaphora. On any approach to donkey anaphora that does not incorporate some version of Dynamic Blocking, it is not obvious how these examples, which clearly fall together with the facts observed by Reinhart, could be dealt with. On the present approach, the contrast in (107) follows in the by now familiar fashion. The topicalized adjunct is linked to a position within IP. Material in that position can be directly bound from the subject position. Hence nothing prevents λ-conversion from lowering the adjunct into the scope of the subject, thereby making the pronoun contained in it accessible to the subject:

(108)   a.   [near it$_i$]$_k$ O$_k$ [[every man who has [a donkey]$_i$] put a bale of hay t$_k$]
         b.   λ α [[every man who has [a donkey]$_i$] put a bale of hay α] (near it$_i$)
               = [[every man wh has [a donkey]$_i$] put a bale of hay near it$_i$]

Dynamic Binding operates in the usual manner in the reduced form of (108b), where *a donkey* semantically binds *it*. Per contrast, if the binder is contained within the object position, scoping will be required. The relevant structure is this:

(109)   a.   [near it$_i$]$_k$ O$_k$ [[every man who had a donkey$_i$]$_j$ [John saw t$_j$ t$_k$]]
         b.   λα [[every man who had a donkey$_i$]$_j$ [John saw t$_j$ α]] (near it$_i$)
               ≠ [[every man who had a donkey$_i$]$_j$ [John saw t$_j$ near it$_i$]]

But QR in (109a) calls for a static semantics. Hence the conversion corresponding to (108a) is invalid and the pronoun in the preposed adjunct cannot be bound. The parallelism with the previous cases is obvious.

3.4.4 Donkey Crossover

A further set of cases I would like to discuss involves an analogue of Weak Crossover with non-c-command anaphora. Consider first the following sentence:

(110)   a.   An advisor discussed the program with every student.
         b.   [every student$_i$ [an advisor discussed the program with t$_i$]]

The universal quantifier can have scope over the subject. The relevant reading is obtained in the usual manner by QR'ing *every student,* as illustrated in (110b). In light of this fact, the ungrammaticality of sentences of the following kind might well be surprising:

(111)   a.   *An advisor discussed it$_j$ with [every student that had a problem$_j$]$_i$.
         b.   *Its$_i$ mother kicks [every farmer who beats a donkey$_i$]$_j$.
         c.   [[every student that had a problem$_j$]$_i$ [an advisor discussed it$_j$ with t$_i$]]

The ungrammaticality of (111a–b) cannot be attributed to Principle C, for *with every student that had a problem* is an adjunct and hence *it* does not c-command its antecedent. So, after QR, we have LFs like the one in (111c), which appears to be perfectly well-formed in terms of all the familiar principles. Note in particular that Weak Crossover (in our terms, Leftness) is not violated, as the relevant configuration is not met. Now, if the mechanism we have proposed to deal with donkey anaphora is available in (111b), nothing would prevent *a problem* from anteceding the pronoun *it*. In our theory this doesn't happen. Once we QR the relevant phrase as in (111c), Dynamic Binding is blocked and hence *it* cannot be bound by *a problem*. This provides us with further independent evidence that whatever is at play in donkey anaphora must be incompatible with ordinary scoping.[21]

Higginbotham (1980) considers examples parallel to (111a) that involve *wh*-movement rather than QR:

(112)   a.   [which man who owns a donkey$_i$]$_j$ t$_j$ hates it$_i$?
         b.   *[which man who owns a donkey$_i$]$_j$ does it$_i$ hate t$_j$?

By marrying the present approach with Chomsky's proposal concerning *wh*-traces we can explain this contrast. In what follows, I present the steps in the derivation of the relevant structure proposed in Chomsky 1992. Under the copy theory of traces, the structure of (112a–b) is as follows:

(113)   a.   [which man who owns a donkey$_i$]$_j$ [[which man who owns a donkey$_i$]$_j$ hates it$_i$?
         b.   *[which man who owns a donkey$_i$]$_j$ does it$_i$ hate [which man who owns a donkey$_i$]$_j$?

According to Chomsky, the *wh*-operator, in order to be interpreted, has then to be extracted from the containing NP and adjoined to it, resulting in the following structure:

(114)   a.   [which [e man who owns a donkey$_i$]] [[which [e man who owns a donkey$_i$]] hates it$_i$]]
         b.   [which [e man who owns a donkey$_i$]] [does it$_i$ hate [which [e man who owns a donkey$_i$]]]]

At this point, according to Chomsky, the *wh*-operator in situ and the restriction in A'-position are deleted (again for interpretive reasons):

(115)   a.   [which [[e man who owns a donkey$_i$] hates it$_i$]]
         b.   [which [does it$_i$ hate [e man who owns a donkey$_i$]]]

On the present theory, it is clear why (115b) is impossible on the intended reading. In (115a), the NP containing *a donkey* is in subject position. Thus, no QR is necessary and Dynamic Binding can apply in the usual way. But in (115b), the pronoun in subject position is not accessible to *a donkey*. And if we raise the subject via QR, Dynamic Binding is blocked. Hence there is no way for the pronoun in subject position to be bound.

In section 3.3.1 we noted that a semantic treatment of reconstruction in principle needs just one component of Dynamic Binding, namely abstraction over assignments. If we had just that, we could try to account for Reinhart's generalization by having QR block abstraction over discourse markers, without bothering with the rest of the dynamics. As already mentioned, a coherent approach along these lines can be developed, and someone might want to pursue it. However, besides the conceptual reasons pointed out in section 3.3.1 for going dynamic, we now have further empirical motivation to do so. To see this, suppose, for example, that we are in a static framework augmented by the possibility of abstracting over assignments to deal with reconstruction. Suppose that, consequently, we handle donkey anaphora not dynamically but, say, as in classical DRT by means of a set of construal rules. Now consider again sentence (111a) on the analysis in (111c). Clearly, suspending in such case the possibility of abstracting over assignments would leave us completely in the dark as to why (111a) is deviant. To account for (111a)'s deviance, we either must prevent the indexing in (111c) or else we must prevent the construal algorithm from taking its usual course just in case QR is involved. But this amounts to missing a clear empirical generalization, namely that the blocking of reconstruction and the donkey crossover cases both crucially involve an element scoped out of its original site. On the present dynamic approach, shutting off abstraction over assignments is part and parcel of the blocking of the dynamics. This immediately explains, besides Reinhart's generalization, the ungrammaticality of sentences like those in (111). The same holds, mutatis mutandis, of the cases discussed in section 3.4.3. Thus the empirical coverage of the present approach is broader than that of a static alternative, even if the latter is augmented by facilities to abstract over assignments.

3.5 CONCLUDING REMARKS

The starting point of the present approach is a rather simple partition algorithm for sentences containing adverbs of quantification. The adverb selects its scope by adjoining to it at LF. The restriction is whatever locally c-commands the adverb. The resulting structures are interpreted using Dynamic Binding. On the basis of the analysis of backwards donkey dependencies we are led to the following conclusion:

(116)   Backwards anaphora into a left-adjoined adjunct is made possible by "reconstructing" the adjunct into its IP-internal position.

As is clear from its formulation, (116) applies to any kind of topicalized adjunct (not just to those involving donkey-type anaphora). The generalization in (116) follows from a couple of things. If we adopt a CP-recursion analysis of topicalization, under the assumption that QR is IP-adjunction, a topic is too high up for an NP to bind into. Moreover, under a Leftness-based approach to Weak Crossover, such an adjunction would be ruled out in the relevant cases, even independently of locality considerations.

The second main aspect of our proposal can be schematically summarized as follows:

(117)   a. Aside from the copy theory of traces, there exists a purely inter-
            pretive "reconstruction" (= λ-conversion).
         b. The binding theory is formulated in terms of chains.

Something like (117a) seems to be necessary in order to interpret base-generated phrases linked to operator–variable constructions (such as at least some topics appear to be). As these structures often display connectivity effects, (117b) is called for. In a theory that has chains, this does not appear to be a particularly costly move.

The kind of λ-conversion we need for interpretive reconstruction requires abstracting over assignments, which is a key component of dynamic semantics. We have also discovered that QR (i.e., scoping) in a sense inhibits the use of abstraction over assignments, which leads to a disactivation of the dynamics. This principle, dubbed Dynamic Blocking, is the last central plank of our proposal and turns out to have a rather extensive empirical coverage. At present I don't know of any way to achieve these results with fewer stipulations. Even though aspects of our approach could be developed independently of each other, we have argued that the various principles just mentioned form a particularly integrated and coherent whole in a dynamic setting. To the extent that any of this discussion is on the right track, it shows that the fruitfulness of a dynamic approach goes well beyond the set of data originally taken to be its primary motivation (viz., basic cases of donkey anaphora).

APPENDIX

I. Left-Adjoined *If/When*-Clauses

The interpretive procedure for "reformed" tripartite structures can be stated as follows:

(1) $[CP \; ADV_{i1, \ldots, in} \; IP]$
   $\Rightarrow ADV \; (^\wedge \underline{\lambda} \; x_{i1}, \ldots, {}_{\underline{\lambda} \, xin} \; CP) \; (^\wedge \underline{\lambda} \; x_{i1}, \ldots, {}_{\underline{\lambda} \, xin} \; IP)$
   where '$\underline{\lambda}$' is the Disclosure operator:
   $\underline{\lambda} \; x_i A = \lambda \; u_i \; [A \; \triangle \; \uparrow \; u_i = x_i]$

This interpretation can also be achieved in a stepwise fashion, as follows:

(2) $[ADV_{i1, \ldots, in} \; IP]$
   $\Rightarrow \lambda\phi \; ADV \; (^\wedge \underline{\lambda} \; x_{i1}, \ldots, {}_{\underline{\lambda} \, xin} \; {}^\vee\phi) \; (^\wedge \underline{\lambda} \; x_{i1}, \ldots, {}_{\underline{\lambda} \, xin} \; IP)$

As an example, consider the object-asymmetric reading of (3a), represented as (3b):

(3)   a. If a painter lives in a village it is usually pretty.
   b.

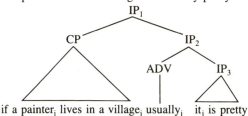

   if a painter$_i$ lives in a village$_j$ usually$_j$ it$_j$ is pretty

I assume that *usually* translates as MOST', which is a relation between dynamic properties defined in terms of MOST, the usual static generalized determiner. The interpretation of (3b) according to (2) proceeds as follows:

(4) $IP_3 \Rightarrow \; \uparrow \; pretty(x_j)$
   $IP_2 \Rightarrow \lambda\phi \; MOST' \; (^\wedge \underline{\lambda} \; x_j \; {}^\vee\phi) \; (^\wedge \underline{\lambda} \; x_j \; \uparrow \; pretty(x_j))$
   $CP \Rightarrow \exists \; x_j \; \exists \; x_i \; [\; \uparrow \; painter(x_i) \; \triangle \; \uparrow \; village(x_j) \; \triangle \; \uparrow \; lives \; in(x_i,x_j)]$
   $IP_1 \Rightarrow \lambda\phi \; MOST' \; (^\wedge \underline{\lambda} \; x_j \; {}^\vee\phi) \; (^\wedge \underline{\lambda} \; x_j \; \uparrow \; pretty(x_j)) \; (^\wedge \exists \; x_j \; \exists \; x_i \; [\; \uparrow \; painter(x_i)$
   $\triangle \; \uparrow \; village(x_j) \; \triangle \; \uparrow \; lives \; in(x_i,x_j)])$
   Reductions:
   a. $MOST' \; (^\wedge \underline{\lambda} \; x_j \exists \; x_j \exists \; x_i \; [\; \uparrow \; painter(x_i) \; \triangle \; \uparrow \; village(x_j) \; \triangle \; \uparrow \; lives \; in(x_i,$
      $x_j)]) \; (^\wedge \underline{\lambda} \; x_j \; \uparrow \; pretty(x_j))$ (λ-conv., $^\wedge \; {}^\vee$-canc.)
   b. $MOST' \; (^\wedge \underline{\lambda} \; x_j \exists \; x_i \; [\; \uparrow \; painter(x_i) \; \triangle \; \uparrow \; village(x_j) \; \triangle \; \uparrow \; lives \; in(x_i,$
      $x_j)]) \; (^\wedge \underline{\lambda} \; x_j \; \uparrow \; pretty(x_j))$ (def. of $\underline{\lambda}$)
   c. $MOST \; (\lambda \; u_j \; \exists \; u_i \; [painter(u_i) \; \wedge \; village(u_j) \; \wedge \; lives \; in(u_i, u_j) \; (\lambda u_j$
      $pretty(u_j))$ (def. of MOST')

II. Type Shifting

We define here a type-shifting device that maps dynamic generalized quantifiers into Context Change Potentials.

(5) $!\wp = \wp\ (^{\wedge}\lambda\ x\ \uparrow\ [x = x])$

Example:

(6) $!a\ painter_i = !\lambda P\ \exists\ x_i\ [\uparrow\ painter(x_i)\ \Delta\ P(x_i)]$
       Reductions:

a. $\lambda\ P\ \exists\ x_i\ [\uparrow\ painter(x_i)\ \Delta\ P\ (x_i)]\ (^{\wedge}\lambda\ x\ \uparrow\ [x =$ [def. of '!']
   $x])$

b. $\exists\ x_i\ [\uparrow\ painter(x_i)\ \Delta\ ^{\vee\wedge}\lambda\ x\ \uparrow\ [x = x]\ (x_i)]$ [λ-conv.]

c. $\underline{\exists}\ x_i\ [\uparrow\ painter(x_i)\ \Delta\ \uparrow\ [x_i = x_i]$ [˅-canc., λ-conv.]

d. $\underline{\exists}\ x_i\ [\uparrow\ painter(x_i)]$ [taut.]

e. $\lambda\ p\ \exists\ x_i\ [painter(x_i) \wedge\ ^{\vee}p]$ [def. of $\underline{\exists}$, $\uparrow$]

Formula (6e) can undergo $\exists$-Disclosure in the usual way.

III. Right-Adjoined *If/When*-Clauses

In general, a tripartite structure involving a right-adjoined *if/when*-clause will schematically look as follows (irrelevant details aside):

(7)

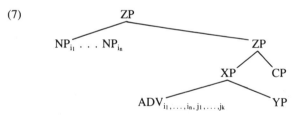

Here, YP is the scope and $NP_{i_1}, \ldots, NP_{i_n}$ plus CP are the restriction of ADV. The NP_is come from the main clause. The indices on the adverb in part match the indices on the NPs that originate in the main clause (i.e., $i_1, \ldots, i_n$); in part they disclose indefinites within the *if/when*-clause (i.e., $j_1, \ldots, j_k$). The assumption is that Q-adverbs are indexed freely; if, however, one of the indices on the Q-adverb doesn't match that of an NP in the restriction (whatever its source), the sentence will be ruled out by the Contentfulness Presupposition discussed in chapter 2, section 2.4.2. As the reader might recall, the Disclosure operation introduces an equation of the form '$x_i = u_i$'. If i is not the index of an open quantifier, this will introduce a free variable in the restriction, which winds up making the Q-adverb contentless.

The interpretation of (7) proceeds as follows:

(8) $ADV\ (^{\wedge}\underline{\lambda}\ x_{i_1}, \ldots, \underline{\lambda}\ x_{i_n}\ \underline{\lambda}\ x_{j_1}, \ldots, \underline{\lambda}\ x_{j_k}\ [!NP_{i_1}'\ \Delta \ldots \Delta\ !NP_{i_n}'\ \Delta\ CP'])$
       $(^{\wedge}\underline{\lambda}\ x_{i_1}, \ldots, \underline{\lambda}\ x_{i_n}\ \underline{\lambda}\ x_{j_1}, \ldots, \underline{\lambda}\ x_{j_k}\ YP')$

It can also be specified in a stepwise fashion, by assigning to the indexed adverbs the following interpretation:

(9) $\lambda\Psi\lambda\phi\lambda\wp_1, \ldots, \lambda\wp_n$ ADV ($^\wedge\underline{\lambda}\ x_{i_1}, \ldots, \underline{\lambda}\ x_{j_1}, \ldots, \underline{\lambda}\ x_{j_k}$ [$!\wp_1 \vartriangle \ldots \vartriangle$ $!\wp_n \vartriangle \check{}\phi$]) ($^\wedge\underline{\lambda}\ x_{i_1}, \ldots, \underline{\lambda}\ x_{i_n}\underline{\lambda}\ x_{j_1}, \ldots, \underline{\lambda}\ x_{j_k}$ [$\check{}\Psi$])

This operator combines first with the scope, then with the *if/when*-clause, and finally with an NP sequence. If the number of NPs taken as arguments by the operator in (9) doesn't match the number of those effectively found in the structure, the sentence will be uninterpretable. Here is an example:

(10)   A computer usually$_i$ routes a plane$_i$, if$_i$ it$_i$ is modern.
   a. LF: [a plane$_i$ [usually$_i$ [a computer routes t_i] if it$_i$ is modern]]

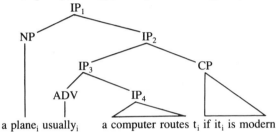

   The IP nodes are indexed for ease of reference. I first provide the interpretation of the leaves of the tree in (a):
   b. [$_{IP_4}$ a computer routes t_i] $\Rightarrow$ $\exists y$ [$\uparrow$ computer(y) $\vartriangle$ $\uparrow$ route(y, x_i)]
   c. [$_{CP}$ it$_i$ is modern] $\Rightarrow$ $\uparrow$ modern(x_i)
   d. [$_{NP}$ a plane$_i$] $\Rightarrow$ $\lambda P \exists x_i$ [$\uparrow$ plane(x_i) $\vartriangle$ P(x_i)]
   e. usually$_i$ $\Rightarrow$ $\lambda\Psi\lambda\phi\lambda\wp$ ADV ($^\wedge\underline{\lambda}\ x_i$ [$!\wp \vartriangle \check{}\phi$]) ($^\wedge\underline{\lambda}\ x_i$ [$\check{}\Psi$])

   I now turn to the interpretation of the nonterminal nodes of tree (a):

   f. [$_{IP_3}$ usually$_i$ [a computer routes t_i]]
      $\Rightarrow \lambda\Psi\lambda\phi\lambda$ MOST' ($^\wedge\underline{\lambda}\ x_i$ $!\wp \vartriangle \check{}\phi$) ($^\wedge\underline{\lambda}\ x_i\ \check{}\phi$) ($^\wedge\exists y$ [$\uparrow$ computer(y) $\vartriangle$ $\uparrow$ route(y, x_i)])
      = $\lambda\phi\lambda\wp$ MOST' ($^\wedge\underline{\lambda}\ x_i$ $!\wp \vartriangle \check{}\phi$) ($^\wedge\underline{\lambda}\ x_i\ \exists y$ [$\uparrow$ computer(y) $\vartriangle$ $\uparrow$ route(y, x_i)])
   g. [$_{IP_2}$ usually$_i$ [a computer routes t_i] if it$_i$ is modern]
      $\Rightarrow$ $\lambda\phi\lambda\wp$ MOST' ($^\wedge\underline{\lambda}\ x_i$ $!\wp \vartriangle \check{}\phi$) ($^\wedge\underline{\lambda}\ x_i\ \exists y$ [$\uparrow$ computer(y) $\vartriangle$ $\uparrow$ route(y, x_i)]) ($^\wedge$ $\uparrow$ modern(x_i))
      = $\lambda\wp$ MOST' ($^\wedge\underline{\lambda}\ x_i$ $!\wp \vartriangle \uparrow$ modern(x_i)) ($^\wedge\underline{\lambda}\ x_i\ \exists y$ [$\uparrow$ computer(y) $\vartriangle$ $\uparrow$ route(y, x_i)])
   h. [$_{IP_1}$ a plane$_i$ [usually$_i$ [a computer routes t_i] if it$_i$ is modern]]
      $\Rightarrow$ $\lambda\wp$ MOST' ($^\wedge\underline{\lambda}\ x_i$ $!\wp \vartriangle \uparrow$ modern(x_i)) ($^\wedge\underline{\lambda}\ x_i\ \exists y$ [$\uparrow$ computer(y) $\vartriangle$ $\uparrow$ route(y, x_i)]) ($\lambda P \exists x_i$ [$\uparrow$ plane(x_i) $\vartriangle$ P(x_i)])
      Reductions:
      i. MOST' ($^\wedge\underline{\lambda}\ x_i$ $!\lambda P \exists x_i$ [$\uparrow$ plane(x_i) $\vartriangle$ P(x_i)] $\vartriangle$ $\uparrow$ modern(x_i)) ($^\wedge\underline{\lambda}\ x_i\ \exists y$ [$\uparrow$ computer(y) $\vartriangle$ $\uparrow$ route(y, x_i)])   [λ-conv.]

ii. MOST' ($^\wedge\lambda$ x_i $\underline{\exists}$ x_i [$\uparrow$ plane(x_i)] $\triangle$ $\uparrow$ modern(x_i)]) ($^\wedge\lambda$ x_i $\exists y$ [$\uparrow$ computer(y) $\underline{\triangle}$ $\uparrow$ route(y, x_i)])   [def. of '!']

iii. MOST' ($^\wedge\lambda$ x_i [$\uparrow$ plane(x_i) $\triangle$ $\uparrow$ modern(x_i)]) ($^\wedge\lambda$ x_i $\underline{\exists}y$ [$\uparrow$ computer(y) $\triangle$ $\uparrow$ route(y, x_i)])   [def. of λ]

iv. MOST (λu [plane(u) $\wedge$ modern(u)]) (λu [plane(u) $\wedge$ modern(u) $\wedge$ $\exists y$ [computer(y) $\wedge$ route(y, u)]])   [def. of MOST']

IV. Dynamic Blocking

In what follows I provide the rule for quantifying-in:

(11)   [NP_i S] $\Rightarrow$ $\downarrow$ NP'(λ x_i $\downarrow$ S')
where:

i. $\downarrow$ A = $\downarrow$ [λ v_1, . . . , λ v_n A ($^\wedge u_n$) . . . ($^\wedge u_n$)], A of type cc; v_i, . . . , v_n are all the variables free in A of type $\langle s,a \rangle$, for some type a, and for any i, $1 \leq i \leq n$, u_i is a variable of type a with the same index as v_i.

ii. $\downarrow$ $\wp$ = λX $\downarrow$ [$\wp$ ($^\wedge\lambda$u $\uparrow$ X(u))], $\wp$ a dynamic generalized quantifier, X of type $\langle e,t \rangle$

Example:

(12)   a. In front of his house, every man smokes.
b. [[in front of his$_i$ house]$_k$ O_k [every man$_i$ [t_i smokes t_k]]]

Since *every man* in (12b) has undergone QR, it triggers Dynamic Blocking. Let us see how this works in detail. In what follows, let us assume that the adjunct *in front of his house* and its trace are interpreted as properties of events.

(13)   Interpretations of the parts of [every man$_i$ [t_i smokes t_k]]
a. [t_i smokes t_k] $\Rightarrow$ $\exists e$ [$\uparrow$ smoke(x_i, e) $\triangle$ $^\vee P_k$(e)]
b. every man$_i$ $\Rightarrow$ λ $\overline{Q\forall}$ x_i [$\uparrow$ man(x_i) $\underline{\to}$ $^\vee Q(x_i)$]

(14)   [every man$_i$ [t_i smokes t_k]]
$\Rightarrow$ $\downarrow$ $\lambda Q\forall$ x [$\uparrow$ man(x) $\underline{\to}$ $^\vee Q(x)$] ($^\wedge\lambda$ u_i $\downarrow$ [$\exists e$ [$\uparrow$ smoke(x_i, e) $\triangle$ $^\vee P_k$(e)])

Reductions:

a. $\downarrow$ [$\exists e$ [$\uparrow$ smoke(x_i, e) $\triangle$ $^\vee P_k$(e)] = $\downarrow$ λ P_k [$\exists e$ [$\uparrow$ smoke(x_i, e) $\triangle$ $^\vee P_k$(e)] ($^\vee V_k$)
= $\downarrow$ [$\exists e$ [$\uparrow$ smoke(u_i, e) $\triangle$ $^{\vee\wedge} V_k$(e)]   [λ-conv.]
= $\exists e$ [smoke(u_i, e) $\wedge$ $\downarrow$ V_k(e)]   [$^{\vee\wedge}$-canc., def. of $\downarrow$]
b. $\downarrow$ λ $Q\forall$ x_i [$\uparrow$ man(x_i) $\underline{\to}$ $^\vee Q(x_i)$] = λ $X\forall$ x_i[man(x_i) $\to$ X(x_i)]
c. λ $X\forall$ x_i [man(x_i) $\to$ X(x_i)] (λ u_i $\exists e$ [smoke(u_i, e) $\wedge$ $\downarrow$ V_k(e)])
= $\forall$ x_i [man(x_i) $\to$ $\exists e$ [smoke(x_i, e) $\wedge$ $\downarrow$ V_k(e)]]

(15)   a. in front of his$_i$ house $\Rightarrow$ λe $\uparrow$ [in front of x_i's house](e)
b. [[in front of his$_i$ house]$_k$ O_k [every man$_i$ [t_i smokes t_k]]]
$\Rightarrow$ λ V_k $\forall$ x_i [man(x_i) $\to$ $\exists e$ [smoke(x_i, e) $\wedge$ $\downarrow$ V_k(e)]] (λe $\uparrow$ [in front of x_i's house](e))

This formula cannot be further reduced, hence on this reading his_i cannot be bound by *every man*$_i$.

The same sentence has an analysis where the subject does not undergo QR, in which case we get the following:

(16)   [[in front of his$_i$ house]$_k$ O$_k$ [every man$_i$ smokes t$_k$]]
         $\Rightarrow \lambda$ P$_k$ $\underline{\forall}$ x$_i$ [$\uparrow$ man(x$_i$) $\underline{\rightarrow}$ $\exists$e [$\downarrow$ smoke(x$_i$, e) $\wedge$ ˆP$_k$(e)]] (ˆλe $\uparrow$ [in front of x$_i$'s house](e))

In this formula the λ-conversion is valid, and hence his_i can get bound by *every man*$_i$.

V. Binding Without Quantifying-In

(17)   [NP$_i$ VP] $\Rightarrow$ NP (λ x$_i$ VP)

(18)   Example:
         [every man$_i$ [t$_i$ thinks that Mary hates him$_i$]]
         a. every man $\Rightarrow \lambda$ P$\forall$ x [man(x) $\rightarrow$ P(x)]
         b. [t$_i$ thinks that Mary hates him$_i$] $\Rightarrow$ think(x$_i$, that Mary hates x$_i$)
         c. [every man$_i$ [t$_i$ thinks that Mary hates him$_i$]]
            $\Rightarrow \lambda$ P$\forall$ x [man(x) $\rightarrow$ P(x)] (λ x$_i$ [think(x$_i$, that Mary hates x$_i$)])
            = $\forall$ x [man(x) $\rightarrow$ think(x, that Mary hates x)]

This can be generalized to every case of functional application, but I will not pursue that point here.

4 Presuppositions and Definites

4.1 INTRODUCTION

In the present chapter, I will discuss how a dynamic semantics of the kind we have been developing deals with presupposition projection and the related issue of the interpretation of definite NPs. In particular, I will address the following questions:

(i) How do determiners affect presuppositions?

(ii) What is the relationship between anaphoric and non-anaphoric uses of definites?

Question (i) concerns the following pattern:

(1)　　a. John saw the doctor.
　　　　b. No one has spoken to the doctor.
　　　　c. No one who was seen by a nurse and a doctor has spoken to the doctor.

Sentence (1a) presupposes the existence of a unique relevant doctor, a presupposition which is triggered by the definite article *the*. Sentence (1b) shares this presuppositions with (1a). This shows that the presupposition associated with *the* "passes through" the determiner *no*. However, sentence (1c) does not seem to carry any presupposition. Unlike (1a–b), it can be uttered in a context where nothing is known about doctors. The material in the relative clause attached to *no one* seems to "cancel" the presupposition associated with *the*. This pattern is completely general and can be reproduced, as we will see, with every determiner. It constitutes an illustration of the so-called projection problem for presuppositions, which we will review shortly. While there are promising theories of presupposition projection, to my knowledge cases such as those in (1) and, in general, the projection properties of determiners have not been dealt with in full generality.[1]

Question (ii) has to do with two prominent uses of definites, the anaphoric and the non-anaphoric. The anaphoric use is illustrated in (1c). In this sentence, the value of the NP *the doctor* seems to be determined by the indefinite *a doctor*. In fact, the definite in (1c) seems to act essentially as a variable bound by *a doctor*. This contrasts, for example, with the following kind of use of definites:

(2)　　　I will meet the first baby to be born in the year 2000.

In (2), the definite is not anaphoric to another NP, nor does it presuppose any kind of familiarity with the thing being described. While there are good theories of the use exemplified in (1c) and good theories of the use illustrated in (2), there are no theories, as far as I know, that handle both examples in an equally enlightening manner.

Questions (i) and (ii) are interconnected, partly because the definite article is itself a determiner and partly because one cannot discuss definites without getting into presuppositions. In fact, as we will see, these questions will lead us to several others also related to the interaction between quantification and presuppositions.

The plan of this chapter is as follows. In the remainder of the present section I give some preliminary background concerning presuppositions and their projection and discuss the specific form that the problem takes within the framework I am adopting. In section 4.2, I articulate my approach and show how it deals with the presuppositional properties of standard connectives and quantifiers. In section 4.3, I present specific applications of the framework developed in section 4.2 to the behavior of verbs of propositional attitude and, especially, to determiners. In section 4.4, I address the issue of definites, and finally in section 4.5 I discuss some further consequences and loose ends of the theory.

4.1.1 The Projection Problem in a Dynamic Setting

Since the early work on this issue, it was observed that the presuppositions of simple, atomic sentences are projected in regular ways to the sentences of which they are part, so that the presuppositions of a complex sentence are in a way compositionally predictable. A particularly clear case, much discussed in the literature, is that of the standard logical connectives. Generally speaking, the presuppositions of a sentence of the form [ϕ Conn ψ] are a simple function of the presuppositions of ϕ and ψ and the nature of the connective Conn. So, for example, the presuppositions of a sentence of the form $\neg\phi$ are the same as the presuppositions of ϕ (i.e., in Karttunen's 1974 terms, negation is a "hole"). The presuppositions of a conjunction, by contrast, are the presuppositions of both conjuncts, *unless* the first conjunct entails the presuppositions of the second, in which case the presuppositions of the second are "filtered out." This is illustrated in (3):

(3)   a. John too likes Mary.
       b. John, in addition to some x (contextually specified), likes Mary.[2]
       c. John too likes Mary, and he is not happy.
       d. John is not happy, and he too likes Mary.
       e. Bill likes Mary, and John too likes her.

To utter sentence (3a) felicitously we must assume that the truth of something like (3b) is taken for granted (this presupposition is triggered by *too*). Sentence (3a) is the first conjunct of sentence (3c), and we see that (3c) as a whole inherits (3b) as a presupposition; that is, we would normally utter something like (3c) only in a context where (3b) is known to hold. The same applies to (3d). The situation is distinctly different for (3e). Sentence (3e) does not require that (3b) is already taken for granted at the time of utterance. We can felicitously utter (3e) in a context where nothing is known as to whom John likes. This means that the presupposition of the second conjunct in (3e) is, as it were, filtered out by the fact that it is entailed by the first conjunct.

The pattern of presupposition inheritance illustrated in (3) is also associated with conditionals and, as we will see, is very general indeed. Disjunction has a different projection pattern instead. [ϕ or ψ] inherits the presupposition of both disjuncts, unless the negation of one of them entails the presuppositions of the other. This is illustrated by the following example:

(4)   a. John likes Mary too, or he is unhappy.
        b. Either John doesn't likes Sue, or he likes Mary too.
        c. John likes Mary too, or he doesn't like Sue.

While (4a) requires that John loves somebody else besides Mary, (4b–c) do not; that is, they can be uttered naturally in a context where it is not known whether John likes anybody.

It is not just logical connectives that display a regular behavior with respect to presupposition projection. Other constructions do as well. For example, as argued by Karttunen (1974), a sentence like (5a) seems to presuppose something like (5b).

(5)   a. John hopes that Mary too will be present.
        b. John believes that somebody (contextually specified) other than Mary will be present.

In fact, prima facie (5a) might be thought to have the stronger presupposition that the speaker has the belief attributed to John in (5b). But Karttunen points out examples of the following kind:

(6)   John erroneously believes that Sue will be present and hopes that Mary too will be.

The felicity of (6) indicates that what (5a) presupposes must indeed be something along the lines of (5b).

In considering this and other examples below it should be borne in mind that presuppositions in certain cases can be "accommodated," as Lewis (1979) puts it. So I can say, for example, "I don't regret that John will not be able to come," to convey, indirectly, that John will not be able to come. That is, in a context where it is not taken for granted that John will not be able to come, an addressee, upon hearing the sentence in question, will tend to automatically modify the context by entering into it that John will not be able to come, if she has no independent evidence against this presupposition. In general, the hearer tends to accommodate the presuppositions of a sentence, in the absence of evidence to the contrary. While most theories agree on the fact that processes of accommodation such as the one just sketched are possible, they differ greatly on the *extent* to which it is possible to accommodate. On this issue we will side with those that try to narrowly constrain the ways in which accommodation can take place.

Dynamic semantics not only offers a descriptive apparatus within which the projection problem for presuppositions can be captured. It also arguably sheds some light on the reasons why the projection properties of various elements are what they are. Let me try to illustrate in a very sketchy form how such a case can be made. As we know from chapter 1, illocutionary agents must rely on a body of shared information to successfully engage in a conversational exchange. Following Stalnaker (1978), this body of shared information can be thought of as a set of worlds, namely those compatible with such information—in Stalnaker's terms, the *context set*. The utterance of ϕ against the background of a given context set c typically narrows down the set of live alternatives by excluding those incompatible with ϕ. In a dynamic setting (putting aside for the moment the treatment of anaphora developed so far), we can represent this by interpreting ϕ in terms of a function $+ \phi$ from context sets into new context sets. The utterance of ϕ in c takes us into $c + \phi$, which will include those members of the original context c in which ϕ holds.[3] As we will see more clearly below, the function $+ \phi$ is related to, but somewhat different from, Context Change Potentials (CCPs) as defined in the previous chapters. Following the terminology of Veltman (1990), we will call $+ \phi$ an *update function*. Presuppositions, then, can be thought of as felicity conditions on context sets. A context set c must satisfy ϕ's presuppositions for ϕ to be interpretable in c. In other words, the update function $+ \phi$ is a partial one. It yields a value only for the contexts sets in whose worlds ϕ's presuppositions are true.

Assuming that (atomic) sentences are interpreted as update functions, there are natural ways of recursively defining the contribution of various sentential operators, from which the projection behavior of the operators follows. For example, the update function of negative sentences can be defined as in (7):

(7) $c + \neg\phi = c - (c + \phi)$ (where for any set of worlds a,b: a $-$ b $= \{w \in a: w \notin b\}$)

According to (7), uttering $\neg\phi$ in c amounts to subtracting from it the worlds in which ϕ holds. Notice now that (7) immediately explains why negation is a hole with respect to presuppositions: in order to compute $c + \neg\phi$, we must first compute $c + \phi$. Hence $c + \neg\phi$ will be defined iff $c + \phi$ is. By the same token, the update function of conjoined sentences can be represented along the following lines:

(8) $c + [\phi \text{ and } \psi] = (c + \phi) + \psi$

In (8), conjunction is represented simply as a composition of functions. To compute $c + [\phi \text{ and } \psi]$, we first compute $(c + \phi)$. This provides us with the new context in which ψ is evaluated. A definition of this sort predicts that *and* is a filter and what its filtering properties are. It is easy to see that if the presuppositions of ϕ and ψ are independent of one another, the initial context c will have to satisfy them both, or else $c + [\phi \text{ and } \psi]$ will be undefined. But if ϕ entails ψ's presuppositions, then obviously so does $(c + \phi)$; since ψ operates on $(c + \phi)$, its presuppositions are guaranteed to be satisfied. Consequently, the original context c must only satisfy ϕ's presuppositions. This is just what the filtering effects of *and* amount to.

Similar considerations can be developed in connection with other connectives as well. At this introductory level, we are interested in underlining a general point that has already emerged from these sketchy considerations, namely that by viewing meanings as update functions, we can come to a better understanding of how the projective behavior of various connectives is related to their content as standardly conceived. This seems to be a step forward that the dynamic approach can claim to its credit, a point made forcefully in Heim 1983.

4.1.2 Presuppositions and Anaphora

In the informal discussion of update functions in section 4.1.1, we have temporarily disregarded the treatment of anaphora developed in the previous chapters. One of our goals is to integrate that treatment with an approach to presuppositions along the lines suggested above. This turns out not to be so straightforward. To see why, let us compare the approach just sketched with the extensional theory we have been working with so far. In such a theory, we represent the CCP of a sentence φ as the set of its admissible continuations, namely $\lambda p[\phi \wedge \check{~}p]$. Consider now an update function $+ \phi$. Note that while c in c + φ represents the initial context in which φ is processed, p in $\lambda p[\phi \wedge \check{~}p]$ represents what remains open after processing φ. This difference is clearly reflected in the definition of conjunction of CCPs, repeated here from chapter 2 (56i):

(9) $A \triangle B = \lambda p(A(\hat{~}B(p)))$

This should be contrasted with the definition we have in (8). There we applied the *first* conjunct to the initial context and the *second* conjunct to the result. In (9) we first apply the *second* conjunct to possible continuations and then we apply the *first* to the result. The definition in (8) works well for presuppositions. The one in (9) works well for binding. How can they be integrated in a unitary view of information flow?

There is an answer to this question which prima facie seems to be promising. We might build information states out of pairs ⟨w,g⟩ of worlds and assignments. The world coordinate can be used to represent factual knowledge and presuppositions, while assignments can be used to encode information on binding (e.g., which discourse referents are "alive"). Viewing CCPs as functions that simultaneously manipulate worlds and assignments, we can hope to arrive at a unified account of the various facets of context change. File Change Semantics as originally formulated by Heim (1982) is built on this idea. And virtually all the work done within dynamic semantics that deals with both presuppositions and binding (e.g., Dekker 1993 and Beaver 1994) follows essentially this same line.

I have some misgivings about viewing context change as a single function that operates simultaneously on world–assignment pairs. They have to do with the observation that the two coordinates in question behave independently of each other with respect to many phenomena, which makes it of little use to deal with them in terms of a single function. I will illustrate this with three cases. The first has to do with sentence embedding. Consider a sentence like (10a) and its natural interpretation in terms of world–assignment pairs given in (10b):

(10)   a. He_1 is a genius.
          b. $\lambda c.\{\langle w,g \rangle \in c: g(he_1)$ is a genius in w$\}$

The function in (10b) takes as input sets of world–assignment pairs and returns as outputs new sets in which the g-coordinate maps he_1 into individuals that are geniuses with respect to the w-coordinate. Now, normally one assumes that sentence-embedding verbs take as arguments the (intensional) semantic value of their complements. Thus, one might naively expect the interpretation of a sentence like (11a) to be something like (11b):

(11)   a. Mary believes that he_1 is a genius.
        b. believe $(\lambda c.\{\langle w,g \rangle \in c: g(he_1)$ is a genius in $w\})$(Mary)

But this seems wrong. A predicate like *believe* does not seem to operate on an object like (10b), where the value of *he₁* is abstracted over. Intuitively, in (11a) the value of *he₁* is kept constant: *believe* only cares for the w-coordinate of (10a). To account for this we must be able to abstract over worlds independently of assignments.

Second, there are also cases where we want to do the opposite, namely abstract over assignments but not over worlds. In chapter 3, section 3.2.4, I have argued that sentences like (12a) have the syntactic structure displayed in (12b), which is interpreted as in (12c):

(12)   a. If it has blue eyes, a cat is usually intelligent.
        b. [if it has blue eyes]$_k$ [a cat is usually intelligent t$_k$]
        c. $\lambda \beta \ [most_x \ [cat(x) \ \wedge \ ^{\vee}\beta][intelligent(x)]](^{\wedge}has\text{-}blue\text{-}eyes(x))$
           $= [most_x \ [cat(x) \ \wedge \ has\text{-}blue\text{-}eyes(x)][intelligent(x)]]$

In (12b), it is assumed that the left-adjoined *if*-clause is fronted from an IP-internal position. The interpretation of this structure is simply taken to be a conversion of the meaning of the *if*-clause back into its extraction site, along the lines indicated in (12c). In this way, the clause *has-blue-eyes(x)* is incorporated in the restriction of the quantifier *most*. As we noted, in this conversion a pronoun which is seemingly free winds up in the scope of a binder. We have seen that on our treatment of binding, an operation of this sort is straightforwardly available, for the ^-operator abstracts over assignments. Note, now, that the operation in (12c) manipulates only assignments; it doesn't affect content or presuppositions. Thus the content and projection properties of (12a) appear to be the same as those of its counterpart *A cat is usually intelligent if it has blue eyes*. (The two sentences can, of course, have a different focal structure.) Hence the operation in (12c) only affects the g-coordinate.

A third order of considerations has to do with the different properties that the aspect of context change relating to presuppositions and the one relating to anaphora seem to have. For example, there are connectives, such as negation, that let presuppositions go through but generally shut off discourse reference. The opposite is also attested. Connectives such as conjunction can filter out the presuppositions of their second conjunct while passing on discourse markers. If context change is, in a sense, made up of two autonomous functions (one operating over worlds, the other over assignments), differences of this kind are to be expected. If, on the other hand, context change is made up of just one function, these differences are less clearly expected.

In the early times of the study of context dependency (e.g., in Montague 1968), it was argued that the meaning of a sentence can be represented as a function from a sequence of coordinates (like a speaker, a hearer, a time, a world, . . .) into truth values. In this view, the contributions to meaning of context and content were treated on a par, which prima facie appeared to be the simplest option technically. However, Stalnaker (1974) and Kaplan (1977) have countered that it is ultimately preferable to keep the contribution of context distinct from that of content. Kaplan, in particular, has proposed a distinction between "character" and "content," where a character is a function from contexts into contents. There is an obvious parallel between Kaplan's distinction and the behavior of the assignment coordinate with respect to the world coordinate in dynamic semantics. In fact, the above argument about embedding is modelled on one by Stalnaker and Kaplan.

On the basis of these considerations, I am inclined to think that it is useful to maintain a distinction in a dynamic setting that is in some ways analogous to the one advocated by Kaplan. The idea is that there are two autonomous and interacting components to discourse dynamics. One involves checking whether the input context meets the presuppositional requirement of a sentence. This aspect is inherently backward-looking: it looks at the context as it is, prior to the processing of the sentence. The second aspect is the introduction or subtraction of discourse referents. This second aspect is inherently forward-looking. It sets up "hooks" onto which new pieces of incoming information can be hung. Taking this intuition at face value, we will formulate a two-layered dynamics. First, update functions will be introduced to deal with the projection problem. Then full-blown Context Change Potentials will be (re)defined out of update functions, to deal with binding. Finally, within this setup, we will look at the projection properties of quantifiers. This project can be schematized as follows:

	Updates	*Context Change Potentials*
Type	Functions from context sets into context sets	Relations between input contexts and admissible continuations
Coverage	Content, presuppositions	Binding, anaphora

This is still a rough approximation. The task now is to fill in the details.

4.2 A FRAMEWORK FOR PRESUPPOSITIONS AND ANAPHORA

In the present section, I will present in more detail a presuppositional dynamics. In doing so, I will follow a general strategy advocated by various researchers (e.g., Beaver 1994) and mentioned in section 4.1, namely that of limiting accommodation to a minimum. In particular, I will only admit "global" accommodation of the input context. Here is what I mean by that. A discourse of the form $[S_1, \ldots, S_n]$ will be construed as a complex function that operates on an input context and progressively modifies it. Some adjustment of the input context will be allowed, but ideally, "intermediate" or "local" accommodation will not be. I will call this the *Root Context Constraint*. Examples of global accommodation are those originally discussed by Lewis (and presented in section 4.1.1). As an example of local accommodation, we might recall Heim's (1982) treatment of the following sentence (discussed in chapter 1, section 1.7.3):

(13)   Everyone$_i$ likes his$_i$ father.

According to Heim (1982), definites must be linked to already established discourse referents. However, (13) can be uttered felicitously in a context where no discourse referent associated with *his$_i$ father* has been explicitly introduced. Hence we need accommodation. In Heim's (1982) framework, accommodating globally in the initial context amounts to assuming that everyone has the same father, which runs against common sense. Hence we have no option but to accommodate more locally, thereby obtaining the interpretation 'Everyone who has a father loves him'.

Now, I doubt that this is even descriptively adequate, for consider the following sentences:

(14)   a. In this community everyone likes his doctor.
        b. In this community everyone likes the doctor.

Imagine talking about a small community where, for all we know, everyone might or might not have the same doctor. If Heim's suggestion is correct, in such a situation global accommodation should be preferred, and (14a) should be interpreted just like (14b). But this is clearly not so. There is no detectable difference in interpretation between (13) and (14a).

At any rate, independent of empirical shortcomings, the main reason for sticking to the Root Context Constraint is that while, as Beaver puts it, judicious use of intermediate and local accommodation can lead to a descriptively adequate characterization of presuppositional dynamics, it arguably does so at the cost of a loss in explanatory force, for at present there are no clear constraints on when and how local or intermediate accommodation is to be used. For this reason alone, it is interesting to see how far one can go with the Root Context Constraint, even if ultimately it turns out to be too restrictive.

4.2.1 Intensionality

Since I find it convenient to couch my approach in a version of Montague's IL (as I have done for anaphora), I will first discuss some preliminary changes in the underlying logic that will facilitate our task. So far the version of IL we have been using, though syntactically identical to Montague's IL, has been a purely extensional one. The operators '^' and '˅' have been used as an abstractor over assignments and as an application to the "current" assignment, respectively. As a first step toward dealing with presuppositions, we need to bring intensions back into the picture. For the reasons laid out in section 4.1.2, we do not want to add worlds as a further parameter with respect to which expressions are evaluated. The other option, then, is to add worlds as a new type, as in Gallin's (1975) TY2. The resulting system will be the union, as it were, of IL and TY2.

As a second step toward an analysis of presuppositions we need to partialize the logic, since some expressions may lack a value due to presupposition failure. This entails, in particular, that formulae may fail to have a truth value in certain contexts. The partial logic I will adopt for our purposes is Kleene's strong logic.[4] The principle underlying such logic is that as soon as we have enough information to determine the truth value of a formula, we do so. Thus, for example, if we a have a conjunction [$\phi \wedge \psi$] and we know that ϕ is false, this suffices to make the whole conjunction false (regardless of whether ψ has a definite truth value). The same applies, mutatis mutandis, to other connectives and to quantifiers. The details of the formal system can be found in the appendix to this chapter, part I. It should be borne in mind that this system does not, in itself, provide a full-blown presuppositional logic. (For example, Kleene's truth table for 'or' does not give us its projection properties.) It merely constitutes a formal frame within which a presuppositional logic can be formulated.

To implement all this, let w be the type of worlds. We will use w', w'', . . . as variables ranging over worlds. Propositions are (total or partial) functions from worlds into truth values (of type $p = \langle w,t \rangle$). If a proposition (and, in general, any function of type $\langle a,t \rangle$) is total we will say that it is a *set*. Ordinary relations (i.e., those used to represent basic verbs) are assumed to have a world argument.[5] Here are some examples:

(15)   a. run(x)(w) = x runs in w   (*run* is of type $\langle e,\langle w,t\rangle\rangle$)
        b. love(x)(y)(w) = y loves x in w
        c. λw run(x)(w) = the proposition that x runs

For ease of readability, I will write '$run_w(x)$' for 'run(x)(w)'. Also, I will often use the relational notation 'run(w,x)' instead of the functional one 'run(w)(x)'.

Though it is not strictly speaking necessary, I find it convenient to rearrange the interpretive procedure so that sentences are assigned type p (as in, e.g., Cresswell 1973) rather than type t (as in Montague 1973). Below I give a list of some category–type associations, together with simple examples. I introduce the following notational convention. If α is a predicate of type $\langle w,\langle e,t\rangle\rangle$, α' is the corresponding propositional function of type $\langle e,\langle w,t\rangle\rangle$.

(16)   *Category*   *Type*   *Example*

Category	Type	Example
VP	$\langle e,p\rangle$	$run' = \lambda x\lambda w[run_w(x)]$
CN	$\langle e,p\rangle$	$boy' = \lambda x\lambda w[boy_w(x)]$
Det	$\langle\langle e,p\rangle,\langle e,p\rangle,p\rangle$	$every' = \lambda P\lambda Q\lambda w\forall x[P(x)(w)\rightarrow Q(x)(w)]$
S	p	$every'(boy')(run') = \lambda w\forall x[boy_w(x)\rightarrow run_w(x)]$

The standard connectives and quantifiers are defined for expressions of type t; in view of the change outlined in (16), it is useful to extend them to propositions as well. This extension is a straightforward pointwise definition:

(17)   If ϕ and ψ are expressions of type p, then:
        a. $\phi \wedge \psi = \lambda w[\phi(w) \wedge \psi(w)]$
        b. $\phi \vee \psi = \lambda w[\phi(w) \vee \psi(w)]$
        c. $\neg\phi = \lambda w\neg[\phi(w)]$
        d. $\exists x\phi = \lambda w\exists x[\phi(w)]$ (similarly for other connectives and quantifiers)
        e. $\phi \subseteq \psi = \forall w[\phi(w) \rightarrow \psi(w)]$
        f. $D'(\lambda x\phi,\lambda x\psi) = \lambda wD(\lambda x\phi(w),\lambda x\psi(w))$
           (where D is of type $\langle\langle e,t\rangle,\langle\langle e,t\rangle,t\rangle\rangle$ and D' of type $\langle\langle e,p\rangle,\langle\langle e,p\rangle,p\rangle\rangle$)

I will use the terms 'property' and 'propositional function' interchangeably for expressions of type $\langle e,p\rangle$.[6] In a system like the one I have just sketched, propositional functions can be *total* or *partial*. Furthermore, when a propositional function is applied to an individual u in its domain, it can yield a total or a partial proposition. I will make rather limited use of these facilities. In particular, simple nonpresuppositional expressions like *woman* or *smoke* are going to be interpreted in the lexicon as total propositional functions[7] that always yield total propositions. In contrast, lexical entries that are presupposition triggers will be associated in the lexicon with (total) propositional functions that yield partial propositions. Thus, for example, for any proposition p and individual x, 'regret$'$(p)(x)' is a proposition that has a definite value only in those worlds where p is true. This "semantic" notion of presupposition will only be used to encode lexical information. It does not coincide with the full-blown pragmatic notion of presupposition, which will be modelled in terms of context updates.[8]

A final preliminary observation concerns Montague-style "intensional" types. We maintain as in standard IL that for any type $a, \langle s,a \rangle$ is a type. Expressions of type $\langle s,a \rangle$ are associated with functions from assignments (i.e., an aspect of the context) into objects of type a. Accordingly, they resemble Kaplanian characters more than ordinary intensions and I shall refer to them by that name.

To summarize, we have outlined a partial intensional logic (formally laid out in the appendix). This system is not yet a theory of presuppositions but has all the basic ingredients we need to formulate such a theory. I should add as an aside that I believe there is some good evidence that the notions of property and proposition we need in semantics cannot be properly defined in terms of possible worlds, but have to be taken as primitives. This means that ultimately the line I am taking here might well need to be revised. But for our purposes this more traditional approach will do.[9]

4.2.2 Updates

In the present section, I will discuss the notion of context update. As argued by Stalnaker, a purely semantic notion of presupposition does not suffice to adequately capture presuppositional phenomena in general. If Stalnaker is right, what is coded in the partiality of propositions can at best be a technical, abstract relation we need to get the system going. Our final goal, though, must be a full-fledged pragmatic notion of presupposition. Such a notion has to do with the way in which the common ground is modified by incoming information. In particular, according to Stalnaker, the content of a proposition p is used to update what was known prior to finding out that p. And if p's presuppositions are not met in c, p cannot be used to update it. What we want to do first is formalize this notion within our framework.

A context set c will be modelled within IL as a total function from worlds into truth values. I will use c as that subtype of p ranging over total functions. When we utter a proposition ϕ in a context set c, ϕ will be felicitous iff c entails φ's presuppositions. This means that the proposition p expressed by φ must be total when restricted to c; for p has a value only in those worlds where its presuppositions hold. Hence, if p has a value in all the members of a context set c, this means that in all such worlds, p's presuppositions are met. This observation leads to the following view on information flow. In trying to add to a context set c the information encoded in p, we first check whether the restriction of p to c (in symbols, 'p↾c') is total. If it is, we exclude from c the world incompatible with p. If it isn't, we stop (and possibly try to accommodate). We can represent this process by defining a context updating function along the following lines:

(18)   a. $[c + p] = [c \wedge p]$, if p↾c is total; else $\perp$, where '$\perp$' stands for 'undefined'.

    b. Example:
        $[c + run'(x)] = [c \wedge run'(x)]$ $(= \lambda w[c(w) \wedge run_w(x)])$, if run'(x)↾c is total; else $\perp$.

The symbol '$\perp$' in (18) stands for "undefined". Note that to say that p↾c is total is to say that p↾c is a set—that there are no worlds such that p↾c(w) is undefined (cf. FACT 1 in the appendix, part II). Hence we can restate (18) as:

(19) $[c + p] = [c \wedge p]$, if $[c \wedge p]$ is a set; else $\perp$.

For any proposition p, the function $\lambda c[c + p]$ (of type $\langle c,c \rangle$) is the formal representation of a context updating function. If the context fails to satisfy p's presupposition, $\lambda c[c + p]$ will yield "error," that is, $\perp$. The newly defined operator ' + ' can be viewed as a way of mapping a proposition p to the corresponding update $\lambda c[c + p]$ (which we will abbreviate as ' +p').

    An update f contains, in some sense, a proposition, which can be compositionally retrieved from f. So, if f is an update function, we define $-f$ (i.e., the proposition associated with f) as follows:

(20)   a. $-f = \lambda w[f(\{w\}) = \{w\}]$, where $\{w\}$ is the singleton that contains only w (formally, $\{w\} = \lambda w'[w' = w]$)

    b. Example:
        $- \lambda c[c + run'(j)] = \lambda w[\lambda c[c + run'(j)](\{w\}) = \{w\}]$
        $= \lambda w[\{w\} + run'(j) = \{w\}]$

As the example should make clear, for every world w, we update w with f and look at the results. Out of what we get, we can reconstruct the proposition contained in f. In particular, the last line of (20b) is a proposition which is provably equivalent to 'run$'($j$)$'. More generally, it can be shown that for any proposition p, $- + p = p$. Thus '$-$' is the inverse of '$+$', (cf. FACT 2 in the appendix, part II). So, the relations between updates and their propositional content can be diagrammed as follows:

(21)   Updates $+$ Propositions

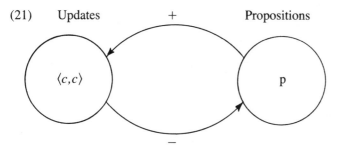

We will soon see the precise role that updates will play in the recursive interpretation of English. However, to anticipate one aspect of the outcome, eventually each sentence will correspond to an update function. So, for example, (22a) will end up interpreted as (22b) and (22c) as (22d):

(22)   a. John is bald.
        b. $\lambda c[c + bald'(j)]$
        c. John is bald and he regrets it.
        d. $\lambda c[[c + bald'(j)] + regret'(j, bald'(j)])]$[10]

It is easy to see that this approach is capable, in principle, of yielding a treatment of the projection problem in the spirit of the one informally discussed in section 4.1.1. Consider, for example, the update function corresponding to sentence (22c) above, which is given in (22d), and imagine evaluating it in a context c*. This amounts to applying (22b) to c*, which in turn involves computing first 'c* + bald$'($j$)$.' The outcome of this will be a contextually supplied set of worlds in which John is bald. But such a set automatically meets the factive presupposition associated with the second conjunct in (22d). Hence the function in (22d) is always defined, for every context, in spite of the fact that its second component is partial. The projective behavior of conjunction seems to be nicely captured.

Updates enable us to define a notion of *felicity* relative to a context set. An update function A is felicitous in a context set c iff A(c) is defined. If an update function A is felicitous in c, we say that it is true in a world w of c if $A(c)(w) = 1$ and false if it $A(c)(w) = 0$. Note that by definition, if an update function is felicitous in c, A(c) is a total function (i.e., a set). Notice also that we limit ourselves to evaluating updates relative to worlds that are considered live alternatives in the context of evaluation (i.e., to worlds that are members of c).

Updates as defined so far handle presuppositions well but have nothing to contribute to the dynamics of anaphora. We now turn to a discussion of how they can be integrated with the approach to pronouns developed in the previous chapters.

4.2.3 Context Change Potentials Revisited

For essentially technical reasons, an update of the form $\lambda c[c + \phi]$ turns out not to have the right structure for dealing with anaphora. However, it also turns out to be the case that if we lift the type of updates to $\lambda c \lambda P[^{\vee}P(c + \phi)]$, we get just what we want. The function $\lambda c \lambda P^{\vee}P(c + \phi)$ (where P is of type $\langle s, \langle c, t \rangle \rangle$) maps an input context c into all the properties of the context that result if we update c with ϕ. Lifted updates can be thought of as relations between an input context and its admissible continuations. From now on, we will reserve the name "Context Change Potential" for lifted updates. The basic idea is that rather than defining CCPs from formulae (i.e., ultimately, propositions) as we have done so far, we define them from updates by means of a type-lifting operation. This means that we redefine ' ↑ ' as follows:

(23)   a. For any update function A (of type 'up' = $\langle c, c \rangle$):
           ↑ A = $\lambda c \lambda P[^{\vee}P(A(c))]$, where P is of type $\langle s, \langle c, t \rangle \rangle$
        b. Example:
           ↑ $\lambda c[c + run'(x)] = \lambda c \lambda P[^{\vee}P(c + run'(x))]$

To better see the relation between the old and the new way of defining CCPs, it might be useful to rewrite them as follows:

(24)   a. New way: $\lambda c \lambda P \exists b[c + run'(x) = b \wedge {^{\vee}}P(b)]$
        b. Old way: $\lambda p[run(x) \wedge {^{\vee}}p]$

The function in (24a) is clearly the same as the function in (23b). However, writing it in this more long-winded form might help bring out the similarity to our old way of defining CCPs. The variable p in (24b) is a placeholder for possible ways of adding to the available information. The content of a new sentence S is going to occupy this slot (and in the process, variables may get bound). The variable P in (24a) plays the same role as the variable p in (24b): that of being the hook to which incoming information is going to be attached. However, (24a) contains an additional hook, represented by the variable c. This stands for the *initial* context, that is, the information that is already there on which the function in (24b) is going to operate. In this sense, (24a) relates an initial context to the set of its admissible continuations. It is simultaneously backward-looking and forward-looking, encoding both aspects of the discourse dynamics. In particular, by setting things up in this way, we can directly lift the logic of CCPs presented in chapter 2.

Before looking at the logic of CCPs, we should check how from a CCP $\uparrow \lambda c[c + p]$ we can retrieve the corresponding update function $\lambda c[c + p]$ in a compositional manner. We do so by redefining ' $\downarrow$ ' as follows.

(25)   For any CCP β: $\downarrow \beta = \lambda c \lambda w[\beta(c)(^{\wedge}\lambda a[a(w)])]$

Intuitively, $\downarrow$ A takes the union of the smallest members of A. Let us consider a simple example:

(26) $\downarrow \uparrow \lambda c[c + d] = \downarrow \lambda c \lambda P \exists b[c + d = b \wedge ^{\vee}P(b)]$

$= \lambda c' \lambda w[\lambda c \lambda P \exists b[c + d = b \wedge ^{\vee}P(b)](c')(^{\wedge}\lambda a[a(w)])]$ (def. of ' $\downarrow$ ')

$= \lambda c' \lambda w[\exists b[c' + d = b \wedge ^{\vee \wedge}\lambda a[a(w)](b)]]$ (λ-conv.)

$= \lambda c' \lambda w \exists b[c' + d = b \wedge b (w)]$ ($^{\vee \wedge}$-canc., λ-conv.)

$= \lambda c' \lambda w[c' + d](w)$ (elementary logic)

$= \lambda c'[c' + d]$ (def. of 'λ')

So ' $\uparrow$ ' takes us from update functions into CCPs, while ' $\downarrow$ ' takes us from CCPs back to update functions. As before, $\downarrow \uparrow A = A$ (as (26) shows), but $\uparrow \downarrow \beta \neq \beta$, for ' $\uparrow \downarrow$ ' "closes off" any quantifier that may be active in β. This can be summarized in the following schema:

(27)   Context Change Potentials   Updates

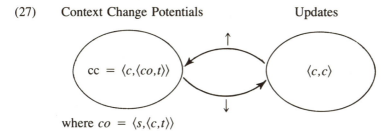

where $co = \langle s, \langle c, t \rangle \rangle$

By putting this together with the schema in (21) (section 4.2.2), which displays the relation between updates and propositions, we get:

(28)   CCPs   Updates   Propositions

The ⇑-operator is simply the composition of ' ↑ ' with ' + ' which will take us directly from a proposition p to the corresponding CCP: ⇑p = ↑ + p. Similarly, '⇓' is the composition of ' − ' and ' ↓ ' and takes us from CCPs into the corresponding propositions (i.e., if A is a CCP, ⇓A = − ↓ A). In virtue of the equivalences previously established, we have that ⇓⇑ p = p, but ⇑⇓ A ≠ A (⇑⇓ A has the effect of closing off all the discourse markers active in A). By exploiting the systematic relationships between these three levels of meaning, we may shift back and forth among them as necessary. This means that we can simultaneously access the CCP of a sentence, the corresponding update, and its propositional content. We will soon find an indication of the usefulness of doing so.

We have already defined what it is for an update to be felicitous and true in a context. Since we can extract from CCPs the corresponding update functions, we can naturally extend these definitions to the former. We can say that a CCP β is felicitous in a context c iff the corresponding update (i.e., ↓ β) is felicitous in c. And if β is felicitous in c, we can say that it is true in a world w of c just in case ↓ β is (i.e., just in case ↓ $\beta(c)(w)$ = 1). So, for example, *John runs* translates as '⇑run′(j)'. We say that this is felicitous in c iff ↓ ⇑run′(x) (i.e., $\lambda c[c + run′(x)]$) is. And we say that if $\lambda c[c + run′(x)]$ is felicitous in c, then it is true in a world w in c iff [c + run′(x)](w) = 1. This leads us to the following general definition:

(29)   a. A CCP β is *felicitous* in a context c iff ↓ $\beta(c)$ ≠ ⊥.
         b. A CCP β that is felicitous relative to c is *true* in a world w in c iff ↓ $\beta(c)(w)$ = 1, and is false in w iff ↓ $\beta(c)(w)$ = 0.

With this in place, it is a relatively easy task to define a logic for CCPs by carrying over what we already have (i.e., essentially, the Dynamic Logic of Groenendijk and Stokhof) to the new type of CCPs. The crucial cases are those of conjunction and existential quantification, which are once more treated as composition operations of a sort. Here are the relevant definitions:

(30)   a. $\beta \vartriangle \gamma = \lambda c \lambda P[\beta(c)(^\wedge \lambda c'[\gamma(c')(P)])]$
        b. $\underline{\exists}x\beta = \lambda c \lambda P \exists x[\beta(c)(P)]$

Intuitively, '$\beta \vartriangle \gamma$' says roughly that there are admissible inputs to γ among the possible outputs of β (in an initial context c). Existential quantification over CCPs is just plain composition.

English sentences are going to be interpreted as CCPs (as reinterpreted here), and various constituents are going to be interpreted as functions that help build CCPs in a Montagovian way. I will not provide a fully explicit characterization of the system, but merely consider the interpretation of the discourse *A man shot at the president. He was caught,* as an illustration of what this approach affords us. First let me give the unreduced translations of the single sentences of the discourse in question:

(31)   a. A man shot at the president $\Rightarrow \underline{\exists}x [\Uparrow man'(x) \vartriangle \Uparrow shot\ at'$ (the president')(x)]
        b. He was caught $\Rightarrow \Uparrow caught'(x)$

As usual, I am disregarding tense here. These readings are compositionally derived by familiar techniques; here is an overview of the steps involved:

(32)

Translation	Type	Description
man $\Rightarrow \Uparrow man' = \lambda x \Uparrow man'(x)$	$\langle e,cc \rangle$	Function from entities into CCPs
shot at the president $\Rightarrow$ shot'(the president')	$\langle e,cc \rangle$	Function from entities into CCPs
a $\Rightarrow \lambda P \lambda Q \underline{\exists}x[^\vee P(x) \vartriangle ^\vee Q(x)]$	$\langle dp,\langle dp,cc \rangle \rangle$	Dynamic generalized determiner
	where *dp* ("dynamic properties") $= \langle s,\langle e,cc \rangle \rangle$	
a man $\Rightarrow$ $\lambda P \lambda Q \underline{\exists}x[^\vee P(x) \vartriangle ^\vee Q(x)](^\wedge \Uparrow man')$ $= \lambda Q \underline{\exists}x[\Uparrow man'(x) \vartriangle ^\vee Q(x)]$	$\langle dp,cc \rangle$	Dynamic generalized quantifiers
a man shot at the president $\Rightarrow$ $\lambda Q \underline{\exists}x[\Uparrow man'(x) \vartriangle ^\vee Q(x)](^\wedge \Uparrow shot'(the\ president'))$ $= \underline{\exists}x[\Uparrow man'(x) \vartriangle \Uparrow shot'(the\ president')(x)]$	cc	CCPs

The interpretation of the discourse as a whole is given in (33a). In virtue of
the definitions in (30), the formula in (33a) is provably equivalent to (33b):

(33)   a. $[\exists x[\Uparrow\text{man}'(x) \;\Delta\; \Uparrow\text{shot at}'(x, \text{the president})] \Delta\; \Uparrow\text{caught}'(x)]$
        b. $\underline{\exists}x[\Uparrow\text{man}'(x) \;\Delta\; \Uparrow\text{shot at}'(x, \text{the president}) \;\Delta\; \Uparrow\text{caught}'(x)]$

The proof is elementary but long (cf. the appendix, part III). The CCP in
(33b) is felicitous in a context c iff the corresponding update is. The context
updating function corresponding to (33b) is the following:

(34) $\downarrow \underline{\exists}x[\Uparrow\text{man}'(x) \;\Delta\; \Uparrow\text{shot at}'(x, \text{the president}) \;\Delta\; \Uparrow\text{caught}'(x)]$
        $= \lambda c \exists x[c \;+\; \text{man}(x) \;+\; \text{shot}(x, \text{the president}) \;+\; \text{caught}(x)]$

The function in (34) maps a context c into the result of adding to it first the
information that there is a man, then the information that that man shot at
the president, and finally the information that that man was caught. If at any
step there is a presupposition failure, the function returns "error." The scope
of the existential quantifier extends itself in the by now familiar manner
beyond its c-command domain.

The remaining aspects of the logic of CCPs can also be defined rather
simply (only disjunction requires special attention):

(35)   a. $\neg\beta \;=\; \uparrow\lambda c[c \;+\; \neg\downarrow\beta(c)]$
        b. $\underline{\forall}x\beta \;=\; \neg\underline{\exists}x\;\neg\beta$
        c. $\beta \underset{\rightarrow}{\rightarrow} \gamma \;=\; \neg(\beta \;\Delta\; \neg\gamma)$
        d. $\beta \underline{\vee} \gamma \;=\; \uparrow\lambda c[\downarrow(\neg\beta \underset{\rightarrow}{\rightarrow} \gamma)(c) \;\vee\; \downarrow(\neg\gamma \underset{\rightarrow}{\rightarrow} \beta)(c)]$

A few remarks may be in order. Beginning with negation, note that its
definition uses the ' $\downarrow$ ' operator, which will make any discourse marker active
in β inaccessible for subsequent pronouns. Notice also that in computing the
value of $\neg\beta$ in a context c, we must first compute the value of β in c. The
fact that negation is a hole for presuppositions is an immediate consequence
of this. It is interesting to remark that in this case the results of the "double
dynamics" diverge radically: presuppositions are inherited, but discourse
referents are shut off. Consider next the universal quantifier. As it is defined
in terms of negation, its closed character follows immediately. We will return
below to a discussion of the projection properties of quantifiers.

The next interesting case is that of implication. As far as anaphora is
concerned, in virtue of the definition in (35c), implication is externally closed
but internally open. That is to say, a pronoun external to a conditional cannot
be bound by an indefinite internal to it, but an indefinite in the antecedent
will be able to bind a pronoun in the consequent. With respect to presupposi-

tions, it is easy to see that conditionals are expected to have the same projection behavior as conjunction. This follows straightforwardly from the fact that negation is a hole and that the definition uses conjunction. Note also that as far as content is concerned, the effect of a conditional on a context set c is that of subtracting from c those worlds in which the antecedent is true and the consequent false.[11]

The definition of disjunction is the most complex and requires a more extensive commentary. First notice that (35d) predicts that disjunctions are closed both externally and internally. This is so because their most embedded occurrence is in the scope of negation or on the right-hand side of a conditional. The projective behavior of disjunction works as follows. In (35d) we take the union of two conditionals. The first conditional requires that (i) the initial context c satisfy β's presuppositions and (ii) c $+$ $\neg\beta$ satisfy γ's presuppositions. If $\neg\beta$ entails γ's presuppositions, then (ii) will hold automatically whenever (i) does. If either condition fails, the first conditional yields '$\perp$'. The second conditional works in the same way, except that the order in which the disjuncts are processed is reversed. Given the definition of '$\bigvee$' as extended to propositions, the final result will be '$\perp$' only if both conditionals yield '$\perp$'. This gives a chance to either disjunct to filter out the presuppositions of the other.[12]

In the present section I have developed a framework for the integrated treatment of anaphora and presuppositions. While sentential meaning is a unitary phenomenon, three levels can in a sense be individuated in its structure: propositions (partial functions from worlds into truth values), updates (partial functions from contexts into contexts), and CCPs (type-lifted updates). The first level of meaning corresponds to the traditional notion of truth-conditional content. The second level is the context updating potential of an expression. The third level specifies how expressions constrain possible continuations. These different levels are linked via general type-shifting mechanisms. We have seen how the resulting system handles the anaphoric and presuppositional properties of the main connectives and quantifiers in a systematic and enlightening way. We now turn to more specific illustrations of how the framework works.

4.3 SOME EMPIRICAL APPLICATIONS

The fruitfulness of a framework rests on whether it enables us to derive empirical generalizations in a principled manner. I will show how this is indeed the case for the framework developed in section 4.2, by giving two unrelated examples. The first concerns verbs of propositional attitude. By couching their meaning in a dynamic setting, we are able to derive their effect on presuppositions and anaphora. This analysis is due to Heim (1992); I merely adapt it here to our notation.[13] The second example concerns determiners. We will see how by simply translating the approach developed in chapter 2 into the present formalism we can explain in a general and direct way the presuppositional behavior of determiners and its interaction with their anaphoric properties.

4.3.1 A Dynamic Semantics for Propositional Attitude Verbs

As mentioned in section 4.1.1, Karttunen (1974) observed that verbs expressing a mental attitude have the following projective behavior:

(36)   a. x believes that ϕ presupposes x believes ϕ's presuppositions
Example:
b. x believes that the king is bald.
c. x believes that there is a king.

It is only felicitous to utter something like (36b) in a context where (36c) is taken for granted.[14] I will now reproduce a variant of Heim's (1992) argument that if we think of the meaning of *believe* as an update function, we can see why it has the projective behavior illustrated in (36).

In classical possible worlds semantics, verbs of mental attitude are analyzed in terms of alternativeness relations among worlds. Let $B(x,w)$ be the set of worlds compatible with what x believes in w, that is, x's doxastic alternatives in w. For x to believe a proposition p in w is for p to be true in every world in $B(x,w)$. Now, in terms of this classical analysis, let us consider what it is to add to a context set c the information that x believes a proposition p. Generally, the knowledge embodied in a context set also includes something about the belief system of relevant individuals. The participants to a conversation will share information concerning what a given relevant individual x may believe. For example, in talking about x in a context c, we may know that x believes a proposition p_1, that x disbelieves p_2, and that x may or may not believe p_3. This means that in every world w of the context c, p_1 is and p_2 is not a subset of $B(x,w)$. In addition, there are some worlds w of c where p_3 is a subset of $B(x,w)$ and some other worlds where it isn't. Adding the information that x believes p_3 is to eliminate the latter kind of world from c. Translating this in terms of doxastic alternatives, the worlds in which x believes a proposition p are the following:

(37)   a. $\lambda w[B(x,w) \subseteq p]$
b. $\lambda w[B(x,w) + p = B(x,w)]$

If we ignore for a moment the partiality of ' + ', (37a) is equivalent to (37b), since to say that A is a subset of B is to say that the intersection of A and B is the same as A. We can exploit this equivalence and define the meaning of *believe*, in first approximation, as follows:

(38) $\lambda x \lambda p \lambda c [c + \lambda w[B(x,w) + p = B(x,w)]]$

The function in (38) maps a proposition and an individual into a context updating function that eliminates from c the worlds in which x does not believe that p. Notice, however, that in virtue of the definition of ' + ', the function in (38) is defined only if for all the worlds w in c, $B(x,w) + p$ is defined. This in turn means that for every w in c, $B(x,w)$ must meet the presuppositions of p. Thus, x's doxastic alternatives throughout c must satisfy p's presuppositions. What this shows is that by thinking of *believe* as an update function, it is easy to see why x believes that p presupposes that x believes p's presuppositions.

We must bear in mind, though, that sentences are interpreted not as propositions but as CCPs. Thus, (38) should look for a CCP, not for a proposition. However, it is straightforward to adjust the type of (37) appropriately.

(39)   believe = $\lambda \beta \lambda x \uparrow \lambda c[c + \lambda w[\downarrow \beta(B(x,w)) = B(x,w)]]$
        where β is of type *cc*

Believe is now a function that takes a sentence meaning (i.e., a CCP) and an individual to return a CCP (so its type is $\langle cc, \langle e, cc \rangle \rangle$). The way *believe* is defined can be viewed as giving three instructions: (i) Extract the corresponding update from β via ' $\downarrow$ ', (ii) use the previous definition of *believe* on the result (i.e., (38)), and (iii) form a CCP via ' $\uparrow$ '.[15] Interestingly, this definition has an immediate consequence for anaphora. Since ' $\downarrow$ ' shuts off all active discourse markers in its scope, it is predicted that no discourse marker active in β can bind something when embedded under a verb like *believe*. The evidence as to whether this is actually so is not univocal, however; some discussion of this issue may be appropriate. Consider:

(40)   a.   ??John believes that Bill bought a car$_i$. It$_i$ is parked over there.
        b.   ?John believes that Bill bought a car$_i$. Mary thinks it$_i$ is parked over there.
        c.   John believes that Bill bought a car$_i$ and hopes that he will lend it$_i$ to him.

Sentence (40a) is fairly marginal. The only plausible way to interpret it is by construing *a car* de re. On a de dicto reading, the anaphoric link in (40a) is ill-formed. Sentence (40b), out of the blue, is also strange. To rescue it, we must be able to interpret the second sentence as something like 'Mary too believes that Bill bought a car and . . . '. Maybe with the help of a suitable context this can be done. Sentences like (40b) are isomorphic to Geach's 'Hob-Nob sentences' (like, *Hob believes that a witch$_i$ killed his horse and Nob believes that she$_i$ scared his cow*), which with the help of an appropriate context (e.g., a widespread witch-hysteria attack) display a seemingly well-formed anaphoric link. We thus face a dilemma. If we stick to (39), we can explain the ungrammaticality of (40a) (on the intended reading) but not the well-formed instances of sentences like (40b). If, on the other hand, we revise (39) so that quantifiers embedded under *believe* can reach beyond it, we have the opposite problem. I am currently inclined to think that the first of these two alternatives is more on the right track. If we extend Dynamic Binding indiscriminately, the danger of massive overgeneration is substantial. If instead we stick to the hypothesis that Dynamic Binding from the complement position of *believe* is impossible, we must treat cases of well-formed anaphoric links differently—say, as instances of E-type pronouns, an option that I claim is independently available.[16] This in turn commits us to seeking an explanation for the possibility (or impossibility) of certain anaphoric links in the relative ease (or difficulty) with which the descriptive content of the pronoun (viewed as a proxy for a description) may be retrieved from the context. So, on this view, (40a) is out because Dynamic Binding is impossible and there is no plausible description that *it* can stand for. Sentences like (40b), on the other hand, are acceptable only to the extent that the context is rich enough to supply an appropriate description. Consider, finally, sentences such as (40c), which involve *believe-hope* sequences with the same subject. Sentences of this sort, which appear to be systematically well-formed, are also discussed by Heim (1992). She shows that by suitably defining the contribution of *hope* to context update, it is possible to see why, for example, *John hopes that p* presupposes that John believes p's presuppositions. Hence, if we take *it* in (40c) to go proxy for something like *Bill's car,* we see why sentences of this sort are always well-formed (in spite of the fact that Dynamic Binding is impossible here). They are well-formed because a description is readily available whose presuppositions are guaranteed to hold, in virtue of the dynamic meaning of *believe* and *hope* and the projection properties of *and.*

4.3.2 The Presuppositions of Determiners

In chapter 2 we have formulated a theory of determiners that arguably handles well their anaphoric properties. By recasting them in terms of updates, we should be able to capture the projection properties of determiners without having to stipulate anything.

Recall that in chapter 2 we argued that existential and quantificational determiners should be treated differently. Let us consider them in turn. Existential determiners are simply obtained by existential closure. Accordingly, the CCP of a sentence like (41a), an example from Heim 1983, will be (41b):

(41)   a. Some fat man was riding his bicycle.
        b. $\exists x[\Uparrow$ fat man$'(x) \triangle \Uparrow[x$ rides x's bicycle]]

where I assume that [x rides x's bicycle] is only defined for individuals who have a bicycle (see section 4.4 below for a treatment of definites that affords us this interpretation). Sentence (41a) contains a presupposition trigger; we can therefore ask how this presupposition is passed up—that is, what presuppositions (41b) as a whole is predicted to have. In order to answer this question, let us extract the update function corresponding to (41b):

(42) $\downarrow \exists x[\Uparrow$ fat man$'(x) \triangle \Uparrow[x$ rides x's bicycle]]
        $= \lambda c \exists x[c$ + fat man(x) + [x rides x's bicycle]]

For which contexts is (42) defined? Clearly, for those where we can find an individual such that [c + fat man(x) + [x rides x's bicycle]] is defined. Contexts of this kind require that some man has a bike. Thus our approach predicts that sentences like (42) have rather weak presuppositions (namely, in the case at hand, only that a man has a bike), which seems to be right. Uttering (41a) in a situation where it is known that no man has a bike would obviously be pointless. The presuppositions of existential determiners like *some* are thus straightforwardly obtained, without our having to resort to accommodation.

For quantificational determiners we have proposed a schema which, adjusted to the current types of CCPs, looks as follows:[17]

(43) $D^+(A,B) = \Uparrow D'(\Downarrow A, \Downarrow[A \triangle B])$

A and B in (43) are dynamic properties and D^+ is a relation between them (more precisely, a function from pairs of dynamic properties into CCPs). This relation is defined in terms of the ordinary static value of determiners (i.e., a conservative relation D' between static properties; cf. (17f) above). These static properties are obtained by means of the $\Downarrow$-operator. What gives the schema in (43) its bite is that we first dynamically conjoin A with B and then get at the corresponding static properties. In this way any discourse marker active in A gets a chance to bind pronouns in B. This schema, it was argued, constitutes a natural extension of conservativity to a dynamic setting. Leaving the technical developments to the appendix (part IV), let me illustrate its application to some basic cases, so that we can test the predictions the schema makes concerning presupposition projections. Here is how the universal quantifier comes out on the basis of (43):

(44)   a. Every man who rides his bike is healthy.
        b. ⇑λw[λx[x is a man who rides x's bike](w) ⊆ λx[x is a man who rides x's bike and x is healthy](w)]
        c. λw[λx[x is a man who rides x's bike](w) ⊆ λx[x is a man who rides x's bike and x is healthy](w)]

The CCP in (44b) is what we obtain by instantiating D′ in schema (43) to the subset relation (and working out the definitions implicit in the schema). Consider now the proposition contained in (44b), which is given in (44c). Such a proposition checks world by world whether the set of men that ride their bike is a subset of the set of men that ride their bike and are healthy. However, something important should be noted. The relation '⊆' is originally defined only for sets. But functions like λx[x is a man who rides x's bike](w) will be undefined for individuals that don't have a bike, and hence these functions do not always identify sets. We have to spell out what happens in these cases. There are essentially two natural ways to proceed. The first is to stipulate that if A and B are not sets, A ⊆ B is just undefined. Under this interpretation, the proposition in (44b) will be defined only in worlds where every man has a bike. Hence a context admits (44c) under this interpretation only if it is taken as a fact that every man has a bike.

The other natural way to extend '⊆' to partial properties is to look at their positive and negative extensions. In general, a partial function λx[x is a man who rides x's bike](w) is true of some individuals, false of others, and undefined for others yet. Its completion, which we will denote with λx[x is a man who rides x's bike](w)*, agrees with λx[x is a man who rides x's bike](w) on the individuals for which the latter is defined and maps the rest of the individuals into false. (And if λx[x is a man who rides x's bike](w) has no positive or negative extension, then it has no completion.) So when A and B are partial, we can interpret A ⊆ B as A* ⊆ B*, (which is defined only if A and B have completions). Applying this to (44b), we immediately see that if we are in a world where at least some man has a bike, then λx[x is a man who rides x's bike](w) will have a completion. Thus (44c), under this second interpretation, will be admitted only by contexts where it is known that at least a man has a bike.

To recapitulate, for quantificational determiners we simply adopt the schema proposed in chapter 2, adjusted to the current type of CCPs and to the fact that we now admit partial functions. If D is a relation between sets, there are two natural ways of extending it to a relation D′ between partial properties, namely:

(45)   *Option 1:* $D'(A,B)(w) = D(\lambda x A_w(x), \lambda x B_w(x))$, if $\lambda x A_w(x)$, $\lambda x B_w(x)$ are sets; undefined otherwise.
         D′ is of type $\langle\langle e,p\rangle,\langle\langle e,p\rangle,p\rangle\rangle$, A, B are of type $\langle e,p\rangle$ and D is of type $\langle\langle e,t\rangle,\langle\langle e,t\rangle,t\rangle\rangle$.
         Option 2: $D'(A,B)(w) = D(\lambda x A_w(x)^*, \lambda x B_w(x)^*)$, where $\lambda x A_w(x)^*$ and $\lambda x B_w(x)^*$ are the completions of $\lambda x A_w(x)$ and $\lambda x B_w(x)$, if $\lambda x A_w(x)$ and $\lambda x B_w(x)$ have a completion; undefined otherwise.

These two options yield slightly different projection properties for determiners. Consider:

(46)   a. Every man who rode his bike was late.
         b. Most men who rode their bike were late.
         c. No man who rode his bike was late.

(47)   a. Every man rode his bike.
         b. Most men rode their bike.
         c. No man rode his bike.

In (46) the presupposition trigger is in the left argument of the determiner; in (47) it is in the right argument. On both Option 1 and Option 2, (46) and (47) are predicted to be deviant in a context where it is known that no man has a bike. Moreover, on Option 1, both (46) and (47) presuppose that every man (in the relevant domain) has a bike. On Option 2, both (46) and (47) presuppose that it be known that some man has a bike.

It is not easy to decide on empirical grounds which of these two predictions is correct, especially given that each determiner occurrence may select its own domain (as, e.g., Westerståhl (1988) argues; cf. chapter 2, section 2.1.3). Consider, for instance, example (46a) on Option 1. The occurrence of *every* in (46a) can select as its domain the set of bicycle-owning men, an option that guarantees satisfaction of the universal presupposition associated with Option 1. Given the flexibility of domain selection, it is very difficult to tease apart existential presuppositions from universal ones, once the latter are suitably restricted to a chosen domain.[18]

Whichever option will ultimately turn out to be correct, there is a particularly clear prediction made by both variants: the projection properties of determiners should be the same as those of conjunction. This is an immediate consequence of schema (43), which defines determiners in terms of dynamic conjunction. Thus for any determiner, the presuppositions of both its arguments should be passed up, unless the left argument entails the presuppositions of the right one. This seems to be exactly right.

(48)   a. Every man who saw the doctor asked her what to do.
        b. Every man saw the doctor.
        c. Every man who saw a doctor and a nurse asked the doctor what to do.
        a'. No man who saw the doctor asked her what to do.
        b'. No man saw the doctor.
        c'. No man who saw a doctor and a nurse asked the doctor what to do.

It is easy to observe that while both (48a–b) and (48a'–b') presuppose that there is a unique relevant doctor, (48c) and (48c') carry no such presupposition. The reason why this is so is clear: the first conjunct entails the presuppositions of the second, thereby automatically satisfying them. In the present framework, this follows from the fact that determiners, being conservative, have conjunction built into their meaning. To the best of my knowledge, such a generalization in this strong form has gone unaccounted for so far (with the exception of Beaver (1994), who has independently arrived at a solution closely related to the present one).[19]

Thus, the present theory comes in two simple variants of a very general and independently motivated schema, namely (45). Both variants correctly predict the presuppositions of determiners in the intuitively clear cases, and they do so without resorting to accommodation. As for choosing between the two variants, at our current level of understanding it just seems too soon to make a call.

4.4 DEFINITES

The main point of this section is to show that within the general framework we have adopted, a simple extension of a classical Frege/Russell-style treatment of definites takes us to a somewhat better understanding of their behavior. The extension of the classical theory that I will adopt consists in the idea that the context dependency of definites has well-identifiable syntactic and semantic reflexes, which must be made explicit. I should add that even though my lines on definites and dynamic semantics support each other rather well, they can be adopted or rejected independently of each other.

Starting with Frege's insight (which we will modify a bit as we go along), we can view definites as (partial) functions from properties into the unique object that satisfies them, if there is such an object. Accordingly, the semantics of the ι-operator can be given as follows:

(49)   a. If x is of type e and ϕ of type t, then $[\![\iota x \phi]\!]^g = u$, where u is the unique object such that $[\![\phi]\!]^{g[x/u]}$, else $\bot$.
    b. Examples:
        (i) the president of the U.S. $\Rightarrow \iota x[\text{president}_w(x, \text{U.S.})]^{20}$
        (ii) the book John wrote $\Rightarrow \iota x[\text{book}_w(x) \wedge \text{wrote}_w(j,x)]$
        (iii) his father $\Rightarrow \iota x[\text{father}_w(x,y)]$

This much is completely straightforward. An example of a simple proposition containing a definite is:

(50) $\lambda w[\text{inhale}_w(\iota x[\text{president}_w(x, \text{U.S.})])]$

This proposition is true in a world w if there is a unique president of the U.S. in w and that person inhales. It is false in a world w if there is a unique president of the U.S. in w and that person doesn't inhale. It is undefined in a world where there is no unique president.

Propositions are uttered in a context. Let us see what (50) would express relative to a given context set c:

(51) $c + \lambda w[\text{inhale}_w(\iota x[\text{president}_w(x, \text{U.S.})])]$

The expression in (51) is defined only if c entails the presuppositions of (50). This means, in our terms, that the proposition in (50) restricted to the worlds in c must be total. For this to be so, it must be the case that in every world of c, there is a unique president of the U.S. So the sentence *The president inhales* will have a well-defined value only in a context where it is known that there is a unique president. (Global accommodation is, of course, possible.)

Exercise

Using this approach, write the reduced translations of (a) *Every boy saw the president* and (b) *Every boy saw his father,* and compute the presuppositions of each. Assume that *father* is a relational noun, so that 'father(x,y)' says that x is father of y. For (b) compute the presuppositions according to both options in (45).

Having spelled out a semantics for the ι-operator, we should now show how it can be used in giving a semantics for the determiner *the*, bearing in mind that we are working with CCPs. In what follows, I will present two approaches to the definite article. On the first approach, the ι-operator combines with a CN denotation to give an individual concept. On the second approach, the ι-operator is used to define a generalized quantifier. It will be shown that these two approaches make slightly different predictions.

4.4.1 Two Possible Implementations

If we want to derive individual concepts from noun denotations, which are of type $\langle e,cc \rangle$, we will need to exploit our $\Downarrow$-operator, which takes us from CCPs into propositions. In particular, we might adopt the following definition, an illustration of which is also provided immediately below:

(52)   a. If β is of type $\langle e,cc \rangle$, $\iota u\beta(u) = \lambda w\iota u \Downarrow \beta(u)(w)$.
         b. Example:
            $\iota u \Uparrow \text{president}'(u) = \lambda w\iota u \Downarrow \Uparrow \text{president}'(u)(w)$
            $= \lambda w\iota u\ \text{president}_w(u)$

Thanks to definition (52a), we can apply the ι-operator directly to noun denotations and obtain individual concepts. Now we have to address a second, related issue. How is a VP (also of type $\langle e,cc \rangle$, and more generally, any predicate, going to combine with a definite (which, according to the present hypothesis, is of type $\langle w,e \rangle$)? Again we have to use our $\Downarrow$-operator, which takes us from cc to p (and, hence, from $\langle e,cc \rangle$ to $\langle e,p \rangle$). We are then left with the further problem of combining propositional functions with individual concepts, which can be managed in a simple way. Given a function β of type $\langle e,p \rangle$, we can shift it to a function $[\beta]$ of type $\langle \langle w,e \rangle,p \rangle$ as follows:[21]

(53)   a. $[\beta] = \lambda a\lambda w[\beta(a(w))(w)]$, where a is of type $\langle w,e \rangle$ and β of type $\langle e,p \rangle$
         b. Example:
            inhale', the president' $\Rightarrow$ $[\text{inhale}'](\lambda w\iota x[\text{president}_w(x)])$
            $= \lambda a\lambda w'[\text{inhale}'(a(w'))(w')](\lambda w\iota x[\text{president}_w(x)])$ (def. of [ ])
            $= \lambda w'[\text{inhale}'(\lambda w\iota x[\text{president}_w(x)](w'))(w')]$ (λ-conv.)
            $= \lambda w[\text{inhale}'(\iota x[\text{president}_w(x)])(w)]$ (λ-conv.)
            $= \lambda w\ \text{inhale}_w(\iota x[\text{president}_w(x)])$ ('-convention, cf. (16) above)

Recapitulating, to combine a VP-denotation, say, $\Uparrow \text{inhale}'$, with a definite, say, 'the president', we first go down to $\lambda u \Downarrow \Uparrow \text{inhale}'(u)$ (i.e., inhale'); we then combine that with $\lambda w\iota x[\text{president}_w(x)]$, via the type-shifting in (53); finally, since we want the value of a sentence to be a CCP, we go up again to cc (i.e., $\Uparrow \lambda w\text{inhale}_w(\iota x[\text{president}_w(x)])$). So in conclusion, under this approach, the analysis of the sentence *The president inhales* works as follows:

(54)   the president inhales $= \Uparrow [\lambda u \Downarrow \Uparrow \text{inhale}'(u)](\iota u \Uparrow \text{president}'(u))$

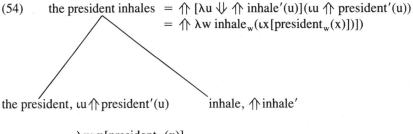

$= \Uparrow \lambda w \, \text{inhale}_w(\iota x[\text{president}_w(x)])])$

the president, $\iota u \Uparrow \text{president}'(u)$ inhale, $\Uparrow \text{inhale}'$

$\lambda w \iota x[\text{president}_w(x)]$

In other words, on this view of definites we need a modest amount of housekeeping devices, in the form of type-shifting mechanisms, all of which are quite straightforward within our general setup.

A consequence of this approach is that definites are closed. So, for example, in an NP like *the man who has a credit card,* the indefinite *a credit card* will not be able to bind outside of its c-command domain. This is a straightforward consequence of the fact that definites are treated here as individual concepts, which do not have enough structure to carry information about possible discourse markers associated with a definite. Formally, this restriction manifests itself in the need to use '$\Downarrow$' when combining 'ι' with a noun denotation (cf. (52)), which has the effect of shutting off all discourse referents active within the noun denotation. The empirical effect of this is that reference to, for example, *a credit card* in *the man who has a credit card* has to happen via the E-type strategy, which is supposed to trigger a uniqueness/maximality effect. So there should be a systematic contrast between the (a)- and the (b)-cases in examples like the following:

(55)   a. Yesterday, every man who had a dime used it for the the parking
            meter.
        b. The man who had a dime put it in the parking meter.

(56)   a. Every man who has a hat must wear it.
        b. The man who has a hat must wear it.

It seems to me that there is in fact a uniqueness presupposition present in the (b)-cases (in spite of the pragmatic context, which strongly disfavors it). But not every speaker agrees.

I now turn to a second way of implementing the theory of definites just sketched, one that doesn't have this consequence. Let me illustrate the basic idea by means of an example. We assume that the determiner THE applied to a noun denotation, say, the denotation of *man that has a donkey,* gives the following generalized quantifier:

(57)   a. THE(man that has a donkey)
$= \lambda Q \exists y [\iota u [\text{man that has a donkey} (u)] = y \,\triangle\, \text{man that has a}$
donkey $(y) \,\triangle\, Q(y)]$

If we combine this generalized quantifier with a predicate, say, *beats it*, we get:

(58) $\exists y [\iota u [\text{man that has a donkey} (u)] = y \,\triangle\, \text{man that has a donkey}$
$(y) \,\triangle\, \text{beat it}(y)]$

While I must leave technical details to the appendix (part V), it should be fairly clear what the truth-conditional content of (58) is; namely, that some y is the unique donkey owner and that y has a donkey that he beats. This will be felicitous only in contexts where it is known that there is a unique donkey owner. Moreover, it makes definites open, using essentially the same idea we used for other quantifiers. Maybe this is engineering rather than real insight. But it nicely marries the Fregean approach with our treatment of generalized quantifiers. As a result, definites are open while at the same time carrying uniqueness/maximality presuppositions and projecting in the appropriate way.

As pointed out above, these two implementations do not differ in the way they behave with respect to presuppositions. They probably are not to be thought of as being in competition with one another but as complementary (although the predictions made by the first theory with respect to uniqueness are closer to my intuitions). At any rate, in what follows I am going to think in terms of the first approach, the one that treats definites as singular terms, as it is slightly simpler. I think that what I have to say can also be couched, with relatively minimal changes, in a generalized quantifier framework.

4.4.2 The Functional Theory of Definites

In this section we will extend the theory of definites sketched above to cases of anaphoric and indexical uses, which so far are not handled by it. As pointed out in the introduction to section 4.4, this involves being explicit as to the role of context in the interpretation of definites. Beginning with indexical uses, consider the following sentence:

(59)   a. Look, the table is dirty.
          b. $\text{dirty}_w (\iota x \, \text{table}_w(x))$

One way to remedy the obvious inadequacy of (59b) might be via domain selection. Perhaps we could say that a felicitous utterance of a sentence like

(59a) requires a contextually salient domain of objects with only one table. We know that each quantifier may select its own domain; definites surely will be no exception. In spite of the plausibility of this view, there are reasons to doubt that it is the whole story. For example, a sentence like (59a) can be uttered felicitously in a room with two tables by speakers who are fully aware of this fact. All that is required is that the speakers' attention be focused on one of the tables, which can be achieved by a gesture, a stare, or the like. The parallel with the way we use indexicals is evident. So an alternative way to analyze (59a) might be as follows:[22]

(60)   a.   The table over there is dirty.
        a'. $\text{dirty}_w(\iota x[R_w(o,x) \wedge \text{table}_w(x)])$ o = a location,
                                                                   R = is occupied by
        b.   The table we are looking at is dirty.
        b'. $\text{dirty}_w(\iota x[R_w(y,x) \wedge \text{table}_w(x)])$ y = the speakers,
                                                                   R = is looking at

A sentence like (59a) might be taken to be shorthand for something like (60a) or (60b). The logical form of (60a–b) is given in their primed counterparts. What characterizes these formulae is the presence of a relational variable and its arguments. The values of these variables must be something salient in the context. In other words, when the descriptive content of a definite is too poor to identify the intended object, the context has to supply the necessary information. And it does so not only by selecting an appropriate domain but also by linking the intended object to something that is already given to us somehow.

Extrapolating from these simple cases, we can take the interpretation of a definite of the form *the N* to be as follows:[23]

(61)   a. $\iota x[R_w(y_1,\ldots,y_n,x) \wedge N_w(x)]$
        b. $\iota_{i_1,\ldots,i_n} x[N_w(x)]$

where $R, y_1, \ldots, y_n$ are simply free variables. I abbreviate (61a) as (61b), by attaching to the ι-operator the indices of the variables. Note that given the semantics of the ι-operator, assuming that definites translate as shown in (61a) amounts to saying that the contextually supplied value of R must be an n-place function with the denotation of N as its range.[24] In other words, the context has to supply a function with range N. The classical Fregean theory arises as a special case, namely when the function is a 0-place one. This happens when the descriptive content of N is sufficiently rich to individuate the intended object. For example, 'the first boy to be born in the year

2000' can be viewed as a 0-place function with the denotation of 'first boy to be born in the year 2000' as range. Or, alternatively but equivalently, in these cases the function is a function just of the property associated with N. These considerations justify the label "functional theory of definites."

To put it in slightly different terms, the idea here is that the ι-operator, besides combining with a property, may have some further hidden parameters. When it has none, it is because the descriptive content associated with the property suffices. The classical theory, therefore, can be viewed as providing the default interpretation of definites, appropriate for cases of sufficient descriptive content.

This proposed enrichment of the classical theory is rather simple. Everybody accepts the idea that the classical theory of definites needs to be supplemented somehow by an injection of contextually supplied information. The claim put forth here is that the assumption that contextual information is packaged in this way suffices to handle the multiple uses of both nominal and pronominal definites (the latter to be discussed in section 4.5). In fact, we can sharpen our views a bit further, as follows. On the assumption that there is a syntactic level of LF at which anaphoric relations are overtly displayed, one is led to conclude that the indices of the contextually supplied variables are present at this level. Accordingly, the structure of a definite NP can be taken to be the following:

(62)   a. $[_{NP_j} \text{ the N}]^{i_1, \ldots, i_n}$
         b. $\iota_{i_1, \ldots, i_n} x[N_w(x)]$

That is, a definite NP, besides carrying its own referential index ('j' in (62a)) may carry one or more "anaphoric indices" ("a-indices", for short; '$i_1 , \ldots , i_n$' in (62a)). These anaphoric indices act like phonologically null pronominals, in fact, and are interpreted as arguments of the contextually supplied function that constitutes the interpretation of the definite. The interpretation of (62a) is given in (62b). Within the syntactic theory we have adopted, it is in fact tempting to hypothesize that a-indices are associated with empty pronominals (presumably, small *pro*'s). Their exact nature depends on the structure of NPs. For example, some of them may be implicit arguments of the head noun (as with relational nouns like *mother* or *author*). Others may be implicit adjuncts, possibly licensed by the definite determiner *the*. Being more explicit would involve delving deeply into the issue of NP structure, which would take us too far afield.[25] For our purposes, the key point is the assumption that a-indices are linguistically real. If definites are implicit functions of contextually supplied arguments and if LF is a disambiguated level of syntax at which scope and anaphora are structurally represented, then a-indices must be present at LF. In what follows I will explore some consequences of this view.[26]

4.4.3 Consequences

The observations below provide evidence in favor of the functional theory mainly in two ways. On the one hand, the functional approach allows a uniform interpretation of a variety of uses of definites that previously could not be treated in an integrated way. On the other, these observations show that various grammatical processes appear to be sensitive to the presence of a-indices.

4.4.3.1 Anaphoric Uses of Definites

As pointed out in section 4.1, typical anaphoric uses of definites are the following:

(63)   a. A boy saw a man in the distance. The man was carrying a gun.
        b. Every student who was given a pen and a notepad lost the pen.
        c. When a painter lives in a village, the village is usually pretty.

Here definites appear to be anaphoric to an antecedent. We have argued that they are generally interpreted as functions of implicit variables. Now, the value of a variable can be contextually supplied (as with (59a) above). But of course it can also be bound by a suitable antecedent. Anaphoric uses of definites constitute this second case. Let us see how the examples in (63) can be analyzed. Beginning with (63a), we can say that the first sentence introduces a seeing event and its protagonists (i.e., the agent and the patient of the seeing), thereby making them highly salient. In this situation, it makes sense to conjecture that the definite is interpreted as something like 'the man who is the patient of the seeing' (or as 'the man the boy saw'). In our framework, the discourse in (63a) could be interpreted as follows:

(64)   a. $\exists e[e$ is a seeing of a man by a boy $\wedge \exists e'[$wear a hat $(\iota_e u$
        $man_w(u),e')]]$
        b. $\exists e'$wear a hat$_w(\iota u[Theme_w(e,u) \wedge man_w(u)],e')$

Let me explain the hybrid notation in (64). First of all, here and throughout, I am only giving a rough rendering of the propositional content of the examples under discussion. So for example, whenever possible I omit writing the possible-world argument. I am also assuming that each verb has an existentially closed event argument (which I will likewise omit to represent when it is not directly relevant). Now, in a discourse like (64a), the scope of existential quantifiers expands beyond their c-command domain, and hence the existential quantifier associated with the event argument in the first clause can bind a variable in the second clause. The definite is interpreted as a function mapping the first event into the man who is its theme (i.e., the man who is seen by the boy). (64b) gives the semantics of the second sentence in primitive notation, along with the interpretation for the relational variable R.[27]

Let us consider next (63b). Here we have the option of interpreting the definite as a function of giving-events or as a function of students. On the first option, the representation of (63b) parallels that of (63a). On the second option, the interpretation of the sentence would be as follows:

(65)   a. $\forall x[[\text{student}(x) \wedge \exists y \exists z[\text{notepad}(y) \wedge \text{pen}(z)]] \rightarrow \text{lost}(x, \iota_x \text{ u pen}(u))]$

   b. $\iota_x \text{ u pen}(u) = \iota \text{ u}[\text{was-given}(x,u) \wedge \text{pen}(u)]$

In (65b), the definite is given in primitive notation, along with the intended interpretation of the relational variable.

Consider finally (63c). As we know from chapter 2, this sentence has various readings. Let us examine, for example, its subject-asymmetric reading:

(66)   a. Most $(\lambda x[\text{painter}(x) \wedge \exists y \text{ village}(y) \wedge \text{live-in}(x,y)], \lambda x[\text{painter}(x) \wedge \exists y \text{ village}(y) \wedge \text{live-in}(x,y) \wedge \text{pretty}(\iota_x \text{ u village}(u))])$

   b. $\iota_x \text{ u vilage}(u) = \iota \text{ u}[\text{live-in}(x,u) \wedge \text{village}(u)]$

In (66a) we give the reading our interpretive procedure delivers. The definite can be naturally interpreted as a shorthand for 'the village x lives in', where 'x' is bound by 'a painter,' which is quantified over by 'usually.' The other readings are obtained in a similar way.[28]

Other uses that come out naturally on the present theory are the so-called "associative anaphoric" uses of definites, illustrated by the following example:

(67)   a. Every boy played a piece and then put the music sheets away.

   b. $\forall x[\text{boy}(x) \rightarrow \exists y[\text{piece}(y) \wedge \text{played}(x,y) \wedge \text{put-away}(x, \iota_y u[\text{music-sheets}(u)])]]$

   c. $\iota_y u[\text{music-sheets}(u)]) = \iota u[\text{contains}(y,u) \wedge \text{music-sheets}(u)])]$

Here *the music sheets* (which, nota bene, is not a relational noun) is naturally understood as anaphorically linked to *a piece,* which is in the scope of the subject and extends its own scope over the second VP-conjunct in the by now familiar way.

The general picture is the following. Definites may be linked to contextually supplied arguments. These arguments are taken to be part of their logical form as variables (or, in syntactic terms, phonologically unrealized pronominals). We then expect that such variables can be bound by some suitable antecedent or else that their value can be indexically specified, as is the case for variables in general.

The unaugmented classical theory is incapable of dealing with anaphoric uses. In particular, no simple manipulation of the domain of quantification will account for the cases considered in the present section. In fact, it was primarily this shortcoming that led Heim (1982) to abandon the classical theory in favor of her familiarity-based approach. Heim's approach, on the other hand, has difficulties with the cases that work well in the classical theory, namely those where the descriptive content of the definite is sufficiently rich to identify the intended object. The reason for this difficulty is intuitively clear: if the definite is rich in content, there is no natural sense in which the thing described has to be "familiar." Massive use of accommodation can get us out of this trouble, of course, but at the cost of a loss in explanatory force (and at any rate, certain descriptive difficulties remain; cf. example (14) above). The present analysis is an attempt to integrate these two views. When the descriptive content is too poor, the context has to integrate it with relevant information, by relating the intended object to familiar ones. Thus the description takes the form of a function from these familiar objects into the intended output. For the arguments of the function to be familiar they must either have been introduced previously or be prominent in the context.

4.4.3.2 A-Indices and Weak Crossover

It turns out that the syntactic and semantic structures we need for definites are independently needed. Consider the question–answer pair in (68):

(68)   a. Who does no one like?
         b. His mother-in-law.
         c. Which function f makes the following true: no one$_i$ likes $f(x_i)$

As the answer in (68b) shows, the question in (68a) seems to request information concerning a certain connection between people. The meaning of (68a) can be represented as in (68c). The functions that the question in (68a) quantifies over is exactly the type of functions we need to interpret definites.[29]

In addition, I have argued in Chierchia 1993 that the traces of *wh*-phrases, interpreted functionally, carry a-indices, just like definites. So for example, the LF of (68a) would be something like (69):

(69)   who$_j$ does no one$_i$ like $[e_j]^i$

I've shown that adopting a structure of this sort explains a number of interactions between *wh*-phrases and quantified NPs. For example, it explains the absence of a functional reading for questions like the following:

(70)   a.   Who likes nobody?
         b.   *His mother-in-law.
         c.   who$_j$ $[e_j]^i$ likes nobody$_i$?

It is impossible to answer question (70a) in a manner which is parallel to (68b). Why? On the present assumptions, the LF of (70a) would be (70c). Here the potential antecedent 'nobody$_i$' does not c-command the a-index of the trace. In order for it to c-command the trace, it would have to raise over it, giving rise to a crossover configuration. This explains the impossibility of a functional answer for questions like (70a).

If this view of functional questions is correct, it would seem surprising that a-indices are to be confined to *wh*-traces. Why shouldn't a-indices ever show up on phonologically realized NPs? The present view of definites makes what would otherwise look like an arbitrary gap disappear. Moreover, if a-indices are present at LF on definite NPs, syntactic constraints should "see" them, just like they see them on *wh*-traces. Hence we ought to find Weak Crossover effects with definites as well. I think that we do indeed. Consider:

(71)   Every young author will have a new book at the fair.
         a.   Every author$_i$ will personally present the book^i to the critics.
         b.   *The book^i will make every author$_i$ rich.

In the given context, where the book is understood as varying with the author, sentence (71a) is perfectly naural. But (71b), though pragmatically plausible, is not nearly as natural. The reason, I submit, is Weak Crossover. In (71b), in order to bind the a-index of *the book,* the NP *every author* would have to cross over it. A similar pattern obtains with *wh*-binders:

(72)   Context (i): In this conservatory each student has a violin and is supposed to take care of it.
         a.   (?)I want to know who$_i$ t$_i$ doesn't take good care of the violin^i.
         Context (ii): In this conservatory each student has a violin that he

must keep on a certain shelf. But the shelves are defective, and
recently some violins fell from the shelves onto some students.

b.   *I want to know who$_i$ the violin^i fell on t$_i$?

Question (72a), though perhaps not perfect in English, is acceptable. Other
languages, like Italian, use the definite article more liberally, and in such
languages (72a) is perfect. But sentences like (72b) tend to be crushingly bad,
in spite of the fact that context (ii) makes the intended reading pragmatically
plausible. Even readers who don't find (72a) so good tend to get a systematic
contrast with (72b). Question (72a) can be intepreted as in (73a), while (72b)
cannot be interpreted as in (73b):

(73)   a. I want to know which x's are such that x doesn't take care of
            x's violin.
        b. I want to know which x's are such that x's violin fell on x.

Again, (73b) is a typical crossover configuration. If there was no pronoun-like
element in the logical structure of definites, there would be no reason to
expect any contrast whatsoever in these cases.

4.4.3.3 Accessibility

We have seen in the course of the present work that the antecedent–pronoun
relation is not only sensitive to syntactic conditions (such as Weak Crossover)
but also to semantic ones. In particular, a pronoun has to be *accessible* to its
antecedent, where accessibility is roughly characterized, descriptively, as
follows:

(74)   An indefinite α can antecede a pronoun β iff the first binder that
        c-commands α also c-commands β.
        Binder: adverb of quantification or NP

In chapter 1, section 2.4 we have illustrated this constraint (which we now
know follows from Dynamic Binding) by means of patterns of the following
sort:

(75)   a.   Usually, if a mean farmer has a donkey$_i$, it$_i$ gets beaten.
        a'. *Usually, if every mean farmer has a donkey$_i$, it$_i$ gets beaten.
        b.   John met a farmer who had a donkey$_i$ and examined it$_i$.
        b'. *John met every farmer who had a donkey$_i$ and examined it$_i$.
        c.   Usually, if John meets a woman with a hat$_i$, he stares at it$_i$.
        c'. *Usually, if John meets every woman with a hat$_i$, he stares at
             it$_i$.

The pattern in (75) is pretty systematic. In (75a) the first binder that c-commands *a donkey* is the adverb of quantification *usually*, which c-commands the pronoun *it*, and *a donkey* can antecede the pronoun. But in (75a') the first binder that c-commands *a donkey* is the quantified NP *every mean farmer*, which does not c-command the pronoun *it*, and the anaphoric link between *a donkey* and *it* is no longer well-formed. The other examples in (75) are similar. The point of relevance to our present concerns is that if the a-indices of definites are pronominals, we expect them to display the same behavior. They should allow only accessible antecedents (E-type anaphora aside, on which more below). This indeed seems to be so. Consider:

(76)   a.   Usually, if a book$_i$ in this shop sells well, the author^i gets rich.

        a'.   *Usually, if every book$_i$ in this shop sells well, the author^i gets rich.

        b.   John met a boy who had an interesting book$_i$ and wrote to the author^i.

        b'.   *John met every boy who had an interesting book$_i$ and wrote to the author^i.

        c.   Usually, if John meets a boy with an interesting book$_i$, he writes to the author^i.

        c'.   *Usually, if John meets every boy with an interesting book$_i$, he writes to the author^i.

The facts in (76) are completely parallel to those in (75). Take (76a), for example. Here the a-argument of *the author* is accessible to *a book*. And in fact we get the reading that if a book in this store sells well, the author of that book gets rich, where the author varies with the book. Such reading is unavailable in (76a'). To the extent that (76a') is interpretable, we have to assume that there is one author for all the books in the store. So the possibility of anaphoric uses of definites (in this case, the possibility of anaphoric associative uses) seems to be governed by accessibility. This is to be expected on the present approach, but it would be unclear how to account for it on a theory that doesn't have a-indices (and the semantics for definites that goes with them) at the relevant level of representation.

4.4.3.4 Other Bound Occurrences of A-Indices

VP anaphora is known to allow for sloppy interpretations in cases like the following:

(77)   a. John likes his mother and Paul does too.
        b. $\lambda x[x$ likes x's mother]

The VP anaphor in the second sentence of (77a) is understood to be something like (77b). Such a property is predicated of *Paul*, which will give us the sloppy reading. The process of abstraction that creates the right antecedent for a VP anaphor must thus be able to bind pronouns contained in the antecedent. If a-indices are pronoun-like, we would expect them to be amenable to abstraction like other pronouns and display sloppy interpretations in VP anaphora contexts. The following example illustrates this point:

(78)   Every student who deserves it will get a prize. Usually we give prizes to first-graders in the morning and to second-graders in the afternoon. But this year, the first-graders will get the prize in the morning and the second-graders will __ also.

The VP we need to interpret the gap in the last sentence of the discourse in (78) is the following:

(79)   a. $\lambda x[\text{get-in-the-morning}(x, \iota_x u[\text{price}(u)])]$
        b. $\iota_x u[\text{price}(u)] = \iota u[\text{deserves}(x,u) \wedge \text{price}(u)]$

So the a-index associated with definites is indeed accessible to the kind of abstraction process necessary to interpret VP anaphors, something we expect on the line we are taking.

   The final case I would like to consider has to do with the interpretation of *only*. This is a complex topic that we certainly cannot address properly here. However, without getting into much detail it is possible to see that our approach to definites, married with any reasonable theory of *only*, makes an interesting prediction. The final interpretation of a sentence like (80a) has to be roughly as in (80b), no matter how one gets there:

(80)   a. John likes only Bill.
        b. The only (relevant) value of x that makes 'John likes x' true is 'Bill'.

It has been known for a long time that sentence (81), where *only* occurs preverbally and *Bill* is focused, receives the same interpretation as (80a):

(81)   John only likes BILL.

In other words, *only* can associate with an element either by forming a constituent with it or via focus. Observe now what can happen with definites:

(82)   a. Each book will be introduced only by the author.
        b. Each book will only be introduced by THE AUTHOR.

In (82a) *only* selects its scope positionally, by being placed next to it. In (82b) such association is gotten by focusing the definite. Both these sentences have an interpretation that can be spelled out as in (83):

(83)   The only (relevant) value of f that makes 'Every book$_i$ will be presented by $f(x_i)$' true is the one that maps each book into its author.

If definites denote functions, as I am suggesting, the availability of this reading is to be expected. Focus-sensitive items like *only* can associate with a definite by the usual mechanisms. And the semantics that works in the general case will take its usual course and deliver the intended reading (which amounts to quantifying over functions). If, on the other hand, definites are not associated with functions, it is not obvious how to obtain this reading.

So there are a wide variety of syntactic and semantic processes that fall into place if we assume that contextually supplied arguments of definites, when present, are projected in their Logical Forms as variables. Or equivalently, natural language grammar treats a-indices to a large extent as if they were "real" pronouns. If definites are context dependent, then by assuming that their context dependency is realized in this way, we can account in a unitary manner for a significant class of cases.

4.5 LOOSE ENDS AND CONCLUSIONS

There are a number of additional issues raised by the approach to definites developed above. Here I would like to discuss briefly the main ones. Most of them fall under the rubric "Open Problems" and/or "Lines for Further Research."

4.5.1 E-Type Pronouns Again

In chapter 2 we have put forth the hypothesis that Dynamic Binding and the E-type strategy (viz., the idea that pronouns can go proxy for definite descriptions) should be viewed as coexisting mechanisms rather than mutually exclusive alternatives. It was argued that this amounts to assuming that pronouns, besides being semantically bound, can also be interpreted through contextually supplied information, which seems to be the null hypothesis. We furthermore sketched the idea that E-type pronouns can be assimilated to functions from individuals into individuals, where the antecedent of the pronoun fixes the range of such function. Now we can see how that idea fits into and flows from a general approach to definite descriptions. E-type pronouns have descriptions as their meaning. Descriptions are, in the general case, context-dependent functions from individuals into individuals. So that must be the logical type of E-type pronouns as well.

More specifically, in overt definite descriptions, the head noun fixes the content of the description. If the descriptive content of the head noun is sufficiently rich, that is done directly; if not, then the head noun fixes the range of a contextually specified function. Now, pronouns lack heads. Hence their descriptive content is inherently defective and they can be interpreted as functions only if the context supplies the relevant information. Moreover, pronouns have antecedents that can partially compensate for the poverty of content. The idea at the basis of the proposal sketched in chapter 2 is that antecedents provide, in part, the kind of information that heads provide in overt definite descriptions. This means, in our terms, that the antecedent of a pronoun determines the range of a contextually specified function.

Let us try to flesh this out a bit more. Since E-type pronouns are like descriptions, we expect them to have the same syntactic makeup as overt definites. Thus, in particular, we expect them to have a (possibly null) sequence of a-indices, as shown in (84a).

(84)   a. $[it_j]^{i_1, \ldots, i_n}$
        b. $\iota_{i_1, \ldots, i_n} u\, P_j(u)$, where P_j is the interpretation of the head of NP_j.[30]

The interpretation of (84a) is given in (84b). The superscripts stand for the arguments of the function. As with overt definites, their value is provided either indexically or anaphorically. The subscript links the pronoun to its antecedent, which doesn't bind it in the standard sense but determines the range of the function. We see, then, that the antecedent-pronoun relationship in the case of E-type pronouns is not purely pragmatic. E-type pronouns are coindexed with their antecedent, and such coindexing has a precise semantic import, spelled out in (84b). Equipped with this sharper formulation of the syntax and semantics of E-type pronouns, we can now reconsider some of the predictions that the theory makes.

We have observed that functional traces (cf. (69) above) as well as overt definites (cf. (71) above) display systematic crossover effects. If this approach is on the right track, we would expect pronouns on their E-type readings to display similar effects. And indeed, such effects can be detected. Consider examples of the following kind (from chapter 3):

(85)   a.   *An advisor discussed it with every student that had a problem.
        b.   [every student$_i$ that had a problem$_j$][an advisor discussed it$_j^i$
              with t$_i$]

We noticed in chapter 3 that the pronoun *it* in (85a) cannot be bound by
a problem. We attributed this to Dynamic Blocking, which switches off the
dynamics when scoping is used. Thus in a configuration like (85b), *it* cannot
be dynamically bound. This prevents sentence (85a) from having a ∃-reading.
But what about ∀-readings? The latter are obtained via the E-type strategy,
to which Dynamic Blocking is irrelevant. After all, uttering (85a) surely
makes a function from students into problems salient. What's to prevent,
then, the pronoun *it* from being interpreted as such a function? The Logical
Form in (85b) would be truth-conditionally interpreted as follows:

(86)   For every student x who had a problem, there is an advisor y such
        that y discussed f(x) with x (where f is a function that maps students
        into their problems).

The interpretation in (86) does not involve Dynamic Binding and corresponds
to the ∀-reading of sentence (85a). But such reading is just as ungrammatical
as the ∃-reading. Therefore, something has to rule it out. What can that be?
We have a ready answer, namely, Weak Crossover. In order to get reading
(86) we have to go through the Logical Form in (85b). But such a structure
clearly violates Weak Crossover (however formulated), since the binder of
the pronominal a-index (namely, *every student*) has to cross over the a-index
in order to bind it. Hence the ungrammaticality of (85a) on the intended
reading seems to provide strong support in favor of the present view of E-type
pronouns. I don't know how any other current proposal could deal with the
ungrammaticality of (85a).

Let us turn next to anaphora across inaccessible domains and test what
predictions the theory makes. Some cases that I think fall out nicely are the
following types of negation and disjunction:

(87)   a.   *John doesn't have a car$_j$. Bill$_k$ has it$_j^k$.
        a'. $c + \neg[c + \exists x[car'(x) \wedge has'(j,x)]] + \lambda w[has_w(b,$
              $\iota_b u[car_w(u)])]$
              where $\iota_b u[car_w(u)] = \iota u[own(b,u) \wedge car_w(u)]$
        b.   It isn't true that John$_k$ doesn't have a car$_j$. It$_j^k$ is parked in the
              back of the house.
        b'. $c + \neg\neg[c + \exists x[car'(x) \wedge has'(j,x)]] + \lambda w[parked_w(\iota_j u$
              $[car_w(u)])]$

c.   Morrill Hall$_i$ either doesn't have a bathroom$_j$ or it$_k{}^i$ is in a funny place.

c'. c + ¬¬[c + ∃ x[bathroom'(x) ∧ has'(M,x)]] + λw[funny-place$_w$(ι_Mu[bathroom$_w$(u)])]

Consider first (87a). The indexing on the pronoun indicates that *it* is interpreted as a car-valued function that has *Bill* as argument. The natural function potentially relevant in a context appropriate to uttering something like (87a) is one that maps people into their cars. In a context c where nothing is known concerning who has cars, (87a) will be interpreted as in (87a'). And in such a context the presupposition of the description that our theory associates with the pronoun *it* will not be met, whence the deviance of (87a). Now suppose that the very same discourse is uttered in a context where it is known that John has sold his car to Bill. In such a case, (87a) will be felicitous, because the presuppositions of the descriptions will be met. I doubt that there are ways of extending Dynamic Binding that can achieve this same level of descriptive adequacy and do so in an equally principled way. Contrast this with what happens with the discourse in (87b), which, given the dynamic semantics for negation, will be interpreted as shown in (87b') in a context c. We see from (87b') that the first sentence winds up adding to c the information that John has a car. Hence the presupposition of the description naturally associated with the pronoun *it* is guaranteed to be automatically met. So (87b) is felicitous (and free of presuppositions). Consider finally (87c). According to the dynamic semantics for disjunction (given in (35d) section 4.2.3 above), to utter [A ∨ B] in a context c involves adding to c [¬A → B]. This, in turn, involves computing as an intermediate step the formula in (87c') (because of the semantics for '→'). But then the presupposition of the definite description is once again guaranteed to be automatically satisfied.

The present approach also rules out in a straightforward way some of the ungrammatical cases, such as the following, taken from Heim (1990):

(88)   a. [Every donkey owner]$_i$ would like John$_j$ to beat it$_i{}^j$.
       b. Speaking of [the successor function]$_i$, no number$_j$ is greater than it$_i{}^j$.

In (88a) *it* cannot look inside the matrix subject (say, because of something like the lexical integrity hypothesis). The indexing shown there is consistent with our approach, but it requires *it* to be interpreted as a function from individuals into donkey owners, and no such function is natural or salient. Similarly, the indexing of *it* in (88b) calls for a function from numbers into successor functions, and no such function is salient or natural. So these examples (which were taken by Heim to show the nonviability of purely pragmatic approaches) are correctly and straightforwardly ruled out.

While the present approach enables us to deal with certain cases of anaphora across inaccessible domains, it doesn't let through just any old anaphoric link. For example, cases of the following sort are not licensed:

(89)   a.   *Every student$_i$ came to the party. He$_i$ had fun.
      b. $\forall x[\text{student}(x) \rightarrow \exists e[\text{come-to-the-party}(x,e)]]$
      c. $\exists e \forall x[\text{student}(x) \rightarrow \text{come-to-the-party}(x,e)]]$
      d.   f: e $\rightarrow$ the agent of e

If we try to make *he* anaphoric to *every student,* it must be interpreted as a function into students. But arguably there is no suitable argument for such function. The two possible interpretations for the first sentence in (89a) are given in (89b–c). As far as (89b) is concerned, *every* is a closed determiner, and hence the variables within its scope are inaccessible from the second sentence. In (89c) the event variable, being existentially quantified, is accessible to the second sentence. But the relevant event is a complex formed by joining together several individual events of student coming. Consequently, it can be argued that it has no agent, at least not in the primary sense in which the single events it is constituted of have agents. If such a plural event has an agent it does so in a derivative sense, see, e.g., Landman 1993 for a theory of events with these features. So one can argue that the ungrammaticality of (89a) is due to the absence of a natural, readily salient function to interpret the pronoun.

Of course, we know that there are sentences isomorphic to (89) that are well-formed (the so-called "telescoping sentences"). For example:

(90)   a.   Every soldier stood up. He then walked to the podium.
      b.   Every chess set comes with a spare pawn. It is taped under the box.   (P. Sells)

The problem is that so far there haven't been many interesting regularities detected in connection with this phenomenon. The main observation is that sentences like those in (90) tend to become acceptable in a kind of newscaster mode, where the speaker is directly reporting a series of ongoing events (or purports to do so). We may conjecture that in newscast-type situations, where we are directly witnessing what is going on, functions from the single events to their agents are promoted to salience. At present, I will leave this as a speculation. Other approaches are also conceivable.[31]

Harder nuts to crack are the following sentences, which involve "virtual antecedents":

(91)   a. A: Each time$_i$ I was there I saw a goat$_j$.
        B: It$_j^{i,t}$ was not a goat. It$_j^{i,t}$ was a sheep.   (P. Strawson/I. Heim)
        b. John has a car$_j$. Or maybe it$_j^s$ is a van.   (D. Beaver)

The problem here is obvious. Our E-type approach predicts that *it* in (91a) should be a goat and in (91b) should be a car. But this cannot be. As far as I know, however, these sentences are problematic for any approach. In spite of the prima facie intractability of cases like this, I still believe the theory outlined in (84) to be on the right track. The clause in (84b) embodies the claim that the head of the antecedent completely determines the range of the function (similar to what happens with the head of overt definites). But the pronoun–antecedent relation is less strict than the relation between a determiner and its head noun. Accordingly, the contribution of the property associated with the head of the antecedent might well be somewhat looser than indicated by (84b): it might constrain the range of the function associated with the E-type pronoun without determining it. If P is the property associated with the head of the antecedent, instead of requiring the intended object to be P, we might require it to be P in some contextually relevant worlds. So, for example, the description that does the job in (91a) is something like 'the object that speaker A calls a goat'. For (91b), 'the vehicle I remember as a car' might do. Under this view, the antecedent still makes a direct contribution to the interpretation of the pronoun. Such contribution is somewhat open-ended but not completely so. It is a modalized form of the property associated with the head of the antecedent. Facts of this sort appear to be within the reach of a pragmatically driven approach to E-type anaphora such as the present one.[32]

In spite of the incomplete and speculative character of these remarks, it seems to me that our initial hypothesis comes out corroborated. Neither Dynamic Binding nor the E-type strategy per se suffices in covering the whole range of data—not, that is, without a considerable amount of ad hocness. On the other hand, two relatively simple integrated mechanisms—the first semantically driven, the second pragmatically—seem capable of taking us quite a few steps forward in understanding how pronouns work.

4.5.2 Existence and External Negation

The line we have taken on definites, being a simple variant of the classical Fregean one, will suffer from some of the same drawbacks that have been discussed in the literature in connection with the latter. Two of these are particularly prominent: the one concerning the verb *to exist* and the one concerning certain uses of negation.

(92)   a. The present king of France doesn't exist.
        b. You have not seen the present king of France because France is no longer a monarchy.

A variety of solutions to these problems have been proposed in the literature, and I do not have much to contribute. I will merely indicate the line I currently feel inclined to follow. Both of the sentences in (92) require very special contexts. For example, (92b) only makes sense as a denial of a preceding assertion. This suggests that (92b) can merely correct a previous claim: we negate a previous assertion in order to negate one of its presuppositions. This use of negation is related to what Horn (1989) calls "metalinguistic negation," a phenomenon he amply and convincingly documents, where negation is used not to deny the truth-conditional content of what is said, but to deny some other aspect of the utterance. For example, I once was told:

(93)   You didn't kiss Isa (pronounced [ki:s], with a tense 'i']). You kissed her (pronounced [kis], with a lax 'i').

What was being objected to in this case was the phonetic component of my English competence. It seems likely that sentences like (92b) are related to metalinguistic uses of negation and hence do not call for any special semantic maneuver.

The case of (92a) presents several points of contact with (92b). Sentence (92a) as well is only natural, if at all, in a situation of denial of somebody's presuppositions. Moreover, both types of sentences have counterparts involving names of fictional characters:

(94)   a. Pegasus doesn't exist.
        b. You didn't see Pegasus because Pegasus doesn't exist.

Though some relation is undeniable, I also perceive a contrast between sentences (94a) (and their positive counterparts, like *Pegasus exists*), which strike me as fairly natural, and (92a) (and their positive counterparts, like *The king exists*), which strike me as very marginal. The natural way to assert or deny the existence of kings is the following, which bypasses problems having to do with definites:

(95)   a. There is a king of France.
        b. There is no king of France.

The contrast between (94a) and (92a) might have to do with the fact that while names of fictional entities may well denote something in a world where those entities do not exist, definites probably simply fail to have a semantic value in a world where nothing satisfies their descriptive content.

At any rate, what emerges from this rather inconclusive discussion is that sentences like those in (92) raise issues that go beyond that of the proper treatment of definites and presupposition. There are various lines one can take on such issues that are consistent with the approach presented here. Which one will turn out to be most satisfactory must be left open at this point.

There is also another issue related to existence presuppositions and quantification that should at least be mentioned. It is sometimes claimed that quantified NPs as in (96a) carry an existential presupposition of the kind exemplified by (96b).

(96)   a. John saw every student.
        b. There are students.

I actually think that a more accurate rendering of the existential commitment of sentences like (96a) is along the following lines:

(97)   For all we know, there may be students.

Evidence in favor of something like (97) is constituted by the felicity of discourses of the following type:

(98)   [Said by a teacher to his/her class]
        a.   It is possible that nobody has done flawlessly. But to everyone who has, I will give a bonus.
        b.   ??I know that nobody has done flawlessly. But to everyone who has, I will give a bonus.

Discourse (98a) seems perfect. If *everyone who has (done flawlessly)* presupposes that someone has, we would expect it to be deviant. Discourse (98b) is in fact deviant, as it denies that there may be students who have done flawlessly. The next question is what triggers the presupposition in (97). The answer to this might be sought in Gricean maxims: a quantifier whose restriction is known to be empty stands no chance of updating the context in an informative manner. However, a detailed analysis of this and related phenomena must be left for future development.

4.5.3 Summary

In the present chapter we have elaborated a version of the dynamics of presuppositions that integrates them with the treatment of anaphora developed in earlier chapters. Our main point has been that by viewing determiners as being dynamically conservative we can derive their observed behavior with respect to presupposition projections in a very direct manner. We have also sketched what we have called the "functional theory of definites," a simple, pragmatically driven extension of the classical theory of definite descriptions. The essential feature of the functional theory is that definites are functions of properties and possibly other contextually supplied parameters. We have tried to provide evidence that this view, in conjunction with our approach to presupposition projection, offers an account of features of definites (including definite descriptions, E-type pronouns, and functional traces) that so far seemed hard to explain in a unitary fashion.

Independent of how convincing each particular proposal put forth in this chapter (and, for that matter, in the rest of this book) may be, I think we have mounting evidence that a dynamic perspective on meaning has profound conceptual and empirical effects on our understanding of what grammar is. Only if interpretation of syntactic structures is viewed as a context-changing process can we state certain generalizations properly and reduce them to simple principles. Moreover, if the level of syntax that feeds into semantics does indeed feed into a *dynamic* semantics, some of its properties may well be different in nontrivial ways from what one might expect.

APPENDIX

I. Partial IL

(1)   *Types:*
    (i) e, w, t are in TYPE.
    (ii)   If a and b are in TYPE, then $\langle a, b \rangle, \langle s, a \rangle$ are in TYPE.

(2)   *Domains:*
    Let E be the set of entities and W the set of worlds.
    (i) $D_e = E, D_w = W, D_t = \{0,1\}$
    (ii) $D_{\langle a,b \rangle} = D_a \to D_b$ (the set of all total and partial functions from D_a into D_b)
    (iii) $D_{\langle s,a \rangle} = G \to D_a$, where $G = \bigcup_{a \in \text{TYPE}} D_a^{\text{DM}}$ (DM are the discourse markers)

(3)   *Structures:*
    $\langle U, W, F \rangle$, where if β is a constant of type a, $F(\beta)$ is in D_a

(4)   *Interpretation:*

(In what follows I omit making explicit reference to assignments to static variables.)

a. $[\![\beta]\!]^g = g(\beta)$, if β is a variable, $F(\beta)$ if β is a constant

b. $[\![\beta(\alpha)]\!]^g = [\![\beta]\!]^g ([\![\alpha]\!]^g)$, if defined, else $\bot$

c. $[\![\lambda u\beta]\!]^g = h$, where for any **u** in the appropriate domain $h(\mathbf{u}) = [\![\beta]\!]^{g[u/u]}$, if defined, else $h(\mathbf{u})$ is $\bot$

d. i. $[\![\neg\phi]\!]^g = 1$ iff $[\![\phi]\!]^g = 0$, else $\bot$

   ii. $[\![\phi \wedge \psi]\!]^g =$ $[\![\psi]\!]^g$

		1	0	$\bot$
	1	1	0	$\bot$
$[\![\phi]\!]^g$	0	0	0	0
	$\bot$	$\bot$	0	$\bot$

   iii. $[\![\phi \vee \psi]\!]^g =$ $[\![\psi]\!]^g$

		1	0	$\bot$
	1	1	1	1
$[\![\phi]\!]^g$	0	1	0	$\bot$
	$\bot$	1	0	$\bot$

e. $[\![\exists x\phi]\!]^g = \begin{cases} 1, & \text{if for some } \mathbf{u} \ [\![\phi]\!]^{g[u/u]} = 1 \\ 0, & \text{if for every } \mathbf{u}, \ [\![\phi]\!]^{g[u/u]} = 0 \\ \bot, & \text{otherwise} \end{cases}$

f. $[\![\forall x\phi]\!]^g = \begin{cases} 1, & \text{if for every } \mathbf{u} \ [\![\phi]\!]^{g[u/u]} = 1 \\ 0, & \text{if for some } \mathbf{u} \ [\![\phi]\!]^{g[u/u]} = 0 \\ \bot, & \text{otherwise} \end{cases}$

g. $[\![{}^\wedge\beta]\!]^g = \lambda g'[\![\beta]\!]^{g'}$

h. $[\![{}^\vee\beta]\!]^g = [\![\beta]\!]^g(g)$

II. Some Elementary Facts about Updates

FACT I. $[c \wedge p]$ is a set iff $p1c$ is total.

Proof:

Assume that $[c \wedge p]$ is a set but that for some w in c, $p(w)$ is $\bot$. Then from the truth table for '$\wedge$' it follows that $[c \wedge p](w)$ is $\bot$ (since $c(w) = 1$ but $p(w) = \bot$) and hence is not a set.

Assume that $p1c$ is total. Then, given that c is total, too, for any w, if $c(w) = 0$, then $[c \wedge p](w) = 0$ (regardless of whether $p(w)$ has a value), and if $c(w) = 1$, then $p(w)$ is defined and hence $[c \wedge p]$ will be, too.$\square$

FACT 2. $-+p = p$

Proof:

$$-+p = -\lambda c[c + p]$$ (def. of '+')
$$-\lambda c[c + p] = \lambda w[\lambda c[c + p](\{w\}) = \{w\}]$$ (def. of '−')
$$\lambda w[\lambda c[c + p](\{w\}) = \{w\}] = \lambda w[[\{w\} + p] = \{w\}]$$ (λ-conv.)

We must now show that for every w, $p(w) = [[\{w\} + p] = \{w\}]$. Suppose that $p(w) = 1$. Then $\{w\}1p$ will be a set and hence $\{w\} + p$ will be defined and equal to $\{w\}$. Suppose next that $p(w) = 0$. Then again $\{w\}1p$ is a set and hence $\{w\} + p$ will be defined and equal to $\varnothing$. Since $\varnothing \neq \{w\}$, we will have that the truth value of $[\{w\} + p] = \{w\}$ is 0. Finally, suppose that $p(w) = \bot$. Then $\{w\} + p$ is $\bot$ and hence $[\{w\} + p] = \{w\}$ is, too. □

It can also be shown that for arbitrary f's of type $\langle c,c \rangle$, $+-f = f$ does not hold. I leave this as an exercise for the reader.

III. The Compositional Derivation of CCPs

We consider here how the readings of sentences like *A man saw Bill* are to be compositionally derived. First, the relevant types are the following:

(5)   *Type*   *Name of Type*

up $= \langle c,c \rangle$ updates
co $= \langle s,\langle c,t \rangle\rangle$ continuations   (characters)
cc $= \langle c,\langle co,t \rangle\rangle$ context change potentials
dpr $= \langle s,\langle e,cc \rangle\rangle$ dynamic properties   (characters)

The derivation involves the following steps

(6)   a. man $\Rightarrow$ ⇑man' $= \lambda x\lambda c\lambda P\exists b[c + \lambda w[man_w(x)] = b \wedge ˘P(b)]$

b. see $\Rightarrow$ ⇑see' $= \lambda y\lambda x\lambda c\lambda P\exists b[c + \lambda w[see_w(x,y)] = b \wedge ˘P(b)]$

c. Bill $\Rightarrow$ bill (of type e)

d. saw Bill $\Rightarrow$ ⇑see'(bill) $= \lambda x\lambda c\lambda P\exists b[c + \lambda w[see_w(x,bill)]$
   $= b \wedge ˘P(b)]$

e. a $\Rightarrow \lambda P\lambda Q\exists x[˘P(x) \Delta ˘Q(x)]$

f. a man $\Rightarrow \lambda P\lambda Q\exists x[˘P(x) \Delta ˘Q(x)](ˆ⇑man')$
   $= \lambda Q\exists x[˘ˆ⇑man'(x) \Delta ˘Q(x)]$ (λ-conv.)
   $= \lambda Q\exists x[⇑man'(x) \Delta ˘Q(x)]$ (˘ˆ-canc.)

g. a man saw Bill $\Rightarrow \lambda Q\exists x[⇑man'(x) \wedge ˘Q(x)]$
   $(ˆ⇑see'(b))$
   $= \exists x[⇑man'(x) \Delta ⇑see'(bill)(x)]$ (λ-conv., ˘ˆ-canc.)

Now we proceed to show the reduction steps of (6g):

(7)   a. $\exists x[\lambda y\lambda c\lambda P\exists b[c + \lambda w[man_w(y)] = b \wedge \;\check{}P(b)](x)$
        $\Delta \Uparrow see'(bill)(x)]$ (def. of $\Uparrow man'$, alphabetic change)
       b. $\underline{\exists}x[\lambda c\lambda P\exists b[c + \lambda w[man_w(x)] = b \wedge \;\check{}P(b)] \Delta \Uparrow see'(b)$
                    (λ-conv.)
       c. $\underline{\exists}x[\lambda c\lambda P\exists b[c + \lambda w[man_w(x)] = b \wedge \;\check{}P(b)]$
        $\Delta \lambda c\lambda P\exists b[c + \lambda w[see_w(x,bill)] = b \wedge \;\check{}P(b)]]$
                    (def. of $\Uparrow see'(bill)$, alphabetic change)

We next compute the value of the subformula of (7c) embedded under $\underline{\exists}x[\ .\ .\ .\ ]$:
(8)   a. $\lambda c\lambda P[\lambda c''\;\check{}\lambda P''\exists b[c'' + \lambda w[man_w(x)]$
        $= b \Delta \;\check{}P''(b)](c)(\char`^\lambda c'[\lambda c'''\;\check{}\lambda P'''\exists b[c''' + \lambda w[see_w(x,bill)]$
        $= b' \wedge \;\check{}P'''(b')](c')(P)])]$ (def. of Δ, alphabetic changes)
       b. $\lambda c\lambda P[\lambda P''\exists b[c + \lambda w[man_w(x)]$
        $= b \wedge \;\check{}P''(b)](\char`^\lambda c'[\lambda P'''\exists b'[c' + \lambda w[see_w(x,bill)]$
        $= b' \wedge \;\check{}P'''(b')](P)])]$ (λ-conv. [twice])
       c. $\lambda c\lambda P[\lambda P''\exists b[c + \lambda w[man_w(x)]$
        $= b \wedge \;\check{}P''(b)](\char`^\lambda c'\exists b'[c' + \lambda w[see_w(x,bill)]$
        $= b' \wedge \;\check{}P(b')])]$ (λ-conv.)
       d. $\lambda c\lambda P[\exists b[c + \lambda w[man_w(x)]$
        $= b \wedge \;\check{}\char`^\lambda c'\exists b'[c' + \lambda w[see_w(x,bill)]$
        $= b' \wedge \;\check{}P(b')](b)]]$ (λ-conv.)
       e. $\lambda c\lambda P[\exists b[c + \lambda w[man_w(x)] = b \wedge \lambda c'\exists b'[c' + \lambda w[see_w(x,bill)]$
        $= b' \wedge \;\check{}P(b')](b)]]$ ($\check{}\char`^$-canc.)
       f. $\lambda c\lambda P[\exists b[c + \lambda w[m,an_w(x)] = b \wedge \exists b'[b + \lambda w[see_w(x,bill)]$
        $= b' \wedge \;\check{}P(b')]]$ (λ-conv.)
       g. $\lambda c\lambda P[\exists b'[[c + \lambda w[man_w(x)]] + \lambda w[see_w(x,bill)]]$
        $= b' \wedge \;\check{}P(b')]]$ (element. logic)
       h. $\lambda c\lambda P[\exists b'[[c + man'(x)] + see'(x,bill)] = b' \wedge \;\check{}P(b')]$
                    (not. conv.)

We now substitute this result in (7c).

(9)   a. $\exists x[\lambda c\lambda P[\exists b'[[c + man'(x)] + see'(x,bill)] = b' \wedge \;\check{}P(b')]]$
       b. $\lambda c\lambda P\underline{\exists}x\ \exists b'[c + man'(x) + see'(x,bill)$
        $= b' \wedge \;\check{}P(b')]$ (def. of $\underline{\exists}$)

At this point, let us compute what the update corresponding to the CCP in (9b) is:

(10)   a. $\downarrow \lambda c\lambda P\exists x\ \exists b'[c + man'(x) + see'(x,bill) = b' \wedge \;\check{}P(b')]$
       b. $\lambda c\lambda w[\lambda c'\lambda P\exists x\ \exists b'[c' + man'(x) + see'(x,bill)$
        $= b' \wedge \;\check{}P(b')](c)(\char`^\lambda a[a\ (w)])]$ (def. of $\downarrow$)

c. $\lambda c\lambda w\exists x\ \exists b'[c + man'(x) + see'(x,bill)$
  $= b' \wedge \lambda a[a\ (w)](b')]$ $\qquad$ (λ-conv., ˆˇ-canc.)
d. $\lambda c\lambda w\exists x\ \exists b'[c + man'(x) + see'(x,bill)$
  $= b' \wedge b'\ (w)]$ $\qquad$ (λ-conv.)
e. $\lambda c\lambda w\exists x[[c + man'(x) + see'(x,bill)](w)]$
  $\qquad\qquad\qquad$ (element. logic)
f. $\lambda c\exists x[c + man'(x) + see'(x,bill)]$ $\qquad$ (def. of $\exists$ on the type $\langle w,t\rangle$)

We now give the interpretation of the discourse *A man shot Bill. He was caught.*

(11) $\qquad$ a. $\lambda c\lambda P\exists x\ \exists b'[c + man(x) + shot(x,bill) = b' \wedge {}^\vee P(b')] \triangle \lambda c\lambda P\exists b$
  $[c + caught(x) = b \wedge {}^\vee P(b)]$
  By the steps shown in (7)–(8) this reduces to
  b. $\lambda c\lambda P\exists x\ \exists b[c + man'(x) + shot'(x,bill) + caught'(x) = b \wedge {}^\vee P(b)]$
  By applying again the definitions of $\underline{\exists}$, $\triangle$, and $\Uparrow$ ("backwards," as it were) this is equivalent to
  c. $\exists x[\Uparrow man'(x) \triangle \Uparrow shot'(x,bill) \triangle \Uparrow caught'(x)]$
  By the same steps displayed in (10) the update corresponding to (11c) is
  d. $\lambda c\exists x[c + man'(x) + shot'(x,bill) + caught'(x)]$

IV. Dynamic Determiners

The objective is to define determiners by lifting their ordinary static meaning to a two-place function from dynamic properties into CCPs. We will do so with the help of some auxiliary definitions, as follows.

First we define the notion of *completion* for expressions A of type $\langle e,t\rangle$:

DEFINITION 1. A* is defined only if A has a positive or negative extension. If so, for any u, A*(u) = 1, if A(u) = 1; A*(u) = 0, if A(u) = 0 or A(u) = $\bot$.

Next, we define two relations between properties in terms of relations between sets (these correspond to Option 1 and Option 2 of (45) in the text):

DEFINITION 2. $D'(A,B)(w) = D(\lambda xA_w(x),\lambda xB_w(x))$,
if $\lambda xA_w(x)$, $\lambda xB_w(x)$ are sets; undefined otherwise.
D' is of type $\langle\langle e,p\rangle,\langle\langle e,p\rangle,p\rangle\rangle$, A, B are of type $\langle e,p\rangle$ and D is of type $\langle\langle e,t\rangle,\langle\langle e,t\rangle,t\rangle\rangle$. (Option 1)

DEFINITION 3. $D'(A,B)(w) = D(\lambda xA_w(x)^*,\lambda xB_w(x)^*)$,
where $\lambda xA_w(x)^*$ and $\lambda xB_w(x)^*$ are the completion of $\lambda xA_w(x)$ and $\lambda xB_w(x)$, if $\lambda xA_w(x)$ and $\lambda xB_w(x)$ have a completion; undefined otherwise. (Option 2)

The next definition extends conjunction to dynamic properties.

DEFINITION 4. If β and ∂ are dynamic properties, then
$\beta \triangle \partial = {}^\wedge\lambda u[{}^\vee\beta(u) \triangle {}^\vee\partial(u)]$

(12)   Example
    a. ˆman that owns a donkey $\triangle$ ˆbeats it
       = ˆλuλcλP∃b∃x[c + man′(u) + donkey′(x)
       + own′(u,x) = b ∧ ˇP(b)]
       $\triangle$ ˆλuλcλP∃b[c + beat′(u,x) = b ∧ ˇP(b)]   (red. transl. of (a))
    b. ˆλu′[ˇˆλuλcλP∃b∃x[c + man′(u)
       + donkey′(x) + own′(u,x) = b ∧ ˇP(b)](u′)
       $\triangle$ ˇˆλuλcλP∃b[c + beat′(u,x) = b
       ∧ ˇP(b)](u′)]   (Def. 4)
    c. ˆλu′[λuλcλP∃b∃x[c + man′(u) + donkey′(x)
       + own′(u,x) = b ∧ ˇP(b)](u′)
       $\triangle$ λuλcλP∃b[c + beat′(u,x) = b ∧ ˇP(b)](u′)]   (ˇˆ-canc.)
    d. ˆλu′[λcλP∃b∃x[c + man′(u′) + donkey′(x)
       + own′(u′,x) = b ∧ ˇP(b)]
       $\triangle$ λcλP∃b[c + beat′(u′,x) = b ∧ ˇP(b)]]   (λ-conv.)
    e. ˆλu′[λcλP∃b∃x[c + man′(u′) + donkey′(x)
       + own′(u′,x) + beat′(u′,x) = b ∧ ˇP(b)]]   (def. of $\triangle$)

The final definition generalizes '⇓' to dynamic properties.

DEFINITION 5. If β is a dynamic property, then
  ⇓β = λu[⇓ˇβ(u)]

(13)   Example:
    a. ⇓ˆ man that owns a donkey′ =
       λu ⇓man that owns a donkey′(u)   (Def. 5)
    b. λu⇓λcλP∃b∃x[c + man′(u) + donkey′(x)
       + own′(u,x) = b ∧ ˇP(b)]]   (red. transl.)
    c. λu↓ − λcλP∃b∃x[c + man′(u) + donkey′(x)
       + own′(u,x) = b ∧ ˇP(b)]]   (def. of ⇓)
    d. λu − λc∃x[c + man′(u) + donkey′(x)
       + own′(u,x)]   (def. of ↓)
    e. λu[∃x man′(u) ∧ donkey′(x) ∧ own′(u,x)]   (def. of '−')

With these auxiliary definitions, we can define Dynamic Generalized Quantifiers in terms of relations between properties (we leave it open as to whether we use DEFINITION 2 or DEFINITION 3 in defining D′):

DEFINITION 6. For any dynamic properties
  D⁺ = λβλ∂⇑D′(⇓β, ⇓[β $\triangle$ ∂])

(14)   Example:
    Most men that have a donkey beat it.
    a. Translations of the components:
       i. most⁺ ⇒ λβλ∂⇑ most′(⇓β, ⇓[β $\triangle$ ∂])

       ii.   men that have a donkey $\Rightarrow$ $^\wedge\lambda u'[\lambda c\lambda P\exists b\exists x[c$ + man$'(u')$ + don-key$'(x)$ + own$'(u',x)$ = b $\wedge$ $^\vee P(b)]]$

       iii.   beat it $\Rightarrow$ $^\wedge\lambda u'[\lambda c\lambda P\exists b[c$ + beat$'(u',x)$ = b $\wedge$ $^\vee P(b)]]$

    b.   most men that have a donkey beat it $\Rightarrow$ most$^+$ ($^\wedge\lambda u'[\lambda c\lambda P\exists b\exists x[c$ + man$'(u')$ + donkey$'(x)$ + own$'(u',x)$ = b $\wedge$ $^\vee P(b)]])(^\wedge\lambda u'[\lambda c\lambda P\exists b$ [c + beat$'(u',x)$ = b $\wedge$ $^\vee P(b)]])$

    c. $\lambda\beta\lambda\partial\Uparrow$ most$'(\Downarrow\beta, \Downarrow[\beta \;\triangle\; \partial])(^\wedge\lambda u'[\lambda c\lambda P\exists b\exists x[c$ + man$'(u')$ + donkey$'(x)$ + own$'(u',x)$ = b $\wedge$ $^\vee P(b)]])(^\wedge\lambda u'[\lambda c\lambda P\exists b[c$ + beat$'(u',x)$ = b $\wedge$ $^\vee P(b)]])$ (def. of most$^+$)

    d. $\Uparrow$ most$'(\Downarrow^\wedge\lambda u'[\lambda c\lambda P\exists b\exists x[c$ + man$'(u')$ + donkey$'(x)$ + own$'(u',x)$ = b $\wedge$ $^\vee P(b)]]$, $\Downarrow[^\wedge\lambda u'[\lambda c\lambda P\exists b\exists x[c$ + man$'(u')$ + donkey$'(x)$ + own$'(u',x)$ = b $\wedge$ $^\vee P(b)]]$ $\triangle$ $^\wedge\lambda u'[\lambda c\lambda P\exists b[c$ + beat$'(u',x)$ = b $\wedge$ $^\vee P(b)]]])$ (λ-conv.)

    e. $\Uparrow$ most$'(\lambda u\exists x[$man$'(u)$ $\wedge$ donkey$'(x)$ $\wedge$ own$'(u',x)]$, $\lambda u\exists x[$man$'(u)$ $\wedge$ donkey$'(x)$ $\wedge$ own$'(u,x)$ $\wedge$ beat$'(u,x)])$ (def. of $\Downarrow$)

V. Definites as Generalized Quantifiers

DEFINITION 7.   THE$'$ = $\lambda\beta\lambda\partial\exists y[\Uparrow\lambda w[\iota u\Downarrow^\vee\beta(u)(w)$ = y] $\triangle$ $^\vee\beta(y)$ $\triangle$ $^\vee\partial(y)]$

(15)   Example:

       The man who had a donkey

    a. $\lambda\partial\exists y[\Uparrow\lambda w[\iota u\Downarrow\lambda c\lambda P\exists x\exists b[c$ + man$'(u)$ + donkey$'(x)$ + own$'(u,x)$ = b $\wedge$ $^\vee P(b)](w)$ = y] $\triangle$ $\lambda u\lambda c\lambda P\exists x\exists b[c$ + man$'(u)$ + donkey$'(x)$ + own$'(u,x)$ = b $\wedge$ $^\vee P(b)](y)$ $\triangle$ $^\vee\partial(y)]$

    b. $\lambda\partial\exists y[\Uparrow\lambda w\iota u\exists x\exists[man_w(u)$ + donkey$_w(x)$ + own$_w(u,x)]$ = y $\triangle$ $\lambda c\lambda P\exists x\exists b[c$ + man$'(y)$ + donkey$'(x)$ + own$'(y,x)$ = b $\wedge$ $^\vee P(b)]$ $\triangle$ $^\vee\partial(y)]$ (def. of 'ι', λ-conv.)

    c. $\lambda\partial\exists y[\Uparrow\lambda w\iota u\exists x\exists[man_w(u)$ + donkey$_w(x)$ + own$_w(u,x)]$ = y $\triangle$ $\exists x\Uparrow[c$ + man$'(y)$ + donkey$'(x)$ + own$'(y,x)$ $\triangle$ $^\vee\partial(y)]]$ (def. of $\underline{\exists}$)

Notes

CHAPTER 1

1. Cf. especially Kamp 1981 and Heim 1982.
2. Heim 1982 (chap. 2) and Kamp 1981 exemplify this approach.
3. Early illustrations are Heim 1982 (chap. 3), Rooth 1987, Barwise 1987, Gärdenfors 1988.
4. Structures of the form [every$_x$ [A][B]] correspond to the more traditional $\forall x[A \rightarrow B]$.
5. This metaphor was originally discussed in Karttunen 1976.
6. *Before/after/because/unless*-clauses also display a similar pattern. We won't be able to discuss these other cases in depth. On *before/after*-clauses cf. Partee 1984 and De Swart 1991. On *unless*-clauses see von Fintel 1992.
7. As we shall see in detail in chapter 2, (17c) turns out to be not quite adequate as an interpretation of (15c).
8. Cf. the definition of "anaphorically related" in Heim 1982 (pp. 195 ff). For an early characterization of the relevant issues, see Karttunen (1969).
9. Assuming that restrictive relatives are internal to the NP's they modify, we should talk of domination rather than c-command.
10. On generics, see Carlson 1977, 1989, Krifka 1988, Carlson and Pelletier 1995 and references therein.
11. The term is due to Evans (1980, 1982). In presenting the notion of E-type pronoun, Evans didn't actually have in mind "paycheck sentences." He had in mind structures like those I will discuss in section 1.4. However, his notion of E-type pronoun does extend naturally to paycheck sentences and has been used in the literature in connection with examples like (48) (cf., e.g., Neale 1990).
12. In the case at hand, it is quite plausible that such a uniqueness assumption would arise as scalar implicature from Gricean maxims; cf. Horn 1972, Kadmon 1987, 1990 for discussion.
13. I use 'o' as a variable over occasions, events, states, processes, situations, etc. The point that I am making can also be made using a situation-based semantics instead of a Davidsonian one. Cf. on this Heim 1990.
14. A possibility here is to claim that a situation in which x lives with y is different from a situation in which y lives with x. This involves making situations as fine-grained as assignments to variables.
15. Classical references on Weak Crossover are Postal 1971 and Jacobson 1977.
16. For a categorical approach to these issues, see Bach and Partee 1980. For a phrase structure approach, see, e.g., Pollard and Sag 1988.
17. Kratzer's analysis in addition employs an "ordering source," which we will disregard here for simplicity.
18. See Rooth 1985, Krifka 1992 for extensive discussion of how focus helps determine the restriction of quantificational adverbs.
19. There remain some cases where modals do appear to actually quantify over instances of the subject, such as in examples of the following kind, discussed originally by Carlson (1977):

    (i)   Texans can be tall.

A natural reading of (i) is that some Texans are tall. There are a variety of ways in which the intended reading might be derived, and I am uncertain at this stage as to which is the best one. However, if what is pointed out in the text (concerning, e.g., the lack of interaction between modals and focal structure) is correct, the fact remains that it is unlikely to be modals which actually determine the quantificational force of indefinites in the absence of an overt quantificational element.

20. On presuppositions, see Karttunen and Peters 1979, Soames 1989 and references therein.

21. Cf. also Chierchia and Rooth 1984, and Theory 6 in Landman 1987.

22. For a radically different view, see Kamp and Reyle (1993).

23. See, e.g., Zeevat 1989, Barwise 1987, Rooth 1987, Pelletier and Schubert 1989, and Groenendijk and Stokhof 1990, 1991, among many others.

24. See Heim 1982, 1983 for discussion. See also chapter 4 of the present work.

25. See Heim 1982 (pp. 337ff.) for an attempt to generalize this definition to arbitrary files (including ones that contain false information).

26. In other words, $C(f)$ is a relation between worlds and assignments, which can also be expressed as a function from worlds into sets of assignments $Sat_w(f)$.

27. See Heim 1982 (pp. 370ff.) for details concerning the formal implementation of these ideas. She also applies her approach to cases like *It is not the case that the present king of France is bald.* Here global accommodation gives us (i) (which is the preferred reading), while local accommodation results in (ii):

(i)   There is a present king of France and it is not the case that he is bald.

(ii)   It is not the case that there is a present king of France who is bald.

Reading (ii) would arise only if it is part of the common ground that there is no present king of France.

28. Kratzer (1988) and Berman (1991), among others, develop theories where accommodation is syntacticized along lines similar to those suggested in the text.

CHAPTER 2

1. The present chapter is a radical reexamination and development of ideas presented in Chierchia 1992a. Most of the examples are taken from there.

2. An important exception is Pelletier and Schubert 1989. Kratzer 1988 also discusses ∃-readings. Since Chierchia 1990, 1992a, there have been a number of works addressing the issue of the distribution of ∃- vs. ∀-readings (e.g., Kanazawa 1993, van der Does 1993).

3. Cf. Rooth 1987, Root 1986, Kadmon 1990, Heim 1990, and references therein.

4. See, e.g., Barwise and Cooper 1981, Keenan and Stavi 1986. There are some alleged counterexamples to the conservativity universal. Some involve *only,* which, however, can be argued to be an adverbial element. Others involve certain readings of *many* and *few.* I am not convinced that non-conservative readings really do exist in these cases. At any rate, even if such counterexamples turned out to be genuine, there would still be an overwhelmingly strong tendency for determiners to be conservative. Most universals in linguistics express general tendencies and scales of markedness rather than absolute constraints.

5. See, e.g., Gazdar 1980, Partee and Rooth 1983, or Keenan and Faltz 1985.

6. The approach sketched in section 2.2.1 was suggested by an anonymous referee as

an alternative to a previous proposal of mine, based on Chierchia 1992a. The referee felt that I was not giving the first soul of DRT a fair chance. The strawman theory discussed in Chierchia 1992a had also been suggested by an anonymous referee, with similar motivations.

7. It is impossible within the limits of the present discussion to give a thorough introduction to Montague's Intensional Logic. Readers who are not familiar with it might want to consult Dowty et al. 1981 or Gamut 1991. Precise definitions for the notions informally described in this section can be found in the appendix to this chapter.

8. In fact, the restriction to individual-level discourse markers is not fundamental. One can introduce discourse markers of any type. See, e.g., Chierchia 1991 on this.

9. This entails that if a formula contains no free discourse markers, its intension is going to be either Ω, if the formula is true, or $\varnothing$, if the formula is false. This counterintuitive situation would not arise in a more intensional setting.

10. Such a system was dubbed 'DTT' (for 'Dynamic Type Theory') in Chierchia 1990. But since it is a minimal variant of IL, I now think that there is no real need for giving it a special name. I should also mention that this system differs from the one of Groenendijk and Stokhof 1990 in that no "case switching" operators are introduced.

11. This is actually only one, highly simplified aspect of context change potentials. Heim uses the related term 'file change potential' for functions from files into files. I am about to introduce a technical use of the term 'context change potential' that does not correspond fully with Heim's 'file change potential', for reasons that will become clear in chapter 4.

12. Here I depart from Groenendijk and Stokhof's definition, for reasons to be discussed later.

13. For ingenious ways of relaxing in restricted ways the closed character of downward entailing operators, see Dekker 1990b, 1993. For some problems with Dekker's approach, see Roberts 1992.

14. See, e.g., Harel 1984 or Janssen 1986. It is also worth adding that while the model theory we are adopting does give an indication of the intended interpretation of dynamic logic, I do not think that it should be identified with it. There are other ways of validating the equivalence '$[\exists x\phi] \wedge \psi \leftrightarrow \exists x[\phi \wedge \psi]$'. In fact, a syntactic (i.e., proof-theoretic) characterization of dynamic logic also appears to be possible (cf. Groenendijk, Stokhof, and de Vrier 1989).

15. Actually, rather than to things of type $\langle\langle s,t\rangle,t\rangle$ context change potentials correspond to things of type $\langle s,\langle\langle s,t\rangle,t\rangle\rangle$. This can be seen by the fact that a formula of the form '$\exists xA$' resets the assignment relative to which it is evaluated. However, for simplicity, I will keep equating cc with $\langle\langle s,t\rangle,t\rangle$.

16. In general, if α is of a type that "ends in t," $\uparrow \alpha = \lambda u \uparrow \alpha(u)$. This is just a pointwise generalization of '$\uparrow$'. For relevant discussion see Partee and Rooth 1983.

17. It is technically possible to have a uniform (parametrized) schema for all determiners (cf. Chierchia 1990). Such a schema can also be used to make open determiners like *every*, in view of cases like (i):

(i)   Every chess set comes with a spare pawn. It is taped under the box.
       (P. Sells)

(Downward entailing determiners can never be made open, in virtue of our Principle of Informativeness; cf. (66) in the text). However, I will not pursue this issue here. We will discuss these cases further in chapter 4.

The approach adopted in the text might fit well with the view that indefinites are precisely those NPs that have a natural predicative use. Thus the basic interpretation of *a boy* and *two boys* might be as in (ii)–(iii).

(ii)   a boy = λx [boy(x) ∧ one(x)]
(iii)   two boys = λx [boy(x) ∧ two(x)], etc.

Consequently, the basic interpretation of indefinite determiners would be as cardinality predicates. In argument position the type of predicative NPs is automatically shifted to that of quantificational NPs, by closing the NP existentially.

18. See, e.g., Higginbotham 1985 and Parsons 1990, among many others.

19. Cf., e.g., Kratzer 1989, Berman 1987, or Heim 1990.

20. See, e.g., Muskens 1989 for work relevant in this connection.

21. Alternatively, by resorting to θ-roles, (85b) could be further analyzed as (i):

(i)   ∃e[singing(e) ∧ agent(e,Pavarotti)]

I will not take a stand on the issue of the status of θ-roles in semantics. Readers should feel free to fill in their favorite view on this topic.

22. Kratzer (1988) argues that individual-level predicates lack the Davidsonian argument, a hypothesis that I am not going to follow here. See e.g., Chierchia 1992a,b for some discussion.

23. It could be argued that a situation-based approach enables one to do away with Dynamic Binding. It might appear that this is so as far as *if/when*-clauses are concerned (but cf. section 2.5.3 below). However, an important motivation for Dynamic Binding is the behavior of determiners (i.e., the relative clause versions of donkey anaphora). And if Dynamic Binding is needed anyway, avoiding it in *if/when*-clauses constitutes no conceptual gain.

24. One needs to keep in mind that Q-adverbs have an additional modal dimension which we are disregarding here. Such a modal dimension can be added more or less in the same way as in classical DRT (cf. the discussion in chapter 1).

25. Contentfulness is the opposite of uniqueness, in a sense. *The* presupposes uniqueness. Quantifiers like *every, most,* and so forth, presuppose that uniqueness does not follow from the common ground. For further discussion, cf. Chierchia 1992a, (pp. 175–176), where the same restriction is called "plurality."

26. The same holds for the symmetric reading of (99). Lappin and Francez 1993 miss this point and erroneously claim that my approach has difficulty with such cases.

27. For more discussion, see, e.g., van Benthem 1989. A strong case for polyadic quantification in natural language has been made by Srivastav (1990). Her treatment of correlatives in Hindi (and crosslinguistically) is very relevant to the issues discussed here, and I believe it may provide a crucial testing ground for the claim that Q-adverbs are polyadic rather than quantifiers over cases à la Lewis.

28. There is, however, unselective abstraction via the ˆ-operator.

29. In the Principles and Parameters framework, indefinites are viewed as R-expressions. Hence (101a) might be ruled out as a Principle C violation (cf. the formulation of Principle C in chapter 1, section 1.5). We must, however, assume that indefinites are exempt from Principle C when coindexed with a Q-adverb, for otherwise we would rule out all the good cases as well, like (i):

(i)   Usually$_i$ [if a cat$_i$ meows][it$_i$ is hungry].

We will come back to this in chapter 3.

30. See the contributions to Carlson and Pelletier 1995 for relevant discussion.

31. For instance, Rooth's (1985, pp. 164ff.) treatment of the following examples can be adopted wholesale within the present approach:

(i)   John usually takes [$_F$Mary] to the movies.

(ii)   John usually takes Mary [$_F$ to the movies].

32. Examples of this sort have been discussed in Kratzer 1988 and especially in Diesing 1992, to which I refer for an interesting explanation of the phenomena under discussion. For a somewhat different view, cf. also Bowers 1993 and Chierchia 1992b.

33. Versions of this view have been proposed by Cooper (1979) and Engdahl (1986). Heim (1990) discusses a related theory, even though she eventually dismisses it. A modified version of Cooper's and Engdahl's approaches, based on choice functions, is explored in Chierchia 1992a and shown to be inadequate in Kanazawa 1993. Finally, a theory very close to the one proposed in the text can be found in Lappin and Francez 1993. Other approaches, rather different from the one adopted here, are presented in Neale 1990 and van der Does 1993.

34. A widely discussed question that arises in this connection is whether E-type pronouns besides, having a pragmatically driven construal, also involve a syntactically instantiated and semantically significant link between the pronoun and its antecedent. In chapter 4 I will side with those who claim that they do. But for our most immediate concerns, it is immaterial to settle this matter.

35. This approach would fit with several current treatments of plurality, but the theory I have in mind as most directly compatible with it is the one developed in Schwarzschild 1991. According to Schwarzschild, predication of pluralities is always relativized to factors (called "covers") that determine the pattern of distribution from a group to its parts. This is particularly relevant to the analysis of sentences like (i):

(i)   Every student who borrowed a book from a teacher returned it to him on time.

On my approach this would be interpreted as 'Every student who borrowed a book from a teacher returned the books he borrowed to the teachers who lent books to him'. The relativization to covers would then narrow down further the interpretation in appropriate ways. However, the proper development of these ideas must be left to another occasion.

36. A similar point is made in Partee 1984, though not in the context of a comparison of DRT with the analysis of donkey-type dependencies in terms of the E-type strategy.

37. I should also point out the main innovations of the Dynamic Binding approach with respect to the framework of Groenendijk and Stokhof 1990, to which Dynamic Binding is most directly linked. From a technical point of view, my version of IL is just a trivial variant of Groenendijk and Stokhof's Dynamic Intensional Logic. The main changes (besides the absence of "state switchers") relate to how one deals with quantification in English. There are two important differences here: the general characterization of conservative determiners—Groenendijk and Stokhof give a nonconservative definition of *every* and do not take a stand on other determiners—and the view developed here of Q-adverbs as polyadic counterparts of determiners.

CHAPTER 3

1. The examples in (6) are odd if pronounced with an unmarked stress pattern. However, if *a mouse* is destressed or the verb in the *if*-clause is focused (as in (i)), some speakers find that the examples in (6) become somewhat better than those in (5).

(i)   If a cat SPOTS it, it attacks a mouse.

I don't know exactly to what this should be attributed. In terms of the approach to be developed, I would say that in (i) cats and mice are discourse topics and *a mouse* behaves like a resumptive quantifier in May's (1989) sense. However, even the speakers that find (6) better than (5) find that (6) is systematically degraded with respect to (2)–(4). My theory aims to account for this contrast.

2. Some speakers (including myself) find (9b–c) somewhat harder to get than (9a). I have no explanatory account for this fact. Everybody, however, tends to find (9a–b) systematically better than (5)–(6), which justifies regarding them as grammatical, at least in first approximation.

3. Notice that if we assume that right-adjoined *if/when*-clauses have also the option of adjoining higher up, (11a) would have an analysis according to which it should be grammatical and an explanation in terms of Principle C could not be maintained. One could explore the possibility of appealing to some version of the Novelty Condition. But it would be very mysterious why such a condition should single out the subject position (cf. the grammaticality of (9b–c).

4. The hypothesis on the nature of tripartite structures presented here affects the definition of accessibility, given in (19), chapter 1, which has to be restated in terms of m-command:

> (i)   A is the closest binder for B iff (a) A is the lowest quantificational NP containing B or (b) A is the highest Q-adverb m-commanding B.
>
> (ii)   B is accessible to A iff the closest binder for A c-commands B.

Instead of m-command, we could use Chomsky's (1992) notion of checking domain. At any rate, this change in the definition of accessibility is of no impact, as the accessibility constraint is a purely descriptive generalization which follows from the way the semantics is set up.

5. One might object that the binding theory concerns A-positions, while the Q-adverb in (18) is in an A'-position. However, the Q-adverb really acts as an intermediary between *an Italian,* which is in an A-position, and *an American.* There might be a need for a tune-up of the technical definition, but it is a fact that the relation we are excluding concerns two A-positions.

6. See also Chierchia 1992b on this.

7. Alternatively, we can quantify the NP into the *when*-clause.

8. While this seems to be true of *if*-clauses, things actually are more complicated for *when*-clauses. Right-adjoined *when*-clauses can sometimes be incorporated in the scope. I will ignore this complication here. See Rooth 1985 for discussion of some relevant cases.

9. This approach probably needs to appeal to some syntactic dependency between the *if*-clause and the Q-adverb (e.g., a mutual government requirement, or the like). Alternatively, one might use semantic types. For example, a compositional step-by-step interpretation of (18b) might proceed as follows. The TP, after *usually* has operated on it, might be a function that looks for a proposition and a noun phrase to give a new proposition. Using type-lifting techniques, we might treat the *if*-clause in turn as a function that takes an object of this kind and returns a function that looks for an NP to yield a proposition.

10. Zimmerman (1992) develops an alternative to Montague's proposals. However, it has the consequence of denying the ambiguous character of (i):

> (i)   Herod wants every male baby of this region.

According to Zimmerman's theory, sentence (i) is predicted to have only a de re reading. I find this prediction to be clearly wrong.

11. It is worth recalling that, in a different framework, an approach in terms of cyclic Quantifier Lowering, such as the one discussed in Jacobson 1977, also achieves the correct effects.

12. After having come to this conclusion, I became aware of Iatridou 1991 (pp. 25ff.), which contains proposals that have several points of contacts with the one I will develop. In particular, Iatridou observes the ungrammaticality of the following sentence:

(i)   *If his$_i$ mother invites Mary$_j$, she$_j$ yells at every boy$_i$.

She argues that if we assume that the *if*-clause in (i) has to be reconstructed, the pronoun *she* would end up c-commanding *Mary*, resulting in a Principle C violation. Hence, if binding into left-adjoined adjuncts is done via reconstruction, we have an account for the ungrammaticality of (i).

The problem I see with Iatridou's suggestion is that it is not clear what forces reconstruction. Note in particular that if we choose not to reconstruct, and if *every boy* in (i) can raise (as Iatridou seems to think; cf. her p. 32), the sentence would be expected to be grammatical. I assume that WCO rules out this option and that therefore reconstruction really is the only way to get backwards binding. I also think that structures involving quantificational NPs like *every boy* have somewhat different properties from those that Iatridou suggests. Cf. section 3.4 below.

13. The possibility of using abstraction over assignments in recursive semantic rules has been considered and discussed in the literature. Cf., e.g., Cooper 1983.

14. One problem with this analysis has to do with the fact that *then,* as an adverbial, is an adjunct, and adjuncts generally cannot be incorporated. This problem also arises for the cliticization of adjuncts in Romance. See Baker 1988 (pp. 467) for relevant discussion.

15. I think that the slight awkwardness of (71b) and (71d) is just a processing effect, due to the complexity of the examples.

16. This is closely related to the general point that Cinque (1990) makes in connection with Clitic Left Dislocation in Italian.

17. This notion of chain is meant to include the kind of operator–variable structures hypothesized for topicalization.

18. Thanks to J. Whitman for bringing the facts discussed in this section to my attention.

19. Stroik (1990) articulates an approach to adverbs as V-sisters, where the surface order is derived via a Larsonian mechanism of verb raising. Stroik's position is incompatible with our account of the asymmetries in (99)–(100). But by treating adjuncts as structurally on a par with arguments, Stroik complicates the treatment of *wh*-dependencies, which are known at least since Huang 1982 to be sensitive to this contrast. See, e.g., Travis 1988 for a treatment of adverbs that deals with Stroik's observations in a way consistent with our proposal.

However, my position is also compatible with approaches that preserve some of the insights of Stroik's line, such as, e.g., Pesetsky's (1994) proposal concerning the simultaneous existence of two levels of structure, "cascades" and "layers" (where it is the "layered" structure that is relevant to interpretation).

20. I owe the following point to F. Landman.

21. On the strong reading of (111a), which does not involve Dynamic Binding, see chapter 4, section 4.4.1.

CHAPTER 4

1. One exception is Beaver 1994, which was written independently from and roughly at the same time as the present chapter. Beaver's proposals and mine have many points in common and are both a development of important ideas put forth in Heim 1983. However,

Beaver couches his approach within a version of TY2 (Gallin 1970), with overt abstraction over assignments, while the system I adopt is closer to Montague's IL. There are various other technical differences between the two approaches that I will not try to evaluate here. In addition, Beaver's treatment of definites is very different from the one I develop.

For another alternative, related to but also rather different from both Beaver's and my approach, cf. van der Sandt 1989.

2. This analysis of *too* is due to S. Kripke and I. Heim. Cf. Heim 1992.

3. This is Heim's 1983 notation. Following her we write 'c + φ' for '+ φ(c)'.

4. For a fuller discussion of the available options, see Muskens 1989.

5. The world argument might eventually be replaced by a situation argument.

6. It might be more appropriate to reserve the term 'property' for expressions of type $\langle w, \langle e, t \rangle \rangle$. But since this would make my prose even heavier than it already is, I will not follow this practice here.

7. This means that I am not taking any stand here on matters of sortal correctness.

8. It is also possible, maybe, to do away altogether with semantic presuppositions, by directly assigning to items like *regret* functions from individuals into updates. (E.g., we could say that for any proposition p, individual x, and context set c, 'regret(p)(x)(c)' yields those members of c in which John regrets that p, if $c \subseteq p$, and is undefined otherwise). I will not follow this course here for three reasons: (i) I do not find encoding lexical presuppositions in terms of truth value gaps conceptually troubling; (ii) there are certain features of definites, to be discussed below, that I am not sure how to deal with without partial propositions; and (iii) even if solutions to such issues can be found, I don't think that the end result would differ substantially from what I am proposing.

9. See Chierchia 1991 for an attempt to integrate dynamic semantics with a more strongly intensional theory of properties and propositions.

10. The reader might wonder why, if sentences are interpreted as updates, the complement of *regret* is a proposition rather than an update. The simplest answer is that, as we have just seen, propositions can always be retrieved from updates and verbs may be sensitive to propositional content alone. However, we will see shortly that the semantics of verbs expressing propositional attitudes is more complex than this. The one in (22d) is just a first approximation.

11. This definition of the conditional in conjunction with the definition of the universal quantifier give rise to ∀-readings of donkey sentences. It should also be noted that the general approach taken here is consistent with other semantics for conditionals as well (cf. Heim 1992 for relevant discussion).

12. Notice that either one of the conditionals in (35d) would suffice to represent the contribution of disjunction to a given context, but it would not be enough to represent its projection properties. So in the case of disjunction it cannot be claimed that its presuppositional behavior follows naturally from explicitly stating its contributions to context change. Thus one might say that the dynamic framework (at least as I understand it) can correctly describe the projection properties of disjunction without achieving a significant level of explanatory value.

13. Use of the formalism of section 4.2, as opposed to some other dynamic formalism, arguably sharpens certain issues pertaining to the anaphoric properties of verbs of propositional attitude.

14. Zeevat (1992) formulates a different generalization and proposes an alternative account.

15. Heim's (1992) formulation is close to our (38). In that paper she deals just with

presuppositions. Notice, however, that if we try to formulate a dynamic meaning for *believe* within File Change Semantics, it is not obvious how to proceed, for the reasons pointed out in section 4.1.

16. But see Edelberg 1986 for some problems stemming from an analysis of "Intentional Identity" statements in terms of E-type pronouns.

17. In chapter 2, I have used 'D' for static determiner meanings (i.e., relations between sets) and 'D′' for their dynamic counterparts. From now on I will use 'D' for static determiners (of type $\langle\langle e,t\rangle,\langle\langle e,t\rangle,t\rangle\rangle$), 'D′' for relations between properties (of type $\langle\langle e,p\rangle,\langle\langle e,p\rangle,p\rangle\rangle$), and 'D$^+$' for their dynamic counterparts (of type $\langle dp,\langle dp,cc\rangle\rangle$).

18. This is reflected in the disagreement one finds in the literature concerning what happens in these cases. Heim (1983) and van der Sandt (1989) make heavy use of accommodation; Lerner and Zimmerman (1983) and Beaver (1994) argue in favor of existential presuppositions.

19. Karttunen and Peters (1979) only treat *every, the,* and *a,* and for those quantifiers the mechanism they set up makes the right predictions. However, their account does not extend to quantifiers like *no* and *most,* nor is it clear how it could be modified so as to work for such quantifiers. Lerner and Zimmerman (1983) note that Karttunen and Peters's approach doesn't work for *no* and propose a way of correcting that. While their proposal seems to be descriptively adequate (but I haven't tried extending it to *most*), it does not give an account of presupposition projection, nor does it make clear *why* all determiners display the same pattern. Heim (1982, 1983) comes closer to identifying the spirit of the solution, without, however, stating it explicitly and in full generality.

20. I am assuming that nouns like *president* or *father* are inherently relational; that is, they denote two-place relations. The relevant relata may or may not be syntactically expressed. More on this below.

21. This type-shifting could be generalized to all types that "end in p"; cf. Partee and Rooth 1983.

22. The representations in (60) are strongly reminiscent of Cooper's (1979) treatment of pronouns. In a sense my proposal is an extension of his view of pronouns to definites in general.

23. In (60b), 'ι' is indexed with the indices of the arguments of R. Strictly speaking, one would also need an index for the relation. But for ease of readibility, I omit that.

24. When I use the term an 'n-place function', I refer to n-individuals. Descriptions, being individual concepts, are always also functions of possible worlds. The idea of definites as functions is similar, I think, to what Loebner (1987) proposes. However, Loebner does not provide an explicit formalization of his proposals, or at any rate, not in the present terms.

25. See Chierchia 1993 for relevant discussion.

26. Within the second implementation discussed in section 4.3.1, definites would have to be functions from individuals into generalized quantifiers, that is, parametrized generalized quantifiers.

27. In (63a), we could also try to interpret the definite as being more directly anaphoric to the NP *a man,* along the following lines:

(i) $\exists x[\text{man}(x) \;\wedge\; \text{was-seen-by-a-boy}(x) \;\wedge\; \text{wearing-a-hat}(\iota y[\text{R}(x,y) \;\wedge\; \text{man}(y)])]$

However, the question here is how to interpret R. The only option that comes to mind is to interpret it as the identity relation. But this looks like a trick. For in what sense does uttering the first sentence of (63a) make identity salient?

28. It might also be worth considering the object-asymmetric reading:

 (i) a. Most $(\lambda x[\text{village}(x) \wedge \exists y\ \text{painter}(y) \wedge \text{live-in}(y,x)], \lambda x[\text{village}(x)$
     $\wedge\ \exists y\ \text{painter}(y) \wedge \text{live-in}(y,x) \wedge \text{pretty}\ (\iota_y u\ \text{village}(u))])$
    b. $\iota_y u\ \text{village}(u) = \omega u[\text{lives-in}(y,u) \wedge \text{village}(u)]$

The reader can verify that (i) assigns the right truth conditions for the object-asymmetric reading. Note that here, as in (63a), it is implausible to make 'the village' dependent on 'a village' for the reasons laid out in note 27 above.

29. Functional readings of questions have been studied most prominently by Engdahl (1986) and Groenendijk and Stokhof (1984). Cf. also Chierchia 1993.

30. Or P_j could be the interpretation of the N'. At any rate, as will immediately become clear, this is just a first approximation.

31. On telescoping, see also Poesio and Zucchi 1992.

32. The present approach has something to offer on Bach-Peters sentences as well, I think. But that development will have to be left to some other occasion.

References

Authier, M. 1992. "Iterated CP's and Embedded Topicalization," *Linguistic Inquiry* 23:329–336.

Bach, E., and B. H. Partee. 1980. "Anaphora and Semantic Structure." In K. J. Kreiman and A. Ojeda, eds., *Papers from the Parasession on Pronouns and Anaphora,* 1–28. Chicago: Chicago Linguistic Society.

Baker, M. 1988. *Incorporation: A Theory of Grammatical Function Changing.* Chicago: University of Chicago Press.

Barss, A. 1986. *Chains and Anaphoric Dependencies.* Ph. D. dissertation MIT.

Barwise, J. 1987. "Noun Phrases, Generalized Quantifiers and Anaphora." In P. Gärdenfors, ed., *Generalized Quantifiers,* 1–29. Dordrecht: Kluwer.

Barwise, J., and R. Cooper. 1981. "Generalized Quantifiers in Natural Language." *Linguistics and Philosophy* 4:159–220.

Beaver, D. 1994. *What Comes First in Dynamic Semantic.* Ph.D. dissertation, University of Edinburgh.

Benthem, J. van. 1989. "Polyadic Quantifiers." *Linguistics and Philosophy* 12:437–464.

Berman, S. 1987. "A Situation-Based Semantics for Adverbs of Quantification." In J. Blevins and A. Vainikka, eds., *UMOP 12.* GLSA, University of Massachusetts, Amherst.

———. 1991. *The Semantics of Open Sentences.* Ph.D. dissertation, University of Massachusetts, Amherst.

Bowers, J. 1993. "The Structure of I-level and S-level Predicates." Paper presented at SALT III, UC Irvine.

Carlson, G. 1977. *Reference to Kinds in English.* Ph.D. dissertation, University of Massachusetts, Amherst. Distributed by the Indiana University Linguistics Club, Bloomington. Published 1980 by Garland Press, New York.

———. 1982. "Generics and Atemporal *When.*" *Linguistics and Philosophy* 3:49–97.

———. 1989. "The Semantic Composition of English Generic Sentences." In G. Chierchia, B. H. Partee, and R. Turner, eds., *Properties, Types and Meaning,* vol. 2, 167–191. Dordrecht: Kluwer.

Carlson, G., and J. Pelletier, eds. 1995. *The Generic Book.* Chicago: University of Chicago Press.

Chierchia, G. 1990. "Anaphora and Dynamic Logic." ITLI Prepublication Series, University of Amsterdam.

———. 1991. "Intensionality and Context Change." Manuscript. Forthcoming in *Journal of Logic, Language and Information.*

———. 1992a. "Anaphora and Dynamic Binding." *Linguistics and Philosophy* 15:111–183.

———. 1992b. "Individual-Level Predicates as Inherent Generics." Unpublished

Manuscript, Cornell University. Published in revised form in G. Carlson and F. J. Pelletier, eds., 1995.

————. 1993. "Questions with Quantifiers." *Natural Language Semantics* 1:181–234.

Chierchia, G., and M. Rooth. 1984. "Configurational Notions in Discourse Representation Theory." In C. Jones and P. Sells, eds., *Proceedings of NELS 14*. GLSA, University of Massachusetts, Amherst.

Chomsky, N. 1976. "Conditions on Rules of Grammar." *Linguistic Analysis* 2:303–351.

————. 1977. "On Wh-Movement." In P. Culicover, T. Wasow, and A. Akmajan, eds., *Formal Syntax*, 71–132. New York: Academic Press.

————. 1981. *Lectures on Government and Binding*. Dordrecht: Foris.

————. 1986. *Knowledge of Language*. New York: Praeger.

————. 1992. "A Minimalist Program for Linguistic Theory." MIT Occasional Papers in Linguistics 1. Department of Linguistics and Philosophy, MIT, Cambridge, Mass.

Cinque, G. 1990. *Types of A'-Dependencies*. Cambridge, Mass.: MIT Press.

Collins, C. 1989. "A Note on Extraction from Conditionals." Unpublished manuscript, MIT.

Cooper, R. 1979. "The Interpretation of Pronouns." In F. Heny and H. Schnelle, eds., *Syntax and Semantics 10*, 61–92. New York: Academic Press.

Cooper, R. 1983. *Quantification and Syntactic Theory*. Dordrecht: Reidel.

Cresswell, M. 1973. *Logics and Languages*. London: Methuen.

Davidson, D. 1967. "The Logical Form of Action Sentences." In N. Rescher, ed., *The Logic of Decision and Action*, 81–95. Pittsburgh: University of Pittsburgh Press.

Dekker, P. 1990a. "Existential Disclosure." ITLI Prepublication Series, University of Amsterdam. A revised version with the same title has been published in *Linguistics and Philosophy* 16:561–587 (1993).

————. 1990b. "The Scope of Negation in Discourse." ITLI Prepublication Series, University of Amsterdam.

————. 1993. *Transsentential Meditations*. Ph.D. dissertation, University of Amsterdam.

De Swart, H. 1991. *Adverbs of Quantification: A Generalized Quantifiers Approach*. Ph.D. dissertation, University of Gröningen.

Diesing, M. 1992. *Indefinites*. Cambridge, Mass.: MIT Press.

Does, J. van der. 1993. "The Dynamics of Sophisticated Laziness." In J. Groenendijk, ed., *Dyana Deliverable* R22A. Amsterdam: ILLC.

Dowty, D., R. Wall, and S. Peters. 1981. *Introduction to Montague Semantics*. Dordrecht: Kluwer.

Edelberg, W. 1986. "A New Puzzle about Intensional Identity." *Journal of Philosophical Logic* 15:1–26.

Engdahl, E. 1986. *Constituent Questions*. Dordrecht: Reidel.

Evans, G. 1980. "Pronouns." *Linguistic Inquiry* 11:337–362.

————. 1982. *The Varieties of Reference*. Oxford: Oxford University Press.

Eynde, F. van. 1992. "Towards a Dynamic and Compositional Treatment of

Temporal Expressions.'' In P. Dekker and M. Stokhof, eds., *Proceedings of the 8th Amsterdam Colloquium*. ITLI, Amsterdam.

Fintel, K. von. 1992. "Adverbs of Quantification, Complex Conditionals and Focus.'' In C. Barker and D. Dowty, eds., *Proceedings of SALT 2*. The Ohio State University, Columbus, Ohio.

Gallin, D. 1975. *Intensional and Higher-Order Modal Logic*. Amsterdam: North Holland.

Gamut, L. T. F. 1991. *Logic, Language and Meaning*. Chicago: University of Chicago Press.

Gärdenfors, P. 1988. *Knowledge in Flux: Modeling the Dynamics of Epistemic States*. Cambridge, Mass: MIT Press.

Gazdar, G. 1980. "A Cross-Categorial Semantics for Coordination.'' *Linguistics and Philosophy* 3:407–409.

Geach, P. 1962. *Reference and Generality*. Ithaca, N.Y.: Cornell University Press.

Groenendijk, J., and M. Stokhof. 1984. *Studies in the Semantics of Questions and the Pragmatics of Answers*. Akademisch Proefschrift, University of Amsterdam.

———. 1990. "Dynamic Montague Grammar.'' In L. Kalman and L. Polos, eds., *Papers from the Second Symposium on Logic and Language*. Budapest: Akadémiai Kaidó.

———. 1991. "Dynamic Predicate Logic.'' *Linguistics and Philosophy* 14:39–100.

Groenendijk, J., M. Stokhof, and R. de Vrier. 1989. "A Natural Deduction System for DPL.'' Manuscript presented at the 6th Amsterdam Colloquium.

Harel, D. 1984. "Dynamic Logic.'' In D. Gabbay and F. Guenthner, ed., *Handbook of Philosophical Logic,* vol. 2. Dordrecht: Kluwer.

Heim, I. 1982. *The Semantics of Definite and Indefinite Noun Phrases*. Ph.D. dissertation, University of Massachusetts, Amherst. Published 1989 by Garland Press, New York.

———. 1983. "On the Projection Problem for Presuppositions.'' In M. Barlow, D. Flickinger, and M. Wescoat, eds., *Proceedings of WCCFL 2,* 114–125. Stanford, Cal.: Stanford Linguistics Association, Stanford University.

———. 1987. "Where Does the Definiteness Restriction Apply?'' In E. Reuland and A. ter Meulen, eds., *The Representation of (In)definiteness,* 21–42. Cambridge, Mass.: MIT Press.

———. 1990. "E-type Pronouns and Donkey Anaphora.'' *Linguistics and Philosophy* 13:137–178.

———. 1992. "Presupposition Projection and the Semantics of Attitude Verbs.'' *Journal of Semantics* 9:183–221.

Heycock, C. 1992. "(Anti)reconstruction and Referentiality.'' Unpublished manuscript, Yale University.

Higginbotham, J. 1980. "Pronouns and Bound Variables.'' *Linguistic Inquiry* 11:679–708.

———. 1983. "Logical Form, Binding and Nominals." *Linguistic Inquiry* 14:395–420.

———. 1985. "On Semantics." *Linguistic Inquiry* 16:547–594.

Horn, L. 1972. *On the Semantic Properties of Logical Operators in English.* Ph.D. dissertation, UCLA. Distributed by the Indiana University Linguistic Club, Bloomington.

———. 1989. *A Natural History of Negation.* Chicago: University of Chicago Press.

Huang, J. 1982. "Logical Relations in Chinese and the Theory of Grammar." Ph.D. dissertation, MIT.

Iatridou, S. 1991. *Topics in Conditionals.* Ph.D. dissertation, MIT. Distributed as MIT Working Papers in Linguistics.

Jacobson, P. 1977. *The Syntax of Crossing Coreference.* Ph.D. dissertation, UC Berkeley. Published 1979 by Garland Press, New York.

———. 1987. "Phrase Structure, Grammatical Relations and Discontinuous Constituents." In G. Huck and A. Ojeda, eds., *Syntax and Semantics 20: Discontinuous Constituency.* New York: Academic Press.

Janssen, T. 1986. *Foundations and Applications of Montague Grammar.* Ph.D. dissertation, University of Amsterdam.

Kadmon, N. 1987. *On Unique and Non-Unique Reference and Asymmetric Quantification.* Ph.D. dissertation, University of Massachusetts, Amherst.

———. 1990. "Uniqueness." *Linguistics and Philosophy* 13:273–324.

Kamp, H. 1981. "A Theory of Truth and Discourse Representation." In J. Groenendijk, T. Janssen, and M. Stokhof, eds., *Formal Methods in the Study of Language,* 277–322. Mathematical Centre, Amsterdam.

Kamp, H., and U. Reyle. 1993. *From Discourse to Logic.* Dordrecht: Kluwer.

Kanazawa, M. 1993. "Weak vs. Strong Readings of Donkey Sentences and Monotomicity inferences in a Dynamic Setting." ILLC, Amsterdam. A revised version was published in *Linguistics and Philosophy* in 1994, Vol. 17.2:109–158.

Kaplan, D. 1977. "Demonstratives." Manuscript, UCLA. Published in 1989 in J. Almog, J. Perry, and H. Wettstein, eds., *Themes for Kaplan.* New York: Oxford University Press.

Karttunen, L. 1969. "Pronouns and Variables." *CLS* 5. Chicago: Chicago Linguistic Society.

———. 1974. "Presuppositions and Linguistic Context." *Theoretical Linguistics* 1:181–194.

———. 1976. "Discourse Referents." In J. McCawley, ed., *Syntax and Semantics 7: Notes from the Linguistic Underground,* 363–385. New York: Academic Press.

Karttunen, L., and S. Peters. 1979. "Conventional Implicature." In C. Oh and D. Dinneen, eds., *Syntax and Semantics 11: Presuppositions,* 1–56. New York: Academic Press.

Kayne, R. 1993. "Antisymmetry in Syntax." Unpublished manuscript, CUNY, New York.

Keenan, E., and L. Faltz. 1985. *Boolean Semantics for Natural Language.*
Dordrecht: Kluwer.

Keenan, E., and J. Stavi. 1986. "A Semantic Characterization of Natural
Language Determiners." *Linguistics and Philosophy* 9:253–326.

Koopman, H., and D. Sportiche. 1982. "Variables and the Bijection Principle."
Linguistic Review 2:139–160.

———. 1988. "Subjects." Unpublished manuscript. UCLA.

Kratzer, A. 1981. "The Notational Category of Modality." In H. Eikmeyer and H.
Rieser, eds., *Words, Worlds and Contexts,* 38–74. Berlin: de Gruyter.

———. 1986. "Conditional." In A. M. Farley, P. Farley, and K. E. McCullough,
eds., *Papers from the Parasession on Pragmatics and Grammatical
Theory,* 1–15. Chicago: Chicago Linguistic Society.

———. 1988. "Stage-Level and Individual-Level Predicates." In M. Krifka, ed.,
Genericity in Natural Language, 247–284. SNS-Bericht 88-42,
University of Tübingen. A revised version was published in G. Carlson
and J. Pelletier, eds., 1995.

———. 1989. "An Investigation of the Lumps of Thoughts." *Linguistics and
Philosophy* 12:607–653.

———. 1991. "Pseudoscope: Ambiguities in Opaque Contexts." Paper presented
at the LSA-ASL Meeting in Santa Cruz, Cal.

Krifka, M. 1988. "The Relational Theory of Genericity." In M. Krifka, ed.,
Genericity in Natural Language, 285–312. SNS-Bericht 88-42,
University of Tübingen.

———. 1992. "A Framework for Focus-Sensitive Quantification." In C. Barker
and D. Dowty, eds. *Proceedings of SALT 2,* 215–236. The Ohio State
University, Columbus, Ohio.

Kuroda, S.-Y. 1988. "Whether We Agree or Not: A Comparative Syntax of
English and Japanese." *Linguisticae Investigationes* 12:1–47.

Ladusaw, W. 1979. *Polarity Sensitivity as Inherent Scope Relations.* Ph.D.
dissertation, University of Texas, Austin. Distributed by the Indiana
University Linguistic Club, Bloomington.

Landman, F. 1987. "A Handful of Versions of DRT." Unpublished manuscript,
University of Massachusetts, Amherst.

———. 1993. "Events and Plurality. The Jerusalem Lectures." Unpublished
manuscript, University of Tel Aviv.

Lappin, S. 1989. "Donkey Pronouns Unbound." *Theoretical Linguistics*
15:263–286.

Lappin, S., and N. Francez. 1993. "E-type Pronouns, I-sums and Donkey
Anaphora." Unpublished manuscript, Israel Institute for Technology,
Haifa.

Larson, R. 1988. "On the Double Object Construction." *Linguistic Inquiry*
19:335–392.

Lebeaux, D. 1988. *Language Acquisition and the Form of Grammar.* Ph.D.
dissertation, University of Massachusetts, Amherst.

Lerner, J.-Y., and T. E. Zimmerman. 1983. "Presuppositions and Quantifiers." In

R. Bäuerle, C. Schwarze, and A. von Stechow, eds., *Meaning, Use and Interpretation of Language*, 290–301. Berlin: de Gruyter.

Lewis, D. 1975. "Adverbs of Quantification." In E. Keenan, ed., *Formal Semantics of Natural Language*, 3–15. Cambridge: Cambridge University Press.

———. 1979. "Scorekeeping in a Language Game." In R. Bäuerle, U. Egli, and A. von Stechow, eds., *Semantics from Different Points of View*, 172–187. Berlin: Springer-Verlag.

Loebner, S. 1987. "Definites." *Journal of Semantics* 4:279–326.

May, R. 1985. *Logical Form: Its Structure and Its Derivation*. Cambridge, Mass.: MIT Press.

———. 1989. "Interpreting Logical Form." *Linguistics and Philosophy* 12:387–435.

Montague, R. 1968. "Pragmatics." In R. Klibansky, ed., *Contemporary Philosophy: A Survey*, vol. 1, 102–122. Florence: La Nuova Italia Editrice. Reprinted in R. H. Thomason, ed., 1974, *Formal Philosophy. Selected Papers of Richard Montague*, 95–118. New Haven, Conn.: Yale University Press.

———. 1973. "The Proper Treatment of Quantification in Ordinary English." In J. Hintikka, J. Moravcsic, and P. Suppes, eds., *Approaches to Natural Language*, 221–242. Dordrecht: Reidel.

Muskens, R. 1989. *Meaning and Partiality*. Ph.D. dissertation, University of Amsterdam.

———. 1990. "Anaphora and the Logic of Change." In J. van Eijck, ed., *Logics in AI*. Berlin: Springer-Verlag.

Neale, S. 1990. *Descriptions*. Cambridge, Mass: MIT Press.

Parsons, T. 1990. *Events in the Semantics of English*. Cambridge, Mass.: MIT Press.

Partee, B. H. 1984. "Nominal and Temporal Anaphora." *Linguistics and Philosophy* 7:243–286.

Partee, B. H., and M. Rooth. 1983. "Generalized Conjunction and Type Ambiguity." In R. Bäuerle, U. Egli, and A. von Stechow, eds., *Meaning, Use, and Interpretation of Language*, 361–383. Berlin: de Gruyter.

Pelletier, J., and L. Schubert. 1989. "Generically Speaking." In G. Chierchia, B. H. Partee and R. Turner, eds., *Properties, Types and Meaning*, vol. 2. Dordrecht: Kluwer.

Pesetsky, D. 1994. "Zero Syntax." Manuscript, MIT. To be published by MIT Press.

Poesio, M., and S. Zucchi. 1992. "On Telescoping." In C. Barker and D. Dowty, eds., *Proceedings of Salt 2*. The Ohio State University, Columbus, Ohio.

Pollard, C. and T. Sag. 1988. *Information-Based Syntax and Semantics*, vol. 1: *Fundamentals*. Chicago: University of Chicago Press.

Postal, P. 1971. *Crossover Phenomena*. New York: Holt, Rinehart and Winston.

Reinhart, T. 1976. *The Syntactic Domain of Anaphora*. Ph.D. dissertation, MIT.

————. 1983a. "Coreference and Bound Anaphora." *Linguistics and Philosophy* 6:47–88.

————. 1983b. *Anaphora and Semantics Interpretation*. London: Croom Helm.

Riemsdijk, H. van and E. Williams. 1981. "NP Structure." *The Linguistic Review* 1:171–217.

Rizzi, L. 1990. *Relativized Minimality*. Cambridge, Mass.: MIT Press.

Roberts, C. 1992. "Domain Restriction in Dynamic Semantics." Unpublished manuscript, Ohio State University, Columbus.

Roberts, I. 1991. "Excorporation and Minimality." *Linguistic Inquiry* 22:209–217.

Root, R. 1986. *The Semantics of Anaphora in Discourse*. Ph.D. dissertation, University of Texas at Austin.

Rooth, M. 1985. *Association with Focus*. Ph.D. dissertation, University of Massachusetts, Amherst.

————. 1987. "Noun Phrase Interpretation in Montague Grammar, File Change Semantics, and Situation Semantics." In P. Gärdenfors, ed., *Generalized Quantifiers: Linguistic and Logical Approaches*, 237–268. Dordrecht: Kluwer.

————. 1992. "A Theory of Focus Interpretation." *Natural Language Semantics* 1:75–116.

Sandt, R. van der. 1989. "Anaphora and Accommodation." In R. Bartsch, J. van Benthem and P. van Emde Boas, eds., *Semantics and Contextual Expressions*. Dordrecht: Foris.

Schwarzchild, R. 1991. *On the Meaning of Definite Plural Noun Phrases*. Ph.D. dissertation, University of Massachusetts, Amherst.

Soames, S. 1989. "Presuppositions." In D. Gabbay and F. Guenthner, eds., *Handbook of Philosophical Logic*, vol. 4, 553–616. Dordrecht: Kluwer.

Speas, M. 1990. *Phrase Structure in Natural Language*. Dordrecht: Kluwer.

Srivastav, V. 1990. *WH-dependencies in Hindi and the Theory of Grammar*. Ph.D. dissertation, Cornell University.

Stalnaker, R. 1974. "Pragmatic Presupposition." In M. Munitz and P. Unger, eds., *Semantics and Philosophy*, 197–230. New York: New York University Press.

————. 1978. "Assertion." In P. Cole, ed., *Syntax and Semantics 9: Pragmatics*, 315–332. New York: Academic Press.

Stroik, T. 1990. "Adverbs as V-sisters." *Linguistic Inquiry* 21:654–660.

Travis, L. 1988. "The Syntax of Adverbs." *Proceedings of NELS 19*, GLSA, University of Massachusetts, Amherst.

Veltman, F. 1990. "Defaults in Update Semantics." In H. Kamp, ed., *Conditionals, Defaults and Belief Revision*. DYANA Report R2.5.A, University of Edinburgh.

Watanabe, A. 1992. "Larsonian CP Recursion, Factive Complements and Selection." *Proceedings of NELS 23*, GLSA, University of Massachusetts, Amherst.

Westerståhl, D. 1988. "Quantifiers in Formal and Natural Languages." In D.

Gabbay and F. Guenthner, eds., *Handbook of Philosophical Logic*, vol. 4, 1–131. Dordrecht: Kluwer.

Zeevat, H. 1989. "A Compositional Approach to Discourse Representation Theory." *Linguistics and Philosophy* 12:95–131.

———. 1992. "Presuppositions and Accommodation in Update Semantics." *Journal of Semantics* 9:379–412.

Zimmerman, T. E. 1992. "On the Proper Treatment of Opacity in Certain Verbs." *Natural Language Semantics* 1:149–180.

Index

The following abbreviations are used throughout this index: DRS, Discourse Representation Structure; DRT, Discourse Representation Theory; FCS, File Change Semantics; IL, Intensional Logic.